THE UNITED

Edited by Tison Pugh and Susan Aronstein

The United States of Medievalism contemplates the desires, dreams, and contradictions inherent in experiencing the Middle Ages in a nation that is so temporally, spatially, and at times politically removed from them. The European Middle Ages have long influenced the national landscape of the United States through the medieval sites that permeate its self-announced republican landscapes and cities. Today, American-built medievalisms continue to shape the nation's communities, collapsing the binaries between past and present, medieval and modern, European and American.

The volume's chapters visit the nation's many medieval-inspired spaces, from Sherwood Forest Faire in Texas to California's San Andreas Fault. Stops are made in New York City's churches, Boston's gardens, Philadelphia's Bryn Athyn Cathedral, Orlando's Magic Kingdom, Appalachian highways, Minnesota's Viking Villages, New Orleans's Mardi Gras, and the Las Vegas Strip. As the editors and their fellow essayists take the reader on this cross-country trip across the United States, they ponder the cultural work done by the nation's medievalized spaces.

In its exploration of a seemingly distant period, this collection challenges the underexamined legacy of medievalism on the western side of the Atlantic. Full of intriguing case studies and reflections, this book is informative reading for anyone interested in the contemporary vestiges of the Middle Ages.

TISON PUGH is Pegasus Professor of English at the University of Central Florida.

SUSAN ARONSTEIN is a professor of English and Honors at the University of Wyoming.

the United States of Medievalism

Edited by
Tison Pugh
and
Susan Aronstein

UNIVERSITY OF TORONTO PRESS
Toronto Buffalo London

© University of Toronto Press 2021
Toronto Buffalo London
utorontopress.com
Printed in the U.S.A.

ISBN 978-1-4875-0738-1 (cloth)   ISBN 978-1-4875-3614-5 (EPUB)
ISBN 978-1-4875-2508-8 (paper)   ISBN 978-1-4875-3613-8 (PDF)

___

Library and Archives Canada Cataloguing in Publication

Title: The United States of medievalism / edited by Tison Pugh and Susan
Aronstein. Names: Pugh, Tison, editor. | Aronstein, Susan Lynn, editor.
Description: Includes bibliographical references and index.
Identifiers: Canadiana (print) 20210204176 | Canadiana (ebook) 20210204257 |
   ISBN 9781487525088 (paper) | ISBN 9781487507381 (cloth) |
   ISBN 9781487536145 (EPUB) | ISBN 9781487536138 (PDF)
Subjects: LCSH: Medievalism – United States. | LCSH: Popular culture –
   United States. | LCSH: United States – Civilization – Medieval influences. |
   LCSH: Europe – History – 476–1492 – Influence.
Classification: LCC CB353.U55 2021 | DDC 306.0973/09051–dc23

___

This book has been published with the assistance of the Wyoming Institute for
Humanities Research, the University of Wyoming's English Department, and UW's
College of Arts and Sciences.

University of Toronto Press acknowledges the financial assistance to its publishing
program of the Canada Council for the Arts and the Ontario Arts Council, an agency
of the Government of Ontario.

  Canada Council   Conseil des Arts
for the Arts   du Canada

To Bonnie Wheeler,
  with love, affection, and admiration,
    for her tireless advocacy of the Middle Ages and medievalists

Contents

List of Illustrations   ix

Acknowledgments   xi

Introduction: Theorizing America's Medievalisms   3
   TISON PUGH AND SUSAN ARONSTEIN

Part One: Building the American Middle Ages

1 *Translatio Horti*: Medievalized Gardens in Boston and Cambridge   21
   KATHLEEN COYNE KELLY

2 Philadelphia's Medieval(ist) Jewels: Bryn Athyn Cathedral, Glencairn, and More   45
   KEVIN J. HARTY

3 The Masonic Medievalism of Washington, DC   63
   LAURIE A. FINKE

4 Medieval Chicago: Architecture, Patronage, and Capital at the Fin de Siècle   84
   ALFRED THOMAS

Part Two: Living in the American Middle Ages

5 Three Vignettes and a White Castle: Knighthood and Race in Modern Atlanta   111
   RICHARD UTZ

6 Medieval New York City: A Walk through *The Stations of the Cross*   130
CANDACE BARRINGTON

7 Minnesota Medieval: Dragons, Knights, and Runestones   157
JANA K. SCHULMAN

8 "I Yearned for a Strange Land and a People That Had the Charm of Originality": Searching for Salvation in Medieval Appalachia   180
ALISON GULLEY

9 Wounded Landscapes: Topographies of Franciscan Spirituality and Deep Ecology in California Medievalism   197
LOWELL GALLAGHER

Part Three: Playing in the American Middle Ages

10 Orlando's Medieval Heritage Project   227
TISON PUGH AND SUSAN ARONSTEIN

11 Saints and Sinners: New Orleans's Medievalisms   246
USHA VISHNUVAJJALA AND CANDACE BARRINGTON

12 Sherwood Forest Faire: Evoking Medieval May Games, Robin Hood Revels, and Twentieth-Century "Pleasure Faires" in Contemporary Texas   264
LORRAINE KOCHANSKE STOCK

13 Las Vegas: Getting Medieval in Sin City   284
LAURIE A. FINKE AND MARTIN B. SHICHTMAN

Selected Bibliography   303

List of Contributors   309

Index   313

Illustrations

1.1	The Monks Garden of the Isabella Stewart Gardner Museum, Boston 28
1.2	Renzo Piano's plan of the Isabella Stewart Gardner Museum 29
1.3	The Monks Garden today 32
1.4	Plan of the Steele Garden 35
1.5	A view of the Steele Garden as designed 36
1.6	The Steele Garden today 36
1.7	The Cloister Garden 38
1.8	Gothic conceit at home: chain-link fence and a neighbour's privacy wall, punctuated by a mirrored arch 40
4.1	The Tribune Building, Chicago 85
4.2	Panorama of downtown Chicago 87
4.3	Panorama of San Gimignano, Italy 87
4.4	La Sainte-Chapelle, Paris 88
4.5	The Chicago Men's Athletic Association, Michigan Avenue, Chicago 93
4.6	The Fisher Building, Dearborn Street, Chicago 98
4.7	Dearborn Street Station, Chicago 99
4.8	The Palazzo Vecchio, Florence 100
4.9	The terracotta façade of 720 Dearborn Street, Printers Row, Chicago 102
6.1	The Cloisters' Gothic Chapel 135
6.2	St. Mary's Episcopal Church 138
6.3	The Cathedral of St. John the Divine 140
6.4	St. Bartholomew's Church 144
6.5	Former Sea and Land Church 150
6.6	Church of the Most Precious Blood 151

x Illustrations

7.1	Scandinavian place names and medievally themed high school mascots throughout Minnesota 159
7.2	Old Joe and Brainerd's warrior mascot 169
7.3	Glaedr the Dragon 171
7.4	Minnesota's tourism districts 174
8.1	Yosef on the Appalachian State University campus 186
8.2	"Maggie Lewis and Wilma Creech, Pine Mountain, KY," by Doris Ulmann, 1934 188
8.3	"Young Man Holding Reins to Two Plowing Horses; Man with Bucket," unknown photographer 189
9.1	Aerial photograph of the San Andreas Fault in the Carrizo Plain 198
9.2	Giovanni Baglione's *The Ecstasy of Saint Francis* (1601) 208
9.3	Mariano Salvador Maella's *Saint Francis of Assisi Receiving the Stigmata* (1787) 209
9.4	Master of Sir John Fastolf 210
9.5	Taddeo Crivelli, *Gualenghi-d'Este Hours* 211
9.6	Map of San Andreas Fault 212
9.7	Map of California mission network 213
9.8	Llagas Creek, California 218
11.1	St. Louis Cathedral from the Mississippi riverbank, with Jackson Square in front 248
11.2, 11.3	The flags along the ceiling of the St. Louis Cathedral, including multiple iterations of the US, Louisiana, and Confederate flags 250
11.4, 11.5	Two views of the Immaculate Conception Jesuit Church from across Baronne Street 252
11.6	The Maid of Orleans, rooting for the New Orleans Saints 261

Acknowledgments

We are grateful to the Wyoming Institute for Humanities Research, the University of Wyoming's English Department, and UW's College of Arts and Sciences for their generous support of this project.

THE UNITED STATES OF MEDIEVALISM

Introduction: Theorizing America's Medievalisms

TISON PUGH AND SUSAN ARONSTEIN

The Middle Ages have always been messed up in order to meet the vital requirements of different periods.

Umberto Eco, *Travels in Hyperreality*

Unlike European nations, the United States has no ruins of the Western medieval past scattered across its landscape, but its more modern geographic medievalisms have their own story to tell about the nation's character, aspirations, and fantasies. *The United States of Medievalism* explores these stories, examining the ways in which the "medieval" structures of our lives – the buildings we work in, the museums we learn in, and the spaces we play in – make America's fabricated fantasy and quasi-historical past very much part of its present and future.[1] These geographic medievalisms are physical places where imaginary pasts are enacted and re-created. Although America's place-based medievalisms may be fanciful, these locations house memories and desires of the past and present, participating in the construction of what Tim Cresswell, citing the work of E.S. Casey, terms "place memory": "the ability to make the past come to life in the present and thus contribute to the construction of social memory."[2]

America's place-based medievalisms are wholly fabricated – no ruin to preserve, no field on which a battle actually occurred. They are material manifestations of a collective memory of the Middle Ages mostly rooted in aesthetic and popular medievalisms: Tennyson, Twain, Disney; Camelot, *Harry Potter*, *Game of Thrones*; knights in shining armour and pastel castles; dragons and wizards; chivalry and barbarity. While heritage sites based on actual history (however selected, interpreted, and commodified) shore up a community's collective memory by providing what Pierre Nora has famously termed *lieux de memoire*, America's medieval sites reify and validate our collective imagination; they are, in the words of Stijn Reijnders, *lieux d'imagination*. Reijnders's analysis of media tourists, those who "starting with their imagination, go in search of physical material references ... to give shape to their ideas – in order literally to give a place to their fantasies, dreams and feelings of fear," can usefully be extended to consider the production and consumption of place-based medievalisms in the United States.[3] The producers of these sites situate their fantasies of the Middle Ages geographically, allowing their "imaginations to take on tangible form"; this tangible form allows consumers to step into these spaces, both real and imaginary, and "to become themselves part of the world of the imagination."[4]

Unlike the literary, cinematic, and digital medievalisms upon which these *lieux d'imagination* are based, geographic medievalisms do not merely evoke the sights, smells, sounds, textures, and tastes of the "Middle Ages"; they offer visitors a chance to experience them. Patrons do not just read about the feast and tournament or observe it on screen; they smell the roasting meat, taste the mead, hear the clanking of the armour, see the dust fly up from the horses' hooves, feel the rough wood of the table. By involving the senses, by providing patrons with "history in place," these sites bring the past into the present. What they choose to "remember," and which Middle Ages they choose to appropriate, constructs a social memory that bears real consequences for national, regional, gender, and ethnic identities.

This introduction maps out the medieval *lieux d'imagination* and their theoretical stakes as explored throughout *The United States of Medievalism*. We begin with a brief discussion of medievalism as both an artistic practice and an academic field and then turn to a historical examination of the United States' ongoing (and conflicted) relationship with the medieval past. The introduction concludes with an overview of the volume's chapters, which discuss varieties of American medievalism that span the nation's geographic and temporal range.

Theorizing Medievalisms

The United States of America's centuries-long return to the medieval past suggests that rather than escaping the Middle Ages, as the nation's originary legends might imply, its citizens have been continually immersed in fantasies of this bygone era, with these fantasies presenting multiple, often contradictory, Middle Ages – a lost golden age, a barbaric past, a chivalric utopia, a Christian kingdom, a mystical land. The list, and the ideological and political uses to which these medieval pasts have been put, could expand extensively. As such, the history of America's engagement with the Middle Ages provides a textbook example of medievalism, defined by Richard Utz as "the ongoing and broad cultural phenomenon of reinventing, remembering, recreating, and reenacting the Middle Ages," a past that need have little real foundation in history so long as it responds to a contemporary need for a fabricated past.[5] Louise D'Arcens distinguishes between "the medievalism of the 'found' Middle Ages and the medievalism of the 'made' Middle Ages," with the former "emerg[ing] through contact with, and interpretation of, the 'found' or material remains of the medieval past surviving into the post-medieval era" and the latter "encompass[ing] texts, objects, performances, and practices that are not only post-medieval in their provenance but imaginative in their impulse and founded on ideas of 'the medieval' as a conceptual rather than a historical category."[6] Within D'Arcens's framework, American medievalisms are, by definition, "made," as they reflect the nation's efforts to define for its citizens the meaning both of the medieval past and of their present moment through a range of cultural artefacts and practices. As Morton Bloomfield observes, "Our deepest dreams and hopes" – and, we would add, our inmost nightmares – "are often clothed in medieval garments," necessitating a closer examination of what such costuming reveals about these medievalist impulses.[7]

Although the *study* of medievalism is relatively new – many scholars identify Alice Chandler's 1970 volume, *A Dream of Order: The Medieval Ideal in Nineteenth-Century English Literature*, as the beginning of the field – the *practice* of medievalism arguably began in the Middle Ages itself, as sundry narratives invent an ideal chivalric past that highlights the lamentable conditions of their authors' contemporary moment. In his twelfth-century romances, Chrétien de Troyes frequently bemoans the loss of courtly manners, as in the opening lines of *Yvain* that recall the feasting at Arthur's court:

> Some told of past adventures, others spoke of love: of the anguish and sorrows, but also of the great blessings often enjoyed by the disciples of its order, which in those days was sweet and flourishing. But today very few serve love: nearly everyone has abandoned it; and love is greatly abased, because those who loved in bygone days were known to be courtly and valiant and generous and honourable.[8]

Chrétien's words evince a longing for a past that is always outside of one's grasp, and it little matters whether he envisioned it as 50 or 250 years prior to penning his poem in the twelfth century. His Middle Ages, as with many such Middle Ages, simply stresses the lamented loss of a better era – along with the paradox that Chrétien would never realize that his contemporary era would later be conscripted to serve as a historical "middle" between the classical past and an as-yet-unrealized future.

As the creation and ideological conscription of the Middle Ages began in the late fifteenth century, various writers and thinkers defined themselves in opposition to a medieval past they figured as synonymous with the barbaric, the violent, and the superstitious. For years, scholars identified this self-fashioned break from the past as the Renaissance; more recently, they have christened it as "early modern," presenting such moments as Poggio Bracciolini's fifteenth-century rediscovery of Lucretius's *De rerum natura* as a pivotal turning point in Western intellectual history – *The Swerve*, in Stephen Greenblatt's famous title, that, as his subtitle promises, explains *How the World Became Modern*.[9] Centuries later, this cultural understanding of the Middle Ages as temporal Other to the Renaissance was nicely captured in the early history of the now-prolific Renaissance faires. Conceived in the early 1960s as a countercultural utopic site returning visitors to a freer, less corporate time, the Medieval Faire was renamed by its first sponsor, the left-wing radio station KPFK, because a board member objected to the name "on the grounds that human rights in medieval Europe were few." The Faire's founder, Phyllis Patterson, "swiftly suggested calling it instead a 'Renaissance Faire.'"[10] Just as few query whether any compliment is indeed intended to the Renaissance in renaming it "early modern," as any number of modernity's innovations are of dubious merit, few note the irony of the boards' embrace of the same faire with a new title but no other changes in costumes, performers, artisans, and entertainments; the Renaissance hardly advanced the cause of universal human rights.

While the Faire's founders renamed it owing to modernity's conception of the Middle Ages as the temporal Other from which we have distanced ourselves – a barbaric past long surpassed – the Faire itself demonstrates the persistence of Chrétien's chivalric vision of the Middle Ages as the site of a lost ideal and a past to which the modern must return. The enchantment with the "modern" – whether during the Renaissance, the 1960s, or today – is not universal. People, almost inevitably, deploy the past in the present to buttress their claims of authority (as Henry VIII did when he appropriated and redecorated the Winchester Round Table) or to lament the loss of a golden past (as did the Faire's artisanal festivals in an age of mass consumption).

From Chrétien's nostalgic gaze towards a past lamentable for its inevitable loss to the Faire's carnivalesque re-creation of that past in the 1960s, it is apparent that the present moment, no matter when that present moment occurs in history, almost invariably requires a past through which its inhabitants can rejuvenate themselves. Furthermore, if the Middle Ages have "always been messed up," as Eco suggests in this introduction's epigraph, to suit the needs and desires of the present, not all of those needs and desires have been benevolent, nor have the uses to which they have been put. As recent academic work, public debate, and current events demonstrate, we need to pay close attention to how and why multiple, contradictory, and particular Middle Ages are created. Medievalism may turn to the past but it operates in the present, and, to put it bluntly, some dreams of the Middle Ages bear ugly consequences. They have been used to shore up the status quo, to valorize martial violence, to urge imperialism, to justify slavery, and to perpetuate racist ideologies and regimes. Examples of malevolent medievalisms run throughout the history of the field, often appearing under the guise of a seemingly innocent longing for a lost golden age and in apparently benign and apolitical popular culture forms. Writing about Hollywood's influence on early twenty-first-century political debates, Tom Shippey worries that "medieval" films such as *Braveheart* (1995), *First Knight* (1995), and *King Arthur* (2004) and contemporary politics are not as separate as we might hope: "It would be sad to think that the highest levels of public policy have been determined, however unconsciously, by a historical awareness derived from medievalizing movies: but in America the movie world and the political world are increasingly closely connected, and the movie world ... has been shown to have had real-world political effects."[11] Whereas Shippey is concerned about the connection between film narratives and political policy, Bruce Holsinger raises the alarm about medievalism in public discourse post-9/11. "Medievalism in this climate," he asserts, "has become the historical handmaiden of a renewed anti-intellectualism that casts suspicion on any politically-minded utterance from within the American university as the sign of a debased leftism that flirts with outright treason."[12] To label one's adversaries as "medieval" is the ultimate insult within political discourse, effectively constructing an opponent as the Other, both morally and temporally excluded from the succours of modernity.

Such connections between medievalism and politics, particularly a politics of "purity," result in one of the most persistent and destructive uses of the Middle Ages: the turn to the medieval past to bolster white nationalism and to perpetuate antisemitism, racism, and other malevolent Otherings. As Robert Chazan demonstrates in *Medieval Stereotypes and Modern Antisemitism*, antisemitism is, in effect, a form of medievalism; he documents the ways in which "long after the Jews had left much of northern Europe, the ideational legacy of the mid-twelfth century maintained its hold on the European imagination," even as "the nineteenth and twentieth centuries added new elements to evolving anti-Jewish imagery."[13] Cord J. Whitaker and Matthew Gabriele explore the intersections of imperialism, medievalism, and racism in the nineteenth century, detailing how "the 1800s saw the zenith of European imperialism, and medievalism was deployed as a tool for the inextricable projects of nation-building and racialization."[14] Similarly, many of the tropes of post-9/11 Islamophobia derive from medieval sources, such as *The Song of Roland*, Chaucer's *Man of Law's Tale*, and romances of the Crusades, at the same time that the Western Far Right has created its own fantasy version of the Middle Ages, one in which a unified – that is, white – Europe resisted Muslim incursions into its landscape and led the attack against "infidels" in the Crusades.[15] The brutal real-world consequences of medievalized fantasies of virile masculinity and white nationality have become only too apparent in the daily news cycle, as images of the angry white men of the alt-right, bearing shields emblazoned with medieval imagery and chanting racist slogans, march for a return to their version of the medieval past, one heavily based on the medievalism of the Confederacy, whose statues and monuments have provided these groups with their rallying cry.

Such are the disturbing undercurrents of medievalism, ones that medievalists – both lay and professional – must acknowledge in the work that we do, the classes that we teach, and the cultural artefacts that we enjoy.[16] As Sierra Lomuto passionately avers, "We have an ethical responsibility to ensure that the knowledge we create and disseminate about the medieval past is not weaponized against people of colour and marginalized communities in our own contemporary world."[17] Theorizing medievalisms necessitates that we recognize their aesthetic allure and their brute force, as well as our complicity in their reproduction in the present and into the future, a process that has unfolded in uniquely American ways since the dawning of the republic, in spite of the fact that the republic was explicitly founded in opposition to the European Middle Ages.[18]

American Medievalisms

It would be a virtually impossible task to tally the complete range of American medievalisms. The US landscape is dotted with tourist castles and neo-Gothic college campuses,[19] as well as with medieval fairs, museums, cathedrals, and attractions offering visitors a chance to step into a history capturing America's wide-ranging artistic, literary, and cinematic engagement with the medieval past. Medieval traditions influenced America's music, as Elizabeth Aubrey documents,[20] and its visual arts, as seen in such works as Edwin Austin Abbey's Quest for the Holy Grail murals in Boston's Central Library in Copley Square.[21] In literature, Chaucer and Dante continue to hold sway over the nation's narrative traditions,[22] while noted works of American poetry and fiction – James Russell Lowell's *The Vision of Sir Launfal* (1848), Mark Twain's *A Connecticut Yankee in King Arthur's Court* (1889), T.S. Eliot's *The Waste Land* (1922), Walker Percy's *Lancelot* (1977), and Marion Zimmer Bradley's *Mists of Avalon* (1983) – attest to the United States' lasting literary engagement with medievalism. Moreover, authors such as F. Scott Fitzgerald and Ernest Hemingway often imbue works set in the modern world with medieval structures and themes.[23] These esteemed works stand alongside the plethora of pop-culture offerings to be found on the shelves of the fantasy and sci-fi sections.

America's medievalisms include Hollywood's medievalisms, and the Middle Ages appears throughout the history of film. Early silent works, including Cecil B. DeMille's *Joan the Woman* (1916) and Allan Dwan's *Robin Hood* (1922), proved that new technologies were compatible with medieval narrative traditions, and the success of these early works paved the way for the ever-expanding corpus of Arthurian adaptations, including such notable examples of this subgenre as *Knights of the Round Table* (1953), *Camelot* (1963), *Excalibur* (1981), *King Arthur* (2004), and *King Arthur: Legend of the Sword* (2017).[24] Robin Hood has likewise inspired a vast oeuvre of Hollywood cinema, and a range of broadly medieval themes and settings continually return to the screen. Even pornography looks back to the medieval past.[25] Hearing, viewing, dreaming the Middle Ages, the nation's citizens also re-embody the medieval past, either by donning armour, tunics, and wimples under the apparently benign auspices of the Society for Creative Anachronism and various cosplay organizations or by taking up shields and torches under the dark influence of the alt-right.

Yet how incongruent this medieval mania appears in contrast to the aspirations of the nation's founders. In *The Federalist Papers*, Alexander Hamilton, James Madison, and John Jay established a spirited opposition between the United States as a forward-looking nation and European countries as mired in the medieval past. These essays, published in 1788 as the states debated whether to ratify the new Constitution, carefully define and defend the authors' vision for America's fledgling "more perfect union." They begin with a continent untouched by the past, waiting to be inscribed with a new form of government:

> One connected, fertile, widespreading country was the portion of our western sons of liberty. Providence has in a particular manner blessed it with a variety of soils and productions and watered it with innumerable streams for the delight and accommodation of its inhabitants. A succession of navigable waters forms a kind of chain round its borders, as if to bind it together; while the most noble rivers in the world, running at convenient distances, present them with highways for the easy communication of friendly aids and the mutual transportation and exchange of their various commodities. (91)[26]

On this blank landscape, blessed by nature and Providence, the authors celebrate "one united people … descended from the same ancestors, speaking the same language, professing the same religion, attached to the same principles of government … fighting side by side," for they "have nobly established general liberty and independence" (91). To allow liberty and independence to thrive, Americans "have not suffered a blind veneration for antiquity, for custom, or for names" (144). This new nation required a clean break with a medieval past of tyrannical monarchs, feuding barons, and corrupt nobility. Its new government, *The Federalist Papers* insists, must be liberated from the European Middle Ages so that it can offer a republic that "derives all of its powers directly or indirectly from the great body of the people" (255). Government must be open to "every citizen whose merit may recommend him to the esteem and confident of his country. No qualification of wealth, of birth, of religious faith, or of civil profession is permitted to fetter the judgement of the people" (344). In fact, "the prohibition of titles of nobility" is "truly … denominated the cornerstone of republican government; for so long as they are excluded, there can never be serious danger that the government will be any other than that of the people" (475).

This fear that the federal government outlined in the new Constitution would fall out of the people's hands was inflamed by the menace of the medieval past, with opposition to the new government, in its fear of regression to tyrants and kings, fanning these flames:

> Calculating upon the aversion of the people to monarchy, they have endeavored to enlist all their jealousies and apprehensions in opposition to the intended President of the United States … He has been shown to us with the diadem sparkling on his brow and the imperial purple flowing in his train. He has been seated on a throne surrounded with minions and mistresses, giving audience to the envoys of foreign potentates in all the supercilious pomp of majesty. (389)

The Federalist Papers promises that the spectre raised in the vision of the president as monarch would never be realized. However, Hamilton, Madison, and Jay also recognized that the country needed to guard against such a return and offered the principles of government laid out in the Constitution as a bulwark against the Middle Ages, assuring that monarchs, barons, tyrants, and sycophants wielding unbridled power would have no place in the new republic. It seems little exaggeration to state that the founding figures of the American revolution fought the residual governmental structures of the Middle Ages as much as they fought King George III.

And yet prior to, concurrent with, and subsequent to *The Federalist Papers*, the United States of America embarked on a long love affair with the Middle Ages: neo-Gothic castles and cathedrals adorned the country's landscape, medieval-inspired literature and art filled its homes, and its citizens admired imagery, institutions, and ideals purportedly drawn from a chivalric and martial past. Rather than rejecting the Middle Ages, the country embraced the era, extolling an Anglophilic medievalism that, as Thomas Bulfinch writes in his *The Age of Chivalry* (1858), offers Americans a "full share in the glories and recollections of the land of our forefathers, down to the time of colonization thence." Through his retelling of the legends of King Arthur, Bulfinch invites his readers to benefit from "the associations which spring from this source," promising that they will be "fruitful of good influences."[27]

To do so, however, Americans needed to invent Europe in much the same way that the early European explorers had invented America.[28] For nineteenth-century American medieval enthusiasts, the Middle Ages was *American* – proto-democratic, youthful, vigorous, natural, manly – a true medieval past prior to the tyrannical, decadent, soft, over-civilized, feminized past from which the founding fathers had freed this new land. These first American returns to the Middle Ages offered the past as a corrective to a present that many of its creators saw as rapidly becoming decidedly *un-American*, in danger of becoming decadent, over-civilized, *European*. With growing antimodernist sentiment among the intelligentsia and the middle and upper classes, some feared that Charles Darwin's evolutionary theories, suffragettes' demands for franchise, the ills of urban life, and unassimilated immigrants threatened the mental, moral, and physical health of the nation and its citizens. T.J. Jackson Lears argues that, by the late nineteenth century, Americans worried that their nation had lost its way – its "apple-cheeked farm boys" and its "manly song" could only be set back on course through a return to an invented medieval past that "exalted robust simplicity, moral certainty … an ability to act decisively, regeneration through preindustrial craftsmanship, and a 'pastoral' simple life," in which "the violent lives of medieval warriors" stood "as a refreshing contrast to the blandness of modern life." In their turn to the past, the antimodernists "longed to rekindle possibilities for authentic experience, physical or spiritual – possibilities they felt had existed once before, long ago."[29] As English Victorians – for instance, Alfred, Lord Tennyson with his *Idylls of the King* and the Pre-Raphaelites with their paintings – turned to the Middle Ages for inspiration against the stultifying effects of the Industrial Revolution, so too did Americans look to the past for rejuvenation in the present, even if doing so required looking back both across the Atlantic and centuries prior in time.

Not all nineteenth-century Americans, however, subscribed to the medieval fad and its nostalgia for a lost golden age. The Middle Ages still represented a barbaric past for many, and its ideals undermined America's founding principles of democratic opportunity, progressive optimism, and technological possibilities. Few authors represent the contrasting receptions of the American Middle Ages in this century as strikingly as Mark Twain – a one-man incarnation of the cultural contradictions of medievalism. With characteristic sarcasm, he skewered neo-Gothic architecture, such as in his snide assessment of Louisiana's Old State Capitol Building in *Life on the Mississippi*, which he blamed on Sir Walter Scott's medievalisms: "Sir Walter Scott is probably responsible for the Capitol building; for it is not conceivable that this little sham castle would ever have been built if he had not run the people mad, a couple of generations ago, with his mediaeval romances."[30] Here Twain's distaste is for medievalism rather than for the Middle Ages, yet he brashly admits in *A Connecticut Yankee in King Arthur's Court* that he has little interest in the actual conditions of the past:

> It is not pretended that these laws and customs existed in England in the sixth century; no, it is only pretended that inasmuch as they existed in the English and other civilizations of far later times, it is safe to consider that it is no libel upon the sixth century to suppose them to have been in practice in that day also. One is quite justified in inferring that wherever one of these laws and customs was lacking in that remote time, its place was competently filled by a worse one.[31]

Despite this dismissive stance, the narrative arc of Twain's protagonist Hank Morgan progresses from his sneering at the medieval past as a hopelessly backward time to his lamenting its loss by the novel's end. And, in his own engagements with the Middle Ages, Twain himself seems to be no less conflicted. He frequently took antagonistic stances towards the Middle Ages, but he also continually returned to medieval themes and storylines in his literature, as evident in his short story "A Medieval Romance" (1869) and his novel *Personal Recollections of Joan of Arc* (1896) – reportedly the work he declared to be his best. No single person can represent a nation's response to a diverse cultural phenomenon, but Twain's conflicting assessments, which collectively suggest his distaste, his ambivalence, and his passion for the Middle Ages, run a startlingly wide spectrum. He metonymically captures the full range of American reactions to medievalisms, attesting through his writings the allure and the inherent awkwardness of the medieval past reborn in the modern United States.

The United States may have been founded in a rejection of the Middle Ages, and many of its citizens over the years have rejected America's medievalism. But just as many Americans have embraced them, and these continuing rebirths of the Middle Ages have indelibly shaped the country's culture and its landscape from its founding in the eighteenth century, through its development in the nineteenth, and into its recent history in the twentieth and into the twenty-first. As Eco phrased it, America is still "living in the Middle Ages" – whether as a long-lost golden age of chivalry and courtly manners, as a Gothic and terrifying inquisitorial reign, or as some distinct hodgepodge of sundry medieval tropes. Dreams of knights and wizards, a chivalric ideal of courtly love, and alarming resurgent dark fantasies of a militantly white nation, among myriad other such re-creations of medieval history, both real and unreal, have a lasting grasp on the public's imagination. This volume acknowledges these conflicting impulses behind the nation's re-creation of a Western European medieval past, illuminating the ways in which the American landscape refracts contradictory visions of idealism and regression.

America's Medievalisms from Sea to Shining Sea

Working from these observations, the contributors to *The United States of Medievalism* contemplate the desires, dreams, and contradictions inherent in experiencing the European Middle Ages in a nation so temporally, spatially, and at times politically removed from them. The first unit, "Building the American Middle Ages," considers the ways in which the European Middle Ages have influenced the national landscape of the United States. In "*Translatio Horti*: Medievalized Gardens in Boston and Cambridge," Kathleen Coyne Kelly tells the story of medievalized gardens, hybridized fantasy spaces that inscribe a medieval else*time* onto the American landscape. Kelly argues that these gardens, inspired by medieval narratives such as Chaucer's *Canterbury Tales*, the *Roman de la Rose*, and illuminated books of hours that were later remediated by William Morris and the Arts and Crafts movement, represent a green medievalism that speaks to the power and privilege of those who designed them, and for whose use their enclosed paradises were reserved. Tracing the histories of three early twentieth-century gardens – Boston's Monks Garden, now part of the Isabella Stewart Gardner Museum, and the Steele Garden and the Cloister Garden, both attached to the Society of St. John the Evangelist Monastery in Cambridge – Kelly examines how these green medievalisms, landscaped into an American city, can still transport visitors to a fantasy of the European medieval past. Kelly's study of Cambridge's and Boston's ecomedievalisms testifies to the attraction of the past in an ostensibly new world, with this allure clearly speaking to Pennsylvania businessman Raymond Pitcairn in the early twentieth century. Pitcairn supervised the construction of both a cathedral to host a denomination of Emanuel Swedenborg's New Church and his own family home, and in "Philadelphia's Medieval(ist) Jewels: Bryn Athyn Cathedral, Glencairn, and More," Kevin J. Harty examines Pitcairn's motivation in building these massive, elaborate "medieval" structures and the ironic relationship between the tenets of Swedenborg's "New Church" and the traditions of the Middle Ages.

Laurie A. Finke continues this discussion of the connections between medievalism, architecture, and cultural traditions in "The Masonic Medievalism of Washington, DC." Focusing on the Freemasons, one of the United States' oldest fraternal organizations, Finke examines the organization's contradictory movement between medieval esoterica and enlightenment rationality, between hierarchy and egalitarianism, in its medieval origin story, as evident in two buildings: the House of the Temple, located in Dupont Circle, and the George Washington Masonic Memorial, located in Alexandria, Virginia. In "Medieval Chicago: Architecture, Patronage, and Capital at the Fin de Siècle," Alfred Thomas turns from architectural style and interior decoration to function, exploring the affinity between the modern American architecture of Chicago, with its towering skyscrapers alongside imposing examples of neo-medieval architecture, and the fortresses of medieval cities, such as those found in Italy's San Gimignano. Observing that these fortresses lend the Italian hilltop town a strangely Manhattan-like look, Thomas argues that both urban spaces, medieval and modern, are characterized by a shared capitalist psychology of acquisitive mistrust.

Part 2, "Living in the American Middle Ages," discusses the ways in which America's built medievalisms, many from the nineteenth and early twentieth centuries, still shape communities, collapsing the binaries between past and present, medieval and modern, European and American, across the United States. In "Three Vignettes and a White Castle: Knighthood and Race in Modern Atlanta," Richard Utz turns to various examples of early twentieth-century Southern medievalism – Stone Mountain, Rhodes Hall (built in 1904), and *Gone with the Wind* (novel 1936, film 1939) – that romanticize the history of the "Lost Cause." These sites and cultural artefacts read the antebellum South through a medievalized lens, interweaving cavaliers and cotton fields, knights and their ladies fair, master and slave, in an act of celebratory remembrance, while using the medieval past to relegate Black bodies to pieces of decoration and furniture. Candace Barrington continues this discussion of how "medieval" structures influence those who view and inhabit them. In "Medieval New York City: A Walk through *The Stations of the Cross*," Barrington undertakes a walking tour of the city based on an art exhibit reimagining Jesus's Crucifixion, visiting such urban landmarks as the Church of St. Vincent Ferrer, the Woolworth Building, City College of New York, and the September 11 Memorial, postulating how the architectures of medievalism intersect with its practices, allowing the residents of the United States' most populous – and often thought of as its most modern – city to travel back to the Middle Ages. Jana K. Schulman explores another American claim to medieval origins, with accompanying attractions, in "Minnesota Medieval: Dragons, Knights, and Runestones," tracing the ways in which Minnesota's Scandinavian immigrants kept their Viking heritage alive in the nineteenth and twentieth centuries through place names, cultural organizations, and college and high school curricula, embracing the romantic notion of the chivalric Viking as central to that heritage. This heritage, Schulman demonstrates, persists across the state, embodied in high school mascots, embraced in the Minnesota Vikings, and marketed to the tourists who come seeking Vikingland and the Kensington Runestone, discovered (or manufactured) in 1898, the *X* that supposedly marked the spot where medieval Vikings landed in Minnesota.

In the final two essays of "Living in the American Middle Ages," Alison Gulley and Lowell Gallagher turn to the intersection of landscape, ecology, and American medievalism. In "'I Yearned for a Strange Land and a People That Had the Charm of Originality': Searching for Salvation in Medieval Appalachia," Gulley compares the temporality of the so-called Dark Ages to the geography of Appalachia, discussing how both an earlier era and a current geography are defined for many through their purported primitivism. Gulley draws out these contrasting impulses that attribute to the Middle Ages and Appalachia a backwardness that also constitutes their allure as idyllic spaces freed from the encroachments of modernity. Gallagher, in "Wounded Landscapes: Topographies of Franciscan Spirituality and Deep Ecology in California Medievalism," employs the metaphors of the state's fault lines and St. Francis's stigmata to analyse the state's network of Franciscan missions and other elements of its history. From these foundations, he theorizes the ways in which the ecological practices of the past influence those of the present, particularly in the contrast between a medieval sense of humility in light of the universe's unknowability and a modern sense of rationality in humanity's attempt to master the unmasterable.

The third and final unit, "Playing in the American Middle Ages," discusses America's medieval play spaces, sites specifically constructed to allow their visitors to immerse themselves in the past. It begins with two chapters that visit locations laying claim to, as well as constructing, a fantasy Middle Ages. In "Orlando's Medieval Heritage Project," Tison Pugh and Susan Aronstein explore the ways in which Orlando has repeatedly invented its own medieval past, from the city's competing nineteenth-century origin stories to its numerous twenty-first-century tourist castles. Pugh and Aronstein's examination of the narratives, genres, and technologies that create the medieval past in Central Florida reveals the ways in which these medieval play spaces don't so much stand in contrast to the real Middle Ages as create a new form of community for the millions of tourists who flock to such attractions as the Magic Kingdom, the Wizarding World of Harry Potter, and Medieval Times. Usha Vishnuvajjala and Candace Barrington's "Saints and Sinners: New Orleans's Medievalisms" shows that America's most European city also engages in medieval time travel. Exploring the contradictory themes of the city's iconic Carnival celebrations – order/chaos, uptown/downtown, white/Black, male/female – Vishnuvajjala and Barrington trace the ways in which medieval social practices affect the structures of life in a city influenced by a range of disparate cultures – French, Spanish, Cajun, Creole, and also American and Southern – examining its churches and its Mardi Gras carnivals as sites of conflicting appropriations of the past.

The final two chapters in *The United States of Medievalism* turn to sites where "authenticity," meticulously re-created, coexists with the knowing wink. Lorraine Kochanske Stock visits two Sherwood Forests in "Sherwood Forest Faire: Evoking Medieval May Games, Robin Hood Revels, and Twentieth-Century 'Pleasure Faires' in Contemporary Texas," observing that the real Sherwood Forest, with its information centre and gift shop, is in many ways less "authentic" than Texas's careful re-creation of Sherwood Forest as it should have been, given its role as the romanticized landscape of the Robin Hood tales. "Las Vegas: Getting Medieval in Sin City," by Laurie A. Finke and Martin B. Shichtman, turns to America's ultimate adult play space, the 4.2-mile stretch of the Vegas Strip that through hyperreal re-creations of everything from fantasy castles to Italian villas caters to a hodgepodge of medieval fantasies and fantasists. By reading a timeshare sales pitch through the lens of Chaucer's *Pardoner's Tale*, Finke and Shichtman argue that Las Vegas's medievalism lies not so much in its Disneyfied castles, Arthurian-themed weddings, and lusty wenches as in its structural function as a pilgrimage site for sin, where people flock to be healed of the "sickness" of the everyday.

These various medievalisms occur in and through time – in the moment of their creation and consumption but also in the nebulous temporality of their medieval roots. Furthermore, they intersect in their organizing principles: one builds a geographic medieval past with the presumption of living in it, and thus of playing in it as well, and so the units of this volume should not be seen as envisioning clean divisions between building, living, and playing as much as in prioritizing modes that then collude. The American landscape, it appears, needs the Middle Ages. "If the Middle Ages hadn't existed, people might have had to invent them, just so that we could safely be non-medieval, and have someplace exotic to fly to when modern life got too, well, modern," Catharine Brown muses.[32] Brown's formulation applies well to the United States of America: in its historical self-construction as a land pushing westward geographically to the Pacific Coast and philosophically into an enlightened future emancipated from European despotism, the nation looks beyond the past yet then inevitably looks back upon it as well. The United States' medievalisms are etched on its landscape and in its cultural practices, as the following chapters, pondering both the regional variations and the historical persistence of the American Middle Ages, so strikingly illustrate. Exploring America's built medieval sites, including the various tourist traps, cultural institutions, and educational venues that create a unique vision of the European Middle Ages for the delight, inspiration, and edification of their consumers, these contributions stretch from sea to shining sea, from New York City across the Midwest and through the plains to Los Angeles, and from the early nineteenth century to the present.

NOTES

1 In referring to America and American medievalisms, we employ a shorthand for the United States of America while acknowledging the semantic slip between two continents (North and South America) and one nation (United States of America). In such instances, the word *American* is used simply as an adjective referring to the United States, despite its potential to denote the diverse cultures of its respective continents.
2 Tim Cresswell, *Place: A Short Introduction*, 2nd ed. (Chichester, UK: Wiley Blackwell, 2015), 121; see also E.S. Casey, *Remembering: A Phenomenological Study* (Bloomington: Indiana University Press, 1987), esp. 189–96.
3 Stijn Reijnders, *Places of the Imagination: Media, Tourism, Culture* (Farnham, UK: Ashgate, 2011), 114.
4 Reijnders, *Places of the Imagination*, 114, 108.
5 Richard Utz, *Medievalism: A Manifesto* (Kalamazoo, MI: Arc Humanities Press, 2017), 81.
6 Louise D'Arcens, "Medievalism: Scope and Complexity," in *The Cambridge Companion to Medievalism*, ed. Louise D'Arcens (Cambridge: Cambridge University Press, 2016), 1–13, at 2.
7 Morton Bloomfield, "Reflections of a Medievalist: America, Medievalism, and the Middle Ages," in *Medievalism in American Culture*, ed. Bernard Rosenthal and Paul Szarmach (Binghamton, NY: Medieval and Renaissance Texts and Studies, 1989), 13–29, at 27.

8 Chrétien de Troyes, *Arthurian Romances*, trans. William Kibler (London: Penguin, 199), 295.
9 Stephen Greenblatt, *The Swerve: How the World Became Modern* (New York: Norton, 2011). For critiques of Greenblatt's argument and its oversimplification of the trajectory from the Middle Ages to the Renaissance, see "Book Review Forum: *The Swerve: How the World Became Modern*," *Exemplaria* 25, no. 4 (2013): 313–70.
10 Rachel Lee Rubin, *Well Met: Renaissance Faires and the American Counterculture* (New York: New York University Press, 2012), 24.
11 Tom Shippey, "Medievalisms and Why They Matter," *Studies in Medievalism* 17 (2009): 45–54, at 52.
12 Bruce Holsinger, *Neomedievalism, Neoconservatism, and the War on Terror* (Chicago: Prickly Paradigm Press, 2007), 14.
13 Robert Chazan, *Medieval Stereotypes and Modern Antisemitism* (Berkeley: University of California Press, 1997), 139–40.
14 Cord J. Whitaker and Matthew Gabriele, "Mountain Haints: Towards a Medieval Studies Exorcized," *Postmedieval: A Journal of Medieval Cultural Studies* 10, no. 2 (2019): 129–36, at 133.
15 For a discussion of the European Far Right's use of medievalism in the service of white nationalism, see Andrew Elliot, *Medievalism, Politics, and Mass Media* (Cambridge: D.S. Brewer, 2017).
16 An excellent example of medievalists addressing these ugly issues can be found in *The Public Medievalist*'s recent series, "Race, Racism and the Middle Ages," www.publicmedievalist.com/race-racism-middle-ages-toc (accessed 14 Dec. 2017).
17 Sierra Lomuto, "White Nationalism and the Ethics of Medieval Studies," inthemiddle.com, n.d. (accessed 31 Dec. 2018).
18 Several scholars have noted that the nation's continual return to the Middle Ages seems incompatible with the American mythos. See, for example, John Fraser, *America and the Patterns of Chivalry* (New York: Cambridge University Press, 1982); and Alan Lupack, "American Arthurian Authors: A Declaration of Independence," in *The Arthurian Revival: Essays on Form, Tradition, and Transformation*, ed. Debra Mancoff (New York: Garland, 1992), 155–73.
19 Counting American castles: Hearst, Sleeping Beauty, Cinderella, Medieval Times Dinner Theater (multiply by eight), Excalibur Hotel and Casino, Knights Inns galore, Bishop, Belvedere, Boldt, Bannerman, Castello Di'Amorosa, Castle Farms, Fonthill, Lyndhurst, Thornewood, Loveland, Ravenwood, Oheka, Gillette, Grey Towers – and many, many more. On Collegiate Gothic, see Jan M. Ziolkowski, "The Rise of Collegiate Gothic," in *The Juggler of Notre Dame and the Medievalizing of Modernity*, vol. 3, *The American Middle Ages* (Cambridge: Open Book, 2018), 189–238.
20 Elizabeth Aubrey, "Medievalism in American Musical Life," in *Reflections on American Music: The Twentieth Century and the New Millennium*, ed. James Heintze and Michael Saffle (Hillsdale, NY: Pendragon Press, 2000), 55–63.

21 On Arthurian images in European and American art, see Muriel Whitaker, *The Legends of King Arthur in Art* (Cambridge: D.S. Brewer, 1990), esp. 287–309.
22 For American adaptations of Chaucer's literature, see Candace Barrington, *American Chaucers* (New York: Palgrave Macmillan, 2007), and Kathleen Forni, *Chaucer's Afterlife: Adaptations in Recent Popular Culture* (Jefferson, NC: McFarland, 2013). For Dante's journeys in America, see A. Bartlett Giamatti, ed., *Dante in America: The First Two Centuries* (Binghamton, NY: Center for Medieval and Early Renaissance Studies, 1983); and Dennis Looney, *Freedom Readers: The African American Reception of Dante Alighieri and the Divine Comedy* (Notre Dame, IN: Notre Dame University Press, 2011).
23 On America's literary medievalisms, see Kim Moreland, *The Medievalist Impulse in American Literature: Twain, Adams, Fitzgerald, and Hemingway* (Charlottesville: University of Virginia Press, 1996).
24 On American adaptations of medieval film, see Susan Aronstein, *Hollywood Knights: Arthurian Cinema and the Politics of Nostalgia* (New York: Palgrave Macmillan, 2005); Laurie A. Finke and Martin B. Shichtman, *Cinematic Illuminations: The Middle Ages on Film* (Baltimore, MD: Johns Hopkins University Press, 2010); and Kevin J. Harty, *The Reel Middle Ages: American, Western and Eastern European, Middle Eastern and Asian Films about Medieval Europe*, 2nd ed. (Jefferson, NC: McFarland, 2006).
25 On medievalism and pornography, see Steven F. Kruger, "Gay Internet Medievalism: Erotic Story Archives, the Middle Ages, and Contemporary Gay Identity," *American Literary History* 22, no. 4 (2010): 913–44.
26 James Madison, Alexander Hamilton, and John Jay, *The Federalist Papers*, ed. Isaac Kramnick (1788; New York: Penguin, 1987); cited parenthetically.
27 Thomas Bulfinch, *Bulfinch's Mythology: The Age of Fable, the Age of Chivalry, Legends of Charlemagne* (1858; New York: Modern Library, n.d.), 299–300.
28 On the point of the United States' and Europe's mutual and "medieval" inventions of each other, see Bernard Rosenthal and Paul Szarmach, "Introduction," in Rosenthal and Szarmach, *Medievalism in American Culture*, 1–12.
29 T.J. Jackson Lears, *No Place of Grace: Antimodernism and the Transformation of American Culture, 1880–1920* (Chicago: University of Chicago Press, 1981), 57.
30 Mark Twain, *Life on the Mississippi*, Oxford Mark Twain, edited by Shelley Fisher Fishkin (New York: Oxford University Press, 1996), ch. 40, pp. 416–17. Of course, Louisiana's "Old State Capitol Building" was simply the State Capitol at the time of Twain's words; the current State Capitol Building was inaugurated in 1932.
31 Mark Twain, *A Connecticut Yankee in King Arthur's Court* (London: Penguin, 1971), preface (unnumbered page).
32 Catherine Brown, "In the Middle," *Journal of Medieval and Early Modern Studies* 30, no. 3 (2000): 547–74, at 549–50.

Part One

Building the American Middle Ages

1 *Translatio Horti*: Medievalized Gardens in Boston and Cambridge

KATHLEEN COYNE KELLY

Gothic is merely architecture, and as one has a satisfaction in imprinting the gloomth of abbeys and cathedrals on one's house, so one's garden, on the contrary, is to be nothing but *riant*, and the gaiety of nature.
 Horace Walpole, letter to Sir Horace Mann

There are many stories that have been told or could be told about medievalized Boston and Cambridge. One might relate the tale of Edward Austin Abbey's wall paintings, *The Quest and Achievement of the Holy Grail* (1895), at the Boston Public Library,[1] or give an account of the late nineteenth-century Viking vogue, which left its mark on Boston's and Cambridge's built environment, including the statue of Leif Eriksson on Commonwealth Avenue (1887) and the Viking prows carved into the Longfellow Bridge over the Charles River (begun in 1900). One might explore the many examples of Gothic architecture: extant examples include Harvard University's Memorial Hall (Robert Ware and Van Brunt, 1878) and the Romanesque Trinity Church (H.H. Richardson, 1877); demolished specimens include Gore Hall, the original library at Harvard College (Richard Bond, 1837–41, razed 1913), and the "Ruskinian Gothic" Museum of Fine Arts on Boylston (Sturgis and Brigham, 1876, razed 1909). One might follow the tale, entwined with the history of newly acquired Gilded Age wealth and the development of an art-collecting Brahmin elite at the end of the nineteenth century, of how medieval manuscripts made their way into area university and museum collections.[2]

Generally – and provocatively – speaking, the Gothic revival in America illustrated by these stories about medievalized Boston and Cambridge was financed by members of the industrialist class who could afford to divest Europe of many of its treasures and sought to build castles and churches of their own in the United States. Such an interest in reproducing the Middle Ages in the New World often represented a desire for a history and a culture that predated

America and, in some quarters, asserted Christianity and even whiteness as supreme.[3] Consider the architectural style known as "Collegiate Gothic" – the fashion of symbolically refashioning American university buildings as medieval universities and cathedrals. Ralph Adams Cram was the chief promoter of Collegiate Gothic and served as the consulting architect at Princeton University from 1907 to 1929. It could be said without exaggeration that Cram viewed the Renaissance and the Reformation as unfortunate interruptions in the project of Christianity.[4] His master plan for Princeton was predicated on recuperating the Gothic; he argued passionately that Gothic architecture was not only "a logical continuation of the great Christian culture of the past" but also "a vital contribution to modern life."[5] Woodrow Wilson shared his sentiments. As president of Princeton, he declared, "Gothic architecture has added a thousand years to the history of the university, and has pointed every man's imagination to the earliest traditions of learning in the English-speaking race."[6] The American Gothic revival was not ideologically innocent.[7]

I want to tell a lesser-known Gothic tale, a tale of secret gardens, of hybridized spaces, of medievalized ecologies, which, in part, contribute to the elitist narrative that often underwrites medievalized American architecture. I'll unpack this narrative later, but for the moment, I want to focus on the garden as an art form, for there is nothing "natural" about gardens. The garden is designed deliberately, and designed to appeal to the senses and to the intellect; furthermore, like any text, gardens and horticultural practices are open to interpretation and theorizing. As do literature, music, and painting, gardens reflect and project the desires of an individual gardener (designers and makers), as well as the desires and values of society and culture at large: "Even the most unique gardens are indicators and traces of the tensions and energies in a constantly changing society," says landscape designer Wade Graham.[8] Indeed, gardens – public and private – have the power to shape individuals and culture.

I am interested in a green medievalism in which the natural world is recruited to simulate a Middle Ages on American soil. I seek the traces of a *translatio horti*, as it were. By saying so, I am adapting the medieval topoi of *translatio studii* ("translation/transfer of studies/learning") and *translatio imperii* ("translation/transfer of empire"), which posit that the history of civilizations is the history of movement, of learning, and of power from one culture to another. The Gothic revival, especially in the hands of Ralph Adams Cram, can be read as the attempt to transfer and preserve a Western European and Catholic past in the United States in quite visible, public ways. It is this very *transference* that I identify as American: Europeans *extended* their past; Americans often *borrowed* a past.[9] The same can be said of the three gardens I focus on, found on both sides of the Charles River: the Monks Garden at the Isabella Stewart Gardner Museum in Boston (completed 1903) and the Fletcher Steele Garden and the Cloister Garden at the monastery of the Society of St. John the Evangelist (built between 1924 and 1936), an Anglican retreat founded by the Cowley fathers in Cambridge. The Monks Garden was designed for private pleasure, the Steele Garden for contemplation for visitors to the monastery, and the Cloister Garden for both pleasure and contemplation for the Cowley fathers. These gardens serve as sensible, substantial, and organic (I intend the pun) representations of medieval ideals deemed worth memorializing in theory, if not in actual practice. To say so is not to criticize; rather, I am struck by the continuities between medieval European enclosed gardens and later iterations of them in which faithful replication, quotation, allusion, and innovation mix – a very American tradition indeed.[10]

What does it mean to create a medieval garden centuries after the Middle Ages ended? Who creates them? And what does it take to apprehend a garden as "medieval"? One way to answer these questions is to invite William Morris into the conversation. Though he was English, his influence is crucial to the American story that I tell.[11] Morris committed himself to reviving, restoring, and redesigning the idiom of the medieval in very material ways, including the gardens at his own houses, both real and fictional. We know Morris best for his artisanal work at the Kelmscott Press and the home furnishings that he elevated to an art form. As a recent exhibit on Morris's art amply demonstrated, Morris took the natural world as inspiration – and, I would argue, a nature filtered through medieval illuminations of garden scenes and the ornamental interweavings of flowers, leaves, and birds in the margins.[12] His famous wallpapers, fabrics, embroideries, and tapestries combine vaguely Eastern Arabesque shapes with the colour and detail of the highly decorated and floriferous borders of the European medieval manuscript. In Morris's art, nature is refracted as if through the Lady of Shallot's mirror: tumultuous but patterned, over-realized but withdrawn. Morris's designs were disseminated widely in England and in North America and became the signature look of the Arts and Crafts movement (c. 1862–1914). He haunts, albeit indirectly, Fletcher Steele and Isabella Stewart Gardner: Steele began as an architect in the Arts and Crafts style; Gardner, in her voracious collecting, assembled a small trove of Arts and Crafts pieces. Architecture critic Robert Campbell notes, "What Fenway Court took from the Arts and Crafts movement ... was not a style or manner. It was rather a love for the crafts of earlier times, and an urge to know that a human hand and mind once shaped the object you are looking at."[13] Gardner shares this affinity for craft with Morris, who sought to re-create the arts of the pre-industrial age, best exemplified, in his mind, by the Middle Ages.

Morris would have agreed with Wade Graham, who, in addition to asserting that gardens embody cultural and aesthetic ideals, also argues that gardens "can express political theories, aesthetic preoccupations, scientific and religious ideas, cultural inheritances, and sheer force of personality."[14] Morris cared a good deal about gardens and exercised his personality in making them. He promoted the enclosed garden as a small civilized and civilizing enclave carved out of the wilder natural world, artfully separated but still connected. Morris, as part of his socialist project, ardently believed that the beauty of the natural world in all of its forms must be preserved:

> There is one duty obvious to us all; it is that we should set ourselves, each one of us, to doing our best to guard the natural beauty of the earth: we ought to look upon it as a crime, an injury to our fellows, only excusable because of ignorance, to mar the natural beauty, which is the property of all men; and scarce less than a crime to look on and do nothing while others are marring it, if we can no longer plead this ignorance.[15]

One may well criticize Morris for his anthropocentricism and his inability to perceive nature in its autonomy. And he often overly aestheticized nature, asserting that "love of nature in all its forms must be the ruling spirit of … works of art."[16] Moreover, Morris makes a claim that modern environmentalists would dispute – that natural beauty is "property." Still, while Morris's proto-conservationist and environmentalist views are sometimes problematic, his fiction, essays, and art earn him a central place in a yet-to-be-written history of what I want to call eco-medievalism.[17]

The Monks Garden, the Steele Garden, and the Cloister Garden (along with many an urban or suburban backyard) are examples of human interventions into natural landscapes in which an indigenous ecosystem is replaced by a more anthropocentric ecosystem. Granted, simply with respect to scale, making a garden does not unleash the same impact on the environment that agriculture, the growth of cities, and manufacturing (and building dams and diverting rivers and adding landfill) do. However, gardens, public and private, frame the natural world into cultural landscapes that produce profound psychosomatic and emotional effects which govern, often unconsciously, not only how humans interact with their environments but also how they make decisions about what to do with and to environments. When geographer Denis Cosgrove describes "the primary act of gardening" as "fixing a boundary between the wild and the cultivated," he is not making a neutral, descriptive statement (as he is aware) but attesting to a human habit that often constructs the "wild" as something other, as gardens from Versailles to Rokuon-ji attest.[18] For millennia all over the globe, we humans have set aside small pieces of wildness and domesticated them for food and ornamentation. We have enclosed and protected such once-wild sites in a variety of ways, using ditches, fences, hedges, and stone walls.[19] In the Germanic and Romance languages, we call it a *garden* (*gartin, jardin, giardino*), a word that assumes enclosure.

English *garden* derives from Anglo-Norman and Old French, Middle French *jardin*, a "cultivated enclosure" or "fertile region," derived from post-classical Latin **gardinus* meaning "'of or relating to an enclosure' [in e.g. **hortus gardinus* enclosed cultivation plot]."[20] We Westerners also went further afield and borrowed the Old Iranian word for "enclosure," *paradise* (Avestan *pairidaēza-* "enclosure, from Old Iranian *pari* around + *daiz-* to heap up, build," from "Persian *pālīz* walled vegetable plot, Armenian *partēz* ... Arabic *firdaws* paradise"), to denote the Garden of Eden, Heaven, or any "place or region of surpassing beauty or delight, or of supreme bliss," and more recently, any "peaceful unspoilt place."[21] An enclosed garden is a little ecological paradise made cunningly.

In its most familiar form, a medieval or medievalesque garden is characterized chiefly by the structure that encloses it; namely, the stone, stuccoed, or brick wall that is both decorative and practical, serving as a boundary and a barrier. The wall defines the *hortus conclusus*, historically and iconographically, literally and figuratively. While the insides of the Monks Garden, the Steele Garden, and the Cloister Garden – plants and hardscape – have changed over the past hundred years, their walls continue to function as the sign of the "medieval" in these gardens. Each garden alludes to a recognizable (even if not always consciously articulated) translated past. They are like the Tardis machines of science fiction: the inside is bigger than the outside, for each garden encompasses a complex, crowded – dare I say sedimented? – history of a European elsewhere and else*time*.

In what follows, I explore how a few determined gardeners and designers created hybridized, medievalized places. Each is a "felicitous space," in Gaston Bachelard's phrase, a beloved space, sometimes even a "eulogized space" – certainly a space "that has been seized upon by the imagination."[22] These gardens are New World bricolaged sites, made up of bits and pieces of Old World architectural and landscape history. They have no connection to the environment that existed before them; in fact, the very soil out of which these gardens were created lacks a history, since these gardens were either built on or adjacent to filled-in marshes, on land claimed from the Charles River – and claimed from the Massachusett, who once grew maize, beans, squash, and tobacco on what they called the Quinobequin ("meandering river"). I begin by furnishing an overview of the features of the historical medieval English garden, and then describe the Monks Garden, the Steele Garden, and the Cloister Garden in a way that emphasizes how they are paradoxically continuous with, yet also deracinated from, their origins. Moreover, as examples of *translatio horti*, these three gardens and their walls speak to privileged desires in very different ways.

The Medieval Urban Garden

There are no extant medieval gardens in Europe, except for a few Hispano-Arab gardens, such as the Generalife and Alhambra (built in the thirteenth and fourteenth centuries CE), both of which have been subjected to a series of unfortunate restorations. Archaeologists have discovered many relict gardens in England and Europe through excavation and, more recently, magnetometry, Light Detection and Ranging (LIDAR), and ground-penetrating radar, technologies that have greatly increased our understanding of gardens in the Middle Ages.[23] It has become clear that we cannot speak of *the* medieval garden; archaeologists and garden historians have found great variety in how gardens were laid out and used, as well as variety in what the word *garden* and its analogues denoted in the Middle Ages. It is also apparent that, while many sites have been gardened continuously since the Middle Ages (if not earlier), the design and arrangement of these gardens have changed dramatically according to prevailing fashions over the centuries. As Derek Clifford in *A History of Garden Design* says, "Gardening, more than architecture, more than painting, more than music, and far more than literature, is an ephemeral art; its masterpieces disappear leaving little trace."[24] Historians must turn to other evidence for medieval gardens to reconstruct them. In addition to household accounts, surveys, and maps, literature and the visual arts offer a good deal of evidence, which, of course, must be tempered by the fact that these representations are often idealized and aspirational – as well as allegorical.

In medieval Christian Europe, when we encounter an enclosed garden in a literary text or medieval painting or manuscript illumination, it is rarely just a representation of a useful or pleasant green space. Rather, every garden, particularly when enclosed, invites us to recall that ur-garden, Paradise. This Paradise is sometimes the heavenly Paradise or the Garden of Eden; it is an analogue for the garden of the lovers in the Song of Solomon ("A garden locked is my sister, my bride, a garden locked, a fountain sealed"; Revised Standard Version 4:12). The Lover in the *Roman de la Rose* (c. 1230–75) says, "Si vi vergier grant et lé / tot clos de haut mur bataillié" (I saw a garden, magnificent and large, completely enclosed by a high crenellated wall).[25] Boccaccio's garden in the *Decameron* (c. 1353) and Chaucer's gardens in the *Parliament of Fowls* (c. 1381–2) and the *Knight's Tale* (c. 1385) evoke Eden and the Song of Songs. Many literary garden descriptions are highly elaborate, complete with walls, trees, shrubs, ornamentals, running water, fountains, statuary, seating, paths, bowers, arbours, singing birds, gentle animals, and delicious food and drink. Since we cannot visit a historical medieval garden (although re-creations exist, such as Queen Eleanor's Garden at Winchester Cathedral and the Cloisters in Manhattan), for most modern people, scenes from the *Très Riches Heures du Duc de Berry* (c. 1412–16) and other iconic medieval illuminated manuscripts offer insights (and entrancing views) into how medieval gardens were designed.

Around the Mediterranean rim and in the East, where the enclosed garden originated, walled gardens were designed to keep the heat out and to provide shade. When walled gardens were adapted to colder climates, the walls functioned to retain the heat. Many gardens or parts of gardens in medieval northern Europe were enclosed by walls, creating an ideal microclimate for growing herbs, vegetables, fruit, and flowers for medicinal purposes and for their beauty. Wind and frost were kept out and tender fruit trees could be espaliered against a south-facing wall. Medieval cities themselves were often walled, and thus many urban gardens backed up against the outer walls.

In addition to gardens attached to monasteries, castles, and manors in the countryside (perhaps our most romantic ideal), cities and towns all over medieval Europe were filled with gardens and orchards. The nobles, merchants, guilds, priests, and monks who held properties in cities made gardens not only for pleasure but also to grow vegetables and fruit for the household, to sell at local markets, and to donate to the poor. Even medieval London was a green city, full of private gardens large and small, lawns, orchards, and vineyards – "precious, savoured enclaves," in John Schofield's words.[26] Recall the garden in Chaucer's *Merchant's Tale* that is jealously guarded by January, who keeps the garden locked until he chooses to use it. This garden, closed off from the city streets ("a gardyn, walled al with stoon"), is so beautiful that it serves as a favourite retreat for Pluto, god of the Underworld, and Proserpina, his stolen bride.[27] January was likely inspired by his real-life counterparts in the Middle Ages: the wealthy often displayed their status and taste through ornamental gardens – but, contra January, they usually built them for the amusement of the women in the family. Even guild workers might own a small plot with space for a single fruit tree and a vegetable garden. If city residents did not have room for a garden or did not own land, they were often permitted to use lands set aside for them by the clergy, the king or lord, or a private landowner – the precursor to the British allotment system and the American community garden.

Just as the wall is a crucial element in realizing a medievalized garden today, so is the visitor's suspension of disbelief – the willingness to play at stepping into a material medieval past. Tourists do so, of course, when they stand on the battlefield in East Sussex where the Battle of Hastings was fought, say, or among the ruins of Glastonbury. What makes the experience of visiting a garden different, however, is the ephemeral nature of plantings and design. Gardening is, in many ways, a performative art. A garden, which changes from hour to hour, week to week, season to season, depends upon its visitors to collude with/in it; a garden requires a kind of *methexis*, a term I borrow from ancient Greek theatre that means "group sharing." Just as a Greek audience may participate in a given performance, improvising as they go, in a medievalized garden, a Gothic arch, a knot garden, a bee skep, a turfed seat, or a wall encourages visitors to locate themselves imaginatively in time and space.

The Monks Garden

Let me begin my discussion of the Monks Garden at the Isabella Stewart Gardner Museum (originally named Fenway Court; 25 Evans Way, Boston, MA) by offering a brief history of the building and the garden. In 1901–3 the building was designed by Willard T. Sears, in collaboration with Gardner; the Monks Garden was designed in 1903 by Gardner. A twenty-five-foot wall was added in 1908 (see figure 1.1). Morris Carter, first director of the museum, redesigned the

1.1. The Monks Garden shortly before Gardener's death (T.E. Marr and Son, 1922; courtesy Isabella Stewart Gardner Museum, Boston).

Monks Garden in 1924, and W.C. Curtis again redesigned the garden, this time according to a Japanese aesthetic, in 1941; 1950 saw the garden's wall lowered to fifteen feet; and from 1971 to 1973, Sasaki Associates completed a third redesign of the Monks Garden. In 1983, the museum was placed on the National Register of Historic Places. It was expanded, and not without controversy, in 2012 by Renzo Piano, who designed a modern glass addition (see figure 1.2). Two milestones occurred in 2013: Michael Van Valkenburgh Associates redesigned the Monks Garden and the museum was designated a Boston Landmark.[28]

The museum and the Monks Garden were originally designed for the private pleasure of Isabella Stewart Gardner (1840–1927). Gardner was avidly interested in everything that wealth and privilege offer: art, music, literature, travel, even sports. (There is a story that she wore a bright-red headband to a Boston Symphony Orchestra performance to show her support for the Red Sox.) She collected European, Asian, and American paintings, sculptures, tapestries, furniture, manuscripts, rare books, architectural fragments, and examples of the decorative arts. In a way, Gardner's building of Fenway Court enshrined her elite lifestyle as an art in itself, for she and her husband John (1837–1898) needed more than simply a

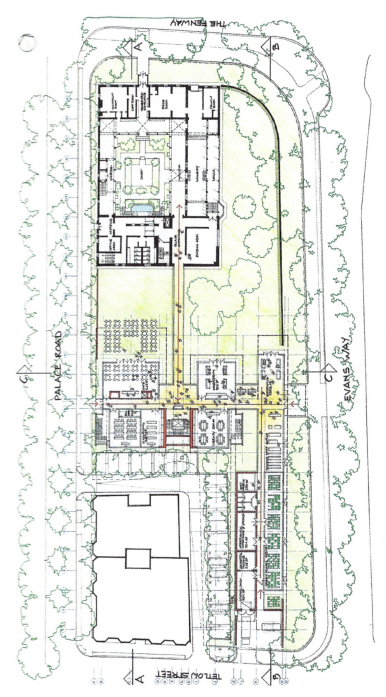

1.2. Renzo Piano's plan of the Isabella Stewart Gardner Museum (2012), in which the Monks Garden is at the lower right, and a view of the Monks Garden as originally designed by Gardner (courtesy Isabella Stewart Gardner Museum, Boston).

residence: they needed a setting – a stage – to highlight their philanthropic work and to display their vast art collection. The garden that Gardner constructed at Fenway Court extended this stage, functioning as an aesthetic statement: horticulture, landscaping, and architecture integrated together and treated as art. Fenway Court was a *maison de plaisance*,[29] and its gardens an extension of that *plaisance* into the western fenny fringes of Boston. At the time, the location seemed folly; in retrospect, Gardner chose her site wisely. Old Boston was outgrowing its narrow geographical confines, and in addition to increasing its footprint through vast landfill projects, the city began to spread west, away from the harbour.

Fenway Court was built in imitation of the fifteenth-century Palazzo Barbaro in Venice, where Gardner and her husband often stayed. (Gardner's palazzo is not "medieval" according to how scholars traditionally mark when, and where and for whom, the Renaissance in Europe began.) The Palazzo Barbaro was built in the "Venetian Gothic" style, which combined the Gothic pointed arch with Byzantine and Moorish details. Gardner's Fenway Court is inspired by a dream of the Italian Renaissance, best realized by the Courtyard Garden, a stunning interior garden enclosed by soaring walls studded with arches upon arches and filled with eclectic statuary and exotic plantings. In keeping with the New England climate, this Courtyard Garden is covered by a glass atrium for year-round enjoyment. Today, it overflows with exuberant flower arrangements, much as it did under Gardner's direction. Most visitors gravitate to this space upon entering the museum. Anne Hawley calls the first view of the courtyard an "epiphanic moment."[30] As visitors move from the modern glass addition into the Chinese Loggia in the original building, they tend to look left, towards the courtyard, and more often than not miss the entrance to the Monks Garden on the right.

The Monks Garden, the wall of which sweeps around the east side following the property boundary, is "medieval" in essence, which is perhaps why Gardner referred to it as "the monks garden," in lowercase letters. It was never planted or designed as a historically accurate medieval garden; it has been redesigned and replanted at least five times, and its current incarnation is stylishly minimalist. The gardens that Gardner visited in Italy served as her primary inspiration for all of the green spaces at Fenway Court, as well as at her Green Hill, Brookline, estate. In her European travels, Gardner would have seen many gardens that originated in the Middle Ages; however, as I noted above, such gardens had been redesigned to suit changing taste (and utility) in the early modern period or later. Still, although the layout of the European medieval garden and the choice of plants changed over the centuries, in most cases, one feature was retained: the surrounding wall, either original, restored, or even newly built, added as a nostalgic "medieval" touch. In addition to seeing such famous Renaissance gardens as the Villa d'Este, Gardner was also familiar with idealized representations of medieval enclosed gardens through the books of hours in her collection, as well as four Renaissance tapestries, the *Château and Garden Series*, that she hung in the Little Salon at Fenway

Court. Given that the "Palace" was sited on a corner, the brick wall of the Monks Garden provided privacy as the construction of new residences in the Fenway began to surround the previously isolated property. Gardner laid the garden along a long axis running parallel with the house, lining the walls with tall Lombardy pines (the vertical evergreens in the background of many Quattrocento portrait paintings). The wall itself is embedded with stone grilles with ogival arches.

Eleanor McPeck writes that the Monks Garden was "a favorite retreat for Mrs. Gardner and her fox terriers. From a small mound at one end she could look through a break in the wall across the new park-land [designed by Frederick Law Olmsted] on the other side of the Fenway. A brick path led through a vine-covered arbor to a gate and the formal perennial garden beyond."[31] This garden is very different today. On the website of its most recent landscape architects, Michael Van Valkenburgh Associates, the Monks Garden as currently constituted is described thusly:

> The original high brick wall of Fenway Court surrounds the garden, and the design aims to soften this enclosure through the creation of a small-scale, dreamlike woodland. Composed of approximately 60 trees including stewartia, paper bark maple, and gray birch, the groves establish a detail-rich palette of colors and textures suitable for intimate appreciation. Winding paths, paved in a striking combination of black brick and reflective mica schist, meander through the trees. Rather than intersecting, the paths playfully meet and diverge, while also gently widening in places to create nooks for garden chairs.[32]

This passage suggests that the wall is a drawback, in need of "softening" – a word used frequently in garden design to describe hiding or minimizing necessary hardscaping. The wall is the main event – medievally speaking – yet the wall in the Van Valkenburgh design seems to disappear as one walks the paths (see figure 1.3). Campbell describes the Monks Garden as "quite small, and it used to feel small ... It now appears to extend far into a shadowy, indeterminate distance ... like the secret hollows of a children's storybook."[33]

As I follow the paths in the Monks Garden, I recall Dante's opening lines of the *Divine Comedy*: "Midway in our life's journey, I went astray / from the straight road and woke to find myself / alone in a dark wood."[34] Instead of Dante's fear and apprehension, one experiences not the *selva oscura* but the sense of wandering in a shimmering, bright wood. The trees in the garden create a painterly effect as the light sifts through their leaves, reminding me of Paolo Uccello's *The Hunt in the Forest* (1470) and its stylized tree canopy, as well as Uccello's play with perspective so that all of the men, horses, and dogs vanish into the far distance – just as we are invited to contemplate a far distance in the Monks Garden, as if there were no wall. I also sense an allusion to the notion of a labyrinth. The labyrinth, with its roots in Greek mythology, was sometimes

1.3. The Monks Garden today (author's photograph, fall 2018).

repurposed in medieval Europe to simulate a pilgrimage to Jerusalem. The most famous pilgrimage-labyrinth is found in the nave of Chartres Cathedral (begun 1145) and is dated to the first part of the thirteenth century.[35] And just outside Chartres, the Jardins de l'Évêché offers a turfed version of the pilgrim's path. Thus, compared to earlier gardens at the Gardner, the Van Valkenburgh design may be the most "medieval" of all. Still, the garden speaks to the new wing of the museum more than it does to the old. It is clearly a repurposed space: constrained by a wall that is now part of a registered Boston Landmark, the current design seeks to obliterate that wall.

But these are the musings of a medievalist who is also a gardener. When compared to the garden-speak on the museum website (quoted above), which is intended to shape visitors' *methexis* in a very particular, à la mode way, my description of my experience of the garden could be deemed idiosyncratic, maybe even peculiar. There is no medieval there there, but that does not prevent me from imagining one.

Gardner was not quite using the Middle Ages as a pretext (in Umberto Eco's sense); rather, given her taste, her vast collections, and her devout

Anglo-Catholicism, I suspect that the notion of a "medieval" garden was an afterthought that simply happened to be congruent with her overall objectives for Fenway Court, and the idea of a "monks garden" more amusing than serious. I wonder if she agreed with fellow fervent Anglo-Catholic Cram, whose guiding principle was, as I have noted, that the Gothic style was superior to all others: "less a method of construction than it is a mental attitude, the visualizing of a spiritual impulse."[36] Perhaps Gardner, like Cram, rejected any notion of a break between the European Middle Ages and the Renaissance, indulging the fantasy that the Reformation never happened. Given her lavish tastes, however, Gardner certainly would have found herself unhappily opposed to Girolamo Savonarola and his bonfire of the vanities.

The Steele Garden and the Cloister Garden

Ralph Adams Cram (Cram & Ferguson) designed the buildings at the Society of St. John the Evangelist Monastery (980 Memorial Drive, Cambridge, MA), and Fletcher Steele designed the courtyard garden, now known as the Steele Garden. A brief history of the site records its beginnings in 1924, when St. Francis House was built, with an addition completed in 1928. A sunken garden on the entry and riverside was added in 1933, and a terrace at grade closer to St. Francis House in 1935. The Chapel of St. Mary and St. John was built from 1936 to 1938, and in 1946 the knot garden was removed and replaced with a patio and mosaic. The buildings were renovated in 2010 and the Cloister Garden redesigned in 2011. The buildings and grounds house the Society of St. John the Evangelist (SSJE), an Anglican religious order for men. In the United States, the SSJE is affiliated with the Episcopal Church, and members take vows of poverty, celibacy, and obedience. The Monastery of St. John the Evangelist sits on Memorial Drive, a parkway that follows the contours of the Charles River on the Cambridge side. Fronted by a stuccoed wall on the left (enclosing the Steele Garden) and a wooden fence painted dark green on the right (enclosing the Cloister Garden) and overhung with London plane trees, the complex of buildings barely registers as one whizzes by in a car or on a bicycle. If one approaches the monastery on foot, however, one feels more in harmony with the spirit of the place. A sign in front of the chapel invites passers-by to enter and "listen to the silence" – although one might also choose to listen to the brothers sing matins, nones, and evensong in plainsong.

Isabella Stewart Gardner owned one of the three parcels on which the monastery was built and suggested to Spence Burton, then Father Superior of the Society, that the riverfront site would be an ideal place for contemplation and prayer. She donated the land and funds to begin the building. Cram designed all of the buildings. Given the Cowley fathers' special devotion to St. Francis (who famously tended his own garden), the austere Romanesque style, which includes a single tower and a vaguely basilica-like chapel with a simple Norman interior, is well suited to the order's ethos. The distinguished landscape architect Fletcher Steele (1885–1971) had collaborated with Cram in the past, most notably on Naumkeag in Stockbridge, Massachusetts, and on Cram's own garden in Sudbury, Massachusetts. Steele began his career under the influence of the English Arts and Crafts style (itself shaped by the Tudor architectural style, which retained elements of the late Gothic "perpendicular" style), best exemplified by the gardens of Gertrude Jekyll (1843–1932), such as Munstead Wood and Hestercombe Gardens. (Jekyll is considered one of the most influential garden designers of the early twentieth century; she often collaborated with the architect Edwin Lutyens.) Although this particular vision was never built, Steele once designed a village centre in which he disguised the water tower as a Gothic church steeple.[37] He was a man of decided opinions: "A good lawn," he declared, "must be enclosed by buildings, walls, or planting," adding as well that "people who live in their gardens must be able to retire in them as to the walled-in rooms of a house. Many of us in these democratic times have forgotten this fact which was obvious to George Washington."[38] For Steele, the enclosed garden is a necessary haven – and privacy from the masses essential, apparently even at the very inception of American democracy.

Steele designed the guesthouse courtyard garden (now called the Steele Garden) in two stages, first installing a sunken garden and then creating a knot garden of clipped boxwood and Alberta spruce at the entrance to St. Francis House. Steele and Cram apparently recruited a group of novices to build the wall – Cram was inspired by tales of medieval monks who supposedly built their own monasteries.[39] The sunken garden included a statue of St. Francis, and Cram selected a wrought-iron cross from his architectural collection for the centre of the knot garden. The area to the right of the garden was, at the time, an open expanse of lawn (and sometime vegetable garden) and is now the site of the St. Mary and St. John Chapel, described by the architectural historian Bainbridge Bunting as as "fine an example of a reproduction of an 'authentic' medieval building as there is in America."[40] The Steele Garden is bounded by a wall on three sides and the chapel on the fourth side. The Cloister Garden is set aside as the private space for the brothers; it is bounded on two sides by an elevated brick cloister or peristyle and on two sides by a wooden fence (see figure 1.4).[41]

Steele planted the guesthouse courtyard garden with linden trees and an array of shrubs, perennials, and bulbs (see figure 1.5). Later, the knot garden was removed and replaced with a bluestone pattern that replicated the in-and-out weavings of the original box and spruce hedge (see figure 1.6). In a nod to Steele's penchant for using marbles as mulch, the interior spaces of the knot were filled with crushed blue glass and white marble stone chips to make a mosaic.[42] These are appropriate colours, given that the chapel is in part dedicated to Mary; moreover, the mosaic connects subtly to the Byzantine-style chapel.

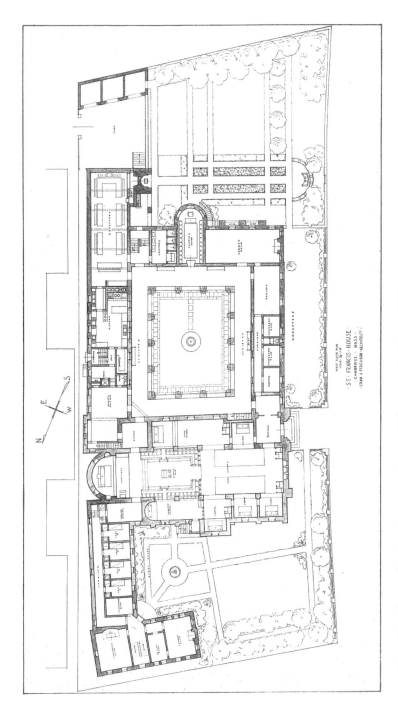

1.4. Plan of the Steele Garden (courtesy Cram and Ferguson Architects LLC).

1.5. A view of the Steele Garden as designed, showing the knot garden (courtesy Cambridge Historical Commission).

1.6. The Steele Garden today (author's photograph, July 2017).

The day I visited, a brother was picking out the pieces of bark that had fallen from the plane trees onto the mosaic. At first, I thought he was adding the glass pieces to make a pattern, in the way that Tibetan Buddhists make sand mandalas. It then struck me that engaging in the endless gardener's task of tidying the garden is rather like making a mandala: gardening can be approached as a devotional act in which contemplatives immerse themselves. I later saw the same brother singing nones in the chapel: complementary work. I include these reflections to underscore how my stepping into a dedicated sacred space affected my perception. Such is the point of many an enclosed garden, secular or religious: the surrounding walls turn the "captured landscape" into a refuge or sanctuary.[43]

The Steele Garden is historically significant because of who designed it. Still, the Cloister Garden appeals to me more because, in its current form, it is lived in and loved. This garden is not public but is set aside for the members of the monastery. It was once a large expanse of lawn (medievals loved turf as negative space, that is, what the Japanese call *ma*, the consciousness of form and non-form, of filled space and empty space). But turf is a waste of real estate because mown grass is a monoculture incapable of sustaining much life. Hence the lawn has been turned into an organic garden with beehives, native plants, and a cutting garden for flowers for the chapel. As in the Monks Garden, wandering paths cut through the plantings; in this case, beds overflow with native plants and grasses (see figure 1.7). An old baptismal font that had been found under a set of stairs has been repurposed as a fountain. This last feature is particularly compelling for its allegorical suggestiveness: the water continuously overflows the lip of the basin – grace never-ending. While other medievalized gardens are designed to invoke the historical medieval garden (such as the garden at the Cloisters in New York) and are intended for show, this "Cloister Garden" is a working garden that makes the labour involved in keeping up a garden quite visible – labour that has changed little since the Middle Ages. Ellis Peters's gardener-monk, Brother Cadfael, surely would feel at home here.

William Morris's Walls

Up to this point, I have attempted to place the Monks Garden, the Steele Garden, and the Cloister Garden in their historical contexts and to convey the experience of visiting a pseudo-medieval garden. The physical features of a medieval garden – plants, fountain, lawn, paths – are common to all gardens, no matter the style. In re-created medieval gardens (recall that in England and most of Europe only the bones of actual medieval gardens are available to us; contemporary simulations are all that we have), the presence of a Gothic arch or a neatly designed herber or woven willow fence serves as the recognizable idiom of the medieval. However, it is the wall that makes a garden most

1.7. The Cloister Garden (author's photograph, July 2017).

"medieval." The respective walls surrounding the Monks Garden, the Steele Garden, and the Cloister Garden, no matter how the plantings may change or the interior design be altered, stipulate, so to speak, the Middle Ages.

It is not surprising that William Morris, who so deftly deployed the semiotics of the medieval, would have strong opinions on the theory and practice of the garden wall. Morris's houses, the Red House (completed 1860) in southeast London and Kelmscott Manor in the Cotswolds (c. 1570), integrate house and garden according to the Arts and Crafts aesthetic. Morris offers the following dictates on the ideal domestic garden:

> Large or small, it should look both orderly and rich. It should be well fenced from the outside world. It should by no means imitate either the willfulness or the wildness of Nature, but should look like a thing never to be seen except near a house. It should, in fact, look like a part of the house. It follows from this that no private pleasure-garden should be very big, and a public garden should be divided and made to look like so many flower-closes in a meadow, or a wood, or amidst the pavement.[44]

In effect, Morris is describing Kelmscott as he found it: the farmstead had been enclosed by stone walls at least a century before he arrived, and within, hedges defined the kitchen garden and ornamental gardens.[45] Note the distinction Morris makes between inside and outside: all within the walls is planned and ordered, creating a feeling of tranquillity and calm, versus the wild wilfulness of "Nature" (reduced to a mere point of departure for a domestic garden), and versus the "outside world," easy enough to parse as nineteenth-century industrialized life. An enclosed garden, made intimate because of its scale, offers the experience of "nature" writ small and deliberate.

In Morris's *News from Nowhere* (1890), William Guest, the dreamer/narrator who awakes in a future English utopia, journeys down the Thames and finds himself outside a beautiful house and garden in full June bloom. "O me! O me! How I love the earth, and the seasons, and weather, and all of the things that deal with it, and all that grows out of it, – as this has done!" cries his companion and guide, Ellen. This is "Kelmscott." As Guest approaches the house, he says that he "looked in vain for the grey walls that I expected to see there."[46] Such a pointed observation seemingly contradicts Morris's dictum that a house "should be well fenced from the outside world." There is no wall preventing all from enjoying dream Kelmscott in the fictional future of England – but there *is* a wall at real Kelmscott. Only *here*, in this dystopia, does one need a wall.

As Fletcher Steele's remarks about privacy and democracy and Guest's narrative suggest, there is another way to see the walls, literally and otherwise, that surround gardens – a way that gestures towards, but is not limited to, a re-created or historical Middle Ages. (As I write in January 2019, Trump's loathsome plan for a border wall – that he calls "medieval" – intrudes on my thoughts.) Walls often reinforce privilege – think of the statement that a twenty-five-foot-high wall makes, as was the case originally at Fenway Court. Gardner's Monks Garden was, and is, an elite, private space. Gardner's home is open to the public but only for those paying a hefty admission fee – though it must be said that students are admitted for a discounted price. The current incarnation of the garden is beautiful, but, in my opinion, lifeless; it exerts a modern pressure on a pseudo-medieval space in which the wall is preserved for its historical significance only. Renzo Piano's 2012 addition consisting of soaring glass walls and a glass atrium applies its own kind of pressure on Gardner's Gothic brick palace. The new wing is open to various interpretations: at one end of the spectrum, as balancing and complementing Gardner's wall, and at the other, as an act of defiance against it.

In Boston and Cambridge, where every architectural style can be found, houses in exclusive older neighbourhoods often have high brick or wooden fences surrounding them – private and precursor variations on the idea of the modern gated (moated?) and planned community. I live in a mixed working-class neighbourhood of two- and three-family houses in Cambridge,

1.8. Gothic conceit at home: chain-link fence and a neighbour's privacy wall, punctuated by a mirrored arch (author's photograph, August 2019).

and even these houses have "walls": chain-link fences a half-century or more in age that say *keep out, this is mine, respect my boundaries* (see figure 1.8 for some of the chain-link around my house – and my vernacularization of the Gothic). William Morris's socialist ideals would have led him to condemn the walls of the rich – he would have been appalled by the modern gated community – but he might have appreciated the chain-link fences, sometimes repurposed as grape arbours, that surround the small garden plots on my block.

Morris believed that everyone, and perhaps especially the working class, needed a respite from the grimy, ugly streets and architecture of urbanized life. Modern Boston and Cambridge are not as grimy as they once were, but they are densely populated cities, and, while both are committed to providing public green space, they are limited in what they can offer. My three gardens contribute to the urban ecology in very different ways. The Monks Garden, surrounded by its imposing wall, offers a respite from the city – if you can afford to pay to walk its paths. The Steele Garden, on the other hand, is left unlocked, welcoming all. It is a curiosity, a kind of remnant garden of the medieval and the medieval revival, which does not diminish its function as a place of contemplation. The Cloister Garden, on the other hand, may be a private space, but it is not an elite one. It is vibrant, uncalculated, abuzz. Morris would have liked to sit in it.

In Time, in Place

A visitor experiences the Monks Garden, the Steele Garden, and the Cloister Garden somatically and sensibly as one moves through three-dimensional space; in this respect, no visitor has quite the same experience as another, though all share immersion in a circumscribed, highly designed ecology. Let me capture this idea through a conceit drawn from the culture of web design. Programmers once used the phrase *walled garden* to denote "an environment that controls the user's access to Web content and services. In effect, the walled garden directs the user's navigation within particular areas, to allow access to a selection of material, or prevent access to other material."[47] Whoever invented the term must have been familiar with the idea of the *hortus conclusus* and, perhaps, was amused to deploy such an esoteric allusion to describe the "path" that a visitor follows through the available content. But even within this enclosed space, most movement is choice-driven, often non-linear, and always interactive.

One does not have to be a programmer, medievalist, landscape architect, or garden historian to enjoy or even recognize the medieval semiotics – and politics – of the Monks Garden, the Steele Garden, and the Cloister Garden. A visitor may well experience the pleasure of moving through time as well as space. No matter that Fenway Park is a fifteen-minute walk from the Gardner Museum and the Monks Garden, or that hectic Harvard Square lies behind the Steele and Cloister Gardens. Visitors may well be persuaded by the dream of an American garden made medieval and find themselves in – or propel themselves into – "a European Middle Ages."

NOTES

1 See Laurie A. Finke and Martin B. Shichtman, "Remediating Chivalry: Political Aesthetics and the Round Table," in *Mediality/Intermediality*, ed. Martin Heusser, Andreas Fischer, and Andreas H. Jucker (Tübingen, Germany: Gunter Narr, 2008), 139–60.
2 See the introductory essay to *Beyond Words: Illuminated Manuscripts in Boston Collections*, ed. Jeffrey Hamburger, William Stoneman, Anne-Marie Eze, Lisa Fagin-Davis, and Nancy Netzer (Chicago: University of Chicago Press/McMullen Museum, Boston College, 2016), and Cynthia Salzman, *Old Masters, New World: America's Raid on Europe's Great Pictures, 1880–World War I* (New York: Viking, 2008).

3   An exception: one might travel south of Boston to Martha's Vineyard to explore the colourful "Carpenter's Gothic" cottages (ca. 1860–79) of Oak Bluffs, once the camp meeting town of revivalist Methodists.
4   For an excellent and lively overview of Cram in his historical context, see Jan Ziolkowski, *The Juggler of Notre Dame and the Medievalizing of Modernity*, 6 vols. (Cambridge: Open Book, 2018), 3:149–238. See also 4:263–98; on Isabella Stewart Gardner in particular, 4:277–82.
5   Quoted in Douglass Shand-Tucci, *Church Building in Boston* (Concord, NH: Rumford Press, 1974), 54.
6   *Princeton Alumni Weekly*, 1902. Quoted in Woodman Ellis, "Porphyrios Associates' Princeton University Whitman Building," *bdonline*, 27 Feb. 2008, www.bdonline.co.uk/buildings/porphyrios-associates-princeton-university-whitman-building/3107462.article (accessed 15 Jan. 2019).
7   Although he assembles much of the evidence for Cram's elitist views, Richard Guy Wilson stops short of critique in "Ralph Adams Cram: Dreamer of the Medieval," in *Medievalism in American Culture*, ed. Bernard Rosenthal and Paul Szarmach (Binghamton, NY: Medieval and Renaissance Texts and Studies, 1989), 193–214.
8   Wade Graham, *American Eden: From Monticello to Central Park to Our Backyards: What Our Gardens Tell Us about Who We Are* (New York: HarperCollins, 2011), xii.
9   See Robin Fleming, "Picturesque History and the Medieval in Nineteenth-Century America," *American Historical Review* 100, no. 4 (1995): 1061–94. Fleming states, "The American producers of medieval buildings and objects … unlike their English contemporaries, were completely uninterested in re-creating academically perfect replicas of the medieval. Instead, by putting together a variety of decorations appropriated from a generic medieval vocabulary, the purveyors of the medieval in America sought to stir the heart and mind and to recall a Romantic and idealized version of the medieval past." She locates the source of American medievalism as "not present in the Middle Ages but in the popular poetry, paintings, and novels of the age" (1072).
10 Of course, Europeans constantly remade their own gardens – but the owners of villas and estates were not borrowing or adapting a tradition but continuing one.
11 See Lindsay Leard-Coolidge, "William Morris and Nineteenth-Century Boston," in *William Morris: Centenary Essays; Papers from the Morris Centenary Conference Organized by the William Morris Society at Exeter College Oxford, 30 June–3 July 1996*, ed. Peter Faulkner and Peter Preston (Exeter: University of Exeter Press, 1999), 156–64. Also useful in the same volume: Pedro Beade, "William Morris in New England: Architecture and Design in Late Nineteenth-Century Rhode Island," 144–55.
12 "Morris & Co. Inspired by Nature," Standen House, West Sussex, UK, National Trust, https://www.nationaltrust.org.uk/standen-house-and-garden/features/morris-and-co-inspired-by-nature-exhibition.
13 Anne Hawley, Robert Campbell, and Alexander Wood, *Isabella Stewart Gardner Museum: Daring by Design* (New York: Skira Rizzoli, 2014), 141.

14 Graham, *American Eden*, xii.
15 William Morris, "The Prospects of Architecture in Civilisation" (1881), in *The Collected Works of William Morris: With Introductions by His Daughter May Morris*, vol. 22 (1910–15; Cambridge: Cambridge University Press, 2012), 119–54, at 135.
16 William Morris, "The Lesser Arts of Life" (1882), in *Collected Works*, 235–69, at 240.
17 Florence Boos argues that Morris's "conviction that spoliation of natural beauty leads straight to other forms of deprivation made him an important predecessor of late twentieth-century environmentalism in all of its varying hues of green—from 'deep' ecological and ecofeminist 'theorists,' to 'pragmatic' activists and resource planners." See Boos, "An Aesthetic Ecocommunist: Morris the Red and Morris the Green," in Faulkner and Preston, *William Morris: Centenary Essays*, 21–46, at 22.
18 Denis Cosgrove, *Geography and Vision: Seeing, Imagining, and Representing the World* (London: Taurus, 2008), 53.
19 John Harvey's *Mediaeval Gardens* (Portland, OR: Timber Press, 1982) remains the best source on the history of medieval gardens; I am greatly indebted to Harvey as well as to Teresa McLean, *Medieval English Gardens* (Minneola, NY: Dover, 1980).
20 *Oxford English Dictionary* [*OED*], s.v. "garden"; https://www.oed.com.
21 *OED*, s.v. "paradise" (3a); https://www.oed.com.
22 Gaston Bachelard, *The Poetics of Space*, trans. Maria Jolas (1969; Boston: Beacon Press, 1994), xxxv–xxxvi.
23 See Oliver Creighton, *Designs upon the Land: Elite Landscapes of the Middle Ages* (Martlesham, UK: Boydell and Brewer, 2013), 45, 50. See also Harvey, *Mediaeval Gardens*, and McLean, *Medieval English Gardens*, 55, 75. For an overview of new archaeological technologies, see *The Conversation*, "Six Tools That Are Revolutionising Archaeology by Helping Us Find Sites without Digging," 7 Dec. 2015, http://theconversation.com/six-tools-that-are-revolutionising-archaeology-by-helping-us-find-sites-without-digging-51826 (accessed 12 Jan. 2019).
24 Derek Plint Clifford, *A History of Garden Design* (London: Faber & Faber, 1962), 17.
25 Guilliam de Lorris and Jean de Meun, *Le Roman de la Rose*, ed. Félix Lecoy, 3 vols. (Paris: Champion, 1965–170), 1.130–1.
26 John Schofield, *Medieval London Houses* (New Haven, CT: Paul Mellon Centre for Studies in British Art/Yale University Press, 1994), 89.
27 Geoffrey Chaucer, *The Riverside Chaucer*, ed. Larry D. Benson, 3rd ed. (Boston: Houghton Mifflin, 1987), 163, line 2029.
28 See *Isabella Stewart Gardner Museum: Boston Landmarks Study Report* (Boston Landmarks Commission, Environment Department, City of Boston, 2011).
29 I quote librarian and curator Philip Hofer, who adapted the term to echo the title of an early nineteenth-century book in Gardner's collection: "A Rare Copy of the … MAISONS DE PLAISANCE." *Fenway Court: Isabella Stewart Gardner Museum* (Boston: Trustees of the Isabella Stewart Gardner Museum, 1977), 9–13, at 9.

30　Hawley, Campbell, and Wood, *Isabella Stewart Gardner Museum*, 61.
31　Eleanor McPeck, "An Eminent Horticulturalist," in *Fenway Court*, 37–8. I am indebted to JoAnn Robinson for her tour of the Monks Garden and for sharing her paper, "The Monks Garden."
32　Michael Van Valkenburgh Associates, "Monks Garden," www.mvvainc.com/project.php?id=104 (accessed 15 Jan. 2019).
33　Hawley, Campbell, and Wood, *Isabella Stewart Gardner Museum*, 138.
34　Dante Alighieri, *The Divine Comedy*, trans. John Ciardi (New York: Penguin/New American Library, 2003), lines 1–3.
35　John James, "The Mystery of the Great Labyrinth, Chartres Cathedral," *Studies in Comparative Religion* 11, no. 2 (1977): 92–155.
36　Ralph Adams Cram, *The Gothic Quest* (New York: Baker and Taylor, 1907), 57. See Robert Muccigrosso, "Ralph Adams Cram and the Modernity of Medievalism," *Studies in Medievalism* 1, no. 2 (1982): 21–42.
37　Robin Karson, *Fletcher Steele, Landscape Architect: An Account of the Gardenmaker's Life, 1885–1971* (1989; Amherst: Library of American Landscape History/University of Massachusetts Press, 2003), 60–1.
38　Quoted in Karson, *Fletcher Steele*, 64 and 119.
39　Brother Eldridge Pendleton, in the afterword to Karen Forslund Falb, "Fletcher Steele and the Guest House Courtyard Garden," *Cowley Magazine: The Society of Saint John the Evangelist* 31, no. 2 (2005): 12–14; issuu.com/ssje/docs/cwlyeaster05 (accessed 15 Jan. 2019).
40　Quoted in "Cambridge Architectural Inventory" (1967), Cambridge Historical Commission, Cambridge, MA.
41　Karen Forslund Falb, "Fletcher Steele and the Guest House Courtyard Garden," photocopied handout, Cambridge Historical Commission.
42　I thank Brother Robert l'Esperance for taking me on a tour of the gardens at SSJE and furnishing some of their backstory. Also see Robert l'Esperance, "Return to Eden," *Cowley Magazine: The Society of Saint John the Evangelist* 38, no. 4 (2012): 10–11.
43　I borrow the term from Kate Baker, *Captured Landscape: The Paradox of the Enclosed Garden* (London: Routledge, 2012).
44　William Morris, "Making the Best of It" (1879), *Collected Works*, 81–118, at 91.
45　The photograph, "Garden Wall Attached Summerhouse and Privy at Kelmscott Manor," makes this quite clear; see *Images of England*, www.imagesofengland.org.uk (accessed 15 Jan. 2019).
46　William Morris, *News from Nowhere*, ed. Krishan Kumar (Cambridge: Cambridge University Press, 1995), 210–11.
47　"Walled Garden," TechTarget, searchsecurity.techtarget.com/definition/walled-garden (accessed 15 Jan. 2019).

2 Philadelphia's Medieval(ist) Jewels: Bryn Athyn Cathedral, Glencairn, and More

KEVIN J. HARTY

First settled in 1682 and granted its charter by William Penn in 1701, Philadelphia by 1750, with its bustling port that attracted thousands of immigrants from across Europe, was among the largest cities in the British Empire. With a population of more than 40,000, the city was in 1790 the financial and commercial hub, and the capital city, of a new nation.[1] Founded by Quakers who were simple in their dress and in their religious practice, Philadelphia grew up long before the Gothic revival would introduce its version of medievalism to both sides of the Atlantic, although church steeples were dotting the nascent city's skyline by 1730.[2] Perhaps not surprisingly then, none of Philadelphia's three most iconic buildings owes any debt, architectural or otherwise, to the medieval. Independence Hall, one-time home to the Liberty Bell and originally designed to house the Colonial Legislature in Pennsylvania, was built of red brick in the Georgian style from 1732 to 1753 – indeed, it is one of the finest examples of American Georgian architecture. Philadelphia's City Hall, a structure with almost 700 rooms, remains the largest municipal building and the finest example of Second Empire style in the country. The Philadelphia Museum of Art, atop the banks of the Schuylkill River at the western end of the Benjamin Franklin Parkway and the eastern end of Fairmount Park, designed in classical Greek Revival style, was built, after much delay and cultural and political wrangling, from 1919 to 1928.[3]

Even the Catholic hierarchy in Philadelphia shunned the medieval when plans were made to build a cathedral farther east down the Benjamin Franklin Parkway from the Philadelphia Museum of Art.[4] Built from 1846 to 1864 in a mix of styles – Roman-Corinthian, Palladian, and Renaissance Revival – from designs originally drawn up by members of the Roman Catholic clergy and then reworked by Napoleon LeBrun and John Notman, the Cathedral Basilica of Saints Peter and Paul is the largest brownstone structure in Philadelphia.[5] The simplicity of the cathedral basilica's exterior, modelled on the Lombard Church of San Carlo al Corso in Rome, is offset by an elaborate interior that features a vaulted dome, an ornate main altar with a baldacchino, and eight side chapels.[6] Begun less than two years after the Philadelphia Nativist Riots, which evidenced the extent of anti-Catholicism and Know-Nothingism in the city,[7] the height of the building's clerestory windows was, according to local legend, determined by how high the builders could throw rocks at them for fear of subsequent outbreaks of anti-Catholic violence in the city.[8]

Philadelphia, however, did not entirely eschew the medieval. Churches in Gothic Revival style were built throughout Philadelphia – though notably in what were then sometimes more rural than urban areas. And situated in what is now Center City Philadelphia is the city's Masonic Temple, built between 1868 and 1873 in Norman Revival style by architect James H. Windrim. Just opposite City Hall on its north side, when it was dedicated on 26 September 1873, the temple was considered "one of the wonders of the Masonic world."[9] The building replaced two earlier structures elsewhere in the city that had proved inadequate for the needs of the Freemasons. Windrim won the commission to design the new temple after what was deemed a fractious competition by the American Institute of Architects.[10] The building's "façade, or front, is a perfect specimen of Norman architecture – notably bold, sharp, and elaborate, with not a trace of flatness or inexpression anywhere on its profile. Its most striking features are the two Towers, which flank it, one of them piercing with its turrets the air to the height of 250 feet; and the wonderfully beautiful Norman Porch, or doorway."[11] Freemasonry flourished in Philadelphia since as early as 1727, and with Windrim's Norman-inspired building, the Freemasons were clearly making a statement about their importance to a city that had fifty years earlier been home to rising anti-Masonic sentiment.[12] Their temple was just north of what William Penn had designated as Centre Square, future home to City Hall, and adjacent to, or opposite, major Presbyterian, Lutheran, and Baptist houses of worship. The temple includes a Norman Hall in Rhenish Romanesque style and a Gothic Hall known as the Asylum of the Knights Templar. In that room, the commander's throne, above which hangs the emblem of the Knights, a cross and crown entwined, is a replica of the throne of the archbishop in Canterbury Cathedral. Five auxiliary rooms, or armouries, provided storage for uniforms, arms, and other ceremonial paraphernalia. The Asylum was "ornamented in the French Gothic style of the fourteenth century," and its adjoining banqueting room featured "the round-arched early Norman style … decorated with the characteristic billet, chevron, and lozenge mouldings." As part of the building's week-long dedication ceremonies in 1873, there was a tournament among the Knights Templar on 25 September and a procession of knights on 29 September.[13]

Equally mammoth is a structure that lies across town from the Masonic Temple and Philadelphia's City Hall, just west of the banks of the Schuylkill River, on the campus of the University of Pennsylvania. Built in Gothic Revival style between 1926 and 1932 from a design by Horace Trumbauer that is clearly an homage to Mont-Saint-Michel, the William B. Irvine Auditorium, with its 11,000-pipe Curtis organ, is now a major performance venue on the campus.[14] But, as interesting, fascinating, and just plain beautiful as these structures are, medieval America is especially alive and well in Philadelphia in four unique structures: the Episcopal churches of St. James the Less and St. Mark's, built in the nineteenth century, and Bryn Athyn Cathedral and Glencairn, built in the early twentieth century under the direction of Raymond Pitcairn. The rest of this chapter explores how the architectural designs of these four buildings, rooted as they are in often conflicting ideas of what constitutes the medieval, reflect a congruence of debates about doctrine, liturgical practice, politics, and architecture, which played out in stone across Philadelphia's landscape.

Architecture and Liturgy: St. James the Less, St. Mark's, and the Oxford Movement

In the nineteenth century, Anglo-Catholic liturgical revival spread from England to Philadelphia's Episcopal congregations. Influential here was the Cambridge Camden Society (later called the Ecclesiological Society) that sought to match the tradition of Gothic architecture with the piety associated with the Oxford Movement for Anglican liturgical reform. The society specifically rejected the Protestant notion of a priesthood of all believers, and that rejection called for the design of churches with markedly pre-Reformation distinct and separate areas for clergy and for laity.[15] The society unequivocally argued that "every church of whatever kind of shape, should have a distinct Chancel at least one-third of the length of the Nave, and separated from the latter, internally at least, if not externally, by a well-defined mark, a chancel-arch if possible, or at least by a screen and raised floor."[16] The finest example of such a church is the Episcopal Church of St. James the Less in what is now the Hunting Park section of Philadelphia. The design for the church takes worship out of the nave and puts it back, as it was in pre-Reformation times, into the sanctuary. Built between 1844 and 1846 in what was then a rural village above the banks of the Schuylkill River known as Falls of Schuylkill, the church became the prototype for American suburban church design, but the Gothic architecture was nearly accidental. The congregation applied to the Cambridge Camden Society, which in 1841 and again in 1844 had published a widely circulated pamphlet on proper church design, for a set of approved plans. The society inadvertently sent drawings prepared by English architect George Gordon Place for St. Michael's Church in Longstanton, Cambridgeshire, built circa 1230, which were then followed in every detail under the supervision of architect John E. Carver.[17] The result is a model church for the sacrament-centred liturgy practised today by Anglo-Catholics and originally advocated for by the Camden Society, and an almost exact replica of a thirteenth-century English country church. It was the first church in America "to be erected under the direct supervision of the English ecclesiologists,"[18] albeit accidentally, and its influence proved especially far reaching "across North America in the decades after the Civil War."[19]

Soon after the construction of St. James the Less was completed, John Notman, who had helped to design the Catholic Cathedral Basilica of Saints Peter and Paul, was commissioned to design another Episcopal church in Philadelphia, St. Mark's, on what is now Locust Street in Center City, in English Gothic Revival style, as suited to the architectural philosophy of the Ecclesiological Society. Notman's design was, in turn, based on a drawing of the now-demolished Gothic All Souls Church in Brighton supplied by English architect Richard Cromwell Carpenter, which the Ecclesiological Society provided to the members of the parish vestry. The church tower, part of Notman's original design, was completed in 1865 by George Hewitt.[20] As Phoebe Stanton approvingly notes, "St. Mark's is as successful a 'town-church' as St. James the Less is a 'rural parish church.'"[21] Within the walls of St. Mark's, "beneath the dark, open timber roof, in the limited light of the nave, the capitals of the arcades, alternately foliated and molded, assist in the composition of the finest church interior of its period in the United States."[22] In 1900, a Lady Chapel, designed by architectural firm Cope and Stewardson in the late decorated Gothic style and with a stone vault ceiling, was added to St. Mark's. Both the construction of the chapel and its furnishings were donated by department store heir Rodman Wanamaker in memory of his late wife, Fernanda.[23] The Lady Chapel now contains a world-renowned silver altar with nearly 150 individually sculpted saints and scenes from the life of the Virgin Mary.[24] Because of a contentious schism that ended up in Commonwealth Court and the resulting legal decision, St. Mark's now administers the slightly older St. James the Less and its campus, running a middle school there in what is one of the few private schools still serving Hunting Park.

Notman would design two other churches for Episcopalians with slightly differently liturgical preferences, each a short distance from St. Mark's: St. Clement's (1855-9), north of Market Street on Twenty-Second Street, and Holy Trinity (1856-9), down the block from St. Mark's on Rittenhouse Square. Both were commissioned by decidedly low church congregations, and their designs reflect liturgical disagreements among Philadelphia's Episcopalians. St. Mark's was intentionally an Anglo-Catholic parish – a visitor's guide to Philadelphia published for the 1876 Centennial described the church as "the property of one of the wealthiest congregations in the city, and its services are grand and impressive."[25] Grand and impressive meant high church and Anglo-Catholic. For these two other churches, Notman turned to Norman Romanesque models that were revived for nonconforming congregations "with an allergic reaction to neo-medieval Gothic styling."[26] St. Clements would, however, undergo a Catholic reawakening within its first decade that pitted the rector against his bishop, "an uncompromising Protestant and militant low churchman."[27] But by 1876, nonconformism had clearly not prevailed: St. Clements "is a handsome edifice, richly decorated within. It is an Episcopal church, and is noted as the most extreme ritualistic establishment in the City."[28]

Notman's Church of the Holy Trinity, dominating Rittenhouse Square with its northern tower and elaborately designed façade (both in Norman Romanesque style and facing east, in contrast to the westward orientation of more Anglo-Catholic structures), remains happily low church, as its relatively simple interior attests.[29] Clearly, Philadelphia's mid-nineteenth-century Episcopalian congregations looked to what they saw as medieval models in designing their churches, but just what form the medieval took (Romanesque, Gothic, or some combination of architectural styles) varied by how much they wanted to distance themselves from the liturgical practices and reforms put in place by the Protestant Reformation.

Organic Medievalism: Architects and Artisans at Bryn Athyn Cathedral and Glencairn

While ecclesiology in Philadelphia "brought a new church style and a new sophistication to American architecture," two of Philadelphia's most notable architectural jewels lie some sixteen miles west of the city limits in the tiny Borough of Bryn Athyn of Montgomery County.[30] These structures, simultaneously very much alike and very much different, are Bryn Athyn Cathedral, the episcopal seat of the General Church of the New Jerusalem, and what is now Glencairn Museum, originally the castle-like home of Raymond Pitcairn, heir to the Pittsburgh Plate Glass fortune, who took over the design for the cathedral and solely designed Glencairn.[31]

Bryn Athyn Cathedral is unique as an example of American medievalism, with its uniqueness stemming from the architectural philosophy and the theological doctrine that made the building of this edifice, whose exterior closely resembles that of England's Romanesque and Gothic Gloucester Cathedral, possible. Land and financial backing for the cathedral were provided by the Scottish-born industrialist John Pitcairn (1841–1916), who made his fortune in railroads and oil and went on to found Pittsburgh Plate Glass. Pitcairn and Bishop William Frederic Pendleton (1845–1927), first executive of the General Church who also established its ritual, initially commissioned the Boston architect Ralph Adams Cram (1863–1942), known for his American Gothic ecclesiastical and collegiate structures, to design the cathedral. Cram and his associates held the original commission for the Cathedral of St. John the Divine and for St. Thomas Episcopal Church on Fifth Avenue, both in New York, and for several buildings on the campuses of Princeton and Rice Universities. Cram also designed the choir rail and gates and the pulpit for St. Mark's Episcopal Church in Philadelphia.[32] But tensions and disagreements with Cram led to the direction of the cathedral's construction being taken over by Pitcairn's son Raymond (1885–1966).

The building of a church, let alone a cathedral, is as much a political and financial as a religious endeavour. As indicated above, nativist anti-Catholic sentiment came to bear on the design of Philadelphia's Catholic cathedral. The first meeting to plan what would eventually become New York's Episcopal Cathedral Church of St. John the Divine was held in secret in 1828: "The old antagonisms between the Dutch and the English had not yet passed from the New York scene, nor had the feeling that the Episcopal Church was a Tory institution."[33] And the efforts to build the great American Catholic cathedrals of the nineteenth century were constantly hindered by financial shortfalls.

Thanks to the deep pockets of the Pitcairn family, cost was not a concern when it came to building Bryn Athyn Cathedral, but major disagreements arose about the building's design that led eventually to Raymond Pitcairn taking on his Suger-like role.[34] Interestingly, Bryn Athyn Cathedral, the Episcopal Cathedral of St. John the Divine in New York, and Washington's National Cathedral – officially the Cathedral Church of St. Peter and St. Paul in the City and Diocese of Washington – all were at one time or another projects directed by Ralph Adams Cram, and all three were in the main constructed beginning in the early twentieth century, some fifty years after the flurry of construction of American Roman Catholic cathedrals in the Midwest and Northeast – although St. John's has been so long in being completed that it has been dubbed "St. John the Unfinished."[35] Because of the break with Cram, Bryn Athyn Cathedral is a decidedly different structure than its Episcopal sisters, which themselves differ markedly from one another.[36] Bryn Athyn Cathedral's uniqueness is directly attributable to the views of Raymond Pitcairn about the way in which cathedrals were once, and in his day ought to be, built. Those views were as much political as they were artistic, although politics would play a more obvious role in the design of Glencairn, a structure more clearly reflective of American medievalism than of the medieval.

From the younger Pitcairn's point of view, Cram was in many ways a victim of his own success. His popularity and his multiple commissions – all of which contributed to the Gothic revival in American architecture, and thus to American architectural medievalism – meant that, for Cram, Bryn Athyn Cathedral was only one of multiple projects that he would design and then pass on to contractors, designers, and subcontractors to complete: "We made our first sketches, as for any ordinary piece of work, with no idea that it would prove anything out of the usual."[37] But Raymond Pitcairn, a student of medieval architecture with no formal training in the field, did indeed want something unusual. His ideas for how Bryn Athyn Cathedral should be built were greatly influenced by the art historian and museum curator William Goodyear, who, in a 1915 series of lectures that Pitcairn attended, advanced the theory that the refinements of the medieval period could be applied to the building of modern churches, even though such a theory might be at odds with contemporary architectural practice.[38] Making that theory a reality required a more hands-on approach than architectural firms could afford to provide in terms of finance and workforce.

Central to Goodyear's thesis was the notion that medieval architecture was organic – medieval structures grew from the ground up, employing unplanned and unexpected refinements and variations in the process as these structures rose towards completion. Where Cram and associates might offer a blueprint that others would follow in constructing the cathedral, Pitcairn wanted the cathedral's builders and their workers on site using materials readily available nearby. When Cram, who in *The Ministry of Art* had earlier referred to medieval practice as "the ideal state of things,"[39] in a letter to Pitcairn dated 3 December 1914, wondered if there was any "necessity of my coming in person … [when] a set of blueprints will be sent to you today,"[40] the seeds of tension between two irreconcilable visions of how a cathedral in the Gothic style should be built in the twentieth century were sown.

Yale and Harvard professor of fine arts Kingsley Porter, an unabashed fan of what Pitcairn achieved with Bryn Athyn Cathedral, pointed out, "The church at Bryn Athyn is an epoch-making masterwork of architectural art, created with joy, full of artistic conscience."[41] And thus, as Porter argues, Pitcairn was correct to follow medieval practice in ways that Cram found abhorrent, if not impossible:

> In mediæval times the man who cut a capital was himself an artist. He designed what he executed. The discovery of paper has made it possible for the architect or his office force to design on paper all the details. The drawings are given to the workmen, who copy them mechanically. The result has been a great decline in craftsmanship … Modern architecture, like everything else modern, has too often been wholesale … One of the most serious, though the least tangible evils of paper architecture is the fact that the architect no longer senses the building growing beneath his hand.[42]

And also,

> No railroads made it possible for the mediæval master-builder to journey from one part of the country to the other, so he was unable to direct the construction of more than a single building at a time. Thus he earned little, but was able to put into the one piece of work which he did do, the energy the modern architect divides between many. The poverty of the mediæval master-builder obliged him

to superintend the actual construction in person, instead of leaving a corps of workers to interpret his drawings … For a true work of art must be executed by the man who designs it.[43]

Under Raymond Pitcairn's direction, the craftsmen and artisans working on the cathedral were directly employed by the church, and creative changes were decided by artists and builders working together.

Pitcairn's ideas led to some unorthodox construction practices. For example, rather than relying on blueprints and plans, almost every aspect of the design was made into scale models by means of which Pitcairn and those working under his direction could easily study, review, and embellish their ideas before constructing the different parts of the cathedral. The design of the cathedral was then organic, following Goodyear's theories ("the Church at Bryn Athyn" is the first "in the last 400 years" to employ the medieval method),[44] and allowed for a continuous series of architectural refinements and variations and for asymmetries and irregularities to be built into the cathedral as they had been built into the great cathedrals constructed in the Middle Ages.[45] Once Pitcairn took over the direction of the construction of Bryn Athyn Cathedral, the structure, properly speaking, ceased to become simply an example of American architectural medievalism. It became something decidedly different, a building reflective of a long-lost practice that saw a seamless link between builder and building, a link forged by faith. The construction of Bryn Athyn Cathedral was then, it is fair to say, a truly medieval undertaking grounded in the artistic vision and the faith of those who built it, for the uniqueness of Bryn Athyn is doctrinal as well as architectural.

The Gothic revival of the nineteenth century, in whatever form it took, was an exercise in medievalism. Architecturally and theologically, it was an attempt to undo changes wrought by the Reformation, but the Church of the New Jerusalem is not an outgrowth of the tension between the Reformation and the Counter-Reformation. Accordingly, the design of the Bryn Athyn Cathedral, which was in the main constructed from 1913 to 1919, reflects the beliefs of the New Church, whose members are sometimes known as Swedenborgians after their founder, Emanuel Swedenborg (1688–1772), a scientist turned theologian who claimed to have received a new revelation from Jesus Christ through continuous heavenly visions experienced over a period of at least twenty-five years. In his writings, Swedenborg predicted that God would replace the traditional Christian Church, establishing a "New Church," which would worship God in one person: Jesus Christ. Central to New Church doctrine is the belief that all people must actively cooperate in repentance, reformation, and regeneration of their own lives.

Members of the New Church do not see themselves as being in either a Catholic or a Protestant tradition. Rather, the church's theology is based on the Old and New Testaments and the theological works of Emanuel Swedenborg, which the New Church teaches are a heavenly doctrine revealed by God in His

Second Coming. The church does not preach Christ crucified. For the church, God is one not trinity:

> The Cathedral is dedicated to the worship of God in a new vision of His Divine Humanity. The "New Church," of which the General Church of the New Jerusalem is an organized body, is not to be regarded as a sect of Protestant Christianity. Founded on the theological writings of Emanuel Swedenborg in the eighteenth century, it is a New Christian Church, distinct from all the branches of the faith founded after the Advent ... [And] as He [the Lord] had chosen Moses, the prophets, and the evangelists to set down His Word in successively deeper penetrations of the human mind and heart, He gave a new revelation of truth through Swedenborg ... He said that He would come again as the Spirit of Truth; and in the apocalyptic vision of John of Patmos. He gave the symbolic prophecy of the New Jerusalem descending out of heaven – a new heaven and a new church on earth, freed from the falsities of human misinterpretation. Indeed, the whole of the book of Revelation is a prophecy of His second coming, now fulfilled in the doctrines given through Swedenborg as the further opening of the Holy Scriptures.[46]

The church's place in theological history is best explained in the cathedral's west window above the narthex and by the main altar. According to church teachings, five churches have existed in succession in which "the true God has been worshipped through His Word": the Most Ancient (represented in the window by Adam), the Ancient (represented in the window by Noah), the Israelitish (represented in the window by Aaron), the First Christian (represented in the window by John the Evangelist), and the New Christian Church (represented in the window by a woman clothed with the sun "who dwelt in the wilderness until the truth which she bore as Manchild might grow to maturity").[47] The New Church was founded on the belief that God explained the spiritual meaning of the scriptures to Swedenborg to reveal the truth of the Second Coming of Jesus Christ. Swedenborg claimed divine inspiration for his writings, and his followers believe that he witnessed the Last Judgment in the spiritual world, along with the inauguration of the New Church. For members of the New Church, Christ will return not in his physical body but in the form of a spiritual reawakening for all men and women.[48]

The interior of Bryn Athyn Cathedral has as its central plan the traditional Gothic cruciform, but the cross itself is absent throughout the cathedral as a symbol. The central focus of the cathedral is "the altar of the Lord and upon it His Word in which is no letter written save by His Divine mind and set down at His command. Perhaps the most solemn moment of the Church's ritual is the opening of the Word upon this altar amid silence at the beginning of each service, representative of the opening of the inner sense of the Old and New Testaments in the Heavenly Doctrines given though Swedenborg."[49] The setting of the sanctuary in which the Word is held up before the eye and mind is a distinctive aspect of a new Christian architecture. The members of the New Church looked backwards some 700 years for an architectural rock on which to sustain their faith. For members of the New Church, Bryn Athyn Cathedral is their St. Peter's and their Canterbury. And its construction was eventually carried out according to principles that Pitcairn argued were nothing short of purely medieval:

> The cathedrals of that bygone [medieval] age are filled with deep religious feeling. The life which has departed from the Christian Church still lingers there to stir our hearts with love and admiration for the living Church, doomed then to perish in the melancholy days that followed. For even in the twelfth and thirteenth centuries – the age of Chartres and Rheims, of Paris, and of Amiens – the Christian Church was slowly dying from evils of life and heresies of doctrine. But it had a span of several years before its doom was sealed by the Last Judgment, which occurred not until the year 1757, thus five hundred years after the zenith of Gothic art was reached in the thirteenth century. In the great cathedral age, the Christian Church still lived; indeed, our European ancestors were not converted to Christianity in large numbers until long after the councils of heresy had foreshadowed the downfall of the Christian Church. It is not an old Church with them, but a new Church, beautiful and living, and there was yet a long time before the Consummation of the Age.[50]

The least strictly medieval feature of the cathedral is the high altar in the sanctuary. Its placement would not be unusual in a medieval cathedral, but its design and symbolism, like almost everything else in the cathedral, is tied to the New Testament's Book of Revelation.[51] Twelve steps lead up to the altar, signifying that in the Word are completed all things of faith. Surrounding the altar are seven golden lampstands that represent the New Church. The altar itself symbolizes the throne found in the fourth chapter of the Book of Revelation and represents Heaven in terms of divine truth. Just as the Word rests on the altar in the midst of seven golden lampstands, so, the Swedenborgians believe, the Lord rests on the truth of Heaven in the midst of the New Church.

The stained-glass windows of Bryn Athyn Cathedral are clearly medieval in inspiration and design. The medieval method of creating stained glass, namely of melting various pigment and metallic oxides into the glass itself and then having a glass blower create a disk of glass with varying degrees of thickness and brightness, was revived. The first glass was blown in 1922, and the last was created in the 1940s; however, the windows were not completed until the 1960s. The windows are of three designs: biblical figures represented in monumental scale; medallions depicting events in the lives either of Christ or of the Old Testament prophets; and grisaille windows of geometric design and pearl-like translucency that fill the cathedral with light. Swedenborgians sometimes seem to have a love-hate relationship with iconography and ecclesiastical decoration, which they associate with the imperfect practice of previous churches.[52] The cathedral windows seem simultaneously, at least to an outsider, to reflect and be at odds with the "newness" integral to the New Church and its movement beyond, if not outright rejection of, the practices and iconography of what it considers earlier churches.

The Ezekiel Tower, located south of the main 150-foot tower, was built between 1920 and 1926. The Choir Hall and Michael Tower lie to the north of the main cathedral. This addition was completed in 1929, and, although these two structures were the last completed portion of the complex, their architectural style is the earliest employed in the cathedral. Today, maintenance of the cathedral requires the employment of a full-time resident master stone carver and his apprentices, just as Raymond Pitcairn imported and housed master European craftsmen almost a hundred years ago when he began to build the cathedral.[53]

Bryn Athyn Cathedral's adoption of a hybrid of the Romanesque and the Gothic as its architectural style is notable for a number of reasons, not the least of which are the date of its building and its denominational affiliation. Generally speaking, the era for building America's great cathedrals and churches on a medieval model was over by the turn of the twentieth century,[54] and such places of worship were almost exclusively home to high church congregations, Catholic or Episcopalian. There were some notable exceptions in Philadelphia such as the Arch Street Methodist Church, standing next to the Masonic Temple and City Hall. Dedicated in 1870, the church, designed by Addison Hutton in a "florid Gothic style of architecture," marked a radical departure from the understated "meeting house plain" structures favoured by nonconforming denominations such as the Methodists and still today stands as the city's central church.[55]

Bryn Athyn Cathedral's uniqueness is directly attributable to the views of Raymond Pitcairn about the way in which cathedrals should be built, and those views were as much political as they were artistic. Politics, however, would play a more obvious role in the design of Glencairn, a structure more reflective of American medievalism than of the medieval, as Raymond Pitcairn would next turn his attention from the ecclesiastical to the secular while building a fitting residence for himself and his family in the Borough of Bryn Athyn adjacent to the cathedral. That residence, Glencairn, today a museum, occupies a curious middle ground between the medieval and medievalism. It is clearly not meant to be an imitation of such stately Victorian follies as Cardiff Castle, which several Marquises of Bute remodelled in various styles, including finally Gothic Revival. Glencairn was built from scratch, employing once again some of the principles of medieval architecture that Pitcairn sought to reestablish for the construction of Bryn Athyn Cathedral. Romanesque in style, Glencairn is a massive structure rising several stories and containing more than ninety rooms. It took a decade to construct (1929–39), with work briefly suspended because of the Depression. It consists of a central tower and two rectangular wings. That the building today should house an eclectic collection of nearly 8,000 works of mainly religious art from the ancient and medieval worlds, as well as representative examples of Islamic, Asian, and Native American art, is fitting because it grew out of Pitcairn's desire to construct a home for his growing collection of medieval art: "I should like to incorporate my little collection into a studio which would be a Romanesque or early Gothic room or small building."[56]

That room or small building grew according to the same organic principles of construction that informed the building of Bryn Athyn Cathedral. And the building, like the cathedral, is filled with the "medieval refinements" so praised by Goodyear and Porter in their assessment of the earlier structure. The family chapel at the top end of the east wing was the spiritual centre of a building that reflected a combination of a fantasy of historical medieval building practices, a faith in the principles of the New Church, and an unswerving patriotism and belief in American constitutional principles.

Raymond Pitcairn was nothing if not a complicated man. He and his family were the driving financial force behind the New Church, and his generosity to the Church and its mission was unmatched. He was also an astute businessman, succeeding his father as chief executive of Pittsburgh Plate Glass, and a successful lawyer. While never holding national political office, he was active in Republican politics. His political leanings were at times far right of centre, as evidenced by his leadership and financial backing of the Sentinels of the Republic, an organization founded in 1922 that favoured less government, opposed the New Deal, and famously lobbied to defeat child labour laws. Faced with charges of antisemitism and a lack of political relevance, the Sentinels disbanded in the early 1940s.[57]

Raymond Pitcairn was, as I have said, a complicated man, and Glencairn reflects that fact. The house is a chapel, a library, a residence, a museum, a public space, and a political statement. According to the New Church, "to strive for freedom and justice in civil affairs is to lay the groundwork for heavenly society."[58] Pitcairn saw his linking of spiritual and civic values as being in the tradition of William Penn and Abraham Lincoln.[59] Nowhere in Glencairn is the connection between spiritual and civic clearer than on the two capitals that connect the great hall to the cloister. To the left, in stained glass, sits the Woman Clothed with the Sun, the symbol of the New Church drawn from the Book of Revelation. To the right, a second stained-glass window depicts the structure of the United States government with the motto "There shall be justice for all" – behind an eagle with its wings spread stand the Capitol, the White House, and the Supreme Court Building.[60]

In the final analysis, Glencairn is more an example of medievalism than the medieval – and as such it differs markedly from Bryn Athyn Cathedral. Glencairn clearly uses the medieval for a modern agenda – it does not, like the cathedral, look backwards or to the future. After visiting the cathedral construction site in 1917, Kingsley Porter wrote to Pitcairn that if the cathedral existed "in Europe, in France or England, it would still be at once six centuries behind, and a hundred years ahead of its time."[61] Glencairn, in contrast, is a structure very much grounded in the time (and the politics) of when it was built. It is, culturally speaking, a prime example of what Umberto Eco characterized uncritically as a "messing up" of the Middle Ages "in order to meet the vital requirements of different periods."[62] With its Norman tower and unbroken massive walls, it lacks the vertical sweep of the Gothic cathedral,[63] and it makes a statement about the values that were important, in Pitcairn's view, to his approach to business, to his religion, to his sense of patriotism, and, most importantly, to himself and his family. Inside, Glencairn is a mixture of the medieval (the great hall, the chapel, the stained glass) and the modern (the carved reproductions of the first eight Pitcairn children, the bedrooms and their furnishings, the Carrara marble bathrooms). The structure is an example of American architectural and design medievalism at its best.

Like any number of American cities that "grew up" in the nineteenth century, Philadelphia did not lack structures inspired by the medieval. While too many of those structures have fallen victim to the wrecking ball, others still stand as administrative, performance, and residential spaces on college and university campuses, as functioning ecclesiastical buildings, or as repurposed structures. But Philadelphia's principal claim to fame as part of "medieval America" lies with two Episcopalian parish churches built in the middle of the nineteenth century[64] and with two structures built in the early twentieth century just outside the city on property belonging to the New Church on which, thanks to the generosity and the hands-on supervision of a multimillionaire member of that church, stand what he considered a proper medieval cathedral and a medievalist manor house castle. Few other American cities can boast of being home to structures with the beauty, majesty, delicacy, mass, and conscious evocation of the medieval that are still displayed in these four unique structures.[65]

NOTES

1 For a brief overview of the history of Philadelphia, see Roger D. Simon, *Philadelphia: A Brief History*, rev. ed. (Philadelphia: Temple University Press, 2017). For details about the city's founding and early growth, see 1–22.

2 Gothic Revival architecture has been used in America for all kinds of structures, most notably for places of worship and for buildings on the campuses of secondary schools, colleges, and universities. In a survey of the sometimes-sorry state of early American church architecture, Henry Russell Cleveland called "the sublime, the glorious Gothic" the architecture of Christianity; see "[Review of] The American Builder's General Price Book and Estimator," *North American Review* 43, no. 93 (Oct.

1836): 380. The Gothic first gained popularity with American architects and their clients in the 1840s, in part thanks to James Renwick Jr.'s Smithsonian Institution Building and to the vigorous defense of its style in Robert Dale Owen's *Hints on Public Architecture* (New York: Putnam, 1849): "[The Smithsonian] is the first edifice, in the style of the twelfth century and of a characteristic not ecclesiastical, ever erected in this country" (109). The popularity of the Gothic would fade in the early 1870s but would enjoy a revival in the 1880s and 1890s. See Carroll L.V. Meeks, "Romanesque before Richardson in the United States," *Art Bulletin* 35, no. 1 (Mar. 1953): 17–33.

3 For further details on Independence Hall and its construction, see John Andrew Gallery, *Philadelphia Architecture: A Guide to the City*, 4th ed. (Philadelphia: Paul Dry Books, 2016), 20–1; and Roger W. Moss, *Historic Landmarks of Philadelphia* (Philadelphia: University of Pennsylvania Press, 2008), 24–31. For further details on Philadelphia's City Hall and its construction, see Gallery, *Philadelphia Architecture*, 74–5; and Moss, *Historic Landmarks*, 180–5. For further details on the Philadelphia Museum of Art and its construction, see Gallery, *Philadelphia Architecture*, 116–17; and Moss, *Historic Landmarks*, 278–83.

4 The decisions of the Catholic hierarchy in Philadelphia about how to design their cathedral stood in stark contrast to those of their counterparts in New York, who, a decade later, modelled the exterior of St. Patrick's Cathedral on the Gothic cathedrals of Cologne and Rheims and the interior on that of Amiens – see John Tauranc, *Essential New York* (New York: Holt, Rinehart, Winston, 1979), 52–3.

5 Notman would soon, however, become a key architect for Episcopal parish churches built in Philadelphia in the Gothic Revival style.

6 For further details on the Cathedral Basilica of Saints Peter and Paul and its construction, see Gallery, *Philadelphia Architecture*, 58; and Roger W. Moss, *Historic Sacred Places of Philadelphia* (Philadelphia: University of Pennsylvania Press, 2005), 152–7.

7 From the city's founding days, Catholics were not always welcome in Philadelphia despite William Penn's vision of a colony founded upon the principle of religious toleration – see Simon, *Philadelphia*, 4, 14–15. Penn's 1701 Charter of Liberties guaranteed religious freedom to all who believed in "One Almighty God," but British law prohibited the public celebration of Catholic Mass. The Nativist riots occurred in 1844 between 5 and 8 May and on 6 and 7 July and resulted in more than twenty deaths. Catholic churches, a convent, and a school, as well as homes and business belonging to Catholics, were burned to the ground, and the local militia was called to restore order. The pretext for the riots was a rumour that Catholics were planning to remove Bible readings from public schools. On the riots, see Amanda Beyer-Purvis, "The Philadelphia Bible Riots of 1844: Contest over the Rights of Citizens," *Pennsylvania History* 83 (2016): 366–93; and Kenneth W. Milano, *Philadelphia Nativist Riots: Irish Kensington Erupts* (Charleston, SC: History Press, 2013).

8 See Virginia Dugan, *A History of the Cathedral Basilica of Saints Peter and Paul* (Philadelphia: [Cathedral Basilica of Saints Peter and Paul?], 1979), 20.

9 *Masonic Temple Philadelphia, Pennsylvania: A Souvenir Album* (Philadelphia: Grand Lodge of Pennsylvania, 1993), [3].

10 Windrim had apprenticed under, and then worked for, John Notman. On the competition for the design of the Masonic Temple, see John C. Poppeliers, "The 1867 Philadelphia Masonic Temple Competition," *Journal of the Society of Architectural Historians* 26, no. 4 (1967): 278–84; and Michael R. Harrison, *Masonic Temple: 1 North Broad Street, Philadelphia, Pennsylvania*, National Park Service, Heritage Documentation Programs, Historic American Buildings Survey, No. PA-1532 (Washington, DC: US Department of the Interior, 2010), 14–24.

11 Unattributed reaction to the building quoted in Moss, *Historic Landmarks*, 176–8.

12 Gallery, *Philadelphia Architecture*, 70.

13 On the design of the Norman and Gothic rooms and the medieval trappings of the dedicatory ceremonies, see *Masonic Temple Philadelphia, Pennsylvania: A Souvenir Album*, [32–5]; and Harrison, *Masonic Temple*, 45–7, 69–71, 84–8.

14 See George E. Thomas, *The University of Pennsylvania: An Architectural Tour* (New York: Princeton Architectural Press, 2002), 30, 46–7. Henry Adams's influential study, *Mont-Saint-Michel and Chartres*, first published privately in 1903, was made more widely available when it was republished by the American Institute of Architects in 1913.

15 Moss, *Historic Sacred Places*, 250.

16 Quoted in Moss, *Historic Sacred Places*, 250. For the full details of the society's "rules for church-building," see James White, *The Cambridge Movement: The Ecclesiologists and the Gothic Revival* (London: Cambridge University Press, 1962), 80–116.

17 The society also supplied the vestry with a copy of *Instrumenta Ecclesiastica: A Series of Working Designs for the Furniture, Fittings, and Decorations of Churches and Their Precincts* (London: John van Voorst, 1847), written by their chief designer, William Butterfield; this text was consulted frequently. See Moss, *Historic Sacred Places*, 248.

18 Phoebe B. Stanton, *The Gothic Revival and American Church Architecture: An Episode in Taste, 1840–1856* (Baltimore, MD: Johns Hopkins University Press, 1968), 91.

19 Moss, *Historic Sacred Places*, 253.

20 Moss, *Historic Sacred Places*, 162–6.

21 Stanton, *Gothic Revival*, 124–5.

22 Stanton, *Gothic Revival*, 125.

23 Moss, *Historic Sacred Places*, 166–7.

24 No such altar had previously been crafted for a church in North America, and the silver Lady Chapel altar in St. Mark's is arguably one of the greatest works of "English ecclesiastical art in Twentieth Century America"; see Claude Gilkyson, *St. Mark's: One Hundred Years on Locust Street* (Philadelphia: St. Mark's Church, 1948), 60. The most exhaustive study of the altar is Addie Peyronnin, "'To Beautify

His House': Rodman Wanamaker's Sacramental Silver Commission" (master's thesis, University of Delaware, 2012). Rodman Wanamaker also built the bell tower at St. James the Less in honour of his late brother, Thomas. The Wanamaker Family Mausoleum lies beneath the bell tower and is the final resting place for Thomas and Rodman Wanamaker and their parents. See Millicent E. Norcross Berghaus, *The Church of St. James the Less, 1846–1971: One Hundredth and Twenty-Fifth Anniversary* (Philadelphia: [St. James the Less?], 1971), 21, 27–8.
25 James D. McCabe, *The Illustrated History of the Centennial Exhibition* (Philadelphia: National Publishing Company, 1876), 192.
26 Moss, *Historic Sacred Places*, 168.
27 Moss, *Historic Sacred Places*, 171.
28 McCabe, *Illustrated History*, 192.
29 Gallery, *Philadelphia Architecture*, 64–5.
30 Stanton, *Gothic Revival*, 124–5.
31 Bryn Athyn means "hill of unity." The borough covers roughly 1.9 square miles and, according to the 2010 census, has a population of 1,375. It was founded in the late nineteenth century as a religious community. In addition to Bryn Athyn Cathedral and Glencairn, it is home to Cairnwood, a Beaux-Arts country house built in 1895 for the industrialist John Pitcairn, Raymond's father; Cairncrest, the home of one of John's other sons, Harold, and now used for office space by the New Church; and Bryn Athyn College, a small liberal arts church-affiliated institution, originally established as the Academy of the New Church to train its ministers. See Ed Gyllenhaal and Kristen Hansen Gyllenhaal, *The Bryn Athyn Historic District* (Charleston, SC: Arcadia, 2011).
32 Moss, *Historic Sacred Places*, 167.
33 George Wickersham II, *The Cathedral Church of Saint John the Divine: A House of Prayer for All Nations* (New York: C. Harrison Conroy, 1978), 5.
34 Suger (ca. 1081–1151) is often credited with inventing Gothic architecture owing to his work in overseeing the building of the Abbey of Saint-Denis in what is now a northern suburb of Paris.
35 Jennifer Kingston Bloom, "Scaffolding Leaving the Cathedral of St. John the Divine: More to Come," *New York Times*, 20 Nov. 1994: CY6.
36 Peter W. Williams, *Houses of God: Region, Religion, and Architecture in the United States* (Urbana: University of Illinois, 2000), 68.
37 Ralph Adams Cram, "A Note on Bryn Athyn Church," *American Architect* 113 (29 May 1918): 710. Cram was, in the end, philosophical about his withdrawal from the project. He had only kind words to say about the Pitcairns and their involvement, but he felt that the construction of the cathedral was a sort of architectural "tragedy," an exercise in architectural socialism that undermined the authority of the architect. Yes, he felt, the building of a structure such as Bryn Athyn Cathedral could restore "the mediæval sense of co-operation which was the essence of mediæval art," but that the architect "must remain not only the

co-ordinating force but the final and sovereign authority in all matters" (712). Cram had earlier expressed his general views on medieval art and architecture in *Church Building: A Study of the Principles of Architecture in Their Relation to the Church* (Boston: Small, Maynard, 1901) and *The Ministry of Art* (Freeport, NY: Books for Libraries Press, 1914). Raymond Pitcairn countered Cram's final verdict of Bryn Athyn Cathedral in "Christian Art and Architecture for the New Church," *New Church Life* 40, no. 10 (Oct. 1920): 611–24, in which he argued that no inspiration could be found in "the dead and ugly [Victorian] Gothic structures of the last century."

38 See the published version of the lectures, William Goodyear, "Modern Church Architecture and Medieval Refinement," *Brooklyn Museum Quarterly* 5, no. 4 (Oct. 1918): 22.
39 Cram, *Ministry of Art*, 162.
40 Quoted in E. Bruce Glenn, *Bryn Athyn Cathedral: The Building of a Church*, 2nd ed. (Bryn Athyn, PA: Bryn Athyn Church of the New Jerusalem, 2011), 46.
41 Kingsley Porter, *Beyond Architecture* (Boston: Marshall Jones, 1918), 190.
42 Porter, *Beyond Architecture*, 156–9.
43 Porter, *Beyond Architecture*, 70.
44 See William Goodyear, "Notes," *Brooklyn Museum Quarterly* 3, no. 2 (Apr. 1916): 88.
45 See Glenn, *Bryn Athyn Cathedral*, 33–74.
46 Glenn, *Bryn Athyn Cathedral*, 19–20.
47 Glenn, *Bryn Athyn Cathedral*, 27.
48 Cram noted that the form of Swedenborgianism practiced at Bryn Athyn is "more mystical than that of the parent sect"; see "Note on Bryn Athyn Church," 710. For a quick summary of New Church beliefs, see Glenn, *Bryn Athyn Cathedral*, 13–14, 19–28.
49 Glenn, *Bryn Athyn Cathedral*, 25.
50 Pitcairn, "Christian Art," 624.
51 On the tension between the medieval and the non-medieval in the cathedral, see Glenn, *Bryn Athyn Cathedral*, 24–8.
52 On the windows, see Glenn, *Bryn Athyn Cathedral*, 135–64. Glenn argues that the use of stained glass for ecclesiastical structures had "degenerated" under the impact of the Renaissance (135). See also Vera P. Glenn, *The Angel of the Lord: Stories about the Angel Windows in the Bryn Athyn Cathedral* (2001; repr., Bryn Athyn, PA: General Church of the New Jerusalem, 2006); Martin Pryke, *A Quest for Perfection: The Story of the Making of the Stained-Glass Windows in the Bryn Athyn Cathedral and Glencairn* (Bryn Athyn, PA: Glencairn Museum, 1990); *A Handbook of Information Concerning the Cathedral-church of Bryn Athyn*, 7th ed. (Bryn Athyn, PA: Cathedral Book Room, 1952); and Lawrence Saint, *The Romance of Stained Glass* (Huntington Valley, PA: [privately printed], 1959).
53 Glenn, *Bryn Athyn Cathedral*, 169–83.

54 Baltimore's original cathedral, the neoclassical National Shrine of the Assumption of the Blessed Virgin Mary, was built between 1806 and 1863. Boston's Gothic Revival Cathedral of the Holy Cross was built between 1866 and 1875. Chicago's Gothic Revival Holy Name Cathedral was dedicated in 1875, replacing a cathedral destroyed four years earlier in the Great Chicago Fire. Cincinnati's St. Peter in Chains Cathedral, designed in a very different Greek Revival style, was dedicated in 1845. Cleveland's Gothic Revival Cathedral of St. John the Evangelist was built between 1845 and 1852. Detroit's original cathedral, the Romanesque Revival St. Patrick's, opened as a chapel in 1862; it was replaced by the Gothic Revival Cathedral of the Blessed Sacrament, which was begun in 1913 but not completed until 1930. New York's Gothic Revival St. Patrick's Cathedral was built from 1858 to 1878, replacing an earlier Gothic Revival cathedral in lower Manhattan that was built from 1810 to 1815. Providence's Romanesque and Gothic Revival Cathedral of Saints Peter and Paul was built from 1878 to 1889.

55 Moss, *Historic Sacred Places*, 140; "Church – Dedicatory Services," *Philadelphia Daily Ledger*, 18 Nov. 1870; James D. Van Trump, "The Gothic Fane: The Medieval Vision and Some Philadelphia Churches, 1860–1900," *Charrette*, Sept. 1963: 20–7; and Frederick E. Maser, *Facing the Challenge of Change: The Story of the City's Central Church* (Philadelphia: Arch Street Methodist Church, 1982), 4–21.

56 Letter written in 1922 to his younger brother, Theo, quoted in E. Bruce Glenn, *Glencairn: The Story of a Home* (Bryn Athyn, PA: Academy of the New Church, 1970), 15.

57 On Raymond Pitcairn's engagement in the civic arena, see Glenn, *Glencairn*, 107–23. On the Sentinels and their disbanding, see George Seldes, *One Thousand Americans: The Real Rulers of the U.S.A.* (New York: Boni & Gaer, 1947), 154, 183.

58 Glenn, *Glencairn*, 111.

59 Glenn, *Glencairn*, 110.

60 Glenn, *Glencairn*, 110–16.

61 Quoted in Glenn, *Glencairn*, 44.

62 Umberto Eco, *Travels in Hyperreality: Essays*, trans. William Weaver (San Diego: Harcourt Brace, 1986), 68.

63 Glenn, *Glencairn*, 48.

64 Anna Nua has recently suggested that the "'Englishness' of ... [St. James the Less and St. Mark's] went beyond religious concerns and was symptomatic of their [vestries'] desire to project, through the architecture of their churches, a distinct English-American identity in an era of any increasingly diverse Philadelphia population." See Nua, "English-American Identity and the Gothic Revival," *Nineteenth Century* 33, no. 1 (2013): 10–19, at 18.

65 Once again, I am happy to acknowledge the invaluable, tenacious, and generous research assistance provided by my very good colleagues in the Interlibrary Loan Department of La Salle University's Connelly Library, Gerard Regan and Megan Bennis.

3 The Masonic Medievalism of Washington, DC

LAURIE A. FINKE

Washington, DC, does not immediately recommend itself as a city steeped in the medieval. Designed to celebrate US and Enlightenment values of equality and freedom, the city draws inspiration in its architecture from the neoclassicism of familiar landmarks like the Capitol (completed in 1800), the White House (completed in 1800, burnt in 1814, and subsequently reconstructed), the Library of Congress (1890–7), the Supreme Court Building (1935), and the National Portrait Gallery (1968), with these later monuments celebrating as well "America's status as an emerging world power" by the start of the twentieth century.[1] Washington boasts a monumental architecture that hearkens back to ancient Greece and Rome rather than, say, the medieval cathedral or castle. As befits a new democracy born of revolution and a rejection of the old medieval order, the United States of America required a new capital, a city created to reflect the Republican virtues of the new nation. In the words of Frederick Douglass, this capital ought to be "the living center of our social as well as of our political civilization and ... incorporated with all our national thoughts and feelings."[2]

Construction of a new federal city was authorized in 1790. The city was created out of land ceded by the states of Maryland and Virginia and named after its founder, the first president of the United States, George Washington. The French architect Pierre Charles L'Enfant was commissioned to lay out a plan for the city, which he delivered in 1792. Construction, which relied heavily on slave labour (the site was chosen largely to reassure Southern landowners that the "peculiar institution" would be protected), began soon thereafter, and the government moved in 1800.[3] The American citizen in 1875, when Frederick Douglass gave his *Lecture on Our National Capital*, might visit Washington, DC, as a pilgrim, but not a medieval one: "He need not go there as a Mohammedan goes to Mecca, nor as a Catholic goes to Rome, nor as an Israelite goes to Jerusalem, but he should go in the spirit of intelligent patriotism, the better to appreciate the value of his country and the excellence of free institutions."[4] The pilgrimage to our nation's capital, Douglass suggests, demands not a religious but a secular commitment to democratic values: "Under the majestic dome of the American Capitol, as truly as under the broad blue sky of heaven, men of all races, colors, and conditions may now stand in equal freedom, thrilled with the sentiment of equal citizenship and common country."[5] The medieval seems poorly suited to carry the various meanings associated with a capital meant to represent the "Great Republic." And yet one does catch glimpses of the medieval in buildings like the National Cathedral (begun in 1907 but not completed until 1990) or the Castle housing the Smithsonian Institution (1855).

My exploration of Washington, DC's medievalism investigates the historical presence in that city of the oldest fraternal organization in the United States, the Freemasons, an organization carrying contradictory meanings that move between the extremes of enlightenment rationality and egalitarianism on the one hand and medieval esotericism and hierarchy on the other. This chapter begins by describing these tensions, focusing on the medieval origin stories that form the basis of Freemasonry. It then explores expressions of Masonic medievalism in two buildings in the DC area: the House of the Temple, the headquarters of the Scottish Rite of Freemasonry, Southern Jurisdiction, located in the Dupont Circle neighbourhood; and the George Washington Masonic Memorial, situated across the river in Alexandria, Virginia. While the external architecture of both buildings is decidedly non-Gothic, their interiors display the medievalism of modern Freemasonry. Here expressions of the medieval seem the beating heart of Masonic secrecy and esotericism.

My argument has three claims. First, there is an institutional (and not coincidental) connection between the city of Washington, DC, and Freemasonry. And not in a conspiracy theory kind of way, in which colonial Freemasons wove demonic symbols into the street plan of the city, or the Dan Brown way, in which esoteric Masonic pyramids constitute a threat to national security,[6] but in the ways in which both city and fraternity embodied – gave concrete and fleshly form to – the political theories that enabled the new republic. Second, despite, or even because of, its foundation in the Enlightenment, Freemasonry looks to the medieval for its origins and its rituals. Finally, I argue that the fraternity provided medieval models of a hegemonic masculinity that were from the start built into the politics of civic republicanism and into the very buildings in which it was enacted. Civic republicanism in the United States has always been, as Dana Nelson notes, a form of national manhood.[7]

Most people are vaguely aware that Masons played important roles in building the city. Besides giving it his name, George Washington, in full regalia, laid the cornerstone of the new US Capitol on 18 September 1793, in a Masonic ritual.[8] L'Enfant may have been at least an Entered Apprentice (first degree) in the fraternity.[9] Other prominent early Masons include Benjamin Franklin, John Hancock, and Supreme Court justice John Marshall. Thomas Paine, who was likely not a Mason, nonetheless wrote a pamphlet called *The Origin of Freemasonry* (1818). Even more significantly, the trowel that Washington used to lay the cornerstone of the Capitol has since been used repeatedly in similar Masonic ceremonies for other important Washington buildings, including the Washington Monument (1885), the Smithsonian, the Thomas Jefferson Memorial (1943), the Supreme Court Building, and the National Cathedral (1990).[10] But more than the mere presence of prominent Masons at our nation's founding (there were of course Masons on both sides of the war for independence), Freemasonry contributed to the emergence of new forms of power in the eighteenth and nineteenth centuries. As a practical instantiation of political theories that would be put into practice in the new capital, Freemasonry helped to determine who could participate in these new forms of government and who would be excluded.

My argument that Masonic medievalism helped to define the national manhood of civic republicanism requires a brief foray into political theory. In a series of lectures at the Collège de France in 1977 and 1978, Michel Foucault coined the term "governmentality" to describe the art of government: "how to govern oneself, how to be governed, by whom should we accept to be governed, how to be the best possible governor."[11] The series of revolutions between the sixteenth and eighteenth centuries spurred on by philosophical investigations of governance, according to Foucault, "shattered the structures of feudalism" and led to, among other things, "the establishment of the great territorial, administrative, and colonial states" of the nineteenth century, among them the United States for which Washington serves as capital.[12] Foucault's preference for the portmanteau word *govern/mentality* over the simpler *government* or *governance* differentiates his work from more traditional histories of the state that focus on philosophies of government.[13] Instead it allows for investigations not only of the processes of governing but also of the mentality of governing itself, that is, for thinking about how abstract philosophical ideas about governing were translated into specific institutions, practices, and techniques. The new discourses and philosophies of liberal government that emerged in the seventeenth and eighteenth centuries in Europe and America required specific practices and techniques to become institutionalized, to take concrete form in a new capital for a new nation. We are used to thinking of Washington, DC, as an object, a finished place occupying a specific location, but what if we try to understand it as the outcome of a set of practices of governmentality that produced the city as an effect: practices and techniques that educated both leaders and populace on how to conduct themselves in this new government? The new American capital city that would embody Enlightenment ideals about government coincided with the professionalization of architecture and a belief that architecture could express these ideals while building a physical public sphere where white men of a particular class could come together to govern themselves and others. Built for new purposes, Washington, DC, required legislative assemblies, government offices, monuments, universities, and museums rather than the castles and cathedrals of monarchs and church. Such buildings, however, were far from being merely "empty or neutral containers" to "facilitate the free interaction of bodies in space."[14] The city required spaces in which government could be both inculcated and practised, spaces that would educate "members of the public so that they would be able to assume the new civic duties to which they aspired."[15] Washington's public architecture both reflected and created citizenship.

Classical architecture "was to be the guiding light for the initial monuments of the United States and its new empire," and as Steven Bedford further explains, "In appropriating the architectural forms of Greece and Rome, the intent was to create a monumental architecture that would be the summation of all that had gone before." By the end of the nineteenth century, "this appropriation of form was also an imperialistic expression of America's new status as an emerging world power."[16] Classical architecture epitomized "the masculine shape of civic architecture."[17] From the beginning, American citizenship had been understood as a white male privilege. Only white men voted (until 1870, when the Fourteenth Amendment granted suffrage to Black men), and political and economic power from the federal down to the local level was firmly in their hands. In a culture that encouraged the separation both of male and female and of public and private spaces, even buildings performed gender. Susan Stewart argues that the miniature functions, in relation to the human body, "as a metaphor for interior space and time of the bourgeois subject" (the domestic sphere, the feminine), while "the gigantic serves as a metaphor for the abstract authority of the state and the collective public life."[18] In Washington, DC, the masculine architecture of public life was "rectilinear, symmetrical, mathematically ordered," employing "massive columns," "ponderous masses, and threatening contrasts of light and shadow."[19] It favoured "tall and representative buildings like skyscrapers and civic buildings, mythological symbols of male dominance."[20]

Carole Pateman has shown that the shift in governmentality from feudal to liberal democracy required a concomitant shift in the ideology of male dominance from a patriarchal state – one ruled absolutely by an almost always male sovereign, a father – to a fraternal one, a regime of the brother.[21] Norman Brown's succinct summary of the famous passage in Freud's *Moses and Monotheism* describes this myth of transition: "The sons form a conspiracy to overthrow the despot, and in the end substitute a social contract with equal rights for all ... *Liberty means equality among the brothers (sons)* ... Locke suggests that the fraternity is formed not by birth but by election, by contract."[22] Brotherhood, or fraternity, enabled what Douglass called "the sentiment of equal citizenship and common country."[23] But if fraternity refers to an abstract ideal of mutual social cooperation, it was made flesh in specific homosocial institutions, like Freemasonry, that were designed to encourage solidarity among particular men through the exclusions they made. It "contains and expresses hierarchical as well as egalitarian assumptions about human relations."[24] Inclusion conferred upon the brothers certain privileges. Freemasonry in the nineteenth century was very much a technique of governmentality, one that encouraged the relay "between the governance of the state and the governance of selves and other." The new republic demanded institutions that nurtured citizenship by educating its members both to govern and to be governed, articulating (in both senses of the word) "the interplay between the technologies of the self and the technologies of governing a people, a state or a society."[25] So, while Masonic lodges expressly forbade "any quarrels about religion, or nations, or state policy" – "We are resolved against all Politicks," James Anderson writes in *The Constitutions of the Free-Masons*[26] – their very activities made them "schools of government," inculcating practical lessons about how to practise the kind of democracy articulated by Enlightenment thinkers. As Margaret Jacob argues in *Living the Enlightenment*, Freemasonry taught men "how to integrate enlightened values with the habits of governance ... to speak in public, to keep records, to pay 'taxes,' to be tolerant, to debate freely, to vote, to moderate their feasting, and to give devotion to other citizens of their order."[27] Lodges wrote constitutions; they sent representatives to nationally organized Grand Lodges, modelling federalism. They taught men to govern and to be governed.

Foucault's notion of governmentality refers not only to liberal forms of government that emerged alongside the Freemasons but also to governing in all senses of that term. Earlier forms of power – say medieval governmentalities – did not just appear, do their thing, and then disappear. Rather they remained embedded in many practices that continue and are institutionalized within and beyond the state. Two practices that converge in this chapter – the professionalization of architecture and the growth of fraternities based on architectural symbols – exemplify nongovernmental forms of governmentality. Freemasonry looked backwards to the Middle Ages as its origin and to justify exclusions codified by its founding documents, exclusions based on gender, class, race, and ability. These exclusions are explicitly laid down in Anderson's *Constitutions* in a famous passage outlining the qualifications for membership: "The Persons admitted Members of a *Lodge* must be good and true Men, free-born, and of mature and discreet Age, no Bondmen [i.e., slaves], no Women, no immoral or scandalous Men, but of good Report"; a potential initiate must also have "no Maim or Defect in his Body."[28] Exclusions sanctioned by "Masonic anciency" determined which citizens could benefit from the fraternity's lessons.[29]

Freemasonry's medievalism offers a means of understanding how masculinity was not a by-product but an essential feature of national civic republicanism. Initially the Middle Ages might not seem promising ground for this claim.[30] Freemasonry is envisioned by many as a break with the medieval past and touted, as one critic put it, for "its precocious modernism" in promoting religious pluralism and friendship across class lines.[31] It was a significant nongovernmental institution that facilitated the development of what Jürgen Habermas has called the "public sphere": "The coming together of private people into a public was ... anticipated in secret, as a public sphere still existing largely behind [the] closed doors" of lodges.[32] At the same time, however, Freemasonry looked back to the Middle Ages as its origin and for the source of much of its ritual. Freemasonry has two medieval origin stories that contradict each other. One is based on a more or less democratic imagining of the medieval guild; the other on aristocratic military orders that emerged in Europe during the twelfth century. Both are examples of medieval governmentalities; both remediate medieval masculinities to create exemplars for nineteenth-century men. As the *Freemasonry for Dummies* blog explains, "Freemasonry ... is the largest, oldest and best-known gentleman's fraternity in the world. It is based on the medieval stonemason guilds who built the great castles and cathedrals of Europe. Modern Freemasons ... use the tools, traditions and terminology of those stonemasons as allegories for building Temples in the hearts of men."[33] Despite Masonry's Enlightenment roots, then, we must look to medieval guilds as the earliest models of secular fraternity. The symbolic structure of speculative masonry is modelled on the tools and skills of "the Craft" (operative masonry) and thus on the mysteries of the medieval guild. The Blue Lodge degrees of Entered Apprentice, Fellow Craft, and Master Mason are loosely based on the three grades of medieval guild membership: apprentice, journeyman (fellow crafts), and master. Masonry remediates medieval labour, shaping it into an intellectual enterprise, through initiation rituals that reenact the building of Solomon's Temple (recounted in 1 Kings and 2 Chronicles). By performing these rituals, Masons symbolically take on a masculinity shaped by the trope Michael Kimmel calls the Heroic Artisan, the man who is "unafraid of hard work, proud of craftsmanship and simultaneously values both self-reliance and loyalty to coworkers."[34]

Andrew Prescott argues that medieval guilds pioneered most of the features that define modern fraternities. Guilds were voluntary and self-regulating organizations. They featured feasting and drinking as their most prominent social activities, held regular business meetings and elections of officers, participated in processions to maintain a public presence, administered oaths and required secrecy, used special clothing to signify membership, and provided various forms of assistance to members, including alms, funerals, and prayers for deceased members.[35] In fact, modern fraternities like Freemasonry differ from the medieval craft guild primarily in their separation of these social functions from those involving labour and production and in their exclusion of women from membership; perhaps the two are not unrelated.

The large number of competing historical narratives that purport to trace the origins of Freemasonry make daunting the task of shaping a coherent progressive narrative from medieval stonemasons to the early decades of the eighteenth century and the emergence of the fraternal organization known as Freemasonry, from operative to speculative masonry, from medieval workshops to lodges that admitted only literate gentlemen – "men who had never lifted a brick" as Margaret Jacob quips.[36] If there ever was a continuous Masonic history, that history has long since been lost. Recorded history tells us that 1717 witnessed the formation of the Grand Lodge of London (although that date has come under suspicion).[37] James Anderson's *Constitutions of the Free-Masons*, considered something like a founding document, was first published in 1723 (it was published in the United States in 1734 by Benjamin Franklin); the papal condemnation of Freemasonry occurred in 1738, suggesting that speculative Freemasonry was well established by the early decades of the eighteenth century. Anderson's *Constitutions* traces a fanciful universal history of masonry, much of it drawn from medieval sources like the *Polychronicon*, that runs in unbroken succession from "Adam, our first parent"; through Noah and his three sons, "true Masons all"; through Egypt and that Grand Master, Moses; Solomon's Temple and its master mason Hiram Abiff; the architectural wonders of Greece and Rome; up to Athelstan and his son Edwin, who "took upon him the Charges of a Master Mason."[38]

This account of Masonic origins in medieval stonemason guilds fits within a progressive view of history that incorporates the Middle Ages into a narrative of continuous evolution towards democratic fraternalism. If things had ended there, the story of Masonry's connections to our nation's capital might be far simpler. But the exemplar of masculinity it offered, the heroic artisan, did not satisfy all men, nor did its message of equality among men. The emergence of democratic institutions in eighteenth-century Europe was not inevitable. Democracy was not without its opponents, primarily conservatives and aristocrats who sought to maintain the status quo and their own models of masculinity, so that the narrative of the heroic artisan – of Masonry's origin from medieval guilds – represented by the Blue Lodge degrees does not go unchallenged even in the fraternity's early years. In 1737, a member of the Scottish court in exile in France, the Chevalier Andrew Michael Ramsey (a baker's son who rose to be a baronet in the Jacobite peerage), offered an alternative myth for the origin of Freemasonry, promoting a more exalted genealogy for the fraternity:

> The word *Freemason* must … not be taken in a literal, gross, and material sense, as if our founders had been simple workers in stone, or merely curious geniuses who wished to perfect the arts. They were not only skilful architects, desirous of consecrating their talents and goods to the construction of material temples; but also religious and warrior princes who designed to enlighten, edify, and protect

the living Temples of the Most High. This I will demonstrate by developing the history or rather the renewal of the Order.[39]

Ramsey seems appalled to imagine descent (even fraternal descent) from mere craftsmen, and even the profession of "skilful architect" requires martial modification. In his account, the order was created by "an intimate union" with "our ancestors, the Crusaders," so that "kings, princes, and lords returned from Palestine to their own lands, and there established divers Lodges" throughout Europe.[40] The Freemasons, Ramsey argues, grew out of the great military orders of the Middle Ages, the Templars and Hospitalers, crusaders and warriors, to his way of thinking a more appropriate masculinity.

In his 1895 *Book of the Ancient and Accepted Scottish Rite of Freemasonry*, Charles T. McClenachan credits Ramsey with the creation of the Ancient and Accepted Scottish Rite of Freemasonry, one group of degrees "appendant to" the Blue Lodge degrees.[41] The origins of the appendant degrees of Freemasonry, the York and Scottish Rites, are buried in obscurity, amid complex claims and controversies, but many historians believe that the Scottish Rite has Jacobite origins, that it represents the desire of a failed Stuart aristocracy to reclaim, even if only imaginatively, its old status. A complete examination of the appendant bodies and side degrees that have proliferated throughout Freemasonry is beyond the scope of this chapter.[42] Most developed out of a desire to create ever more illustrious exemplars of masculinity. Briefly, Master Masons may be initiated in fifteen higher degrees in the York Rite and twenty-nine in the Scottish Rite (or both). While most Masons remain in Blue Lodges, satisfied with the identity of stoneworker or builder, "those who underwent the higher degrees … received the opportunity to experiment with a range of masculine identities,"[43] primarily the more aristocratic avatars of knight, prince, and commander because many of these degrees are based on legends about the orders of crusading knights. Masons did not simply read these legends; rather, through initiations, they attempted to refashion themselves as knights, to remediate medieval narratives as performances of masculinity. In the Scottish Rite alone a Master Mason might achieve the degrees of Knight of the East or Sword (15th), Prince of Jerusalem (16th), Knights of the East and West (17th), Knight of the Rose Croix (18th), Maochite or Prussian Knight (21st), Knight of the Royal Axe (22nd), Prince of the Tabernacle (24th), and Knight of the Brazen Serpent (25th). The so-called Templar Degrees include the 27th, Knight Commander of the Temple; the 28th, Knight of the Sun; the 29th, Knight of Saint Andrew; the 30th, Knights Kadosh; the 32nd, Master of the Royal Secret; and the 33rd honorary degree, Inspector General.

These higher degrees were called the chivalric degrees because they re-created fanciful versions of the codes of chivalry sworn by medieval knights. In the 29th degree of the Scottish Rite, Southern Jurisdiction, initiates are told what medieval knights once did: "The Order of Knighthood of Saint Andrew of Scotland was instituted to rebuild the Churches destroyed in the Holy Land, by the Saracens; to protect pilgrims journeying to the Holy Sepulchre; and to perform the other active duties of Knighthood."[44] Knighthood, however, must be resignified for fin-de-siècle men (this ritual was published in 1878). Barely more than a decade after the end of a civil war that nearly destroyed the Union and the democratic principles supposedly embodied in the country's capital, Southern Masons were told by a former Confederate general, Albert Pike, that the Knights of Saint Andrew of Scotland now "battle manfully for truth and the right, for free speech and free thought; and to defend the people against all usurpation and tyranny, civil or military, in peace or in war, under whatsoever color or pretext their rights under the law and Constitution may be invaded."[45] In governing himself, the newly minted Knight of Saint Andrew became a defender of civic republicanism. He would have inculcated its values into his knightly performance and could style himself a defender of free speech, the law, and the Constitution.

While countless Masonic texts assert that the Blue Lodge degrees are the heart and soul of Masonry, the proliferation of higher degrees and the dissemination of the narrative into the chivalric and esoteric make the organizational chart of Freemasonry so convoluted and top-heavy that the Blue Lodge degrees seem buried under the sheer weight of the fraternity's many supplemental degrees.[46] Pike's *Morals and Dogma* explains how the higher degrees supplant the plebian craft degrees: "The Blue Degrees are but the outer court or portico of the Temple. Part of the symbols are displayed there to the Initiate, but he is intentionally misled by false interpretations. It is not intended that he shall understand them; but it is intended that he shall imagine he understands them. Their true explication is reserved for the Adepts, the Princes of Masonry."[47] In the higher degrees, true knowledge that was withheld in the lower degrees is revealed. The symbolic correspondences established by the allegory of Freemasonry – "building temples in the hearts of men" – recedes as the foundational degrees are, as it were, buried in the basement.

Although the creation of higher chivalric degrees began early in the fraternity's history, it reached its zenith in the United States during the so-called Golden Age of Fraternalism, the period roughly from the end of the Civil War until the First World War. During this time, as many as one in five men, over 5,400,000, belonged to at least one fraternal society,[48] and many belonged to two or more, most – hundreds of them – newly minted after 1880.[49] Noel P. Gist estimates that by 1927 nearly 800 different fraternal orders had a combined membership of 30 million men.[50] Freemasonry also benefited during these years of rapid expansion, especially in the aristocratic Scottish Rite, whose numbers swelled from 40,000 men in 1900 to nearly 600,000 in 1930.[51] Mary Ann Clawson argues that the exoticism and theatricality of the Masonic chivalric degrees "had a profound influence on the style and aspirations of subsequent fraternal organizations" during this period.[52] Men joining fraternities seemed to prefer the masculine identity of the knight over the more menial archetype of the builder, trading in their aprons for swords. This growth in membership necessitated larger spaces, including theatres with elaborate props in which to conduct mass initiations, as it also required funds to commission opulent buildings that displayed the fraternity's wealth and influence. The years between 1870 and 1930 saw the construction of sumptuous Masonic "temples" in nearly every city in the country.[53] "Purpose-built" Masonic buildings became "ubiquitous features of the built American landscape" in cities from Boston and Philadelphia to Dubuque and Laramie.[54] Some Masonic writers argued that these buildings ought to feature Gothic architecture because "the spirit of Masonry is the spirit of Gothic … both were born out of the Middle Ages."[55] Temples built during the Golden Age, however, display an eclectic range of architectural styles including Romanesque, Gothic, Moorish, neoclassical, Classical Revival, Beaux-Arts, and Art Deco, sometimes drawing on many styles in a single building.[56] Masonic architecture plundered all pasts to create what Moore calls a "mythic nontemporal realm" that provided ritual spaces in which men could perform various archetypes of masculinity, among them the heroic artisan (Blue Lodge degrees), the warrior (York Rite), the adept or wise man (Scottish Rite), and the jester or fool (Shriners).[57] Erecting temples also ironically allowed speculative Masons – "men who routinely enacted the metaphysical act of constructing an invisible Neoplatonic temple" – to perform operative masonry.[58] A 1914 editor of the *Masonic Standard* proclaimed, "We not only build character in our speculative capacity, but we have not forgotten the arts of operative Masonry."[59]

The use of architecture to inculcate an ideology of masculine citizenship and the ascendency of fraternalism in American life converge in the commissioning at the beginning of the twentieth century of two of Washington's most prominent and opulent Masonic buildings: the House of the Temple and the George Washington Masonic Memorial. Both buildings encode the contradictions of fraternalism described above: its capaciousness and its exclusivity. Commissioned at the height of fraternalism's Golden Age, they ostentatiously display the prosperity and influence of Freemasonry in the capital during this period. Unlike other Masonic temples (even the more sumptuous ones), these two buildings were not created primarily as spaces for initiations but as national expressions of Freemasonry. Like Washington, DC, itself, which functions as a symbol as well as an administrative hub to unite all fifty states, these buildings were meant to give national presence to the fraternity, to mark its extension in time and space, instantiating governmentality, at the same time as they provide space for administrative offices, museums, libraries, and archives. Their cornerstone and dedication ceremonies were attended by members of Washington's elite, whether Masons or not. Former president and Supreme Court chief justice William Howard Taft, a Mason, as well as sitting presidents Calvin Coolidge and Herbert Hoover, neither Masons, attended cornerstone and dedication ceremonies for the Washington Masonic Memorial.[60] Individuals who oversaw the work of these buildings understood that they had to harmonize with the monumental architecture of the capital. James D. Richardson, the Grand Commander who commissioned the House of the Temple, said, "We are building a Temple, a permanent home, in the Great Capital of the Greatest nation of the Earth. I would prefer to be criticized for building a Temple, considered by some, too fine and costly, rather than for a cheap or mediocre building, surrounded as it will be, by the beautiful structures of our Capital."[61] The George Washington Masonic Memorial was erected on Shuter's Hill, a historic site originally considered for the Capitol building.

Both buildings were modelled on one of the Ancient Wonders of the World, connecting the pre-eminence of the fraternity with the glories of the past and the monumental architecture that dominates Washington. The House of the Temple, which serves as the headquarters of the Scottish Rite of Freemasonry, Southern Jurisdiction, was modelled after the tomb of Mausolus – whose name gives us the word *mausoleum* – at Halicarnassus (in present-day Turkey).[62] Opened on 18 October 1915, it is located at 1733 Sixteenth Street NW, in the Dupont Circle neighbourhood, about one mile north of the White House. Richardson was determined to make a "new temple as magnificent as art and money can make it," setting aside a budget of $1.1 million.[63] The building was architect John Russell Pope's first major public commission; it would establish his reputation as an "architect of empire." Pope would go on to design such iconic Washington buildings as the Thomas Jefferson Memorial, the National Archives, and the National Gallery of Art (West Building).

At about the same time (1910) across the river in Alexandria, at the urging of Charles H. Callahan, Grand Master of Alexandria-Washington Lodge no. 22 (George Washington's Lodge), the Grand Lodge of Virginia invited all Grand Lodges in the United States to create an association to oversee the building of a new temple as a memorial and museum dedicated to Washington's Masonic career. In 1917, Harvey Wiley Corbett, a prominent skyscraper designer, submitted a drawing of the proposed monument that was modelled on the Lighthouse at Alexandria in Egypt. The building would be "an allegorical lighthouse projecting enlightenment over a cynical world."[64] Because construction proceeded only as the commission could raise money, the memorial would take most of the twentieth century to build. Ground was broken in 1922 and a cornerstone ceremony took place in 1923, using the trowel with which Washington dedicated the cornerstone of the Capitol. The building was dedicated in a 1932 ceremony. While the building was nine stories high, elevators were not installed until 1947.[65] The interior of the building was finally completed in 1970, and "the resulting eclectic building combined neoclassical austerity common to contemporary American memorials and civic buildings with the excitement and energy of modern skyscraper design."[66]

Classical monuments were chosen as models for these buildings, despite the fact that Masonic ritual borrows little from classical cultures; no degrees or rites incorporate narrative material from classical Greek or Roman texts or history. The European Middle Ages, the eastern crusader states, and biblical narrative dominate the rituals. The classical Greek and Roman past appear only in Masonry's appropriation of the Roman Vitruvius's orders of architecture, in which the architecture features as geometric perfection, the pinnacle of the stonemason's art – the Doric order signifying strength, the Ionic wisdom, and the Corinthian beauty. The Vitruvian connection between building and the male body provided a paradigm for producing the quintessentially masculine buildings that characterize Washington, DC, at the same time they draw on and incorporate Masonic symbolism.[67] The façade of the House of the Temple, for instance, is ringed by thirty-three Ionic columns each thirty-three feet high; the steps that lead to its entrance rise in groups of three, five, seven, and nine, numbers that refer to Euclidean geometry. They are flanked by two seventeen-ton sphinxes representing wisdom and power. Similarly, the George Washington Masonic Memorial stands exactly 333 feet high, consisting of three successively smaller towers, each featuring a different order of Greek architecture, Doric at the bottom, Ionic in the middle, and Corinthian at the top. Its portico features six huge Doric columns. Neither of these buildings needs a sign to say "no girls allowed," at least in the stereotyped architectural idiom of early twentieth-century Washington. Their "flat planes, straight lines, and sheer drop of precipitous walls" declare the buildings a ritual space for men only.[68]

I am less interested here in the showy faces that these buildings turn to the profane world, however, than in their equally showy interiors designed for the use of the brothers.[69] How do they create meanings for the Masons who inhabit them? Inside, the rectilinear masculinity that Carnes attributes to Masonic buildings gives way to more ambiguous ornamentation. A large part of what Masons do in these spaces involves initiation rituals. In these rituals, as in its buildings, Freemasonry copied indiscriminately from a wide variety of pasts, evincing a nostalgic desire to become part of many different, romanticized, pasts, all "cognitively fungible."[70] In the Scottish Rite alone, various degrees need to represent the disparate times and places of "a cavern, a secret vault beneath Solomon's temple, a bridge, the throne room of a Persian king, the road to Jerusalem, the summit of a mountain, a military encampment in the desert, and the court of Saladin."[71] What binds together all these times and places to create this "mythic nontemporal realm" is the exegetical interpretation of historical events and symbols.

In fact, the Masonic view of history will sound familiar to any medievalist who has read Dante or D.W. Robertson or studied biblical exegesis.[72] For

Thomas Aquinas and his twelfth-century predecessors Hugh of St. Victor and Bernardus Silvestris, the meanings of biblical words, phrases, objects, symbols, and narratives are organized systematically and hierarchically on four levels: (1) the historical or literal; (2) the allegorical, which refers to the spiritual meaning in which the Old Law (Old Testament) prefigures the New (New Testament); (3) the tropological, which provides an edifying moral message; and (4) the anagogical, which refers to eschatology, or the end of time. This system of interpretation was introduced in the Latin West by Augustine, reaching the height of its popularity in the twelfth century. Dante's *Il Convivio* extended the method to vernacular literature.

Masons use this method to discover in the events, symbols, narratives, and objects of their rituals many meanings in a single imaginative act. Take, for instance, the lodge or temple in which Masonic rituals are enacted: "The lodge room acted as a multivalent sign for a complex constellation of interrelated abstractions cognitively linked to the temple by the fraternity."[73] Both the House of the Temple and the George Washington Masonic Memorial feature lodges. The rooms in which each initiates their members are significant on a literal level; they have their own histories. Colonial Lodge no. 1821 "works" or "labors" (conducts initiations) in the House of the Temple.[74] The George Washington Masonic Memorial is home to Alexandria-Washington Lodge no. 22. Colonial Lodge holds its meetings in the Temple Room. Only Dan Brown can do justice to this grandiose inner sanctum where Scottish Rite rituals are enacted:

> The room was a perfect square. And cavernous. The ceiling soared an astonishing one hundred feet overhead, supported by monolithic columns of green granite. A tiered gallery of dark Russian walnut seats with hand-tooled pigskin encircled the room. A thirty-three-foot-tall throne dominated the western wall, with a concealed pipe organ opposite it. The walls were a kaleidoscope of ancient symbols ... Egyptian, Hebraic, astronomical, alchemical, and others yet unknown.[75]

Alexandria-Washington no. 22 meets once a year in a replica of George Washington's eighteenth-century lodge room that is also a museum display, housing the Washington "relics" owned by the lodge.

On the allegorical level, when a lodge is "working," the lodge room, whether humble or grand, "figures" the Temple of Solomon, built by the master mason Hiram Abiff: "Upon his first ceremonial entry into this sacred space, every initiate was informed ritually that 'this and every other lodge is, or ought to be, a true representation of King Solomon's temple.'"[76] On the tropological or spiritual level, the temple, in the spirit of Paul's letter to the Corinthians – "Know ye not that ye are the temple of God, and that the Spirit of God dwelleth in you" (1 Corinthians 3:16) – finds its fulfilment in the hearts and minds of individual Freemasons. As Christopher Hodapp explains, "The Lodge, furniture, ornaments and officers are meant to inspire reflection and perfection within the make-up of man."[77] The inscription over the door to the House of the Temple reads, "Freemasonry builds its temples in the hearts of men and among nations." Finally, on the anagogical level, the lodge is all of creation: "The apartment in which Masons assemble is symbolical of the universe, illimitable on every side, the proper temple of Deity, whose center is every-where, whose circumference is nowhere."[78] The light symbolism, which runs through the Temple Room in the House of the Temple, links these last two levels. An oculus one hundred feet high shines down on a marble altar inlaid with Hebrew characters that read, "God said, 'Let there be light' and there was light," a reference to both the enlightenment of learning (the tropological) and the all-seeing architect of the universe (anagogical).

Masonic exegesis is not and has never been a simple substitution code. Like all medieval allegory, the promise of stable signification – meaning and knowledge – held out by the exegetical method is offset by the fact that Masonic texts and symbols are multiple, complex, and elusively polysemous. Its initiation rituals are dramas, acted out with costumes, props (ritual objects), and often elaborate sets, all redolent with symbolism and allegories that have to be explained, often at great length. Encoded in these rituals are borrowings from a number of esoteric traditions – including Hermeticism, Gnosticism, Neoplatonism, alchemy, astrology, Christian theosophy, Kabbalah, and gematria (Hebrew numerology) – not all of them compatible. "Masonry is the veritable Sphinx, buried to the head in the sands heaped round it by the ages," writes Pike in *Morals and Dogma*.[79] The only thing these systems have in common is that, like medieval allegories, they were invented to conceal knowledge considered too dangerous for the "ignorant" or "profane" to possess. Esotericism uses allegory to conceal knowledge, making it intelligible only to adepts, to those "with eyes to see and ears to hear." Esoteric knowledge becomes available to the Scottish Rite Mason only as he moves through the various degrees towards becoming an adept:

> The whole body of the Royal and Sacerdotal Art was hidden so carefully, centuries since, in the High Degrees, as that it is even yet impossible to solve many of the enigmas which they contain. It is well enough for the mass of those called Masons, to imagine that all is contained in the Blue Degrees; and whoso attempts to undeceive them will labor in vain, and without any true reward violate his obligations as an Adept.[80]

The rituals open up a gap between esoteric and exoteric knowledge, between the sign and what it might signify, and into that gap pours more narrative, more symbols, more allegory, more ritual, and more degrees. Both the House of the

Temple and the George Washington Masonic Memorial curate the mass of material culture created by this surplus of signifiers – the aprons, collars, sashes, jewels, swords, trowels, compasses, and hammers, all of which take on meanings that exceed their functions.

My description of Masonic exegesis makes fraternal initiation sound rather dull as a leisure activity. In a world that offers superhero movies, binge television, and video games, contemporary readers are likely to be put off by what one writer describes as Masonry's "mind-numbing verbosity," "the recitation of seemingly endless prayers and dense explications of arcane symbols."[81] Yet these rituals obviously appealed to the men who flocked to fraternities during their heyday. What it meant to them is less obvious now. Undoubtedly some men joined for friendships, some for conviviality, some for social status, some for the promise of esoteric knowledge. But what kept men spending money and time on initiation after initiation, what kept them coming back for yet another degree, probably had less to do with the lure of knowledge than with the uncanny pleasures of dangerous knowledge, of secret knowledge.[82] Knowing and sharing a secret, knowing others do not know it, and the moment of discovering a secret are all pleasurable.[83] These pleasures were wedded to lessons in the governance of the self and other, in philanthropy and civic republicanism, tied to the goal of "making good men better," that is, of creating forms of masculinity suited to modern capitalism. The myth of the Masons as the heirs to a long-buried, ancient knowledge provided the fraternity both a focal point for creating an imagined community and a rationale for self-government and the governing of others.

If today fraternal organizations like the Masons seem fusty, irrelevant, or even silly – "a bunch of overgrown schoolboys rolling up their trouser-legs and engaging in verbal mumbo-jumbo" is one historian's description[84] – I hope I have shown that there are important political principles at stake in the historic connection Freemasonry has enjoyed with our nation's capital. While all but a handful of the 500 or so new fraternities formed at the turn of the century have faded into obscurity and membership in Freemasonry has shrunk from a high of four million men in 1959 to one million in 2017, its lowest point since 1924,[85] we need to remember that fraternity's lessons have been internalized as a governmentality in the places where powerful men can meet away from the scrutiny of the public: in the more than 5,000 college fraternity chapters that infest our colleges and universities, in all-male board rooms, in legislatures, Bohemian Grove retreats where rich and powerful men go to camp out, in the American Legislative Exchange Council (ALEC) where corporate lobbyists secretly meet with lawmakers to draft model bills that those lawmakers can introduce into their legislatures, in the armed forces, on sports teams, in increasingly vocal neo-Nazi groups. By the end of Dan Brown's *The Lost Symbol*, the book's McGuffin, the Masonic pyramid said to possess lost ancient knowledges, reveals no more powerful secret than that, in the heart of our nation's capital in Washington, DC, there is a secret organization where US presidents, senators and representatives, Supreme Court justices, and cabinet members mingle with the wealthy and influential.

NOTES

1 Steven McLeod Bedford, *John Russell Pope: Architect of Empire* (New York: Rizzoli, 1998), 118.
2 Frederick Douglass, *A Lecture on Our National Capital* (Washington, DC: Smithsonian Institution Press, 1978), 18.
3 If Washington, DC, embodies the loftiest American ideals, it also betrays them; Douglass notes that the site of the capital was "sandwiched between two of the oldest slave states, each of which was a nursery and a hot-bed of slavery … It was southern in all its sympathies and national only in name … Slavery was its idol, and, like all idol worshippers, its people howled with rage when this ugly idol was called in question" (*Lecture on Our National Capital*, 21–2). See also Jesse Holland, *Black Men Built the Capitol: Discovering African-American History in and around Washington* (Guilford, CT: Globe Pecquot, 2007).
4 Douglass, *Lecture on Our National Capital*, 19. Douglass's use of the generic masculine in his address, though commonplace for the period, should not go unremarked. In 1865 these ideals of freedom, equal citizenship, and common feeling were reserved specifically for white men and were denied to all women.
5 Douglass, *Lecture on Our National Capital*, 18–19.
6 See David Ovason, *The Secret Architecture of Our Nation's Capital: The Masons and the Building of Washington* (New York: Harper Collins, 2012), and Dan Brown, *The Lost Symbol* (New York: Doubleday, 2009). An internet search yields instructions for a Masonic Pentagram Walk of Washington.
7 Dana Nelson, *National Manhood: Capitalist Citizenship and the Imagined Fraternity of White Men* (Durham, NC: Duke University Press, 1998), ix. National manhood is "an ideology that has worked powerfully since the Constitutional era to link a fraternal articulation of white manhood to civic identity" (ix).
8 A painting displayed in the House of the Temple illustrates the event. His regalia included the symbolic apron of the medieval stonemason. See Mark Tabbert, *American Freemasons: Three Centuries of Building Communities* (New York: New York University Press, 2006), 45.
9 *Pierre de Ravel d'Esclapon*, "The Masonic Career of Major Pierre Charles L'Enfant," 1 Mar. 2011, https://scottishrite.org/blog/about/media-publications/journal/article/the-masonic-career-of-major-pierre-charles-lenfant/.
10 Tabbert, *American Freemasons*, 45.

11 Graham Burchell, Colin Gordon, and Peter Miller, eds., *The Foucault Effect: Studies in Governmentality* (Chicago: University of Chicago Press, 1991), 87.
12 Burchell, Gordon, and Miller, *Foucault Effect*, 87–8.
13 William Walters, *Governmentality: Critical Encounters* (Abingdon, UK: Routledge, 2012), 12.
14 Gerard Lico, "Architecture and Sexuality: The Politics of Gendered Space," *Humanities Diliman* 2, no. 1 (2001): 30–44, at 31.
15 Kathleen James-Chakraborty, *Architecture since 1400* (Minneapolis: University of Minnesota Press, 2014), 244.
16 Bedford, *John Russell Pope*, 118.
17 Raluca Niculae, "Gender Analogies in Architecture," *Journal of Research in Gender Studies* 4, no. 1 (2014): 474–90, at 474.
18 Susan Stewart, *On Longing: Narratives of the Miniature, the Gigantic, the Souvenir, the Collection* (Baltimore, MD: Johns Hopkins University Press, 1984), xii.
19 Mark Carnes, "Scottish Rite and the Visual Politics of Gender," in *Theatre of the Fraternity: Staging the Ritual Space of the Scottish Rite of Freemasonry, 1896–1929*, ed. Lance Brockman (Minneapolis: Frederick R. Weisman Art Museum, 1996), 72–91, at 80, 83.
20 Niculae, "Gender Analogies in Architecture," 482.
21 Carole Pateman, *The Disorder of Women: Democracy, Feminism, and Political Theory* (Stanford, CA: Stanford University Press, 1989); see esp. "The Fraternal Social Contract," 33–53.
22 Norman Brown, *Love's Body* (Berkeley: University of California Press, 1990), 4; emphasis added.
23 Douglass, *Lecture on Our National Capital*, 19.
24 Mary Ann Clawson, *Constructing Brotherhood: Class, Gender, and Fraternalism* (Princeton, NJ: Princeton University Press, 1989), 6.
25 Walters, *Governmentality*, 13. In the words of the Masons, "making good men better" and so making the world better one man at a time (Tabbert, *American Freemasons*, 9), and as Lilith Mahmud describes it, "the very possibility of transforming society by transforming individuals" (*The Brotherhood of Freemason Sisters: Gender, Secrecy, and Fraternity in Italian Masonic Lodges* [Chicago: University of Chicago Press, 2014], 57).
26 James Anderson, *The Constitutions of the Free-Masons: Containing the History, Charges, Regulations, Etc. of That Most Ancient and Right Worshipful Fraternity* (London: Masonic Pub. and Manufacturing, 1866), 54.
27 Margaret Jacob, *Living the Enlightenment: Freemasonry and Politics in Eighteenth-Century Europe* (New York: Oxford University Press, 1991), 22.
28 Anderson, *Constitutions of the Free-Masons*, 51.
29 These exclusions have always been more complex in practice than the interdictions suggest. Several scholars document the gap between Masonic exclusions and "the

social conditions of possibility necessary for an initiation to take place" (Mahmud, *Brotherhood of Freemason Sisters*, 57). Joy Porter has documented the fraternalism of Native American men in *Native American Freemasonry: Associationalism and Performance in America* (Lincoln: University of Nebraska Press, 2011). Prince Hall Masonry has offered Black men access to Freemasonry since 1776; on "Masonic anciency," see Joanna Brooks, *American Lazarus: Religion and the Rise of African-American and Native American Literatures* (Oxford: Oxford University Press, 2003), 125.

30 On eighteenth-century attitudes towards the Middle Ages, see Johannes Fried, *The Middle Ages*, trans. Peter Lewis (Cambridge, MA: Belknap Press, 2015), 505–7. He writes, "No other advanced civilization on Earth has ever dismissed and denigrated a period of its own past so comprehensively, or even wished to airbrush it out of existence entirely through neglect, in the way Europeans have done with the medieval era" (507).

31 Robert Beachy, "Masonic Apologetic Writings," in *Gender and Fraternal Orders in Europe*, ed. Máire Fedelma Cross (Houndmills, UK: Palgrave Macmillan, 2010), 91–101, at 99.

32 Jürgen Habermas, *The Structural Transformation of the Public Sphere*, trans. Thomas Burger (Cambridge, MA: MIT Press, 1989), 35.

33 "Freemasons for Dummies" blog, http://freemasonsfordummies.blogspot.com (accessed 19 Dec. 2018). This introductory paragraph appears on the websites of many masonic lodges.

34 Michael Kimmel, *Manhood in America: A Cultural History*, 2nd ed. (New York: Oxford University Press, 2006), 16. See also William Moore, *Masonic Temples: Freemasonry, Ritual Architecture, and Masculine Archetypes* (Knoxville: University of Tennessee Press, 2006), 5.

35 Andrew Prescott, "Men and Women in the Guild Returns," in Cross, *Gender and Fraternal Orders*, 30–51, at 30.

36 Margaret Jacob, *The Origins of Freemasonry: Facts and Fictions* (Philadelphia: University of Pennsylvania Press, 2006), 6.

37 Andrew Prescott and S.M. Sommers dispute this date, putting the date of foundation in 1721; see "Searching for the Apple Tree: Revisiting the Earliest Years of Organized English Freemasonry," in *Reflections on Three Hundred Years of Freemasonry: Papers from the QC Tercentenary Conference*, ed. John Wade (London: Lewis Masonic, 2016).

38 Anderson, *Constitutions of the Free-Masons*, 7–31.

39 Andrew Michael Ramsey, "Discourse Pronounced at the Reception of Freemasons," in *Encyclopedia of Freemasonry*, ed. Albert Gallatin Mackey and Harry LeRoy Haywood, vol. 2 (Whitefish, MT: Kessinger, 2003), 831.

40 Ramsey, "Discourse Pronounced at the Reception of Freemasons," 831.

41 Charles Thompson McClenachan, *The Book of the Ancient and Accepted Scottish Rite of Freemasonry* (London: Masonic Pub. and Manufacturing, 1868), 11–13.

Appendant degrees may only be pursued by Masons who have achieved the final Blue Lodge degree of Master Mason.

42 A rite is a series of degrees conferred by Masonic organizations that maintain their own national organizations apart from the grand lodges. They were a mechanism for bringing order to the proliferation of irregular and side degrees that began accumulating around Freemasonry.

43 Moore, *Masonic Temples*, 42.

44 Freemasons United States Scottish Rite Supreme Council for the Southern Jurisdiction, and Albert Pike, *Liturgy of the Ancient and Accepted Scottish Rite of Freemasonry: For the Southern Jurisdiction of the United States*, vol. 4 (L.H. Jenkins, 1878), 205.

45 Pike, *Liturgy*, 205. Pike, supreme commander of the Southern Jurisdiction from 1859 until his death in 1892, wrote the rituals for the Southern Jurisdiction of the Scottish Rite. Pike was the only Confederate officer to have an outdoors statue in Washington; it was donated by the Freemasons. The monument was removed by protesters in 2020. His masonic career is celebrated in the House of the Temple, where he is buried. Some Freemasons believe that Pike shared his Scottish Rite rituals with the Prince Hall Freemasons, which also offers initiation into its own versions of these degrees, versions that use much the same chivalric language.

46 Since 1717 over 1,000 "Masonic" degrees have been created.

47 Albert Pike, *Morals and Dogma of the Ancient and Accepted Scottish Rite of Freemasonry* (Whitefish, MT: Kessinger, 2011), 583–4. Until 1974, Pike's book was given to every Mason completing the 14th degree in the Southern Jurisdiction of the Scottish Rite.

48 W.S. Harwood, "Secret Societies in America," *North American Review* 164, no. 486 (1897): 617–24, at 617.

49 B.H. Meyer, "Fraternal Beneficiary Societies in the United States," *American Journal of Sociology* 6, no. 5 (1901): 646–61, at 655–6.

50 Noel P. Gist, "Culture Patterning in Secret Society Ceremonials," in *Secret Societies in America: Foundational Studies of Fraternalism*, ed. William Moore and Mark Tabbert (New Orleans: Cornerstone, 2011), 172–85, at 173.

51 Kenneth Ames, "The Lure of the Spectacular," in Brockman, *Theatre of the Fraternity*, 18–29, at 21.

52 Clawson, *Constructing Brotherhood*, 115.

53 William Moore opens his book on Masonic temples by quoting the editor of a New York Masonic magazine in 1927: "It is undoubtedly a marked feature of present-day American Masonry to erect huge and elaborate buildings ... and to spend on them enormous sums of money" (*Masonic Temples*, xiii).

54 Moore, *Masonic Temples*, xiii.

55 H.L. Haywood, quoted in Moore, *Masonic Temples*, 140.

56 Bedford, *John Russell Pope*, 127. That a building employed an architect and a recognizable architectural style already suggests the status of the commissioning body.

57 Moore, *Masonic Temples*, 120.
58 Moore, *Masonic Temples*, 120.
59 Quoted in Moore, *Masonic Temples*, 120.
60 William Adrian Brown, *History of the George Washington Masonic National Memorial: 1922–1974, Half Century of Construction* (History House, 1980), 70.
61 Scottish Rite of Freemasonry, S.J., U.S.A., "History of the Temple," https://scottish-rite.org/our-museum/history-of-the-temple (accessed 17 Dec. 2018).
62 "Within the United States, two autonomous, geographically defined bodies governed Scottish Rite Masonry. The Southern Jurisdiction, the original body, is composed of the southern states east of the Mississippi river plus all the states to the west; the Northern Jurisdiction, established in 1813, includes the area north of the Mason-Dixon Line and east of the Mississippi" (Mary Ann Clawson, "Spectatorship and Masculinity," in Brockman, *Theatre of the Fraternity*, 52–71, at 54).
63 Bedford, *John Russell Pope*, 118.
64 Michael Curtis, *Classical Architecture and Monuments of Washington, D.C.: A History and Guide* (Charleston, SC: History Press, 2018), 208.
65 The design of the building with its 7.5-degree incline was a challenge for the Otis Elevator Company, which had to place the car vertically on a set of wheels that would ride on a rail (Brown, *History of the George Washington Masonic National Memorial*, 70).
66 "George Washington Masonic National Memorial," Historic American Buildings Survey, 2010, 2, Library of Congress, https://cdn.loc.gov/master/pnp/habshaer/va/va2000/va2095/data/va2095data.pdf (accessed 19 Dec. 2018).
67 In *De architectura*, Vitruvius writes, "Without symmetry and proportion there can be no principles in any design of the temple; that is if there is no precise relation between its members, as in the case of a well-shaped man" (Niculae, "Gender Analogies in Architecture," 475).
68 Carnes, "Scottish Rite," 81.
69 *Profane* is the term that Masons use to describe the non-Masonic world.
70 Moore, *Masonic Temples*, 20.
71 Moore, *Masonic Temples*, 73.
72 Or to those familiar with Jewish hermeneutic tradition (Pardes) that Masonry also appropriates. Masonic rituals also borrow heavily from Jewish history and philosophies and from the Hebrew language.
73 Moore, *Masonic Temples*, 17. Medieval stonemasons' lodges were more like construction site offices today than massive temples.
74 This lodge is unique among US lodges in that it is limited to faculty, students, parents, and alumni of George Washington University. Master Masons of this lodge wear full academic regalia in addition to their Masonic regalia, representing yet another node in the network of connections that link the fraternity with governmentality.
75 Brown, *Lost Symbol*, 3.

76 Moore, *Masonic Temples*, 16; citing *Duncan's Masonic Ritual and Monitor*.
77 Christopher Hodapp, *Freemasons for Dummies* (Hoboken, NJ: Wiley, 2005), 138.
78 Moore, *Masonic Temples*, 17.
79 Pike, *Morals and Dogma*, 584.
80 Pike, *Morals and Dogma*, 584.
81 Carnes, "Scottish Rite," 74.
82 Mark Tabbert estimates that some men spent as much as 50 per cent of their income on their fraternal activities (*American Freemasons*, 50).
83 Michel de Certeau, *The Mystic Fable*, trans. Michael B. Smith, vol. 1 (Chicago: University of Chicago Press, 1992), 97.
84 Rébert Péter, "'The Fair Sex' in a 'Male Sect': Gendering the Role of Women in Eighteenth-Century English Freemasonry," in Cross, *Gender and Fraternal Orders*, 133–55, at 134.
85 Masonic Information Center, "It's About Time: Moving Masonry into the 21st Century" (pamphlet), 2004, p. 3. https://www.yumpu.com/en/document/view/27678628/its-about-time-masonic-service-association-of-north-america (accessed 28 Feb. 2021). In the forums at www.myfreemasonry.com, Simon Christianson produced graphs based on statistics that used to be provided by the Masonic Service Association of North America indicating that these numbers have continued to fall, bottoming out in 2017 at around one million; My Freemasonry, https://www.myfreemasonry.com/threads/membership-statistics-and-trend.29846 (accessed 28 Feb. 2021).

4 Medieval Chicago: Architecture, Patronage, and Capital at the Fin de Siècle

ALFRED THOMAS

When we think of Chicago architecture, functional modernism rather than decorative medievalism, Mies van der Rohe and Bauhaus rather than the builders of the great Gothic cathedrals of France and England, probably come to mind. And yet Chicago boasts many important and imposing buildings in the neo-Gothic style, like the famous Tribune Building (1925) (see figure 4.1).[1] As Katherine M. Solomonson points out, the fact that many of the designs submitted for the Tribune competition were Gothic and that a Gothic design, complete with flying buttresses on its crown, won in 1922 has a great deal to do with the close identification of the building's sponsors with the fate of French (and western European) civilization during the First World War. The runner-up in the competition was a more avant-garde design by the Finnish architect Eliel Saarinen, evidence that Chicago's elites preferred the more traditional idiom of the neo-Gothic. But the key point was that an American design won, thus demonstrating that the United States had surpassed its great European rivals, France and Germany (which did not even get a mention). In erecting a building closely modelled on Chartres, Antwerp, and Rouen cathedrals, the Americans were in a sense transferring the greatness of European culture to American shores, thereby both showing their solidarity with their European allies and demonstrating their superiority to a ruined European civilization.[2]

Conversely, when we think of medieval cities, we are hardly inclined to picture American skyscrapers. And yet high-rise buildings were a major feature of the cityscapes of medieval Florence and Siena. The well-preserved Tuscan hilltop town of San Gimignano – with its bristling array of fortified towers – affords us a tantalizing glimpse of what Florence must have looked like before Christian morality served as a brake on the erection of excessively high buildings. The height of buildings in late medieval Florence and Siena was carefully restricted to avoid the sin of pride (*superbia*), the biblical example of the Tower of Babel serving as a warning against the dangers inherent in hubris. San Gimignano thus survives as a snapshot of medieval Florence before it

4.1. The Tribune Building, Chicago. (All photographs in this chapter are the author's.)

was remodelled on Renaissance lines – something akin to the crowded modern American skyline. Indeed, San Gimignano is often popularly referred to as the "Medieval Manhattan" (see figures 4.2 and 4.3).

This chapter proposes that the medieval idiom of Chicago's modernist skyline should not be seen simply as a rejection of capitalism but as an attempt to reconcile prevailing notions of medieval artisanry with American capitalism. In the words of Alan Trachtenberg, "The message was plain in the imperial facades that dressed the new railroad stations, courthouses, department stores, office buildings and mansions of the rich ... which in their eclectic composition of classical, Gothic, and Renaissance styles, suggested a new cultural imperialism, a confidence of appropriation."[3] Moreover – and perhaps more controversially – I will argue that the medieval world fetishized by the antimodernist bourgeois elites of late nineteenth- and early twentieth-century America was itself far from anticapitalist. The rise of a money economy in the twelfth century and the emergence of banking families as political power brokers like the Italian Medici and the German Fuggers of Augsburg made the later Middle Ages congenial to their American counterparts – not because its ideology was radically different from their own but, on the contrary, because the later Middle Ages in Italy and Germany provided a paradigm of what the commercial elites were seeking: not a repudiation or outright rejection of bourgeois capitalism but a reinforcement of it. Indeed, the French Annales school historian Fernand Braudel detects a close similarity between Italy's cultural and economic hegemony between 1450 and 1650 and the superpower status of the United States today.[4]

Medieval France and England versus Italy and Germany

The special prestige attached to medieval French cathedrals was exemplified by Henry Adams's influential study *Mont-Saint-Michel and Chartres*, first published in Boston in 1904, which went into several editions.[5] St. James Chapel (835 Rush Street) in Chicago embodies this particular reverence for French medieval architecture. Completed in 1919 soon after the end of the First World War, this beautiful vaulted chapel with stained-glass windows was modelled on the Sainte-Chapelle in Paris, built in 1248 by the Crusader King Louis IX to house his precious collection of Passion relics, including the Crown of Thorns that he had bought from the bankrupt Latin emperor of Constantinople in 1239 (see figure 4.4).[6] The Sainte-Chapelle served an ideological as well as religious purpose in making Paris (and by extension France) the heart of Western Christendom, with the religious prestige attached to the relics of the Passion being merely an extension of France's geopolitical aspiration to become the most powerful country in Europe. Having annexed most of the ancestral lands of the Angevin kings (Normandy, Anjou, and Aquitaine) following the disastrous

Medieval Chicago: Architecture, Patronage, and Capital at the Fin de Siècle 87

4.2. Panorama of downtown Chicago.

4.3. Panorama of San Gimignano, Italy.

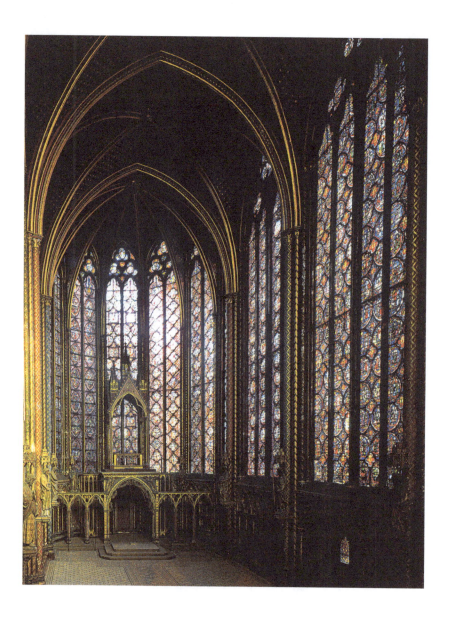

4.4. La Sainte-Chapelle, Paris.

rule of King John of England, Capetian France was now poised to dominate the Continent.[7] In the second half of the fourteenth century, France's European hegemony went into decline following Edward III's successful attempt to reclaim his ancestral lands. It is hardly coincidental, therefore, that the Holy Roman emperor and king of Bohemia, Charles IV (1316–1378), emulated the practice of King Louis by assembling Passion relics of his own (including a thorn from the Crown of Thorns presented to him by his cousin the king of France), which he deposited in his residence at Karlstein Castle near Prague. Emperor Charles was attempting to relocate Christianity's centre away from France to his own kingdom of Bohemia after France's military defeat in the Hundred Years' War. Piety and geopolitics went hand in hand in the late Middle Ages, but the same is also true of early twentieth-century America. In re-creating the Sainte-Chapelle in the St. James Chapel, the Roman Catholic archdiocese of Chicago was in a sense consistent with the secular architectural sponsors of the city in reinventing French medieval civilization in the Midwest. This was not simply an act of cultural veneration but also a supersessionist gesture intended to make Chicago the spiritual heir to Paris and America the geopolitical inheritor of a destroyed European civilization following the devastation of the Great War.

The popularity of the Gothic and Romanesque revivals in American cities like Chicago and New York owed an immense debt to the British art critic John Ruskin, whose writings promoted medieval art as a necessary and salubrious antidote to the anonymous impersonality of mass-produced modernity. Ruskin saw the Renaissance as the slippery slope that led to the drab uniformity of modern art and architecture. Closely associated with the Pre-Raphaelite School of English painters, he regarded the Middle Ages as superior to the Renaissance and shared the Pre-Raphaelites' idealization of the medieval period as one of steadfast faith, simplicity of thought, and individual craftsmanship. A close friend of Ruskin was the American academic Charles Eliot Norton, the first professor of fine arts at Harvard University and author of *Historical Church Building in the Middle Ages* (1880). Norton was the chief American precursor of the American Arts and Crafts movement.[8] For Norton – as for Ruskin – the Gothic represented nostalgia for an idealized pre-capitalist world in which art was deemed superior to mass mechanization. Ruskin's British disciple William Morris even embraced what he saw as the proto-socialist principles of medieval artisanship and, in later life, became actively involved in radical politics and economic reform.[9]

The same nostalgia for a pre-capitalist utopian world would appear to have inspired the earliest builders of America's skyscrapers. Yet, as Johanna Merwood-Salisbury explores, the Gothic style and its successor, the Romanesque Revival, were intended not to critique capitalism but to celebrate it, not to disparage the present but to justify it by linking it to the heritage of the medieval past.[10] The medieval idiom of the earliest skyscrapers may have paid homage to the great cathedrals of France, but these twentieth-century Americans also attempted to synthesize the European Middle Ages with the optimism and energy of the modern industrial United States. According to the historian T.J. Jackson Lears, the "antimodernism" of American culture between the years 1880 and 1920 has to be understood as more complex than idealistic nostalgia for a bygone medieval past; such antimodernism "was not simply escapism; it was ambivalent, often coexisting with enthusiasm for material progress."[11] A similar ambivalence characterizes Mark Twain's view of the Middle Ages in his novel *A Connecticut Yankee in King Arthur's Court* (1889). The depiction of the American Hank Morgan, who goes back in time to fifth-century Britain and takes over Camelot to become its capitalist "Boss," oscillates between a valorization of capitalist technology and a bleak evocation of its destructive imperialist consequences. The novel starts out as a satirical critique of sentimental medievalism, only to end up becoming nostalgic for its simplicity and purity in the face of destructive modernity – in the words of the Arthurian scholar Andrew Lynch, "a world of machine-guns, dynamite and electrified fences."[12]

As we shall see, ambivalence was the key not only to the capitalist view of the Middle Ages but also to the Decadent movement that was so closely allied with the Arts and Crafts movement. The American exponents of the Arts and Crafts ideology were, in the words of Lears, "neither as articulate nor as clearheaded as Ruskin and Morris," and as the movement spread, it turned from a "critique of modern culture to a new kind of accommodation."[13] Yet there are also real similarities between England and America insofar as the industrial magnates of northern England, the home of the first Industrial Revolution, collected the work of the Pre-Raphaelite painters, which later ended up in the important municipal collections of Manchester and Liverpool. Like their American counterparts, the industrialists of northern England found no contradiction between their commitment to capitalism and their love of medieval art.

The model of Medici Florence (from 1434 onwards) and the Venetian Republic was perhaps especially appealing to the American industrialists who sponsored art and architecture in turn-of-the-century Chicago because it served as a flattering reflection of their own enlightened self-image as philanthropists and patrons of the arts and education. Whether or not fifteenth-century Florence was truly a republic or a de facto *signoria* ("lordship") ruled by the Medici family along the lines of princely states like Milan and Ferrara is still a question hotly debated in Medici scholarship.[14] The British historian Chris Wickham points out that the Italian city states between 1350 and 1500 witnessed a movement away from "republican" rule and a steady transition to larger political units: "The period began to make way for the longer-term rule of single rulers, who tended to gain power as head of a faction and then grab it permanently for themselves and for their heirs."[15] As Wickham states, this development eroded the republican-feudal distinction between old aristocratic families like the

Visconti in Milan (1277 to 1447) and the Este in Ferrara (from 1240 onwards), on the one hand, and the mercantile elites like the Medici in Florence (from 1434) and the Della Scala in Verona (1263 to 1444), on the other. Venice, Genoa, Siena, and Lucca resisted this trend, but, Wickham argues, they did so by "establishing tight and closed oligarchies of leading families that were, in many ways, less open than the still fairly meritocratic governing systems of the *signorie*."[16] Florence and Milan were thus more alike than different by this period, and in both cases, provided an ideological model for late nineteenth-century American industrialists to emulate – an ideology that successfully synthesized democratic-republican ideals with an oligarchic-mercantile reality.

For the purposes of this chapter, the crucial point is that medieval Florence *presented* itself as a republic modelled along classical Roman lines even as it succumbed to Medici control. The discrepancy between image and reality in fifteenth-century Florence is one that we might equally extend to a consideration of late nineteenth-century Chicago and, more generally, to the United States as a whole around the year 1900, as the gulf between the democratic ideals of the Republic and a new corporate reality emerged. Had the corporatization of America reached such an extent by the fin de siècle that we are entitled to speak less of a democracy and more of a ruling business class or corporate oligarchy?[17] As we shall explore, the turn to medieval Italian and German architectural idioms was central to the American elite's attempt not only to reconcile the medieval past with the capitalist present but to reinvent itself as latter-day mercantile oligarchy along the lines of fifteenth-century Florence and Venice.

Inevitably, given the prominence and prestige attached to the Chicago Tribune Building, we tend to think of "medieval" Chicago in terms of the French Gothic cathedral style. But prior to the outbreak of the Great War in 1914 and America's later entry into it in 1917 – when all things German began to fall into disfavour – several key examples of Chicago architecture were modelled on the republican city states of medieval and Renaissance Italy (exemplified by Venice, Florence, and Siena) and the autonomous imperial cities of Germany and the Holy Roman Empire like Strassburg, where Gutenberg established his printing press, and Augsburg, the home of the Fugger banking family. This emulation of the architectural idiom of the German and Italian city states should be understood in terms both of the republican ideals of the American elites and of immigration to the United States from late nineteenth-century Germany and central Europe. The "Second Gutenberg" and the inventor of Linotype, Ottmar Mergenthaler (1855–1899) immigrated to America as a young man and made a fortune in the American printing business. As we shall see, he even bought property in Chicago's burgeoning printers' neighbourhood now known as Printers Row.

None of this is to deny that Ruskin's idealization of the Middle Ages was immensely influential in late nineteenth-century America: his love of the Venetian

Gothic, as laid out in his *Stones of Venice* (1853), is clearly echoed in impressive buildings like the Isabella Stewart Gardner Museum in Boston, designed by Willard T. Sears (begun in 1899 and completed in 1901). Isabella Stewart Gardner was the daughter of a wealthy linen merchant who became an important collector of medieval and Renaissance artworks. Even earlier than this famous museum was the Chicago Men's Athletic Association Building (now Hotel), 12 Michigan Avenue, designed by Henry Ives Cobb in 1893, whose façade closely resembles a Venetian palazzo (see figure 4.5). Far from disparaging the capitalist system, such buildings were intended to celebrate the power, prestige, and vitality of the new industrial elites. The Chicago Men's Athletic Association was not only intended as a recreational space for these (male) urban elites but was also a visual sign of their ideological identification with the European past. The economic elites had no problem reconciling this glorification of the European Middle Ages with their celebration of America's capitalist vitality. Yet this sense of vitalism, rooted in athleticism and bodily exercise, was equally a reaction to a crisis of the ruling classes in the 1890s. The very fact that this was a recreational space intended specifically for the *Athletic* Association of Chicago is highly revealing: cultural pride in these young men's European ancestry went hand in hand with their rejection of the neurasthenia, effeteness, and decadence that appeared to plague late nineteenth-century England and America. As Lears points out, the establishment of the Chicago Arts and Crafts Society four years later in 1897 has to be seen as a similar reaction to the sense of spiritual and cultural malaise afflicting Western industrialized society at the fin de siècle.[18]

American Ambivalence to the Decadent Movement

Indeed, there may even have been an unconscious turning away from English and French influences given the association of these cultures with the Decadent movement in the 1880s and 1890s. Joris-Karl Huysman's cultivation of the inner life at the expense of external action in his novel *À rebours* (*Against Nature*, 1874), which became known as the breviary of the art-for-art's-sake movement, and Oscar Wilde's emphasis on aesthetic sensibility in his novel *The Picture of Dorian Gray* (1891) created a sense of unease among the ruling male elites both in the United States and Britain. Wilde had given a successful lecture tour of the United States in 1882, which included two lectures in Chicago on 12 February and 11 March. These took place in the Central Music-Hall Building on the southeast corner of State and Randolph. The Central Music-Hall, which was demolished in 1900 to make way for the present Marshall Field's Department Store (now Macy's), combined a public lecture hall with a series of stores, revealing that commerce lay at the heart of the city's civic identity. Wilde met the future department store owner Marshall Field at a reception given in his honour, further evidence that the nascent Arts and Crafts movement about

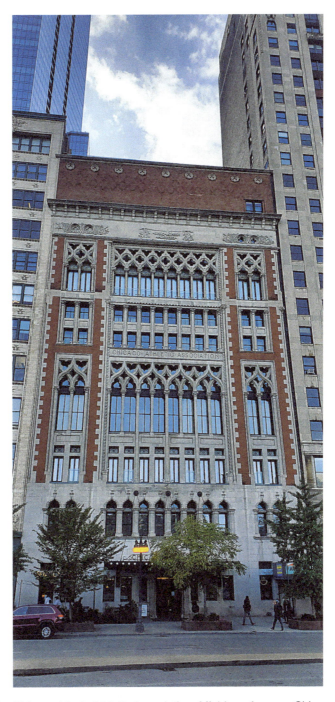

4.5. The Chicago Men's Athletic Association, Michigan Avenue, Chicago.

which Wilde lectured was far from detached from the economic interests of the city's business elites.

But notwithstanding America's enthusiastic reception of Wilde and the spawning of a countercultural aesthetic movement that challenged Victorian social and sexual norms,[19] there was a growing sense of discomfort with his Decadent aesthetic throughout the second half of the decade. At the heart of this unease lay Wilde's cultivation of what Jonathan Dollimore has termed his "transgressive aesthetic" – that is to say, the notion of art as superior to life and therefore independent of its traditional grounding in moral truth.[20] The subordination of art to morality that formed the basis of Victorian respectability appeared to come under attack in Wilde's scandalous novel *The Picture of Dorian Gray*, published simultaneously in 1890 in Britain and in America by the J.B. Lippincott Company of Philadelphia in the July issue of *Lippincott's Monthly Magazine*. As Nicholas Frankel points out, the American editor J.B. Stoddart, who was responsible for editing Wilde's typescript manuscript, "oversaw the elimination of anything that smacked generally of decadence."[21] This drastic mode of editing without consulting the author was, Frankel notes, more characteristic of American than British publishers in this period. But *what* was omitted was also indicative of American responses to the Decadent movement. This included cutting many of the novel's homoerotic allusions and the many instances of paranoia and mistrust that pervade it, including the threat of blackmail. We might say that the novel was carefully trimmed by its American editor to foreground its moralizing message (that sin leads to perdition) at the expense of its atmosphere of aristocratic indolence and sexual deviance – in short, to accommodate it to the work-oriented and moralistic values of its bourgeois American readership. Ironically, the magazine version was more explicitly homoerotic in content than the subsequent 1891 book version from which Wilde, at the publisher's behest, removed more words and passages.

Even before the publication of that most transgressive of novels – and the hostile reaction to it in the British press – the Cleveland Street Scandal of 1889 had implicated members of the British aristocracy in London's homosexual subculture. British aristocrats were often seen as guilty of corrupting the morals of younger, lower-class men and sapping the inherent virility and vitality of the *homo britannicus*. Indeed, the Cleveland Street Scandal reached the top of the British establishment when Lord Arthur Somerset, the Prince of Wales's equerry, was forced to flee to France for fear of prosecution. Even the Prince of Wales's older son, Albert Victor, came under suspicion after he was alleged to have visited the establishment on Cleveland Street.[22] This prince, known in the royal family as "Eddy," was often criticized by members of his family and class for his alleged indolence. Indeed, indolence and sexual aberrance seemed to be linked in the imagination of the British and American Protestant elites. Homosexual acts – "or indecent acts" as they were vaguely termed – had been made illegal by the Criminal Law Amendment Act of 1885; the consequence of that legislation was to create an atmosphere of disquiet, even paranoia, among Anglo-American elites.

This negative association of the British aristocracy with homosexual vice and indolence seems to have coloured American perceptions of British elite culture. The story of Lord Arthur Somerset fleeing England was pruriently reported in the American press, whereas in Britain all such scandals were carefully censored; coverage of the scandal extended to speculating about the involvement of Prince Albert Victor, as indicated by a *New York Times* article dated 10 November 1889 that included a portrait of the prince.[23] No doubt the infamous Oscar Wilde trials in England in 1895, which brought to the surface the implicitly homosexual dimension of Aestheticism, reinforced such American disquiet concerning the moral corruption of the British upper classes.

The medieval idiom of the Arts and Crafts movement was appropriated to the interests of capitalist ideology, but with the added intention of affirming the "masculine" self-reliance and diligence of the medieval artisan in contrast to the effeteness and indolence of the Decadents. There seems to have been an inherent tension between the "masculine" ethos of Arts and Crafts medievalism and the effeteness of the Decadent movement that was recognized by exponents of both creeds. It is significant that Lord Henry Wotton, the spokesman for the Decadent creed in Wilde's novel *The Picture of Dorian Gray*, states categorically, "I believe that the world would gain such a fresh impulse of joy that we would forget all the maladies of medievalism, and return to the Hellenic ideal, to something finer, richer, than the Hellenic ideal, it may be."[24] Through his fictional mouthpiece, Wilde here alludes not to the medieval period per se but to its rehabilitation in the nineteenth century and to its popularity, as we have already seen, in the neo-Gothic architecture of American (and British) cities. It is a swipe against Ruskin as well as an expression of homage to Wilde's Oxford mentor Walter Pater, author of a famous set of essays on the Renaissance, which was more of an appropriation of Renaissance art to the Hellenist principles expounded by the German art critic Winckelmann than an objective, scholarly study of Renaissance art itself. What united Wilde and Pater, and what characterized the Decadent movement, was its rejection of naturalism and its cultivation of artifice and the unnatural. All this would have made the Decadent movement even more suspect in the eyes of the American corporate elites for, as Walter Benn Michaels argues in his discussion of American fiction at the end of the century, there was an inherent complicity between naturalism and the corporation: "In naturalism no persons are natural. Personality is always corporate and all fictions, like souls metaphorized in bodies, are corporate fictions."[25] In its overt preference for artifice and its inherent disavowal of naturalism, Decadence was not only profoundly aristocratic; it was also anticorporation and anticapitalist. The vicious anti-Semitic depiction of the

Jewish manager of the theatre where Dorian Gray first becomes infatuated with the actress Sibyl Vane is further evidence that the Decadents were unashamedly aristocratic and anti-mercantile, even when – perhaps especially when – most of its adherents, like Wilde himself, were would-be aristocrats – "aristocrats of the soul" – rather than the real thing.

Printers Row and Dearborn Station

The turn to the medieval models provided by the city states of fifteenth-century Italy and the independent imperial cities of Germany was therefore more than coincidental. For in favouring the Italianate and German influences on display in the Dearborn Station and the printing buildings on South Dearborn Street, the cultural and economic elites of Chicago were demonstrating a closer affinity with the mercantile ethic of late medieval Italy and Germany than with the "effete" and "decadent" feudal aristocracies of England and France. Ruskin's writings were instrumental in placing an emphasis on the superiority of the Italian republican city states of Venice, Florence, and Siena. It is no coincidence that the Italian city states were thoroughly enmeshed in a proto-capitalist economy, one that was far in advance of medieval England and France. The competitive spirit, which we tend to associate with modern capitalism, already formed the basis of artistic patronage in medieval and Renaissance Italy, as illustrated by the famous competition for the decoration of the northern doors of the Florence Baptistry between Lorenzo Ghiberti, who won the competition, and Filippo Brunelleschi. Competitions of this kind provided the norm for the subsequent rivalry between artists like Caravaggio and Annibale Carracci in seventeenth-century Rome and also the pattern for prestigious architectural commissions in the nineteenth and twentieth centuries.[26] Artistic excellence and capitalist competitiveness were essential concomitants of commissions in both the medieval and modern periods.

The encouragement of artistic competitions had its roots in the mercantile ethos of medieval urban elites like the Medicis of Florence and the banking family the Fuggers of Augsburg, who made no pretence of concealing their non-aristocratic origins. On the contrary, the Medici coat of arms, which consisted of six balls (*palle*), actually depicted six gold coins, thus trumpeting the family's financial success to the world. The same pride in successful business practices was the hallmark of the American urban elites who sponsored and commissioned the earliest skyscrapers in Chicago and New York. It is significant that among the decorations on the façade of the Lakeside Shore Building (located on the corner of Polk and Plymouth Streets and designed by Howard van Doren Shaw in 1897) we find the Medici coat of arms clearly visible (minus one coin) above a rampant lion and an imperial eagle. A more explicit example of family pride can be found on the Fisher Building on Dearborn Street, where the owner's family name is advertised in the shape of a fish in the decorative detail (see figure 4.6). Consciously or unconsciously, the late nineteenth- and early twentieth-century American business magnates were placing themselves in the illustrious tradition of self-made merchant families like the Medici and the Fuggers.

This identification with the urban elites of medieval Italy and Germany rather than with the feudal aristocracies of England and France would go some way to explain the prevalence of the Italianate and German architectural styles in the historic Printers Row in Dearborn Street. Located at the end of this thoroughfare is the neo-Romanesque Dearborn Station, the earliest surviving train station in Chicago, which brought rolls of paper to the printers' shops lining Dearborn Street for the processing of early mail-order catalogues; these were then returned to the train station and shipped across the Midwest. Originally the station and its tower included a wooden mansard roof, which gave the edifice a more eclectic feel, but this was destroyed by fire and not replaced, making the building more closely resemble the Italian palazzo style exemplified by the Palazzo Vecchio, begun in 1298 on the Piazza della Signoria in Florence (see figures 4.7 and 4.8).

Another neo-Romanesque building with a distinctive Italian palazzo look is the eight-storey granite building by Granger and Bollenbacher, completed in 1929 to replace the older building erected by Burnham in 1869, which collapsed during repairs. Originally the home of the Art Institute before it relocated to the other side of Michigan Avenue in 1893, this impressive squat building on the corner of Michigan and East Van Buren houses the Chicago Club (81 East Van Buren Street). Since 1893 it has in fact been a private club for the Chicago commercial elite.

Emblematic of the German mercantile Middle Ages is the Franklin Building (720 South Dearborn Street), designed by George C. Nimmons, a leading member of the Prairie style school of architecture (1916). The eastern façade of the building is decorated with a polychrome terracotta relief depicting the Gutenberg Press ("The First Impression") designed by the Viennese artist Oskar Gross (1871–1963), who was invited to work in the United States by the prominent architect Daniel Burnham (see figure 4.9). Like the printer Mergenthaler, Gross ended up settling in the United States. The first mechanized typesetting machine was invented in 1884 by Mergenthaler, who, in 1886, opened a facility in Printers Row known as the Mergenthaler Linotype Building.[27] Although the new printing method was mechanized – based on a keyboard principle rather like a typewriter – its inventor looked back with pride to the origins of printing in Germany, where the Gutenberg Bible was produced around 1455. The Gutenberg Press terracotta relief on the façade of the Franklin Building was intended to celebrate the medieval origins of printing at the same time as advertising the wonders of modern technology and the glories of American

4.6. The Fisher Building, Dearborn Street, Chicago.

Medieval Chicago: Architecture, Patronage, and Capital at the Fin de Siècle   99

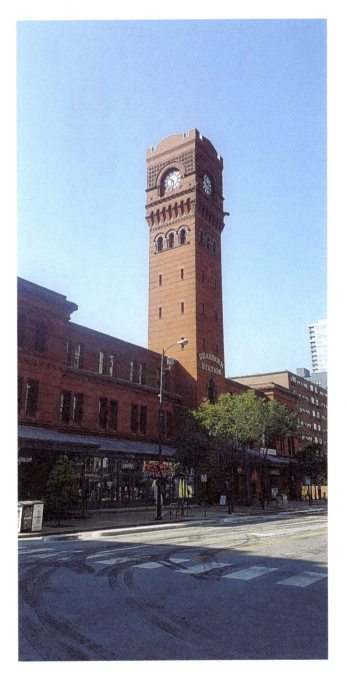

4.7. Dearborn Street Station, Chicago.

4.8. The Palazzo Vecchio, Florence.

republicanism. The figures in the composition "The First Impression" are wearing fifteenth-century clothes, but their fraternal and optimistic spirit (the central two figures are shaking hands) is entirely consonant with the democratic ideals of the American republic. Reinforcing this patriotic ardour and ethos of hard work are miniature reliefs portraying the eponymous Benjamin Franklin in his double role as printer and painter. There was no trace of disavowal of modern industrialization in the ornate façade of the Franklin Building but – to the contrary – a confident appropriation of the medieval past, a syncretization of the Arts and Crafts movement with the latest manufacturing inventions and techniques. More importantly, the celebration of American democracy on this façade can be seen as a form of mystification intended to conceal the new corporate reality at work behind the picturesque surface. As Alan Trachtenberg states, the practical effect of the skyscrapers "was to dress new structures bearing modern functions in old garb, confusing their identity with spectacle" so that "their inner works as corporate headquarters or clearing houses of arcane transactions receded from view, from intelligibility, and from criticism."[28] Above all, the indolent lives of the corporate elites, which ironically resembled the aristocratic world of *The Picture of Dorian Gray*, had to be disguised at all costs and made to masquerade as a democratic exercise in hard work and diligence.

Chicago versus New York and the East Coast

All of this brings us back to the curious phenomenon of the medieval "skyscrapers" of San Gimignano. The political elites of Italian medieval cities built upwards both to save valuable real estate space (again like Chicago) and to provide a safe haven for themselves against rival families in the volatile and frequently violent world of medieval Italy. Although the Holy Roman emperors of Germany had nominal suzerainty over medieval Italy, the city states like Venice and Florence were de facto independent political entities frequently at war with one another and – as in the notorious case of Dante's Florence – riddled with internecine conflicts. The proto-skyscrapers of medieval Florence, Siena, and San Gimignano reflect the rivalries and competitions among the various members of these urban mercantile elites.

This shared context of economic rivalry sheds light on the skyscraper formation of modern American cities like Chicago. Conventionally interpreted as necessary to conserve space in a marshy hinterland, Chicago's bristling modern skyline can also be read as a reflection of the competitive and rivalrous spirit of capitalism itself and thus a mirror image of its medieval proto-capitalist predecessors like Venice and Florence. The influence of the medieval style on modern American cities like Chicago and New York has been traditionally understood in terms of admiration for and rivalry with their European counterparts. But

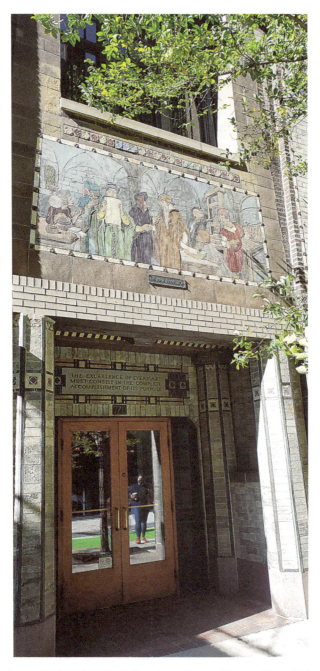

4.9. The terracotta façade of 720 Dearborn Street, Printers Row, Chicago.

we should not forget that rivalry existed not just between America and Europe but also between American cities. Such rivalry is exemplified by Chicago's attempt to outstrip New York as the greatest American city. This rivalry with New York is exemplified not merely by Chicago's burgeoning modern architecture but also by its growing private and municipal art collections in the early years of the twentieth century. The Art Institute of Chicago vied with the New York Cloisters special collection of medieval art, which opened to great fanfare in 1914. Wealthy Chicagoans like the hotel magnate Potter Palmer and his wife, Berthe Honoré Palmer, and Martin A. and Carrie Hutchinson Ryerson became notable collectors of medieval art, the latter collecting for their home and for the Art Institute.[29] Martin Ryerson was the heir to a Michigan timber fortune and, by the age of thirty-six, the richest man in Chicago.

The connection between mercantile wealth and artistic patronage was not exclusive to modern industrial magnates like Ryerson. The Medici rulers of Florence were powerful bankers and politicians but also, needless to say, great patrons of the arts. The rule of Cosimo de' Medici represented the apotheosis of the family's status as prestigious patrons of the arts. Cosimo, the first Medici ruler of Florence, commissioned famous works by Donatello (the statue of David) and Benozzo Gozzoli, whose *Journey of the Magi* (1439) decorates the walls of the Medici Palace in Florence and depicts the Medici as members of the three kings' entourage. This close association of power, wealth, and civic piety can be seen as the precursor of the similar role played by American businessmen like Palmer and Ryerson, for whom artistic patronage and philanthropy were regarded as potent expressions of civic virtue and social responsibility to the community. Underlying both medieval and modern modes of patronage was the patriarchal spirit of civic and political leadership. *Pietas*, the sacred Roman republican principle of devotion to father and country, lay at the heart of Cosimo's philosophy and led to him being dubbed *pater patriae* (father of his homeland) after his death. As Dale V. Kent has shown, the subject of the designs commissioned for the north doors of the Florence Baptistry in 1401 – the *Sacrifice of Isaac* – emphasized the awe and power of the father and thus echoed the authority enjoyed by Cosimo as *pater patriae*. This paternal authority is particularly apparent in Brunelleschi's striking panel, which did not win the competition yet remained powerfully present in the consciousness of the Florentine public.[30]

This patriarchal Roman ideal is not very far from the republican spirit that animated the terracotta relief known as "The First Impression" on the eastern façade of the Franklin Building discussed earlier. Nor is it dissimilar to the philanthropy that motivated Martin A. Ryerson to patronize the Art Institute of Chicago and to serve as president of the executive board of trustees at the University of Chicago, another significant example of neo-Gothic architecture in the Hyde Park area of Chicago's South Side. The campus was laid out in 1891 to the specifications of Ryerson, was designed by Henry Ives Cobb in the neo-Gothic style, and was influenced by the University of Oxford with its emphasis on collegiate quadrangles. Complicating the picture further, the architectural idiom of the University of Oxford was itself influenced by Ruskin's infatuation with medieval Venice, as can be seen in the case of the "copy" of the Rialto Bridge erected in 1914 to join the two halves of Hertford College. Seen in this light, the University of Chicago's architectural emulation of Oxford begins to look like a simulacrum of a simulacrum. The quest for authenticity that informs these modern modes of emulation suggests the circular and illusory nature of capital founded on a gold standard that was undermined during the Civil War when paper money was introduced. By the end of the century, the struggle between silver and gold was reflected in the culture at large.[31] Consciously or unconsciously, the ornamental use of the Medici coat of arms (six gold coins) on the Lakeshore Building in Printers Row would appear to camouflage the complex reality of an economy in which silver and gold competed.

The University of Chicago's rivalry with Old World Oxford is obvious enough, but there may be a more subtle rivalry with an increasingly prestigious East Coast university: Harvard. It is significant that Ryerson was educated in Paris and Geneva and received his law degree from Harvard before returning to the Midwest.[32] It was at Harvard that Ryerson came under the influence of Ruskin's American disciple, Charles Eliot Norton. It is probable that the Ruskinian love of late medieval Italy was transmitted to Ryerson via Norton and that when he returned to the Midwest, the Michigan timber magnate was inspired to collect art that would not only reflect his own tastes but also serve to put Chicago "on the map" as a cultural centre on a par with New York and as an educational centre equal to his alma mater Harvard. A contemporary photograph of the interior of Ryerson's residence on Chicago's Drexel Avenue (from 1924 to 1937) clearly demonstrates the businessman's particular fondness for medieval and Renaissance Italian art.[33] Ryerson wrote to the director of the Art Institute, Robert Harshe, from Italy, where he records his favourable impressions of Perugia and Siena and that he was making purchases intended for the Art Institute.[34] Ryerson's generous gifts – and ultimate bequest – to the Art Institute likely reflect his desire to rival the Cloisters collection of New York.

Conclusion

This chapter has argued that the creation of "medieval" Chicago, in the erection of neo-Gothic and neo-Romanesque buildings and in the private and municipal accumulation of medieval works of art in the years 1880 to 1920, was inseparable from the city's rivalrous relations to – and capitalist affinities with – the European past and the American present. But it has also suggested that the medievalism that is such an important part of Chicago's architectural landscape reflects an ambivalent reaction to the Decadent movement in the late 1880s and 1890s. Although Wilde's tour of America (including two lectures in Chicago) in 1882 had been a great success, his popularity was mingled with growing misgivings about the apparently immoral underpinnings of Wilde's insistence that art was not only superior to life but was morally independent of it. With its profound associations of self-reliant artisanry, medievalism seemed to offer a healthy "masculine" antidote to such antibourgeois aristocratism – indeed, a blueprint for this most American of cities eager to present itself as wholesome and democratic even in the face of corporate expansion and polarized wealth. In this sense its resistance to Decadence was more significant and profound than its alleged rejection of capitalism. Medievalism was a means of accommodating capitalism and celebrating its "athletic" and "masculine" power and vigour, as well as asserting the superiority of the German and Italian mercantile elites over their degenerate English and French counterparts.

But underlying such confidence in capitalism lay a profound crisis of identity in the cultural elites of America. However much these cultural and economic elites took pride in their business accomplishments as self-made men and successful exponents of capitalism, such confidence was brittle. They knew on some deeper level that their real lives were much closer to the effete, indolent, and privileged aristocratic world depicted in *The Picture of Dorian Gray* than they were prepared to admit to themselves or to the world at large. Just as the ugly, corrupt portrait in Wilde's novel is banned to his obscure attic by its beautiful and perpetually youthful owner, so the corporate reality of fin-de-siècle America – as Trachtenberg has so illuminatingly pointed out – had to be hidden from view behind the picturesque façades of the Franklin Building and the Fisher Building. Behind the imposing pseudo-medieval exteriors lurked a grim interior of industrial grind and exploitation, the air loud with the noise of rumbling Linotype machines and thick with the stench of printing chemicals. This gulf between surface beauty and industrial ugliness is beautifully encapsulated in the horrific scene in *The Picture of Dorian Gray* when Dorian blackmails his former lover, the scientist Campbell, into using chemicals to dissolve the murdered corpse of the portrait's painter, Basil Hallward: "As soon as Campbell had left, he (Dorian) went upstairs. There was a horrible smell of chemicals in the room. But the thing that had been sitting at the table was gone."[35] It may not be entirely coincidental that the most famous painterly representation of the novel – a picture of Dorian's corroded soul by the Illinois artist Ivan Albright commissioned for the 1945 Hollywood film version of the novel – is now prominently displayed in the Art Institute of Chicago, a visual icon of the human cost of corrosive, unalloyed capitalism.

NOTES

1. I would like to thank Professors Tom Bestul, Walter Benn Michaels, and Beryl Satter for their helpful insights into an earlier version of this essay.
2. See Katherine M. Solomonson, "Tribune Tower: Medievalism and Memory in the Wake of the Great War," in *Skyscraper Gothic: Medieval Style and Modernist Buildings*, ed. Kevin D. Murphy and Lisa Reilly (Charlottesville: University of Virginia Press, 2017), 112–33.
3. Alan Trachtenberg, *The Incorporation of America: Culture and Society in the Gilded Age* (1994; repr., New York: Hill and Wang, 2007).
4. Fernand Braudel, *Out of Italy: Two Centuries of World Domination and Decline*, trans. Sian Reynolds (New York: Europa Editions, 2019), 16.
5. Solomonson, "Tribune Tower," 19.
6. Andrew Jotischky, *The Crusades: A Beginner's Guide* (London: Oneworld, 2015), 122.
7. See Stephen Church, *King John and the Magna Carta* (New York: Basic Books, 2015).
8. T.J. Jackson Lears, *No Place of Grace: Antimodernism and the Transformation of American Culture, 1880–1920* (Chicago: University of Chicago Press, 1981), 66.
9. See Fiona MacCarthy, *Anarchy and Beauty: William Morris and His Legacy, 1860–1960* (London: National Portrait Gallery, 2014).
10. Johanna Merwood-Salisbury, "The Gothic Revival and the Chicago School: From Naturalistic Ornament to Constructive Expression," in Murphy and Reilly, *Skyscraper Gothic*, 88–111.
11. Lears, *No Place of Grace*, xv.
12. Andrew Lynch, "Imperial Arthur: Home and Away," in *The Cambridge Companion to the Arthurian Legend*, ed. Elizabeth Archibald and Ad Putter (Cambridge: Cambridge University Press, 2009), 171–87, at 179.
13. Lears, *No Place of Grace*, 64.
14. See the essays in *The Medici: Citizens and Masters*, ed. Robert Black and John E. Law (Florence, Italy: Villa I Tatti, Harvard Center for Italian Renaissance Studies, 2015).
15. Chris Wickham, *Medieval Europe* (New Haven, CT: Yale University Press, 2016), 223.
16. Wickham, *Medieval Europe*, 224.
17. Here I am indebted to Alan Trachtenberg's classic study, *The Incorporation of America*.
18. Lears, *No Place of Grace*, 67.
19. See Mary Warner Blanchard, *Oscar Wilde's America: Counterculture in the Gilded Age* (New Haven, CT: Yale University Press, 1998).
20. See Jonathan Dollimore, *Sexual Dissidence: Augustine to Wilde, Freud to Foucault* (Oxford: Clarendon, 1991).

21 See the introduction to Oscar Wilde, *The Uncensored Picture of Dorian Gray*, ed. Nicholas Frankel (Cambridge, MA: Harvard University Press, 2012), 47.
22 See Theo Aronson, *Prince Eddy and the Homosexual Underworld* (New York: Barnes and Noble, 1994).
23 Aronson, *Prince Eddy and the Homosexual Underworld*, 146.
24 Wilde, *Uncensored Picture of Dorian Gray*, 74.
25 Walter Benn Michaels, *The Gold Standard and the Logic of Naturalism: American Literature at the Turn of the Century* (Berkeley: University of California Press, 1988), 213.
26 Andrew Graham-Dixon, *Caravaggio: A Life Sacred and Profane* (New York: Norton, 2010), 212–13.
27 Ron Gordon and John Paulett, *Printers Row, Chicago* (Charleston, SC: Arcadia, 2003), 43.
28 Trachtenberg, *Incorporation of America*, 119.
29 See Christina Nielsen, "'To Step into Another World': Building a Medieval Collection at the Art Institute of Chicago," in *Devotion and Splendor: Medieval Art at the Art Institute of Chicago* (Chicago: Art Institute of Chicago, 2004), 6–17, at 8–9.
30 See Dale V. Kent, "Patriarchal Ideals, Patronage Practices, and the Authority of Cosimo 'il Vecchio,'" in Black and Law, *Medici: Citizens and Masters*, 221–37, at 222–3.
31 See Michaels, *Gold Standard*.
32 Nielsen, "To Step into Another World," 9.
33 For the photograph of the interior of the Ryerson residence, see Nielsen, "To Step into Another World," 9.
34 Nielsen, "To Step into Another World," 9.
35 Wilde, *Uncensored Picture of Dorian Gray*, 206.

Part Two

Living in the American Middle Ages

5 Three Vignettes and a White Castle: Knighthood and Race in Modern Atlanta

RICHARD UTZ

At first sight, few cities could have less of a link with the Middle Ages than Atlanta. Founded in 1837 to provide a train terminus connecting the seaport of Savannah with the Midwest, and about 3,500 miles and at least 500 years removed from Old Europe, Georgia's state capital must count as quintessentially modern. Nevertheless, an observant first-time visitor might notice a host of medieval signposts. Imagine the following scenario: At the baggage claim of the world's busiest airport, a colourful plasma screen displays to the visitor an invitation to be "swept away to an age of bravery and honor" and partake in "a feast of the eyes and appetite with all the splendor and romance" of medieval Spain at the Atlanta Castle of Medieval Times, a dinner theatre chain. A courtesy van, which treats her as if she were a noble lady at a medieval court, takes her to a downtown hotel, the Knights Inn. After a change of clothes, a Lyft driver delivers her to the Catholic Cathedral of Christ the King, where she attends her college roommate's wedding, which includes the celebration of the Eucharist, a sacramental ritual originating in the Fourth Lateran Church Council's decision on transubstantiation in 1215. The visitor particularly enjoys the performance of the Atlanta Early Music Alliance, which performs wedding songs from before 1800, accompanied by instruments painstakingly crafted according to pre-modern building instructions. As the guests exit the cathedral, a Knights of Columbus honour guard from the groom's home parish greets them, and guests are then bussed to the wedding reception at the High Museum of Art, in a space next to an exhibit entitled "Habsburg Splendor," which displays masterpieces from a family whose members served as emperors of the Holy Roman Empire, the highest secular authority in medieval and Renaissance Europe. As our visitor's day ends, she returns to her hotel. In the lobby, she picks up a brochure for the Georgia Renaissance Festival which, April through June, promises to transport her back to pre-modern England, on a thirty-two-acre village "filled with over 150 artisan craft shoppes, 10 stages of endless entertainment, wonderful pubs and taverns," and "giant roasted turkey legs, fish and chips, hearty ales, mead and more." Finally, as she is almost ready to fall asleep, she researches Oglethorpe University, a private institution that offers to match flagship state tuition in all fifty states to high-performing student applicants. As Oglethorpe's magnificent Gothic Revival architecture appears on her laptop screen, she imagines her son, a high school junior, attending this kind of picturesque small liberal arts college.

This fictional narrative compresses a number of features from Atlanta's present and immediate past to reveal the omnipresence of medievalist features all over the city. However, most or all of these medievalist features and practices also exist in other cities and metropolitan areas in the United States: New York, Chicago, and Boston boast "medievalist" cathedrals and churches; several other cities in the US and Canada feature locations of Medieval Times; and examples of neo-Gothic architecture are synonymous with college campuses everywhere. What differentiates Atlanta and other cities in the Southeast from the rest of the country may be the degree to which questions of race are imbricated into the region's reception of medieval culture, as will become apparent in the following examination of the connections between medievalism and the nostalgia for a white past in post–Civil War Atlanta through three vignettes – the history of Stone Mountain; the conception, reception, and remediation of Margaret Mitchell's *Gone with the Wind*; and the city's 1906 Race Riots – along with Amos Rhodes's medieval fantasy castle, with its wistful paean to "the Lost Cause" etched in stained and painted glass.

Vignette One: Stone Mountain

In her brilliant 1998 study, *Making Whiteness: The Culture of Segregation in the South, 1890–1940*, Grace Elizabeth Hale offers a haunting description of Stone Mountain, a unique Atlanta-area geological formation that attracts several million visitors annually:

> It rises, gray and ringing, 1,686 feet of solid granite, straight up from the rippling land of northern Georgia. The foothills surrounding the stone only quote its majesty and make its sudden presence, its hovering bald bulk visible as the pilgrim tops a rise in approach, that much more sublime. Scientists have estimated that at its slow rate of erosion, Stone Mountain will stand its eternal vigil little changed as modern civilization and perhaps even humanity itself disintegrate into dust. Nature has crafted a rock immense, singular, and enduring upon the landscape a mere sixteen miles from Atlanta.[1]

Unsurprisingly, Stone Mountain's commanding presence as an isolated mountain, 1,686 feet tall and 3.8 miles in base circumference, has drawn humans to its proximity at least since North America's early Archaic age, circa 9,000 years ago, and European traders and slave raiders reached the location for the first time in the late seventeenth century.² As Native Americans were gradually pushed out and the region became settled by Europeans, Stone Mountain gained increasing importance as a signpost of a regional racial identity that imagined its roots in medieval culture. This process of medievalist identity formation culminated in two early twentieth-century events.

Stirred by the nostalgic depiction of the nineteenth-century history of the (first) Ku Klux Klan in D.W. Griffith's 1915 silent film, *Birth of a Nation*, minister and activist William Simmons, together with sixteen other men, revived the Klan on Thanksgiving Day 1915. Atop Stone Mountain they ignited a flaming cross according to the following ritual:

> The ceremony began around an altar made of stones contributed by each klansman. On this altar was erected a fiery cross in the halo of whose light the men, with uncovered heads, assumed the oath of the klan, and upon bended knees were dedicated with pure water to the service of country, homes and humanity. On the altar were placed a silk flag of the United States that was carried in the battle of Buena Vista of the Mexican War, a copy of the Bible [opened to Romans 12], the Constitution of the United States, the Declaration of Independence, and the laws of the order. After an impressive prayer of dedication, the company was duly knighted with a saber that was used in the Battle of the Seven Pines of the Civil War. On its blade were rust marks from the blood of the North and the South. The saber was draped with a silk flag of the United States. Each klansman received the saber from the hands of the imperial wizard with both hands and pressed it to his lips, and said, "The klan, my country, my komrades, and my home."³

This event brought about the most powerful movement of the Far Right in US history, attracting perhaps as many as five million adherents to embrace its mélange of paramilitary paternalism, reactionary Evangelical populism, sexism, nativism, and racism.⁴ The link between the white staking of a claim to Stone Mountain with medieval knighthood was expressed by preacher, legislator, and lawyer Thomas Dixon Jr., whose 1905 novel, *The Clansman*, was the literary inspiration for Griffith's movie. Dixon had romanticized the nineteenth-century Klansmen's struggle in terms of the Klan's charter, which enshrined "Chivalry, Humanity, Mercy, and Patriotism: embodying in its genius and principles all that is chivalric in conduct, noble in sentiment, generous in manhood and patriotic in purpose."⁵ So influential were Dixon's narratives that adolescents like fifteen-year-old Margaret ("Peggy") Mitchell, who would later write *Gone with the Wind*, organized neighbourhood children to dramatize his novels.⁶

Dixon, Griffith, Simmons, and many of their contemporaries viewed the Klan's actions in terms of a modern crusade, only this time mostly for an empire of white nativist masculinity, and they relied for foundational inspiration on what David Matthews has called the nineteenth-century "boom" of medievalism in the spheres of art, architecture, and poetry in Britain and most other Anglophone countries.[7] In the Southern United States, this boom had, by the early twentieth century, found almost omnipresent expression in nostalgic narratives in which "Christendom," "Caucasian supremacy," and "masculine strength" were memorialized as the central virtues of "the blessed days of the Old South."[8] "Yes, say what you may of it," reminisced author and former Confederate army chaplain James Battle Avirett in 1901:

> There was an engaging race in the chivalry that tempered even quixotism with dignity, in the piety which saved master and slave alike, in the charity that boasted not, in honor held above estate, in the hospitality that neither condescended nor cringed, in frankness and heartiness and wholesome comradeship, in the reverence paid to womanhood and the inviolable respect in which woman was held, the civilization of the old slave *régime* in the South has not been surpassed and perhaps will not be equaled among men.[9]

Southern masculinity relied on medieval conceptions of chivalry to bolster its claims.

If the first major event in the modern medievalist history of Stone Mountain, the founding of the (second) Ku Klux Klan, involved the South's "chivalric sons," the second one was orchestrated by the South's "beautiful daughters."[10] In 1914, the United Daughters of the Confederacy, an organization of middle- and upper-class white women to sustain antebellum culture and extol Confederate heroism, settled upon the imposing butte outside Atlanta as the perfect site to memorialize the "Lost Cause." Neatly complementary to the KKK's goals regarding gender, UDC leaders opposed women's suffrage, argued that women should be deferential to men and remain in the home, and exalted the plantation mistress as the ideal female role model.[11] In the UDC's original plan for the memorial, Confederate general Robert E. Lee was to be displayed leading Confederate troops as well as KKK members across the mountain's summit. However, various events, especially the two world wars, prevented its completion. It was only in 1970, in direct opposition to the rising tide of two decades of post–Second World War African American activism, that white politicians in the state of Georgia moved to finish and inaugurate the gigantic three-acre relief sculpture, 400 feet above the ground, featuring Confederate icons Robert E. Lee, Thomas "Stonewall" Jackson, and Jefferson Davis. Fittingly, the three Confederate cavaliers were depicted sitting on their favourite horses, Blackjack, Traveller, and Little Sorrel, who, during and after the Civil War, were as recognizable as their owners.

Vignette Two: *Gone with the Wind*

In the summer of 1949, Atlanta's Peachtree Art Theatre showed Michael Powell and Emeric Pressburger's black-and-white movie *A Canterbury Tale*. Originally released in Britain in 1944 as a patriotic war movie, a slightly revised version reached United States cinemas by the late 1940s. Based very loosely on Geoffrey Chaucer's late medieval *Canterbury Tales*, the movie draws attention to the daily wartime experiences of regular citizens, specifically the friendship between two army sergeants (one American, one British) and a young woman from Kent. Clearly intended to exemplify and further solidify the friendship between these allied countries, the narrative shows the three young people collaborating to solve a series of strange attacks, in which a man pours glue on local women's hair at a train station. They identify the culprit, a magistrate who wants to "encourage" the young women to remain faithful to their absent British boyfriends. The movie ends happily for all three protagonists and the magistrate, whom the three decide not to report to the authorities. The real "hero" of the movie is the country, which takes centre stage during the final scenes when English solders march towards their deployment areas for crossing the Channel to Normandy on D-Day.[12]

At 8:15 p.m., on 11 August 1949, a middle-aged Atlanta couple strolled towards the Peachtree Art Theatre, eager to enjoy the patriotic and superficially medievalist movie. As they crossed Peachtree Street, near Thirteenth Street, a taxi sped towards them. The woman stepped back; the man stepped forward. The off-duty taxi driver, who had had too much to drink, applied the brakes, skidded, and hit the woman. Although she was immediately taken to Grady Hospital, she never regained consciousness. During the next five days, crowds waited outside for news, and President Harry Truman, Georgia governor Herman Talmadge, and Atlanta mayor William Hartsfield all requested updates on her condition. The woman died on 16 August 1949.[13]

The woman was none other than Margaret Mitchell, a native and lifelong resident of Atlanta and one of the first female columnists at the *Atlanta Journal*, the South's largest newspaper. One of her most brave and daring assignments as a young reporter was to agree to be strapped into a boatswain's chair and then shoved out the window of the top floor of a fifteen-story Atlanta building to simulate what the workers on the Stone Mountain site would experience as they prepared the gigantic Confederate carving.[14] Quite obviously, Mitchell's views on the role of women and men did not conform with what the Ku Klux Klan, the United Daughters of the Confederacy, or numerous nineteenth-century Southern romantics promulgated and thought about gender roles and plantation-owning cavaliers and their ladies. In fact, critics generally agree that *Gone with the Wind*, which won the US National Book Award for Most Distinguished Novel (1936) and the Pulitzer Prize in Fiction (1937), presents a more nuanced picture of the Civil War South, at least regarding the roles of white women.

However, screenwriter Ben Hecht, in David O. Selznick's film version of *Gone with the Wind* (1939), preferred to return to many of the banal clichés about the Old South, including the depiction of the Southern plantation as an aristocratic, feudal utopia. In the opening intertitle, Hecht wrote for a worldwide audience to see and read:

> There was a land of Cavaliers and Cotton Fields called the Old South.
> Here in this pretty world Gallantry took its last bow.
> Here was the last ever to be seen of Knights and their Ladies Fair, of Master and Slave.
> Look for it only in books, for it is no more than a dream remembered
> A civilization gone with the wind …

Alexandra Cook, in an essay comparing *Gone with the Wind* with Thomas Nelson Page's 1898 "Reconstruction" novel *Red Rock*, summarizes how Mitchell's intent was to challenge the mythical narrative of the South as a pre-industrial idyll populated by knights and ladies. According to Cook, Mitchell tried to depict crude upcountry North Georgia

> "as it [really] was": "I certainly had no intention of writing about Cavaliers," she protests in a letter to historian Virginius Dabney, "and most of my characters, apart from the Virginia Wilkes, were yeoman farmers." Furthermore, while Mitchell does deploy the tradition of southern medievalism that Hecht's roll-up uses to such cloying effect, she bends its idioms to different ends. When Rhett Butler voices the traditional comparison between southern agrarianism and medieval feudalism, he is not sentimentalizing but lambasting the antiquated "southern way of living." While Mitchell compares aristocratic planter Ashley Wilkes to a knight, he is a distinctly enervated and ineffectual one, and though Scarlett may long for Ashley because to her he seems "the young girl's dream of the Perfect Knight," she herself is not one of Hecht's "Ladies Fair." In fact, Mitchell goes so far as to liken Scarlett herself to a knight. She is brave: Ashley reflects "he had never known such gallantry as the gallantry of Scarlett O'Hara going forth to conquer the world in her mother's velvet curtains and the tail feathers of a rooster." What is more, Mitchell relegates Ashley, the object of Scarlett's desire, to the position that was traditionally held by what W.S. Cash characterized as the lovely and exquisitely remote southern lady. Through such critiques and reversals Mitchell discovers new possibilities latent in the stereotypical retrograde fantasy of southern medievalism to which Hecht's text refers.[15]

Even if Mitchell may have questioned some of the facets of this fantasy in her novel, her advocacy for women's rights and agency excluded African Americans, whom she deprived of emotional, intellectual, and spiritual depth. Her innovative use of medieval tropes did not extend to all.

Vignette Three: Race Riots

Young Peggy Mitchell's formative years were spent in an Atlanta rife with racial conflict, and one specific childhood event would mark her more than any other:

> It is the late afternoon of Monday, September 24, 1906, and five-year-old Peggy had spent the entire day nervous because she had heard that a race war was going on in other parts of Atlanta. While she wasn't sure about what exactly that means, she, her brother, and her father (the mother was away) heard gunshots not too far away from their two-story Victorian house in the fashionable Jackson Hill neighborhood. Their neighbor has come over to recommend that Eugene Mitchell, a prominent attorney and real estate developer, arm and ready himself in case any of the black rioters might attack the house.

Mark Bauerlein summarizes what happened after the neighbour left:

> Eugene shuts the door and asks his daughter to leave the room. As the evening shadows lengthen, he retrieves a large ax and an iron water key, leaning against the front door and setting up a chair behind the window. Twilight falls and her father anticipates an all-night vigil, while Margaret retires to her bedroom upstairs. Everything is quiet outside, but she can't sleep. Eugene hears a footstep and turns to find Margaret holding a large sword kept in the house, offering it as another weapon of defense. He grasps it with care as she scampers back to her room, slipping underneath her bed and remaining awake the entire night, listening for sounds of an approaching invasion.[16]

Little Peggy's resorting to the knightly sword to help her father defend their home against potential Black rioters offers more than a symbolic link to her city's and region's racist medievalism in the late nineteenth and early twentieth century. She would return to reading essential periods of her life as related to medievalia. For example, she described her desire to travel independently after divorcing her first husband in terms of the adventuresome knight-errancy of the character Dom Manuel in James Branch Cabell's *The Biography of the Life of Manuel*, a series of speculative novels, essays, and poems produced between 1901 and 1929. According to Darden Asbury Pyron, Mitchell's idea of female knighthood included "freedom of movement," the "very antithesis of women's roles: stability, home immobility, even sequestration."[17] At the age of eight or nine, she wrote the story "Knighthood," which tells "of a beautiful and 'very rich' lady who lived in a valley between two high mountains. While everyone loved her, a 'wild rough knight' worshiped her, but she did not love him. Rejected he decided to seize her by force. A 'good but poor knight' lived nearby, heard about the plot, and defended the lady. The story ended (with all its childish errors): 'Both knight drew there swords and rushed togeth. The good knight hit the bad one such a blow that he was killed. The lady fel in love with her rescueuer, and they were married.'"[18]

The knights of the Atlanta chapter of the Klan would enshrine racist medievalism in their official charter some years after the 1906 race riots. White Southerners not only intended "to commemorate the holy and chivalric achievements of our fathers," but also saw it as their specific "sacred duty" to protect "womanhood" and "to maintain forever the God-given supremacy of the white race."[19] The riots, which made the headlines in numerous national and international newspapers, began on the afternoon of Saturday, 22 September 1906, when newsboys in Atlanta's Five Point neighbourhood tried to attract customers with sensationalized headlines like "Third Assault on White Woman by a Negro Brute!," "Bold Negro Kisses White Girl's Hand!," and "Bright Mulatto Insults White Girls!"[20] These accusations, none of which were ever substantiated, and other similar headlines, stories, and cartoons appeared in the Atlanta papers as a by-product of an adversarial gubernatorial race. Both candidates, Clark Howell and Hoke Smith, two of Atlanta's most prosperous citizens and champions of white supremacy, did everything in their power to fault their opponent for being too friendly with the city's Black citizens. The *Atlanta Constitution*, published by Howell, accused Smith of courting "Negrophile Allies" by appointing Black people to federal positions during his time as secretary of the interior under Grover Cleveland.[21] The *Atlanta Journal*, published by Smith, claimed to expose Howell's tendencies not to sufficiently oppose African American franchise and access to education.

It mattered little that the *Atlanta Independent*, a Black weekly, pointed out how both campaigns disenfranchised "every decent and helpful negro citizen and enfranchize[d] every venal and vicious white thug."[22] Atlanta, the city that prided itself as an exception to the racially divided cities of the South, quickly succumbed to the lurid and dramatic news hype spread by the major newspapers: "With his yellow lips forming insulting phrases," the *Evening News* exclaimed, "Luther Frazier, a young negro, attacked Miss Orrie Bryan, the pretty 18-year-old daughter of Thomas L. Bryan, in her home." And the journalists urged on local men by asking, "What will you do to stop these outrages against the women? Shall these black devils be permitted to assault and almost kill our women, and go unpunished?"[23]

As a result of this and other inflammatory rumours, white men and boys gathered all over Atlanta, attacked Black-owned businesses, pulled Black men out of streetcars and trolley cars, and hunted down others in the streets. Long-held fears, especially of Black sexual violence against white women, continued to lead to attacks by white mobs on Black citizens during the following days, even after the state militia entered the city to stop the violence.

In the end, about forty African Americans were killed, along with two whites. All the elements of an invented modern white knighthood had finally found a violent outlet, and in the only US city with a thriving African American middle class.

A White Castle

The career and aspirations of Amos Giles Rhodes (1850–1928) offer an excellent example of the ways in which deeply racist medievalism trickled down into the upwardly mobile white working class of modern Atlanta. Born in Henderson, Kentucky, in 1850, he came to Atlanta as a simple labourer for the L&N Railroad in 1875, owning only a horse and buggy and with $75 in cash.[24] In 1876, he married Amanda Dougherty (1847–1927) and soon started earning good money by operating a chain of medium-sized furniture stores. By the 1890s, his entrepreneurial spirit – he is credited with inventing the instalment payment plan, allowing customers to make weekly payments on purchases[25] – had turned the company into a large furniture business and made him one of the wealthiest and most prominent citizens of the quickly growing modern city, a city which, in part because of its modernity and rapid growth, offered better living conditions and career opportunities not only for whites but also for Black workers and businesses than any other city in the late nineteenth-century South. Between the 1890s and 1910, Atlanta's population soared from 80,000 to 150,000; the Black population was approximately 9,000 in 1880 and reached 35,000 by 1900. This precipitous growth put pressure on municipal services, increased job competition between Black and white workers, heightened class distinctions, and led the city's white leadership to respond with restrictions intended to control the daily behaviour of the growing working class, with mixed success. Such conditions caused concern among elite whites, who feared the social intermingling of the races, and led to an expansion of racial segregation, particularly in the separation of white and Black neighbourhoods, including separate seating areas for public transportation.[26]

On the white side of Atlanta, Amanda and Amos Rhodes had become enamoured with living the medievalist dream. While on a leisurely boat trip down the Rhine River during a European vacation, they determined to build a new private residence in a similar style. They began multiple land purchases to create an estate of 114 acres along one of the most highly prized Atlanta thoroughfares, Peachtree Street.[27] In 1902, four years before the Atlanta race riots, construction began on a large private castle they originally referred to as Le Rêve ("The Dream") but later decided to call Rhodes Hall. For maximum visibility, the couple situated it on a slight rise at a prominent curve of Peachtree Street. The white granite for the mansion was quarried from the same Stone Mountain that would, in 1915, become the site for the founding of the second

Ku Klux Klan and for which, also in 1915, the Daughters of the Confederacy would commission the carving of Confederate icons Lee, Jackson, and Davis.

By the time Rhodes Hall was built, the Rhineland castle style the Rhodes envisioned had passed out of fashion, and architect Willis F. Denny II (1874–1905), who also designed Atlanta's First United Methodist and St. Mark's United Methodist churches in the style of the popular Gothic Revival, created an example of Victorian Romanesque Revival, which was intended to adapt the medieval Romanesque style to the design of a twentieth-century private home. As so often in modern medievalism, the Victorian Romanesque Revival typically made only superficial reference to the actual architecture of the medieval period. The style, best exemplified by San Francisco's St. Mark's Lutheran Church (1895), Chicago's Marshall Field's Wholesale Store (1887), and Sydney's Queen Victoria Building (1898), featured buildings of substantial weight and mass; a rock-faced foundation; masonry walls highlighted by rock-faced arches, lintels, and sills; semicircular arches in windows, doors, and porches; polychrome masonry; and tower roofs topped with finials.

Owing to its massive and expensive construction requirements, the Romanesque Revival style was normally employed for grand public buildings such as courthouses, churches, libraries, university buildings, department stores, and train stations. Rhodes Hall, which cost the Rhodes family $50,000 to build in 1904 (at least $6 million in today's currency), is an exception to this general picture. According to contemporary records, the house was an immediate success in the Atlanta papers and social scene. One author remarked that "in the war of wealth and opulence waged along Peachtree Street at the time, it can probably be said that Amos Rhodes' fortress won hands down."[28] And it won this "war" not only through its typically Victorian obsession of connecting with the medieval past, or its display of exotic scenes from the Rhodeses' beloved Florida, but also by weaving into these temporally and spatially removed features the most advanced contemporary technology. Over 300 light bulbs illuminated the house, producing a blaze of light uncommon in 1904, and most rooms boasted electric call buttons as well as a state-of-the-art security alarm.

At the very centre, visually and symbolically, of the castle on Peachtree is a massive mahogany staircase, which leads up to the private and much less expensively decorated areas of the Rhodes home. The staircase, for which the architect used mahogany imported from the West Indies, attracts a visitor's eyes to a three-panel series of stained and painted glass. The owners and their architect created a church-like shrine in these panels to the "Lost Cause," romanticizing the rise and fall of the Confederacy, from the first shots initiating the Battle of Fort Sumter on 12 April 1861 to the Battle of Appomattox, after which General Robert E. Lee's army surrendered on 9 April 1865. The windows were executed by the brothers Theodore and Ludwig Von Gerichten, who, with studios in Columbus, Ohio, and Munich, Germany, created windows for more than 800 churches in the United States and who were recognized with a grand prize and several gold medals at the St. Louis World's Fair of 1904.[29]

The glass panels, which vary somewhat in length because of the space they cover from the bottom to the top of the staircase, consist of two longer sections depicting recognizable seminal historical moments: the election of Jefferson Davis as president of the Confederate States of America (1861); dramatic battle scenes and nostalgic scenes of the Old South; and medallion-like portraits of Confederate politicians and generals, including opponents of Reconstruction and members of the first Ku Klux Klan. To ensure a lifelike depiction, the portraits were based on drawings, paintings, and photographs.[30] Each window is crowned by rounded arch illustrations of abstract national virtues, such as the Constitution supported by Wisdom, Justice, and Moderation, or mottoes and seals celebrating various Confederate states.[31] The window panels with scenes from the Old South provide perhaps the most direct commentary on race relations in Atlanta between 1890 and 1930. The numerous medievalizing gestures in Rhodes Hall conflate and conjoin the medieval past, the antebellum past, and the twentieth century. For the owners and visitors of the residence, these three time periods inhabit the same space.

One panel exudes happiness and pride: a Confederate soldier on a horse, probably an officer, gallantly waves goodbye to his wife, son, and daughter, who return his gesture. Portrayed in the dark, on the left of a stately manor house and close to the shade of some trees, stand six Black figures in beige work clothes. They watch the departure scene without observable emotion. Their hands are at their hips or down on the side of their bodies, but their motionless and unfree status provides the symbolic backdrop in front of which the gallant manhood and freedom of the white male hero may be portrayed. In a second window panel, clearly situated years later, a bearded patriarch with a cane stands by as his wife greets their son who, now without his steed, has returned at the end of the war. Their yard is overgrown with ivy and other abundant flora, and an askew shutter on the Classical Revival antebellum plantation manor communicates that the place has seen better days. The cavalier's wife and children are nowhere to be seen, and all slaves are gone. If what can be inferred about Amos Rhodes's taste for the Romantic and exotic in other rooms is any indication – his own favourite room in the building features paintings with "noble native savages" as idealized objects of another bygone era in the Atlanta region – he felt a deep yearning for a time when medieval knights and ladies (that is, Southern gentlemen and their belles) and medieval peasants and serfs (that is, African American slaves) all knew their "rightful" place. Therefore, it is no surprise that the final panel with scenes from the Old South focuses on what the Confederate officer was willing to fight and die for. It is a bucolic still life of four African Americans occupied with providing the economic foundation for the Southern economy and lifestyle: they are picking cotton. The packed basket in the foreground and the ample future harvest still on the healthy cotton bushes celebrate an agrarian and anti-industrialist economy built on the backs of slave and low-wage labour.

Two generations after the American Civil War, Rhodes Hall celebrated the Confederate heritage and well represented the medievalist fortress mentality of Atlanta's white citizens, as would the founding of the second Klan on Stone Mountain in 1915, the writing and reception of Mitchell's *Gone with the Wind* in the 1930s and 1940s, and the race riots of 1906.[32]

Medieval Atlanta Today

Most twenty-first-century visitors to Atlanta will never see Rhodes Hall. No longer the commanding social and geographic presence it used to be until the 1930s, it is now dwarfed by the nearby Equifax Building, the Federal Home Loan Bank of Atlanta, Invesco Global Asset Management, and WSB-TV News 2. Its romantic alterity as a former medievalist private residence now impresses a handful of visitors during the weekly building tours and, more importantly, the guests at numerous weddings, holiday parties, and corporate events. The nonprofit Georgia Trust for Historic Preservation supports the successful renovation of the castle via its Cupid at the Castle program, which boasts having received the Bride's Choice Awards since 2012.[33] Careful to avoid attracting white supremacist attention on the one hand and desirous to invite wedding parties on the other, the newly designed 2018 website for Rhodes Hall omits any sensitive issues. The closest it comes to revealing its troubling historical connections is when the edifice is said to exemplify "the depth of feeling for the 'Lost Cause' as the old heroes passed away."[34] Instead of historical transparency, the Georgia Trust would rather focus on the future, specifically its laudable commitment to adopting greener practices and policies and conserving energy.[35] And so couples from all kinds of racial backgrounds will continue to have their wedding photos taken in the castle, blissfully unaware that the church-like portrait gallery around them includes the likes of Robert Toombs, an impassioned opponent of Reconstruction; Nathan Bedford Forrest, Grand Wizard of the (first) Ku Klux Klan; and John B. Gordon, head of the (first) Ku Klux Klan in the state of Georgia.

The Margaret Mitchell House belongs among the Atlanta attractions managed under the umbrella of the Atlanta History Center. Like the managers of Rhodes Hall, its administrators are careful not to bother site visitors with sensitive issues and instead centre its 2018 activities and exhibits on "lighter" topics: "Margaret Mitchell: A Passion for Character" (career as a reporter, girlhood writings, philanthropy), "The Making of a Film Legend: *Gone with the Wind*" (transformation of the novel into the film classic), and "Stars in Atlanta: The Premiere of *Gone with the Wind*" (events around the world premiere of

Knighthood and Race in Modern Atlanta   123

December 1939).³⁶ However, as a museum, research facility, and centre for educational and public outreach to the citizens of Atlanta and all other visitors, the Atlanta History Center also provides a host of opportunities to learn about the less glorious aspects of the city's and region's history, including the "Confederate Monument Interpretation Guide," which critically examines "the 'Lost Cause,' the notion that white Southerners fought a just cause in the Civil War and won morally, even if they lost on the battle field."³⁷

While owned by the State of Georgia, Stone Mountain is now operated by Herschend Family Entertainment, which is headquartered in Atlanta and operates dozens of other theme parks and attractions throughout the United States, including Dollywood (Pigeon Forge, Tennessee), Silver Dollar City (Branson, Missouri), Pirate's Voyage (Myrtle Beach, South Carolina), and the Harlem Globetrotters International (Phoenix, Arizona). Except for its location – 1000 Robert E. Lee Boulevard, Stone Mountain, Georgia – the company has cleansed its website and public relations materials from any reference to the problematic moments surrounding the site. The "History and Nature" section of the website, for example, focuses on

> the fascinating geology and ecology of Stone Mountain. Visitors can explore the gallery, experiencing everything from interactive science exhibits to the life-size cave with a video about the origin of the mountain. Guests can also view the educational documentary "The Battle for Georgia – a History of the Civil War in Georgia," which has been updated to a large screen video format in the new Confederate Hall Theater. The 25 minute film … features hundreds of archival photographic images and reenactment footage from the Civil War. In addition, guests can learn how the Confederate Memorial carving came to be by viewing the 11-minute feature film "The Men Who Carved the Mountain."³⁸

The historical timeline elides the founding of the second Ku Klux Klan for the year 1915. For that year it only mentions the first plans for a memorial by the United Daughters of the Confederacy.³⁹ For 1963, it elides Dr. Martin Luther King Jr.'s "I Have a Dream" speech, in which King specifically asked to "let freedom ring from Stone Mountain of Georgia!," and rather mentions the opening of the Antebellum Plantation.⁴⁰ Since taking over operations in 1998, Herschend Family Entertainment renovated Confederate Hall as an Environmental Education Center and a museum on Stone Mountain's geology and ecology and added an Indian Festival & Pow Wow, an Outdoor Quarry Exhibit, a Pumpkin Festival, a Southern Christmas (later named Stone Mountain Christmas), and a Kid's Spring Break Festival. As with Rhodes Hall, a focus on "green" activities seems to have been chosen to engage with a positive future instead of a contentious past. The only remaining medievalist connection, limited to friendly Highland Dancing, Piping and Drumming, and Clan Challenge

Athletic events, is the annual Highland Games.[41] Perhaps it is the aggressive silencing of any and all historical engagement with Stone Mountain's Klan history that makes it possible for the festival's "Clan Registration Information" to state, clearly without irony: "It is all about the clans after all. Seriously, the Stone Mountain Highland Games would not exist if it were not for the Clans."[42] The Highland Games were first held at Stone Mountain in 1972, the same year in which the Confederate carving was finally completed.

Despite all efforts to turn Stone Mountain into an anodyne tourist attraction, it is simply too big and public not to remain a major stumbling block in Atlanta's path towards (actively) forgetting its modern white supremacist past. With events similar to those of approximately one hundred years ago, a white supremacist political movement developed concomitant with the primaries and presidential campaign in 2015 and 2016. The shooting of nine African American churchgoers by an avowed white separatist on 17 June 2016 in Charleston and, in response, civil rights groups' call for the eradication of Confederate symbols, led to hundreds of demonstrations and counterdemonstrations all across the nation. In Georgia, the NAACP proposed that the Confederate carving be removed from Stone Mountain. Several other groups and organizations attempted to revive the Confederate history of Stone Mountain and invited "every able bodied soul of our race" to defend "these lands of green glens, rolling hills, and deep glades" from "being purposely flooded with hordes of raping scoundrels."[43] A number of events like "Rock Stone Mountain" (2016) united several hundred neo-Nazis, Klan members, Sons of Confederate Veterans, Neo-Confederate Leaguers, and members of the heavily armed Georgia Security Force III% at Stone Mountain; it also brought together numerous counter-protesters (NAACP, Black Lives Matter, All Out ATL), many of whom also realized the historical symbolism of the site. Unlike at the Unite the Right rally at Charlottesville, Virginia, on 11 and 12 August 2017, which abounded with medievalist connections, symbols, slogans, and memes (for example, Odal rune, Black Sun, Iron Cross, Valknut, Deus Vult crosses), the demonstrations at Stone Mountain showed no symbols or gear that specifically referenced medievalia.[44] Could it be that Atlanta has overcome its nineteenth- and early twentieth-century desire for deriving its identity via various forms of medievalism?

Were history our guide, we should be careful with such predictions. In a 2012 landmark study, Nico Voigtländer and Hans-Joachim Voth showed how persistent medieval anti-Jewish prejudice has proved over centuries. Using data on plague-era pogroms as an indicator for local and regional medieval antisemitism, they could reliably predict violence against Jews in the 1920s, votes for the Nazi party, deportations after 1933, and attacks against synagogues, thus revealing a continuity of cultural traits spanning 600 years.[45] Therefore, those entrusted with the preservation of Atlanta and Georgia history may want to learn a lesson from the creative way in which the congregation of Washington National Cathedral dealt with a series of Confederate War–themed stained-glass windows in their place of worship. The windows depict Generals Robert E. Lee and Stonewall Jackson as exemplary Christians, representations that present a serious problem for the contemporary members of this active place of worship. Cathedral leaders agreed to remove all the Confederate flag images in the windows and to replace them with plain glass. The images were originally installed in 1953 after lobbying by the United Daughters of the Confederacy, an organization founded ten years before the construction of Atlanta's Rhodes Hall and dedicated to heroic readings of the Civil War and the "Lost Cause." Before executing these changes, however, the National Cathedral resolved to make this process a public moment of communal learning and mourning, with discussions and presentations over an entire year. Thus, instead of "simply taking the windows down and going on with business as usual," the removal process served to "provide an opportunity ... to begin to write a new narrative on race and racial justice at the Cathedral and perhaps for [the] nation."[46] There are currently no plans for a similarly conscious public engagement with Atlanta's past.

NOTES

1 Grace Elizabeth Hale, *Making Whiteness: The Culture of Segregation in the South, 1890–1940* (New York: Random House, 1998), 241.
2 See Bruce E. Stewart, "Stone Mountain," *New Georgia Encyclopedia*, http://www.georgiaencyclopedia.org/articles/geography-environment/stone-mountain, last updated 31 Oct. 2016 (accessed 31 Aug. 2018); and Lorraine Boissoneault, "What Will Happen to Stone Mountain, America's Largest Confederate Memorial?," *Smithsonian*, 22 Aug. 2017, https://www.smithsonianmag.com/history/what-will-happen-stone-mountain-americas-largest-confederate-memorial-180964588.
3 *The Georgian*, 27 Nov. 1915, quoted in Mark Bauerlein, *Negrophobia: A Race Riot in Atlanta, 1906* (San Francisco: Encounter, 2001), 288.
4 The fullest historical analysis of the chivalric Klan is Nancy McLean's *Behind the Mask of Chivalry: The Making of the Second Ku Klux Klan* (Oxford: Oxford University Press, 1995).
5 Thomas Dixon Jr., *The Clansman: An Historical Romance of the Ku Klux Klan* (1905; repr., Lexington: University Press of Kentucky, 1970), 320.
6 Andrew Leiter, "Thomas Dixon, Jr.: Conflicts in History and Literature," *Documenting the American South*, https://docsouth.unc.edu/southlit/dixon_intro.html (accessed 13 Sept. 2018). As an adult, in a letter to Dixon dated 10 Aug. 1936, Mitchell wrote, "I was practically raised on your books, and love them very much"

(*Margaret Mitchell's "Gone with the Wind" Letters, 1936–1949*, ed. Richard Harwell [New York: Macmillan, 1976], 52–3).
7   David Matthews, *Medievalism: A Critical History* (Cambridge: D.S. Brewer, 2015), 119–21.
8   James Battle Avirett, *The Old Plantation: How We Lived in Great House and Cabin before the War* (New York: Neely, 1901), 8–9. As early as 1857, Avirett stated that it was "a mistake to say that the age of chivalry has passed" ("Knights and Courtly Ladies: The Romantic Ultimate," in *The Romantic South*, ed. Harnett Kane [New York: Howard-McCann, 1961], 182).
9   Avirett, *Old Plantation*, 19–20. Another example is found in David R. Hundley's *Social Relations in Our Southern States* (New York: Henry B. Price, 1860): "The gentlemen of the South owe their physical perfectness in part, doubtless, to those mailed ancestors who followed Godfrey and bold Coeur de Lion to the rescue of the Holy Sepulchre or to those knightly sires, may be, who, like Front de Boeuf, and most of the other gallant gentlemen of those days, were great with battleaxes" (29).
10 Avirett, *Old Plantation*, 160.
11 Angelo Esco Elder, "United Daughters of the Confederacy," *New Georgia Encyclopedia*, last updated 30 July 2018, http://www.georgiaencyclopedia.org/articles/history-archaeology/united-daughters-confederacy (accessed 31 Aug. 2018).
12 For a critical reading of the movie in the context of medievalism, see Carolyn Dinshaw, *How Soon Is Now? Medieval Texts, Amateur Readers, and the Queerness of Time* (Durham, NC: Duke University Press, 2012), 153–61.
13 See Richard Cavendish, "The Author of *Gone with the Wind* Dies," *History Today* 49, no. 8 (1999): 51–2.
14 See the entry on sculptor Gutzon Borglum in Anita Price Davis, *The Margaret Mitchell Encyclopedia* (Jefferson, NC: McFarland, 2013), 41–2. Mitchell's article, "Hanging over Atlanta in Borglum's Swing," was published in the *Atlanta Journal* on 5 May 1923.
15 Alexandra Cook, "Critical Medievalism and the New South: *Red Rock* and *Gone with the Wind*," *South Central Review* 30, no. 2 (2013): 32–52, at 32.
16 Bauerlein, *Negrophobia*, 192–3.
17 Darden Asbury Pyron, *Southern Daughter: The Life of Margaret Mitchell* (New York: Oxford University Press, 1991), 195–8.
18 Pyron, *Southern Daughter*, 49.
19 *Constitution and Laws of the Knights of the Ku Klux Klan* (Atlanta: Knights of the Ku Klux Klan, 1921), 5. On the strong role of Protestantism for the programmatic goals of the second Klan, see Charles Reagan Wilson, *Baptized in Blood: The Religion of the Lost Cause, 1865–1920* (Athens: University of Georgia Press, 1980).
20 A detailed narrative of the events surrounding the 1906 race riot can be found in Gary Pomerantz, *Where Peachtree Meets Sweet Auburn: A Saga of Race and Family* (New York: Penguin, 1997), 69–77.

21 For additional information and the role of newspaper articles in inciting violence, see "The Atlanta Race Riot of 1906," PBS, https://pba.pbslearningmedia.org/resource/d537b305-c6b0-4f50-8139-d603fa7ddf18/the-atlanta-race-riot-of-1906 (accessed 27 Feb. 2021).
22 *Atlanta Independent*, 6 Jun. 1906; quoted in Pomerantz, *Where Peachtree Meets Sweet Auburn*, 73.
23 *Atlanta Evening News*, 22 Sept. 1906; quoted in Pomerantz, *Where Peachtree Meets Sweet Auburn*, 73–4.
24 Shorter versions of this section on Rhodes Hall were previously discussed in Richard Utz, *Medievalism: A Manifesto* (Kalamazoo, MI: ARC Humanities Press, 2017), 53–68; and Richard Utz, "Cupid at the Castle: Romance, Medievalism, and Race at Atlanta's Rhodes Hall," *Public Medievalist*, 4 Apr. 2017, https://www.publicmedievalist.com/rhodes-hall.
25 See the entry on the "Rhodes Family Papers" at the Atlanta History Center, https://aspace-atlantahistorycenter.galileo.usg.edu/repositories/2/resources/282 (accessed 15 Sept. 2018).
26 Newcomers to Atlanta often marvel at how so many of the city's thoroughfares frequently and unexpectedly change names. The cause is, as Kevin M. Kruse documents, that white Atlantans tried very hard to avoid having a "black address" (*White Flight: Atlanta and the Making of Modern Conservatism* [Princeton, NJ: Princeton University Press, 2005], 62).
27 On Peachtree Street and Rhodes Hall as one of its most spectacular residences, see William Bailey Williford, *Peachtree Street, Atlanta* (Athens: University of Georgia Press, 1962), 100–1. The official Georgia Trust for Historic Preservation website for Rhodes Hall contains basic information on the history and current use of the building: http://www.rhodeshall.org (accessed 15 Sept. 2018).
28 Cited according to the entry on "Rhodes Memorial Hall" by the City of Atlanta's Urban Design Commission, http://www.atlantaga.gov/index.aspx?page=427 (accessed 25 Aug. 2018). For an informative overview, see also the entry "Rhodes Hall" in the Society of Architectural Historians *Archipedia*, https://sah-archipedia.org/buildings/GA-01-121-0045 (accessed 16 Sept. 2018).
29 On the medievalist stained- and painted-glass productions of the von Gerichten brothers, see John M. Clark, *German Village Stories behind the Bricks* (Charleston, SC: History Press, 2015), 140–3.
30 The portraits show Albert Sidney Johnston; Nathan Bedford Forrest; Joseph Eggleston Johnston; Franklin Buchanan; Raphael Semmes; Josiah Tattnall; Howell Cobb; Alexander Hamilton Stephens; Robert Augustus Toombs; Clement Anselm Evans; John B. Gordon; Joseph Wheeler Jr.; Marcellus A. Stovall; Pierre Gustave Toulant Beauregard; and James Longstreet. Most of them were born in or had some other connection with the state of Georgia.
31 I am indebted to Dr. John Turman, novelist and tour guide at Rhodes Hall, who, on 14 May 2013, provided me with an eleven-page document, "The Rise and Fall

of the Confederacy: Art Glass Windows in Rhodes Memorial Hall," which includes a detailed description of all windows.

32 After Amanda Rhodes's death in 1927 and Amos Rhodes's in 1928, their children deeded the house to the State of Georgia, specifying that the property should be used for "historic purposes." Between 1930 and 1965, the building served as the home of the State Archives. (Margaret Mitchell conducted research there.) In 1983, the nonprofit Georgia Trust for Historic Preservation signed a long-term lease with the State of Georgia. Serving as headquarters for the Georgia Trust, Rhodes Hall has undergone significant restoration, most importantly the return of the original mahogany staircase and stained-glass windows in 1990.

33 See "Event Rentals," Rhodes Hall, http://www.rhodeshall.org/event-rentals (accessed 17 Sept. 2018).

34 See "History & Tours," Rhodes Hall, http://www.rhodeshall.org/history-tours (accessed 17 Sept. 2018).

35 See "Going Green," Rhodes Hall, http://www.rhodeshall.org/a-greener-rhodes-hall (accessed 17 Sept. 2018).

36 "Margaret Mitchell House," Atlanta History Center, http://www.atlantahistorycenter.com/explore/destinations/margaret-mitchell-house (accessed 17 Sept. 2018).

37 "Confederate Monument Interpretation Guide," Atlanta History Center, https://www.atlantahistorycenter.com/research/confederate-monuments (accessed 24 Sept. 2019).

38 "Historical & Environmental Education Center," Stone Mountain Park, http://www.stonemountainpark.com/Activities/History-Nature/Confederate-Hall (accessed 18 Sept. 2018).

39 "History," Stone Mountain Park, http://www.stonemountainpark.com/About/History (accessed 18 Sept. 2018).

40 Martin Luther King Jr., "I Have a Dream," https://www.archives.gov/files/social-media/transcripts/transcript-march-pt3-of-3-2602934.pdf (accessed 27 Feb. 2021).

41 "Stone Mountain Highland Games," www.smhg.org (accessed 18 Sept. 2018).

42 "Clan Registration Information," http://www.smhg.org/clans.php (accessed 18 Sept. 2018). Several of the organizations affiliated with the Stone Mountain Highland Games, including the Claranald Trust for Scotland, are actively involved in medieval reenactment and living history events.

43 "A Mission Statement," #Rock Stone Mountain (blog), 10 Feb. 2016, https://rockstonemountain14.blogspot.com/2016/02/a-mission-statement.html (accessed 18 Sept. 2018).

44 The Klan's Blood Drop Cross could be seen as an exception. However, as the Anti-Defamation League (ADL) explains, this symbol's complex modern history does not include overt medieval connections. See the ADL's entry on "Blood Drop Cross," https://www.adl.org/education/references/hate-symbols/blood-drop-cross (accessed 15 Sept. 2018).

45 Nico Voigtländer and Hans-Joachim Voth, "Persecution Perpetuated: The Medieval Origins of Anti-Semitic Violence in Nazi Germany," *Quarterly Journal of Economics* 127, no. 3 (2012): 1339–92.

46 Statement by the Reverend Dr. Kelly Brown Douglas, the cathedral's canon theologian, on the cathedral's website: "Cathedral to Explore Racial Justice through Public Forums, Arts, Worship," Washington National Cathedral, 8 June 2016, https://cathedral.org/press-room/cathedral-to-explore-racial-justice-through-public-forums-arts-worship (accessed 3 July 2019).

6 Medieval New York City: A Walk through *The Stations of the Cross*

CANDACE BARRINGTON

New York City worked itself into my life at walking pace.

Teju Cole, *Open City*

My account of medieval New York City traces a series of three walks, *pilgrimages* one might say, that I made to better understand this modern American city's engagement with the Middle Ages, a historical period that might seem unrelated to a city not founded until 1624.[1] Previously, study of New York's urban engagement with the medieval past – that is, its "medievalism" – has often been structured around buildings designed and built during the Gothic and Romanesque Revival (and re-revival) between 1830 and 1930. Because limiting my study to these buildings seemed to ignore the breadth and depth of New York City's multiple medievalisms, I made two decisions. One, I would experience New York's medievalisms by walking, the most purposeful way for listening to the conversations among the city's varied medievalisms and the people who lived within them. Two, I would structure my walks as a pilgrimage following *The Stations of the Cross: Art. Passion. Justice*, a 2018 public art installation inviting "people of all faiths and spiritualities … on a creative and contemplative journey through Manhattan to consider injustice across the human experience."[2] Part of a project co-founded by Dr. Aaron Rosen and the Reverend Dr. Catriona Laing, *The Stations of the Cross* re-creates itself every year with different artwork in a different global city. In its 2018 Manhattan iteration, the pilgrimage's fourteen stops included nine installations housed in examples of architectural medievalism and another two installations invoking medievalism in other ways. Podcasts associated with each stop placed the artwork in purposeful dialogue with the installation's larger themes – art, passion, justice.

Although *The Stations of the Cross* does not require following the pilgrimage route on foot, I found – as does the narrator in Teju Cole's medievalizing novel of New York City, *Open City* – walking from one station to the next opened my eyes to the city's medievalism riches.³ Consequently, my walking pilgrimage revealed medievalism's role in furthering (or hindering) the installation's dialogue with the themes of art, passion, and justice.

The Stations of the Cross's fourteen stops temporarily mapped a medieval devotional practice, the Stations of the Cross, along Manhattan's twelve-mile north-south axis. (I italicize the art installation to distinguish it from the devotional practice.) Drawing on the Via Dolorosa, a pilgrimage within Jerusalem where the devout retrace the sites associated with Christ's Passion from his sentencing to his entombment, the medieval Stations of the Cross repackaged this pilgrimage for European cities and churches.⁴ Whereas Jerusalem's Via Dolorosa began as a way to collapse the time between the Passion's *then* and the pilgrim's *now* (thereby allowing the pilgrim to witness imaginatively and affectively the events of centuries past), the Stations of the Cross (which were fixed at fourteen after the medieval period) collapsed not only time but also the space between Jerusalem and Europe (thereby allowing the pilgrim to experience distant events). By designating local shrines to represent Jerusalem's traditional stations, Europeans were able to bring Roman-occupied Jerusalem to the pilgrim (rather than the pilgrim to the holy city). Time and space further collapsed when the devotional practice of the Stations of the Cross was compressed to fit within the confines of a local parish or church sanctuary. *The Stations of the Cross*'s Manhattan installation reversed that trajectory by lifting the devotional event from the confines of any single parish and stretching the procession from the island's northern tip to the 9/11 Memorial at its southern end. In this expanded urban environment, *The Stations of the Cross* provided more than opportunities to meditate on the fourteen sets of images. By linking medieval devotional practice to contemporary messages of social justice, *The Stations of the Cross* harnessed medievalism to promote "the spiritual dimensions of the refugee crisis and immigration reform."⁵

This lengthy pilgrimage through an urban environment provided the basic itinerary of my three walks down the island's spine and scaffolds my account of New York City's medievalism. Additionally, in ways likely unanticipated by the installation's creators, the walking space between each station allowed me to absorb how the city's other medievalisms contributed to the installations' objectives; I was interested equally in the fourteen stations *and* in the spaces between them. Although my walks followed *The Stations of the Cross*'s numerical order, generally moving south, my path from one station to the next followed both my personal inclinations and my arbitrary curiosities. Imagining New York City as the Via Dolorosa, a pilgrimage, a Jerusalem, the centre of the universe, I discerned the cultural power of the city's saturating medievalisms, so embedded that they no longer feel static or foreign, so integral that they turn Manhattan into a potent platform for *The Stations of the Cross* and its messages.

Before recounting my walks, I should mention three overlapping categories of medievalism that contextualize the role of medievalisms in New York City's development and self-presentation. Few medievalisms I encountered on my walks fall squarely into any of these three categories; nevertheless, as my walks illustrate, the categories highlight the way medievalisms in New York City create a complex exchange between the present and the past, a conversation that binds communities and justifies (and sometimes dismantles) social hierarchies.

First are the *transplants,* verifiable medieval artefacts brought to the United States for limited display to the public and for preservation and study by certified experts. Transplanted medievalism provides the centre of gravity for academic medievalists, who generally focus on "pastist medievalist studies."[6] The Cloisters (along with its mother institution, the Metropolitan Museum of Art, and other repositories of medieval manuscripts and artwork at Fordham University, Columbia University, and the Morgan Library and Museum) hosts some prominent examples.[7] The justifications for these cultural transplants echo the reasons for other varieties of cultural expropriation: safekeeping, education, passion. Buttressing these avowed justifications is "tycoon medievalism," Kathleen Davis's term for an instance of philanthropy described by Pierre Bourdieu as "the conversion of economic capital into symbol capital, which produces relations of dependence that have an economic basis but are disguised under a veil of moral relations."[8]

In the second category, self-conscious *re-creations* evoke a medieval past and assert a degree of authority tied to that past through a visual culture that limns and maintains traditional boundaries.[9] Some powerful examples are architectural, whose visual, spatial, and material ties to the medieval past assert the legitimacy of institutions those buildings house. Religious and public institutions built during the Gothic revival (1830–1930) are obvious examples. These purposeful re-creations, some nearly two centuries old now, prove difficult to modernize and plead for expensive restoration. Cursory observations reveal that only a few receive the necessary resources. The ones that retain their grandeur are supported by hefty endowments or enormous grants. Some, stranded in neighbourhoods no longer associated with luxury and wealth, are relegated to the poor, providing housing and social services. New York City's medievalizing re-creations measure, then, the growing distance between the infamous 1 per cent and the rest.

The third category comprises continuing *residual* practices rooted in the Middle Ages, including religious ceremonies, rituals, burial practices, and modes of civic and social organization. Although these residual rituals and other "religious subject matter" are sometimes overlooked in medievalism studies, this category structures communities by helping them maintain their collective identity through ties to the past.[10]

Along the way, I make a secondary argument that New York City provides an excellent laboratory for testing the concept of global medievalism.[11] From the moment the Dutch West India Company established a settlement on Manhattan Island in the 1620s, the city's founding was a global rather than a local act, bringing together people and practices from at least three continents: North America, Europe, and Africa. Settlement brought to the island practices that had evolved over the long global Middle Ages, a temporal category bookended by two periods of heightened global engagement, the first ending around 500 CE, the second beginning around 1500 CE. Both the global and medieval features have persisted as the city expanded across the subsequent 400 years to encompass the entire island and four more boroughs. Like European medievalism, global medievalism's manifestations fall into three categories: curated items dating from the global Middle Ages and imported for their prestige value; re-creations inspired by artefacts associated with the global Middle Ages; and rituals and practices that continue from the global Middle Ages. By noting these previously overlooked manifestations, we can see that New York City's medievalism is both broad *and* global.

Station 1: Jesus Is Condemned (at the Cloisters)

My pilgrimage began on a northwestern promontory whose visibility up and down the Hudson River made it the spot where Revolutionary War military strategists chose to defend (unsuccessfully) the lower Hudson from the British.[12] For that same long view, John D. Rockefeller Jr. chose it a century and a half later as the site for his gift to New York City: the Metropolitan Museum's medieval outpost, the Cloisters. To reach the site, visitors can follow a paved road by foot, automobile, or bus, but I climbed a series of narrow stone stairs with crooked handrails and worn stones winding through a series of hillside gardens. The trees and undergrowth muffled the traffic from Riverside Highway and the Henry Hudson Parkway skimming the park's lower edge. This urban wilderness, Fort Tryon Park, was designed by Frederick Olmsted Jr. around four naturalistic elements (the beautiful, the picturesque, the sublime, and the gardenesque) and is maintained with funds donated by David Rockefeller. The park grants visitors a sense of entering an enchanted European past where knights fought, monks prayed, and churls delved.[13] Moving away from the busy neighbourhood at the park's base – more densely populated and developed today than a century ago – conveys the sense of walking into another space and time whose shadows withhold secrets from the uninitiated. The picturesque, terraced gardens with arched gateways and collapsing tunnels left from a previous estate evoke an archaic past so strongly that it accommodates both an annual Medieval Festival and such theatrical events as Robert Steven Ackerman's theatre piece *Joan of Arc*.[14] While neither European nor medieval, Fort Tryon Park illustrates New Yorkers' efforts to transport an ethos of ontological stability across an ocean and many centuries.

At the top of the park, the Cloisters continues this time and space travel, exuding an orderly monastic calm that begins with the cool smell of old stone, much of it dismantled in Europe and reassembled in New York during the years surrounding the Great War. The transported stones preserve in Manhattan a medieval past – with its supposed ontological stability promising quiet hierarchies and unquestioned religiosity – that no longer seemed tenable in Europe. Built of *spolia* abandoned to farmers for barns and stables, the Cloisters testified to the United States' growing dominance in the new world order and its commitment to preserving Old World remnants that Europe had neither the will nor the ability to preserve. Once built, the pristinely maintained facility housed fragile artworks from throughout the European Middle Ages, and its manicured gardens preserved a contemplative way of life seemingly lost in war-ravaged Europe but safe in America. Ostensibly a sober memorial to Europe's medieval past, the Cloisters serves equally as a monument of American exceptionalism and dominance (here grounded in a medieval past translated to the United States), messages clearly conveyed before a visitor enters the museum proper.

To begin at the Cloisters is to begin at the motherlode of American medievalism. Built in the 1930s with the funds and supervision of John D. Rockefeller Jr. (1874–1960) to house his medieval collection numbering more than 2,000 objects, the Cloisters operates in a tension between generous authenticity and imperious vandalism. Rockefeller bought property and paid for buildings that provide international tourists and Americans of all stripes the opportunity to grasp in an afternoon the best of medieval European culture. They can stroll through a series of cloisters and gardens surrounded by sacred and secular spaces, constructed with stones, columns, and other salvaged *spolia* (from Saint-Michel-de-Cuxa, Saint-Guilhem-le-Désert, Trie-sur-Baïse, Froville, and other European sites) and arranged to create a microcosm of western European architecture spanning every style from the Romanesque to the High Gothic.[15] The rooms are tastefully enhanced with artistic treasures and relics plucked from a war-ravaged continent, including a twelfth-century ivory cross, possibly from Bury St. Edmunds; stained-glass windows from the castle chapel at Ebreichsdorf, Austria; a mid-thirteenth-century sculpture of the Virgin taken from a Strasbourg Cathedral choir screen; and the exquisite late medieval Unicorn Tapestries from Charente, France.[16] The museum's initial champions claimed their efforts had saved the stones from being turned into barns or paving stones, and the artwork from being melted down, taken apart, or allowed to waste away. Because something always seems in the process of being restored, the fear was not unfounded (see figure 6.1). Offering "a harmonious and evocative setting for more than 2,000 exceptional artworks and architectural elements from the medieval West," the Cloisters was Rockefeller's gift not only to New York City but also to Europe.[17] The American robber baron claimed to have saved medieval Europe when Europeans could not. At the same time, he created a monument to social stratification as eternal and divinely ordained.

As the first stop for *The Stations of the Cross*, the Cloisters and its four selected illuminated manuscripts showed how medievalism could be appropriated to

Medieval New York City: A Walk through *The Stations of the Cross* 135

6.1. The Cloisters' Gothic Chapel, where the tombs are being studied for conservation. (All photographs in this chapter are the author's.)

ends different from those conservative values generally associated with it (and contributing to the creation of the Cloisters). Rather than justifying entrenched social hierarchies, established Anglo-American institutional norms, and ingrained white supremacy, the medieval illuminations contributed to the larger purpose of *The Stations of the Cross*: to address the ways racism, income inequality, and xenophobia pervert the pursuit of justice. Station 1 invited viewers to contemplate Jesus's trial before Pilate with exquisite illuminations from four manuscripts: Jean Pucelle's *The Hours of Jeanne d'Avreux, Queen of France* (c. 1324–58); the Cloisters Apocalypse (c. 1330); the Limbourg Brothers' *The Belles Heures of Jean de France, duc de Berry* (c. 1405–8/9); and Simon Bening's *Book of Hours* (c. 1530–5).[18] Of the four, only Pucelle's includes an illustration of the trial; the other displayed images focus on the Holy Family's flight from Egypt, and the accompanying podcast reinforced that family's sense of peril as parallel to the current plight of refugee families. To be sure, these Christian devotionals illustrating the passions of Christ and Christian saints are concerned with saintly suffering and divine justice. Nevertheless, the four manuscripts belong to the Cloisters' collection for their exceptional beauty and artistry; given their production history, provenance, and current display in the Cloisters, they fit into that part of American medievalism used to assert the wealth and privilege of the elite. Whereas the manuscripts' original devotional and social purposes aligned with each other, in an egalitarian society (such as the United States aspires to be), these two purposes are in conflict, a conflict Station 1 foregrounds.

Station 2: Jesus Takes Up the Cross (at City College of New York)

My walk from Station 1 to Station 2 passed through lower Inwood Heights and Washington Heights, where scattered examples of re-created medievalisms appear to mean little to residents. They convey no prestige, and these deteriorating, faded medievalisms now shelter and serve the working poor. My path through these neighbourhoods aptly led to an institution founded on being "controlled by the popular will," the City College of New York. The first free institution of higher education in the United States, CCNY was founded in 1847 by Townsend Harris and moved to its current location in the middle of Harlem at the turn of the twentieth century. Reminiscent of the stark two-toned features of the Duomo in Florence and Catholic University in Leuven, the neo-Gothic buildings of dark stone and white terracotta ornament stand out from the surrounding urban drab.[19]

CCNY's ambitions – to be an institution of higher learning on par with Europe's best universities, for all people, without regard for creed or ethnic origins – are reflected in its 14,000-square-foot Grand Hall.[20] As with the Cloisters, CCNY and its architectural medievalism result from a wealthy benefactor's gift to the city; that gift, however, has been more expensive to maintain than the donor anticipated. In 1997, CCNY spent $12,800,000 to bring back the

Grand Hall from the brink of ruin. At the time, the City University of New York (CUNY) system (of which CCNY is a part) faced dire financial straits. Deficits and cuts in state contributions required a 10 per cent cut in faculty positions and a 40 per cent increase in tuition.[21] Back-of-the-envelope calculations show that the restoration and modernization costs for the Great Hall would have paid the increased four-year tuition costs for 900 students. As inspirational as these buildings are, they (like other old buildings of any style) are expensive to maintain. Institutions like CCNY see value in these buildings and commit to preserving and maintaining them because they are viewed less as exotic imports and more as aesthetic statements of institutional values. These medieval re-creations, as costly and irrational as their upkeep might seem, work with the university's inherent residual medievalism – the continuation of the functions and ideals of its medieval university progenitors – to justify their preservation.

The art installed for the second station, Aithan Shapira's *Hope* (2012–18), features white life preservers – circular flotation devices – cast in concrete. Disastrously ineffective if ever put to their nominal purpose of saving a drowning person, the concrete life preservers simultaneously reflected and questioned the host institution's values (and its white terracotta facing). At the same time that *Hope* reflected the fact that CCNY has historically provided educational opportunities to those (such as Jews and other minorities) denied admission elsewhere, the installation also questioned CCNY's ability to deliver on that promise by suggesting both are heavy objects unable to float or provide rescue from desperate situations. Shapira describes the inherent contradiction the art shares with its title, *Hope*, and (I argue) with the college itself: "Hope is integral – some is collected, some is inherited. I want, I think we all want, for it to be a simple, beautifully elegant thing, but the more you draw from it, it begins to look more like despair, or re-purposed despair."[22] Although speaking to the contemporary moment, Shapira's *Hope* also embodied medievalism's inherent tensions between the past and the present, utility and aesthetics, and benefit and cost.

Station 3: Jesus Falls for the First Time (at St. Mary's Episcopal Church)

After blocks of nondescript post-war architecture along Amsterdam Avenue, the sight of St. Mary's Gothic belfry peeking over the clutter is startling (see figure 6.2). Compared to the grand examples of the Cloisters and CCNY, St. Mary's modest eloquence exemplifies the changing uses of medievalism.[23] Built by affluent congregants, the small 1908 sanctuary would have fit well into the rural parish it served then, effortlessly melding medieval elements with a modest clarity associated with earlier American religious buildings and suggesting a certain continuity in American architecture with medieval precedents.[24] The church now serves a much poorer parish than the one that built it. Maintaining the buildings and grounds presents a struggle for the parish, especially in conjunction with

6.2. St. Mary's Episcopal Church, whose simple Gothic elements stand out from the surrounding urban drab.

the pressing needs of those it serves. Like many other examples of Manhattan's re-created medievalism, St. Mary's has deteriorated severely. Paradoxically, the decay makes it feel more medieval to twenty-first-century observers accustomed to modern cinema's visual codes, which often depict the Middle Ages as having always appeared darkly aged.[25] Not only does it resemble the current state of its (unrestored) European antecedents, but the changing demographics of its parish and its urbanized context mean that its residual medievalism is foregrounded.

The parish hosted Mark Dukes's *Our Lady of Ferguson and All Those Killed by Gun Violence* (2016). On loan from Trinity Church Wall Street, *Our Lady of Ferguson* was proudly exhibited as a centrepiece on the front altar. St. Mary's was one of the few sites that posted signs outside inviting passers-by to view its station. With its use of embossed gold leaf and its depiction of the Virgin and the Child in the traditional orans gesture, the art resembles a medieval Russian Orthodox icon. Powerfully, that orans gesture echoes the "Hands up! Don't shoot!" pose associated with Michael Brown of Ferguson, Missouri. By transforming Brown into a Christlike figure, the image asserts that he (and others killed by gun violence) have been sacrificed while leaving unanswered the purpose behind that sacrifice.[26] Dukes's icon also confronts the conversation regarding Black Madonnas. Unlike the Black Madonna in Chartres (recently whitened during a restoration process, removing centuries of smoky residue darkening the face in the image) and more in keeping with the Black Madonna in Soweto (whose dark skin is intentional and speaks to the Black people oppressed by apartheid and murdered during riots), *Our Lady of Ferguson* imagines a holy mother who suffers for all the fallen, not just those of European ancestry.[27] Placed at Station 3 (Jesus Falls for the First Time), the icon reminds us that unjust burdens continue to be imposed on the oppressed.

I found it difficult to leave this poignant station, where residual medievalism and the church's mission align. Surrounded by collapsing buildings and utility repairs that tear up nearby Amsterdam Avenue, St. Mary's has been humbly maintained with loving care, but a sign on the wall informing visitors of the need to raise money for repairs indicates the strain maintenance places on the congregation. When I asked about the competing needs the parish faced – new roof and homeless souls – the rector saw those needs as working together. With its commitment to community, the congregation carries its mouldy medievalism not as a burden but as a sign of its deep roots in and commitment to the neighbourhood it serves.

Station 4: Jesus Meets His Mother (at the Cathedral of St. John the Divine)

South of St. Mary's along Amsterdam Avenue, transplanted and re-created medievalism gradually returns, first modestly in such tokens as arched doorways and Gothic-inspired rooftop metalwork and then grandly in the massive tower of Riverside Church looming over the squat Collegiate Gothic campus of Union Theological Seminary, not far from Columbia University's Butler Library and its preserved medieval manuscripts. Medievalism reaches its full majestic presence on Amsterdam Avenue at the Cathedral of St. John the Divine. While the Cloisters might be the *locus classicus* of New York medievalism, with its imported medieval objects and its deep commitment to creating an aura of medieval authenticity, the cathedral at 113th Street might be the most medieval edifice in the city. Under construction for 125 years and following medieval construction methods, it remains unfinished, with no immediate plans to complete the towers or to add the southern transept. From the outside, that incompletion feels more like deterioration and diminishment, with pollution staining the older stones and mortar, leaving distinctions between old and new construction, while surrounding high-rise buildings diminish the towers' stature (see figure 6.3). On the other side of the large bronze doors, however, the cathedral reveals its grandeur, asserting itself as America's cathedral, a role parallel to London's Westminster Abbey. Its American Poets' Corner commemorates

6.3. The Cathedral of St. John the Divine and adjacent buildings that make the medieval building appear smaller and older than it is.

Walt Whitman, Emily Dickinson, and Langston Hughes. The simple concrete nave floor is embedded with bronze medallions representing pilgrimage sites from around the world. The Great Rose Window in the west façade glows with blue tones. The cathedral incorporates playful elements, such as Keith Haring's 1990 artwork *The Life of Christ* (a bronze and white-gold triptych) and Tom Otterness's cartoonish *memento mori* (ceramic figures mischievously tucked into niches on the Zipper Arch and other columns). It also displays near the choir and altar several pieces signalling the cathedral's embrace of non-European cultures and faith traditions: Siamese book cabinets, Japanese cloisonné vases, Jewish menorahs, and Persian lamps. This most medieval of New York City edifices refuses to pigeonhole "medieval" as exclusively European or Christian.

The cathedral's established sensibility of bridging faith traditions and embracing non-traditional art forms fits well with Station 4, Jesus Meets His Mother, and the associated art installation, *Marsiya*, a 2018 video by Pakistani artist Dua Abbas. Situated in St. James Chapel, south of the altar and adjacent to the apse's radiating Chapels of the Tongues dedicated to seven immigrant groups, the installation reiterated the cross-cultural conversations the cathedral promotes: it interprets Mary's mourning through Shiite women's mourning rituals that stem from the seventh-century martyrdom of the imam Husayn ibn Ali (grandson of the Prophet). Fusing Persian, Arab, Hindi, and Christian traditions, the video's stop-action animation integrates images from original family photographs with images based on a fifteenth-century altarpiece at the Cloisters. Abbas states that she "was interested in similarities between the figures of Mary (mother of Jesus) and Fatima (mother of Husayn) and the cultures of remembrance that have developed around the sufferings of their sons."[28] Abbas's *Marsiya* melded European and global medievalism, reflecting the cathedral's ongoing ecumenical efforts and sense of community.

My pilgrimage coincided with the cathedral's Holy Week observations, so I witnessed the ecumenical spirit of the cathedral during its Maundy Thursday service, where repeated efforts to level the social and global hierarchies (hierarchies that allowed the cathedral to exist in the first place) were mixed with high Anglican ritual (best described as high Victorian medievalism, in which the bishop wore his mitred hat and carried a crozier; the children's choir wore high ruffled robes; and everything was orderly and rehearsed, with carefully detailed instructions provided the attendees). The congregation's commitment to the poor made certain no one was left out of the foot-washing, the centrepiece of Maundy Thursday services; worshippers in expensive business suits sat alongside worshippers in threadbare sweatshirts for the ritual. The leadership resisted the antisemitism inherent in the Holy Week scriptures with a note from the Ecumenical and Interfaith Commission that "'the Jews' … [refers not] to Jews as a people, then or now." At the end, the altars were stripped and prepared for the Good Friday vigil, followed by a three-hour reading of selected cantos from Dante's *The Divine Comedy*, a twenty-five-year tradition at the cathedral. With his Italian and Englished verses read by eminent poets and translators, the medieval poet led us down to Hell, up through Purgatory, and into Paradise. And thus ended the first segment of my medieval New York City walk.

Station 5: Simon of Cyrene Helps Jesus Carry the Cross (at the Riverside Church)

My walk resumed at the Riverside Church, where Siona Benjamin's *Exodus: I See Myself in You* (2016) stretched across the altar of Christ Chapel. Benjamin's seven brightly hued panels amalgamated the iconography of multiple religions and cultures, without letting one dominate. Instead, the panels ask the onlooking pilgrim to accept the burdens of the dispossessed, the persecuted, and the marginalized – to be like Simon who helped Jesus carry his cross, to be like her painting's blue-skinned angel who helps Syrian refugees in their exodus from their homeland.[29] The Riverside congregation has been grappling with such requests for thirty years. On the one hand, they meet in a Gothic edifice built and financed by John D. Rockefeller Jr. as the Roaring Twenties gave way to the Great Depression. Designed by Charles Collen, the same architect Rockefeller later commissioned for the Cloisters' final design, Riverside Church and its chancel-floor labyrinth are modelled on Chartres Cathedral in France.[30] Completely finished and scrupulously maintained, the church declares the benefits of a wealthy benefactor and his endowment. On the other hand, the magnificent building masks the repeated financial and spiritual crises the shrinking congregation has faced since 1988, as its membership has shifted from predominantly mainline Protestant to Black Gospel. By suggesting that any skin colour can carry compassion, Benjamin's painting awakens the residual medievalism of the parish church and its obligations to model itself on Simon as it compassionately aids its local community.

In many ways, Riverside shares the precarious fate of other examples of New York City's high architectural medievalism. To its south is St. Michael's Episcopal Church (Ninety-Ninth Street and Amsterdam Avenue), built in the 1890s in an "imagined Romanesque and Byzantine style" and featuring a series of Tiffany stained-glass windows.[31] It too has faced the problems of an expensive building in a changing neighbourhood. By the late twentieth century, poorer congregants outnumbered affluent ones, and the church could no longer balance a budget that included extensive maintenance and building refurbishments. To recover financially and to find a way forward, the church sold 70,000 square feet of air rights for $12.5 million in 2005 to a developer. With those rights, the developer constructed a pair of (for now) anomalous condominium high rises to the west; with a quarter of the proceeds, the church restored its dilapidated buildings. St. Michael's dilemma (how to both rescue its building and serve its parish community) and its bargain with the devil (selling air rights) are not uncommon. Similar strategies were followed by congregations at Riverside Church, the Cathedral of St. John the Divine, the Byzantine-style Christ Church (Park Avenue and Sixtieth Street), the Italianate Gothic Holy Cross Church (Forty-Second Street in Hell's Kitchen), and the Romanesque Revival St. John Nepomucene Parish (East Sixty-Sixth Street). These compromises result from a loathing to tear down or abandon grand medieval revival buildings so difficult to maintain.

No less easy to maintain are residual medievalisms. On the opposite side of the island, in Spanish Harlem, Pallottine fathers continue to say the Latin Tridentine Mass (as well as masses in English, Spanish, Polish, and Haitian Creole) at Our Lady of Mount Carmel, home of the Pontifical Shrine of Our Lady of Mount Carmel. The church, in a neighbourhood once home to Italian immigrants, now serves a Latinx parish. Congregants for the pre–Vatican II Latin Mass, however, represent a wide swath of believers. Despite its efforts at authenticity, the mass felt hurried and bungled; attendants unfamiliar with the extra accoutrements and the priest's shaky Latin demonstrated the difficulty of returning to "original" or "authentic" practices when participants have pushed this particular form of residual medievalism to the margins of their lives.

Station 6: Veronica Wipes the Face of Jesus (at the Church of the Heavenly Rest)

South and west of Spanish Harlem, transplanted and re-created medievalisms thrive in the Upper East Side. Here, Station 6's host, the Church of the Heavenly Rest, sits atop Carnegie Hill across from Central Park's Jacqueline Kennedy Onassis Reservoir. Its truncated sanctuary, with many neo-Gothic hallmarks such as the tripartite division of space, a rose window, ample stained glass, and an altar reredos, was built with Art Deco details between 1926 and 1929. Although the church clearly announces its modernity, it displays a deeply affecting blend of medieval features, especially on first entry. Missing, though, is the unmistakable scented mixture of old stones, layers of incense, and damp wood. Heavenly Rest instead features faint wafts of coffee, floating up from the undercroft converted into a coffee shop, with communal tables for well-to-do mothers of preschool children and others with free weekday mornings. Creating a neighbourhood gathering spot that welcomes people of every denomination, gender, and heritage for music, edification, and refreshment has become the hallmark of expensive Upper East Side medievalized churches, such as Heavenly Rest and, further south, St. Bartholomew's (St. Bart's) and Christ Church (see figure 6.4).

Inside Heavenly Rest's sanctuary, Michael Takeo Magruder's *Lamentation for the Forsaken* (2016–18) stood in sharp contrast to the cosy comfort of the coffee shop.[32] This video installation juxtaposes images of the Shroud of Turin with images of refugees fleeing the violence and genocide of the Syrian civil war. To enhance the identification between the crucified Christ and the Syrian war's victims, Magruder has engraved the Shroud's image with the names of individuals unable to find sanctuary (within or beyond Syria's borders) and therefore

6.4. St. Bartholomew's Church and its street-facing eatery, a trend among churches in high-end neighbourhoods.

killed in the deadly war. And the video's Syrian women (who all wear hijabs) remind us that a Syrian woman's physical appearance is akin more to that of Veronica, Jesus's veiled comforter, than to that of European women. In this historical dialectic between victim and comforter, their roles become indistinguishable with time. Moreover, by appearing in a church centred in one of New York's wealthiest neighbourhood, Magruder's video implored congregations like Heavenly Rest to integrate the re-created medievalism of their sanctuary with the residual medievalism of "sanctuary," a medieval practice in which human compassion suspends the inevitability of legal prosecution by allowing a space where divine protection is inviolate.[33]

Whatever other residual medieval practices are found in eastern Manhattan's midsection (such as the Mass for Souls in Purgatory, a remnant of a distinctly medieval theology and ritual performed monthly by the New York Purgatorial Society at Lexington Avenue's Church of St. Vincent Ferrer), the area boasts an abundance of striking re-created architectural medievalisms.[34] The Upper East Side and Lenox Hill, two neighbourhoods long associated with wealth, retain some remarkably varied examples. The main thoroughfares are studded with Gothic churches, including Central Presbyterian (formerly Park Avenue Baptist Church), the first of Rockefeller's grand-scale medievalisms designed by Collen. Numerous homes and large institutional buildings were designed in the Romanesque, Gothic, and Tudor styles. Although many homes have been razed, small reminders remain, such as the unusual ironwork on the 1925 entryway at 820 Park Avenue, with its "dark, hammered shapes worked in medieval designs, including the shapes of blades and a knight."[35] The remaining venerable examples have generally been converted into condominiums or otherwise repurposed.[36] Of these restorations, perhaps the most breathtaking is Park Avenue Armory, one of several nineteenth-century armouries evoking medieval military embattlements built in all five boroughs.[37] More gentlemen's club than military barracks, the Armory's front rooms suggest baronial quarters, part of the medieval imaginary the American elite laid claim to. Now it serves as a venue for experimental dramatic, visual, and musical productions that take advantage of its large, unobstructed space. Supported by a nonprofit institution that oversees the building's restoration and offers educational arts programming to underserved students, the Park Avenue Armory exemplifies the best imaginative repurposing of the city's re-created medieval architecture.

Embedded in this medievalism dreamscape are museums housing artefacts of transplanted and re-created medievalism, both European and global. The Smithsonian's Cooper Hewitt Museum of Design displays furniture, skyscrapers, light fixtures, cigarette boxes, and numerous metal-worked and woodworked decorative arts inspired by medieval tapestries and cathedrals. The Metropolitan Museum displays transplanted medieval art and armour, and its gift shop artefacts (ranging from museum-quality reproductions to dime-store trinkets) sometimes blur the distinction between transplanted and re-created medievalism. The Jewish Museum includes medieval artefacts only recently seen in dialogue with the Christian Middle Ages. The Asia Society and Museum hosted an exhibit of the ninth-century Tang Shipwreck Treasure, an important collection of metal coins, golden dishes, and ceramic ware (whether in fragments or whole) attesting to the mercantile and cultural contacts connecting western Europe, the Middle East, and Asia during the early medieval period. Together with its re-created and residual medievalisms, these museum-worthy transplanted medievalisms contribute to the Upper East Side's reputation as "the Silk Stocking District."[38]

Station 7: Jesus Falls for the Second Time (at the Church of St. Paul the Apostle)

Reaching the next station, located on the southwest corner of Central Park at Columbus Circle, requires leaving New York City's grand precinct of medievalism and entering the region of modernism and postmodernism (which themselves do not totally abandon medievalism).[39] The Church of St. Paul the Apostle, "the Mother Church of the Paulist Fathers," is one of the neighbourhood's few remaining examples of full-blown architectural medievalism and features a sanctuary with the openness of early Christian Roman basilicas and a subdued Romanesque exterior.[40] Dedicated in 1885, St. Paul's was built with stonework recovered when the Croton Aqueduct was decommissioned and dismantled. At the time, it was Manhattan's second-largest church and included an adjoining school and convent. In the past fifty years, increasing financial pressures and a diminishing parish community have forced the Paulist fathers to subdivide the adjoining property and to sell development rights to avoid bankruptcy. These difficult decisions have allowed the parish to maintain its historical character – for now.[41]

Inside, Nicola Green's *Day 6, Sacrifice/Embrace* (2010) speaks to the uncertainties and frequent falls associated with any large project, such as serving a parish and building a church. Depicting Barack Obama in silhouette after his 2008 election, Green's canvas shows only his arms and head as a "distillation of [her] experiences in Chicago on the night Obama was elected President. He was embracing a new beginning, but it was also a moment of sacrifice as he prepares to become the most powerful man in the world." Neither "an image of triumph [n]or a happy ending," the painting signals "the beginning of a long road."[42] Midway through *The Stations of the Cross*, Green's *Day 6 Sacrifice/Embrace* sparked a politically charged conversation concerning the Obama presidency, "Jesus Falls for the Second Time," and the Church of St. Paul the Apostle. This conversation illustrates that we can mark the starting point of our pilgrimage and our walks, but the end point is more elusive, a reminder both for those concerned with social justice and for such groups as the Student March against Gun Violence that passed by this station on 24 March 2018. This mass movement (unwittingly, most certainly) takes its cues from and finds its roots in medieval mass revolts, like England's 1381 Peasants' Uprising and France's 1358 Jacquerie, which protested the ruling order and sought greater social justice without certainty of the outcome.

Station 8: Jesus Meets the Women of Jerusalem (at St. Peter's Church)

From Columbus Circle, my pilgrimage continued back east through Midtown, another neighbourhood bedecked with such monumental medievalisms as St. Patrick's Cathedral on Fifth Avenue. These medieval revival marvels, however, did not host Station 8. Instead, it was found in the Erol Beker Chapel of the Good Shepherd at the decidedly non-medieval St. Peter's Church. Comparable to the decision to identify Station 1 with objects already possessed by the Cloisters, Station 8 made use of the chapel's permanent altarpiece, Louise Nevelson's "Cross of the Good Shepherd" (1977).[43] This icon made of recycled material and broken objects found on the city's streets rejects the imported history and grandeur inherent in Manhattan's Gothic homages. For Nevelson, this chapel records her efforts as a Jewish woman to encounter the Christian Jesus, "to bring Jewish feelings and connections into a Christian space."[44] Although Nevelson's "Cross" represents the moment when "Jesus Meets the Women of Jerusalem," the icon just as accurately represents the moment when "The Woman of Jerusalem Meets Jesus."

Although *The Stations of the Cross* remained within the confines of Manhattan, moving towards the East River provides glimpses of Brooklyn Bridge's iconic Gothic towers. This medieval entryway to Brooklyn anticipates the borough's multiple examples of medievalism – both European and global – that include former armouries turned into homeless shelters, the Williamsburg Bank building, numerous Collegiate Gothic schools, and the Brooklyn Museum's collection of both medieval Islamic art (ceramics, textiles, manuscripts, calligraphy, and paintings) and late medieval African art (masks, wooden figures, and metalwork). Similar lists could be compiled for the city's other boroughs: Staten Island, the Bronx, and Queens.

Station 9: Jesus Falls for the Third Time (at the Raoul Wallenberg Memorial)

The ninth station stood across from the United Nations, another iteration of the dream of a world government – or the fear of global domination – that repeatedly made itself known during the Middle Ages with the Holy Roman Empire and such threats from the east as the Mongol Empire. The Raoul Wallenberg Memorial includes Gustav Kraitz's *Hope* (1998), a permanent cluster of monumental columns (and a poignant bronze briefcase) dedicated to the memory of the Swedish diplomat and his diversion of nearly 100,000 Hungarian Jews (the last large Jewish community in Europe) from being sent to Nazi concentration camps during the Second World War. As spare as the memorial might be, it does not allow us to forget that an ugly part of medievalism has been antisemitism. Not only are the Middle Ages filled with anti-Semitic activities, but the Nazis used medievalism to promote National Socialism, to fuel their propaganda machine, and to justify mass extermination of Jewish people and other "undesirables." Medievalism was and continues to be harnessed to despicable ends, and the Wallenberg Memorial reminds us of the work needed to sever that connection. Here, on this sombre note, I closed the second segment of my walk.

Station 10: Jesus Is Stripped of Garments (at the General Theological Seminary)

My third and final walk was confined to the lower third of Manhattan. Here, the city's earliest skyscrapers (like the extraordinary Woolworth Building across from City Hall Park) evoke medieval cathedrals, Europe's first high-rise buildings. As I headed south, I moved back in time to the earliest years of the island's settlement by the Dutch. En route to the General Theological Seminary in Chelsea, I passed by 15 West Twenty-Fifth Street, where "a rugged version of English Gothic Revival, 'reinforced with large buttresses which give it both durability and permanence,'" housed a Trinity Church chapel until 1943.[45] After being sold to the Serbian Eastern Orthodox Church of St. Sava, it later became the first Serbian Orthodox cathedral in the United States.[46] It is one of the many religious structures that have changed hands from (once) elite congregations to immigrant and other marginalized congregations, serving neighbourhoods with needs much greater than the desire to affirm their social and material aspirations. They follow in the late classical/early medieval model of taking pagan buildings and putting them to new, Christian uses. These decaying structures provide a paradoxical link to Europe in that they replicate the decrepit condition of medieval European structures at the time the new Romanesque and Gothic structures were fancifully re-created in New York City between 1830 and 1930, thereby creating a nostalgic bridge not only to the European past but also to many immigrants' own pasts, no matter how Americanized the replicas were. Perhaps the extent to which the city's architectural medievalisms have been preserved can be explained by their ability to cater to the needs and desires of both the elites who built them and the larger populace who later acquired them.

To find Station 10 (Jesus Is Stripped of Garments), I had to enter the Chapel of the Good Shepherd, encompassed within the medieval close of the General Theological Seminary's neo-Gothic buildings. Inside the chapel, Diego Romero's *Saints and Sinners* (2017), which draws on the medievalism of Spanish colonialism, hung in contrast to the decidedly English medievalism surrounding it. A Cochiti Pueblo artist, Romero combines images and techniques from Native American, western European (both classical and medieval), and contemporary popular cultures. In *Saints and Sinners*, male and female Native Americans are stripped naked, whipped, and brutalized by Old World conquerors, men who purport to represent Christianity, in order to deprive them of their "territory, traditions, and basic rights."[47] By echoing the stripping and flagellation of Christ – going so far as to equate the stripes of blood on the victim's back with the bleeding Sacred Heart that the soldiers assume authenticates their authority – the artistic work ambiguates the terms "saints" and "sinners." Here, medieval images demonstrate that dispossessed pagans have as much a claim to Christian salvation as soldiers; moreover, the dispossessed have a greater claim to the culture and territory taken from them. By having Romero's artwork depicting Native Americans and Old World conquerors in a Gothic seminary a few blocks from the waterfront where Europeans first encountered Manhattan's Indigenous peoples, Station 10 gestured towards global medievalism, which emphasizes the continuity between the global Middle Ages and the period of increased contacts among peoples after 1500.

Station 11: Crucifixion (at the Leslie-Lohman Museum of Gay and Lesbian Art)

The Leslie-Lohman Museum of Gay and Lesbian Art hosted Tommy Kha's transfixing installation *Today Was a Good Day* (2018).[48] Kha's series of photographic images of the childhoods of Southern AIDS victims – many of whom were abandoned and rejected by their birth families – forces the viewer to confront a truth: these forsaken men had once been beloved children, embraced and active members of their churches. Heartbreaking, from the first boyhood photos to their funeral ephemera, the images silently document the lives the men lived and the deaths they died, often far from the families who originally nurtured them. Alongside New York City's lost medieval architecture, these earliest AIDS victims shared the poignant trajectory from treasure to cast-off.

Located in the southern part of the island, the Leslie-Lohman Museum is surrounded by evidence that this area is a refuge for newcomers, who bring their own medievalisms or reclaim the cast-off medievalisms of groups who moved out of the neighbourhood. Chinatown duplicates the Asian past with alleyway markets and shrines associated with medieval Yuan beliefs. St. George Ukrainian Catholic Church (30 East Seventh Street), a miniature Byzantine-style cathedral with sparkling mosaic panels and an oxidized copper dome, was built in the 1970s to counter Western European influences.[49] Nearby, the former Sea and Land Church (now the First Chinese Presbyterian Church) needs repair (see figure 6.5) This 1819 Gothic-Georgian building is the second-oldest church building in the city and is designated as a landmark by the city's Landmark Preservation Commission. At the time of my walk, it was surrounded by scaffolding, the iron fringe for much of the city's re-created medieval architecture. The Church of the Most Precious Blood, on the border between Chinatown and Little Italy, preserves religious practices of medieval Italian villages. Quiet and unattended, the church is busy with nooks and crannies filled with plaster sculptures and friezes. Banks of candles lit for the dead testify to the continuing belief in Purgatory (see figure 6.6).

Station 12: Jesus Dies on the Cross (at the African Burial Ground and Visitor Center)

The African Burial Ground and its Visitor Center provide the sites for Station 12 (Jesus Dies on the Cross), linking the deaths of Africans who built Manhattan to the sacrificial death of Jesus. Sitting inconspicuously inside a large office building atop the burial site, the Visitor Center requires no fee, only that visitors reorient their understanding of enslaved people, slavery, and New York City. The exhibit explains the essential roles Africans played in establishing the Dutch West India Company's New Amsterdam. The enslaved people brought from "'Congo, Guinea, &

6.5. Former Sea and Land Church, the city's second-oldest Gothic building.

Angola, / [with their] feet tuned to rhythms of a thumb piano'" were not brutes, the exhibit calmly explains; "they were individuals with histories shaped by cultures as complex and beautiful as [those of] their enslavers."[50] These African peoples shaped New York City in ways ignored until recently. They cut roads and erected buildings, possibly according to practices brought from medieval Africa. The displays also show the ornaments – buttons and jewellery – they might have brought with them. To keep the Africans' medieval traditions alive, the centre celebrates Pinkster, the oldest African American holiday in the United States.[51] Although the holiday originated as a medieval Dutch religious holiday tied to Pentecost, American versions are infused with fifteenth-century Bantu cultures from Congo and Angola. In this way, the centre works to correct the long-told history of Manhattan's origins. And like the followers witnessing the Crucifixion, the centre's visitors have been led to feel grief, sympathy, regret, and guilt.

Outside, Rodney Leon's *African Burial National Monument* (2007) permanently marks the burial ground as a sacred space. Its granite "Ancestral Libation Chamber" pours into a "Circle of Diaspora," a map with western Africa at the centre and surrounded by the regions that traded Africans as slaves. Because it covers the burial ground where the seventeenth-century bodies were re-interred, the descendants of enslaved people use this site to pay homage to their ancestors by pouring libations.

6.6. The Church of the Most Precious Blood, where burning candles attest to the continuing belief in the efficacy of prayer for souls in Purgatory.

By giving the dead the drink's first taste, the descendants affirm the bridge between the living and the dead, between earthly life and the afterlife, an affirmative remnant of African spiritual beliefs.[52] Thus, the centre and the monument restore medieval Africa and its people as integral to New York City history.

Station 13: Jesus Is Taken Down from the Cross (at Trinity Church)

Near Trinity Church (one of the earliest Gothic Revival churches in the United States) can be found the most recent large-scale re-created architectural medievalism: a shopping area at the Wall Street Subway Station that opens into an interior space like a Gothic cathedral with flying buttresses. The largest shopping mall in Manhattan, it begs to be called a cathedral to consumer capitalism. At Trinity Church, G. Roland Biermann's *Stations* (2016–18) continued the references to capitalism, this time only as a critique and with no playful irony. Comprising oil barrels painted fourteen shades of blood red, stacked to form a wall and held in place with two crossing guardrails, *Stations* evokes the wars fought, the despots supported, and the Indigenous peoples displaced to feed Americans' dependence on fossil fuels. The installation's placement at Trinity echoed its churchyard burial grounds. With these juxtapositions that materially evoke Christ's death as well as the deaths of people near and far, Biermann's *Stations* implicated Americans who ignore the sacrificial deaths at the foundation of capitalist culture.

Station 14: Entombment (at the National September 11 Memorial)

The final stop for *The Stations of the Cross* is the memorial "Reflecting Absence" (2011), which approximates the footprints of the World Trade Center's two towers destroyed by the 2001 al-Qaeda attacks.[53] With water streaming from their sides, collecting, and then draining through central basins, its two black granite pools mark the jarring absences left by the destruction of Wall Street's monuments to American capitalism and, more so, by that day's deaths of nearly 3,000 men and women (and from these the more than 1,100 for whom no remains have been recovered) and subsequent deaths of hundreds more.[54] Through its dark yet simple visual and aural images, the memorial calmly acknowledges that ongoing absence. Between and below the memorial's pools, the site includes a museum that re-creates the honour of those lives and the horror of their deaths. Woven within these stories is a second set recounting the rescue efforts. Together, the two sets of stories counterbalance the memorial's overwhelming sense of loss. Perhaps the least medieval in appearance, the memorial and the museum together participate in residual medievalism by recalling the practice of enshrining individual lives in the floors, walls, and windows of medieval churches and cathedrals, where stained-glass windows, brass plaques, personal artefacts, crypts, and floor burials provide daily remembrances of local congregants; long after their individual lives may be forgotten, the commemorations ensure their names are occasionally whispered.[55] So too with the September 11 Memorial. It continues the medieval Christian effort to keep names alive through memorialization. And as the fourteenth station, it is consecrated as a spot marking the end of *The Stations of the Cross* and my walks.

By ending here, I recognize that my account of New York City's medievalisms is painfully partial, mapping only a small fraction of its potential artefacts and sites. This is partially due to my decision to organize my walks around *The Stations of the Cross*. Not only did I concentrate on a narrow strip traversing Manhattan's north-south axis, but *The Stations*' Lenten focus on social justice led me to more sober examples of medievalism. As a result, I left out such playful and comic aspects as the Medieval Festival at Fort Tryon Park, East Harlem Giglio Dance and Feast, Burp Castle, or Medieval Times (across the Hudson in New Jersey).[56] Because *The Stations of the Cross* was fully contained within Manhattan, my walks minimized the extensive medievalisms in the other four boroughs. Medievalisms are so densely packed into New York City's five boroughs that devoting an entire book to each borough's medievalisms would be insufficient. Beyond the limitations of innumerable examples, other factors complicate a full accounting of New York City's medievalisms. The most obvious factor is identifying now-vanished medievalisms. For example, numerous buildings and houses inspired by the medieval revival disappeared before anyone thought to record them. Despite the valiant efforts of architectural critics and bloggers to document these re-created medievalisms before they are demolished, many Gothic and Romanesque Revival buildings have disappeared, their existence noted only in City Hall records and newspaper accounts. A less obvious factor is discovering medievalisms that have not disappeared but remain elusive because they have so thoroughly saturated New York City culture. These practices constitute my third category, residual medievalism. They are difficult to identify because they emerge as organic to contemporary culture. Finally, some global inheritances were previously not visible to us as medievalisms. Despite New York City's 400-year role as a global meeting place, the potential insights of global medievalism remained unexplored. With these complicating factors in mind, my accounting of New York City's medievalisms should be seen as akin to a photograph, that "uncanny art" described by Cole's wandering narrator in *Open City* as capturing a "selected moment ... saved, for no other reason than its having been picked out by the camera's eye."[57] I leave it to other pilgrims to discover more of New York's unrecognized medievalisms.

NOTES

1 I briefly note here my enormous gratitude for the brilliant support generously given by my colleagues Jaclyn Geller, Heidi Hartwig, and Katherine Sugg – as well as by my in-house editor, Mike Shea. I write this in memory of Leslie McGrath, beloved poet and friend, who set me on this pilgrimage's path.
2 "Stations of the Cross: Art. Passion. Justice" [brochure], 2018. See also "Stations of the Cross," Wayback Machine, https://web.archive.org/web/20180401081559 /http://www.artstations.org (accessed 1 March 2021); "Stations of the Cross," Henry Luce III Center for Art and Religion, https://www.luceartsandreligion.org /stations-of-the-cross (accessed 1 March 2021); and the Alight podcasts, both of which feature images of the fourteen stations.
3 Teju Cole, *Open City* (New York: Random House, 2011).
4 Leslie Ross, "Stations of the Cross," in *Medieval Art: A Topical Dictionary* (Westport, CT: Greenwood, 1996), 233; "Stations of the Cross," in *New Catholic Encyclopedia*, 2nd ed., vol. 13 (Detroit: Gale, 2003), 499–501.
5 Kathy Bozzuit-Jones, "Reflect: A Devotional Guide for Groups and Individuals," Wayback Machine, https://web.archive.org/web/20180410090927/http://www .artstations.org/engage/reflect (accessed 1 March 2021).
6 Richard Utz, *Medievalism: A Manifesto* (Kalamazoo, MI: ARC Humanities Press, 2017), 72.
7 For a useful survey of these resources, see the website created by Paul Halsall's students, "Medieval New York," Fordham University, 1998, https://sourcebooks .fordham.edu/med/medny.asp (accessed 20 Sept. 2018).

8   Kathleen Davis, "Tycoon Medievalism, Corporate Philanthropy, and American Pedagogy," *American Literary History* 22, no. 4 (2010): 781–800; and Pierre Bourdieu, *The Logic of Practice*, trans. Richard Nice (Stanford, CA: Stanford University Press, 1990), 123.
9   Umberto Eco, *Travels in Hyperreality*, trans. William Weaver (New York: Harcourt Brace, 1986), 73–85.
10 Utz, *Medievalism*, 82. These three categories best suited the limited aims of this essay. Another examination of New York City medievalism could easily consider another set, such as Stephanie Trigg's recently rearticulated four categories: (1) traditional (overlapping with my transplants and residual practices), (2) modernist and (3) postmodernist (collectively corresponding with my re-creations), and (4) neomedievalism (a "meta-medievalism that … deploys other medievalisms rather than claiming any direct connection to the Middle Ages") (Thomas A. Prendergast and Stephanie Trigg, *Affective Medievalism: Love, Abjection and Discontent* [Manchester: Manchester University Press, 2019], 8).
11 Candace Barrington and Louise D'Arcens, "Introduction: The Global Middle Ages and Global Mediealism," *Digital Philology* 8 (2019): 1–13.
12 Following the pattern set by *The Stations of the Cross* installations, the fourteen sections of this chapter are identified by each station's traditional title and by its Manhattan location in the 2018 installation.
13 Niles Eldredge and Sidney Horenstein, *Concrete Jungle: New York City and Our Last Best Hope for a Sustainable Future* (Berkeley: University of California Press, 2014), 172.
14 "Medieval Festival in Fort Tryon Park," Wayback Machine, https://web.archive.org/web/20161117193223/http://metmuseum.org/events/programs/met-celebrates/festivals-and-special-programs/medieval-festival (accessed 1 March 2021).
15 Mary Rebecca Leuchak, "'The Old World for the New': Developing the Design for the Cloisters," *Metropolitan Museum Journal* 23 (1988): 257–77, at 257.
16 Bonnie Young, *A Walk through the Cloisters* (New York: Metropolitan Museum, 1988).
17 "The Met Cloisters," The Met, https://www.metmuseum.org/visit/plan-your-visit/met-cloisters (accessed 1 March 2021).
18 "The Hours of Jeanne d'Evreuz, Queen of France," The Met, http://www.metmuseum.org/toah/works-of-art/54.1.2; "The Cloisters Apocalypse," The Met, http://www.metmuseum.org/toah/works-of-art/68.174; "The Belles Heures of Jean de France, duc de Berry," The Met, http://www.metmuseum.org/toah/works-of-art/54.1.1; and "Book of Hours," The Met, http://www.metmuseum.org/toah/works-of-art/2015.706 (all accessed 20 Sept. 2018).
19 Norval White, *AIA Guide to New York City*, 4th ed. (New York: Oxford University Press, 2000), xiii.
20 "Great Hall at City College of New York," Elemental Architecture LLC, https://www.elementalnyc.com/projects/great-hall-at-city-college-of-new-york (accessed 1 March 2021).

21. Dennis Hevesi, "CUNY Campuses Prepare to Reduce Faculty and Classes," *New York Times* Archives, 14 May 1995, https://www.nytimes.com/1995/05/14/nyregion/cuny-campuses-prepare-to-reduce-faculty-and-classes.html (accessed 20 Sept. 2018).
22. Aithan Shapira, "Hope," 2015, http://aithanshapira.com/hope.html (accessed 20 Sept. 2018).
23. "The 1908 St. Mary's Episcopal Church – 521 West 126th Street," *Daytonian in Manhattan* (blog), 29 May 2014, http://daytoninmanhattan.blogspot.com/2014/05/the-1908-st-marys-episcopal-church-521.html (accessed 20 Sept. 2018).
24. Peter W. Williams, "The Medieval Heritage in American Religious Architecture," in *Medievalism in American Culture*, ed. Bernard Rosenthal and Paul Szarmach (Binghamton, NY: Medieval and Renaissance Texts and Studies, 1989), 171–91, at 171–2.
25. Sarah Salih, "Cinematic Authenticity-Effects and Medieval Art: A Paradox," in *Medieval Film*, ed. Anke Bernau and Bettina Bildhauer (Manchester: Manchester University Press, 2009), 20–39.
26. "New Icon Depicts Black Mary as 'Our Lady Mother of Ferguson,'" *Sojourners*, 11 July 2016, https://sojo.net/articles/new-icon-depicts-black-mary-our-lady-mother-ferguson (accessed 20 Sept. 2018).
27. Benjamin Ramm, "A Controversial Restoration Wipes Away the Past," *New York Times*, 1 Sept. 2017, http://www.nytimes.com/2017/09/01/arts/design/chartres-cathedral-restoration-controversial.html (accessed 20 Sept. 2018).
28. "Past Exhibits: Stations of the Cross."
29. "Meet Siona Benjamin: Transcultural, Indian-Jewish Artist," The Art of Siona Benjamin, https://artsiona.com/about-siona-benjamin/ (accessed 1 March 2021).
30. "History & Architecture," The Riverside Church in the City of New York, http://www.trcnyc.org/history (accessed 20 Sept. 2018).
31. "Our Church," St. Michael's Episcopal Church, https://www.saintmichaelschurch.org/our-church/#art (accessed 1 March 2021).
32. Michael Takeo Magruder, "Lamentation for the Forsaken," 2016, http://www.takeo.org/nspace/2016-lamentation-for-the-forsaken (accessed 20 Sept. 2018).
33. Elizabeth Allen, "'As Mote in at a Munster Dor': Sanctuary and Love of This World," *Philological Quarterly* 87, nos. 1–2 (2008): 105–33.
34. "About," The New York Purgatorial Society, https://nypurgatorial.com (accessed 20 Sept. 2018).
35. Christopher Gray, *New York Streetscapes: Tales of Manhattan's Significant Buildings and Landmarks* (New York: Abrams, 2003), 240.
36. White, *AIA Guide to New York City*, 262.
37. Lisa Keller, "Armories," in *The Encyclopedia of New York*, 2nd ed., ed. Kenneth Jackson (New Haven, CT: Yale University Press, 2010), 61–4.
38. Anthony Gronowicz, "Upper East Side," in *The Encyclopedia of New York City*, ed. Kenneth Jackson, 2nd ed. (New Haven, CT: Yale University Press, 2010), 1352.
39. John Ganim, "Medievalism and Architecture," in *The Cambridge Companion to Medievalism*, ed. Louise D'Arcens (Cambridge: Cambridge University Press, 2016), 29–44.

40. "Art and Architecture," St. Paul's NYC, https://stpaultheapostle.org/about/art (accessed 1 March 2021).
41. Landmarks Preservation Commission, Report on Church of St. Paul the Apostle, 25 Jun. 2013, https://stpaultheapostle.org/about/art (accessed 1 March 2021).
42. "Nicola Green," Candida Stevens Gallery, https://candidastevens.com/artists/25-nicola-green/works/6 (accessed 20 Sept. 2018).
43. "Renewing a Masterwork," Nevelson Chapel, https://www.nevelsonchapel.org (accessed 20 Sept. 2018).
44. "Past Exhibits: Stations of the Cross."
45. David W. Dunlap, "Ruined Serbian Orthodox Church Was a Landmark of Old New York," *New York Times*, 2 May 2016, https://www.nytimes.com/2016/05/03/nyregion/ruined-serbian-orthodox-church-was-a-landmark-of-old-new-york.html (accessed 22 Sept. 2018).
46. "Home," Serbian Orthodox Cathedral of Saint Sava, http://stsavanyc.org (accessed 20 Sept. 2018).
47. "Past Exhibits: Stations of the Cross."
48. Leslie-Lohman Museum of Gay and Lesbian Art, https://www.leslielohman.org/about-us (accessed 1 March 2021). See Tommy Kha's show at "Today Was a Good Day," YouTube, 17 March 2018, http://www.youtube.com/watch?v=iZBPkp3tUPY (accessed 20 Sept. 2018).
49. White, *AIA Guide to New York City*, 383.
50. "The African Burial Ground," US General Services Administration, https://www.gsa.gov/about-us/regions/welcome-to-the-northeast-caribbean-region-2/about-region-2/the-african-burial-ground (accessed 20 Sept. 2018). For the excerpted verse, see Yusef Komunyakaa, "The African Burial Ground," *Poetry*, Mar. 2014, http://www.poetryfoundation.org/poetrymagazine/poems/56829/the-african-burial-ground (accessed 3 Oct. 2019).
51. Claire Sponsler, *Ritual Imports: Performing Medieval Drama in America* (Ithaca, NY: Cornell University Press, 2004), 42–68.
52. Mechal Sobel, *The World They Made Together: Black and White Values in Eighteenth-Century Virginia* (Princeton, NJ: Princeton University Press, 1987), 174–5.
53. Lurking behind the memorial is the medievalizing rhetorical response to the 9/11 attacks; see Bruce Holsinger, *Neomedievalism, Neoconservatism, and the War on Terror* (Chicago: Prickly Paradigm, 2007).
54. "About the Memorial," 9/11 Memorial & Museum, http://www.911memorial.org/about-memorial (accessed 20 Sept. 2018).
55. Paul Binski, *Medieval Death: Ritual and Representation* (Ithaca, NY: Cornell University Press, 1996), 70–122.
56. Carolyn Dinshaw, *How Soon Is Now? Medieval Texts, Amateur Readers, and the Queerness of Time* (Durham, NC: Duke University Press, 2012); Sponsler, *Ritual Imports*, 95–122.
57. Cole, *Open City*, 152.

7 Minnesota Medieval: Dragons, Knights, and Runestones

JANA K. SCHULMAN

From their football team with helmets boasting stylized Viking horns to the likely apocryphal Kensington Runestone, many Minnesotans have a vested and economic interest in keeping their cultural traditions alive, specifically the medievalist myth of Scandinavian Christian Vikings journeying across Minnesota in 1362. Four key events ground the state in the Middle Ages, imbricating the medieval Scandinavian past and modern Minnesota. First, waves of settlement by many Scandinavians, particularly Norwegians, brought their cultures' traditions to the United States, with each wave reinforcing the beliefs of the previous. Second, many of these immigrants and their descendants desired to preserve those traditions, including their faith, customs, literature, and language; third, this desire to maintain their originary culture inspired local high schools to develop curricula and to feature mascots related to the Scandinavian past. Finally, Swedish immigrant Olof Ohman's discovery – or "discovery" – of a runestone in Kensington in 1898 led to an eventual and pragmatic decision to capitalize on the state's Scandinavian history, resulting in Minnesota's professional football team's name – the Vikings – as well as an idea for six tourism regions in the state, one of which was called Vikingland. In fact, Minnesotans may be unusual insofar as much of the state's Scandinavian medievalism focuses on keeping that heritage alive by embracing and advertising it to tourists, as they also, historically and in the present, reimagine myths of Viking masculinity into more palatable and romanticized incarnations.

Mapping the Landscape: Settling a New Scandinavia

Minnesota's Scandinavian medievalisms are rooted in the state's past. The territory clearly appealed to immigrants from Scandinavia. A Swedish visitor in 1850, Frederika Bremer, wrote, "What a glorious new Scandinavia might not Minnesota become!,"[1] and early settlers embraced her vision, immigrating to Minnesota and settling in and around St. Anthony Falls, near what would become Minneapolis.[2] Propaganda capitalized on the connection to Vikings travelling west, and Theodore Blegen tells the story of a Norwegian journalist, Paul Hjelm-Hansen, employed as a publicist by the state of Minnesota in 1869, who wrote newspaper letters for publication in Norway and in America: "I have made a journey, a real American pioneer trip ... with oxen and a farm wagon. I have spent the nights in the open wagon ... and, like Fritchof's Vikings, [with] the blue sky as a tent."[3] Once Norwegians arrived in Minnesota, they concentrated in regions with good land for farming and were among the first to arrive in Swift, Pope, and Lac qui Parle Counties – all in the west or west central part of the state.[4] "By 1890," as Blegen observes, "half of the Norwegian population of Minnesota was in the western counties."[5] Over time, they moved farther west and north into new frontiers, exploring and taking possession of new and fertile ground, just as in the sagas of Erik the Red and Leif Eriksson, tales of young men going a-Viking, searching for land.

No matter where settlers travelled in the territory and state of Minnesota, they did not forget where they came from or the stories of their homeland; numerous post office, village, city, and township names confirm the presence of Scandinavians from the state's earliest years (see figure 7.1). Many places are named after the immigrants' native towns, villages, fjords, or districts. Consider Vasa in the southeast, New Sweden in south central, and Westerheim in the southwest. Normania, Sandnes, Svea, Swede Grove, Swede Prairie, Swenoda, and Wergeland are townships in west central Minnesota;[6] and in the west are located Sverdrup, Tordenskjold, and Trondhjem townships. Names from Scandinavian medieval mythological texts and sagas can be found throughout Minnesota. Multiple entities named Vin(e)land exist, including post offices, a village, a hamlet, and a township; a post office and a township are named after Idun, the goddess of youth; one township is named after Odin, the father of the gods; and one township after Walhalla, Odin's hall, where chosen warriors go after their deaths. Throughout the modern Minnesotan landscape are etched mythographic, geographic, and other such allusions to a historical and mythological Scandinavian past.

Preserving Scandinavian Heritage in Minnesota: Faith, Language, and Civic Organizations

When Norwegians settled in Minnesota, their Lutheran faith and their Norwegian language strongly influenced the culture of this new territory, as they also grappled with shifting cultural contexts in the fledgling United States. Over the next century, organizations and individuals strove to preserve the languages, traditions, and literature of their ancestors in the New World, while maintaining the connections between the United States and Scandinavia. The preservation of Scandinavian languages was a key component in this quest, one in which the Norwegian Lutheran church played a significant role by founding

Minnesota Medieval: Dragons, Knights, and Runestones 159

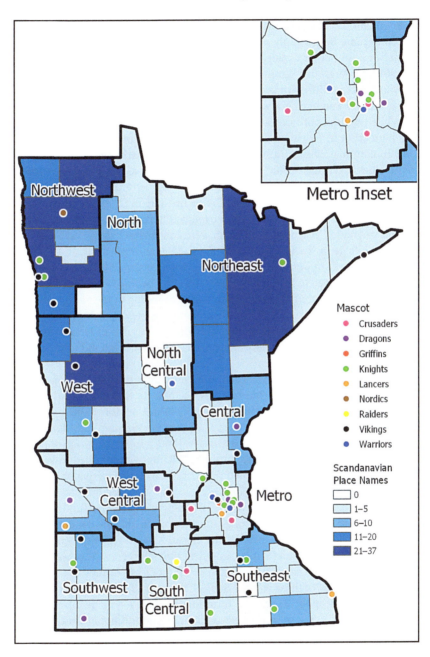

7.1. Locations of Scandinavian place names and medievally themed high school mascots throughout Minnesota. Map created by J. Glatz.

denominational colleges, primarily to train pastors who spoke Norwegian, which became increasingly necessary as time passed and fewer pastors came from Norway.[7] Luther College and Seminary was established in Decorah, Iowa, in 1861, and Augsburg Seminary was founded in 1869 in Wisconsin but moved to Minneapolis, Minnesota, in 1872. St. Olaf College was established in 1875. These schools taught in Norwegian; English was treated as a foreign language.

While English continued as the language of instruction in the common and the high schools, Norwegian remained the primary language in some of the denominational colleges in Minnesota through the early 1900s, as well as in some church settings. After that, Norwegian and Swedish became electives. Teaching Swedish were Gustavus Adolphus College in St. Peter (founded 1862, still offering a major in Swedish) and Bethel Institute in St. Paul (founded 1871 as a seminary, now Bethel University, no longer offering Swedish or any Scandinavian language). Teaching Norwegian were Augsburg College and Seminary, St. Olaf College in Northfield, Concordia College in Moorhead, and Bethany Lutheran College in Mankato. At Augsburg, now a private liberal arts college – the seminary moved to St. Paul in 1963 – it is still possible to study Norwegian. St. Olaf College has taught Norwegian since its founding in 1874 and maintains a Norwegian department offering a major in Norwegian. Bethany Lutheran College still offers Norwegian. Concordia College, founded in 1891 by Norwegian settlers, no longer offers any Scandinavian languages but did offer Norwegian courses in 1939–40.[8]

Members of the Lutheran church and the denominational colleges were among many Norwegians in Minnesota who took steps to preserve their culture, tradition, and language; presses, societies, and organizations of various sorts also sought to uphold the state's Scandinavian culture. The *Minneapolis Tidende* began publication in Minneapolis in 1866, joining the group of nine to ten Norwegian newspapers in the Midwest – all but two published in Wisconsin, a state that, in 1847, had printed the first Norwegian newspaper in America, *Nordlyset*, in the village of Norway.[9] In addition to keeping the language alive, these Norwegian newspapers provided news from Norway and America. While Norwegian newspapers, along with the church and the denominational colleges, kept the language alive, by the close of the nineteenth century and continuing into the twentieth, it became clear that new generations were losing touch with their Scandinavian roots, and several societies formed to counteract this trend. The first of these was the Sons of Norway, a fraternal order founded in 1895 in Minneapolis to provide insurance benefits for its members and to ensure that Norwegian immigrants would enjoy cultural opportunities familiar to them.[10] Following in 1903, Det Norske Selskab i Amerika (the Norwegian Society of America) also formed in Minneapolis, "to unite all Norwegian Americans around the worthwhile cause of Norwegian language, literature, and immigrant history."[11] Two branches of the Norwegian Singers Association of America, renamed in 1910 from an 1891 North Dakotan group, the Northwestern Singers Association, were active in Minnesota,[12] and the Society for the Advancement of Scandinavian Studies, composed of faculty members from various universities offering Scandinavian studies, was formed in 1911. In 1925, the Norwegian-American Historical Society began.

The constitution of Det Norske Selskab i Amerika summarizes the shared goals of these organizations: "The purpose of the Society shall be to work for the preservation by the Norwegian people in America of a) their ancestral tongue, b) their historical memories and traditions, c) their interest in Norwegian literature, art, song, and music, and d) their national characteristics"; and the history of the Sons of Norway exemplifies the ways in which societies and organizations kept the Scandinavian past alive in Minnesota.[13] The society conducted its business meetings in Norwegian until 1942, although requests to have an English-speaking lodge were received – and denied – as early as 1914, and it established a lecture and entertainment bureau in 1907 aimed at keeping Minnesotans connected to their past, featuring a speaker who lectured on Norse mythology in 1908.[14] Even the group's lodge names, echoing the naming practices of their settler-forebears, inscribed Norwegian language and medieval culture into the Minnesota landscape, disseminating Norwegian mythology and medieval history across the state, connecting people and places of the past with their descendants' present. The first lodge was named Nidaros after Nidaros Cathedral in Trondhjem, a medieval cathedral where Norwegian kings were crowned and buried. The Fergus Falls lodge (founded in 1902) was named Heimskringla after Snorri Sturluson's compendia of kings' sagas; the fact that the lodge in Thief River Falls (founded 1907) is named Snorre after the same man confirms this text's influence. A lodge (founded in 1908) named after Thor's hammer Mjølner indicates familiarity with Scandinavian mythology as told in Snorri's *Prose Edda* and the anonymous *Poetic Edda*. The lodge in Cass Lake (founded in 1917) was named for the Norse goddess Freya. Vinland, the name given by Leif Erikson to North America, is the name of the lodge founded in International Falls in 1918. The lodge in Alexandria (founded in 1933) was named Runestone.

The Sons of Norway's lodges inscribed Old Norse–Old Icelandic texts into the landscape, and as they did so they tapped into the heritage brought by Scandinavians immigrating to America, who carried with them books other than just their family Bibles. Many Old Norse texts were translated into modern Norwegian, Danish, and other languages during the early waves of immigration. Snorri's *Heimskringla* and *Prose Edda* were translated into Danish in the seventeenth century, and in 1808, a Danish translation of the *Edda* was published for a general readership.[15] The Danish Romantic poet Adam Oehlenschläger (1779–1850) had read much Old Norse literature, and according to N.F.S. Grundtvig (1783–1872), the nineteenth century's growing interest in Norse mythology was due to the works of Oehlenschläger: "When

Oehlenschläger's harp resounded, a genuine longing to know more about the gods of the North emerged in the hearts of the more advanced people."[16] In addition to Oehlenschläger in Denmark, Bishop Esaias Tegnér of Sweden wrote a narrative poem in Swedish called *Frithiofs Saga* (1824) based on the Icelandic saga of the same name.[17] Hugely popular and Romantic in plot and language, Tegnér's poem was translated into many languages; between 1833 and 1914, "at least 15 independent ... English versions of Tegnér's poem were published."[18] As the nineteenth century progressed, translations of Old Norse-Old Icelandic literature were announced in American newspapers and then picked up in the Norwegian American press. Rasmus B. Anderson, an important contributor to many aspects of Norwegian American life who taught Norwegian at the University of Wisconsin in the 1870s, translated several sagas into English, including *Fridthjofs Saga*.[19]

Fridthjofs Saga and its reception proved particularly significant for the type of Viking medievalism key to the Minnesota medieval. In 1837, Henry Wadsworth Longfellow reviewed W.E. Frye's 1835 translation of Tegnér in the *North American Review*, with little positive to say. In his lengthy review, Longfellow provides some of his own translations of the poem, waxes rhapsodically about the original, and draws his readers' attention to what underlies Tegnér's poem, a fascination with the "spirit of the past; ... the spirit of that old poetry of the North."[20] Longfellow's review is a paean to the Romantic spirit, raising, perhaps, the idea of a Romantic (chivalric) Viking, an idea previously developed in Paul-Henri Mallet's translation into French of the *Poetic Edda* in 1756 and fully articulated in subsequent scholarly interpretation.[21] The Viking, exemplified in Tegnér's story of the valiant Frithiof, resonated both in Europe and in America. On the one hand, according to Andrew Wawn, Frithiof could be said to be the epitome of manliness, "a much-used word in Victorian writings about the North. By it was signified the vigorous, buccaneering spirit."[22] This representation of the Viking may be traced back to Mallet's translation of the *Poetic Edda*. According to Régis Boyer, in eighteenth-century France scholars drew from "Montesquieu's theories about the relationship of climate to character," leading to ideas about the vigorous people of northern Europe juxtaposed against those less-active people found in the south. Boyer concludes that "the figure of the cruel Viking underwent fundamental modification" and that Mallet's translations provided an "admirably energetic Viking."[23] By the end of the eighteenth century in France, another image of the Viking emerged, evolving from the myth of the vigorous Viking. In this new version of Viking history, circulated by French scholars as late as 1911, "the North [was seen] as the source of medieval European chivalry."[24] "As a warrior," in Boyer's words, the Viking "was chivalrous, strong, pure, virtuous."[25] Mallet's translation of *Krákumál*, a poem about Ragnarr Lodbrók, illustrates the new Viking by highlighting Ragnarr's more noble traits: "love for his wife and children, courage, strength of mind and body. With the treatment of Ragnarr, we are much closer to the spirit of the Arthurian Round Table … than to the 'poèms barbares.'"[26] In Longfellow's review, we see glimpses of this chivalrous Viking in Frithiof, and it is worth noting that Xavier Marmier translated Tegnér's *Frithiofs Saga* into French in 1840.

This image of a chivalric Viking, a knight by any other name, joined the other chivalric romances, such as the medieval stories of King Arthur and the Knights of the Round Table, Alexander the Great, Yvain, Erec and Enide, and Roland, which had been widely enjoyed in many languages, including Scandinavian ones, during and after the Middle Ages. There are Old Norse-Old Icelandic versions of *The Song of Roland* (in *Karlamagnús saga*), *Erec and Enide* (*Erex saga*), and *Yvain* (*Ívens saga*), for example. The Middle High German *Nibelungenlied* is a version of the story of Sigurd the dragon slayer, related in Snorri Sturluson's *Prose Edda*, the anonymous *Poetic Edda*, and *Saga of the Volsungs*. In the Scandinavian story, Sigurd is a warrior; in the German, Siegfried is a knight and the story is set against the backdrop of chivalry and knighthood. These stories, like the sagas, constituted a key part of the immigrants' cultural heritage and would have also made their way to Minnesota as early as the mid- to late 1800s; together these literary traditions helped to shape the state's concept of its Viking heritage.

Next-Generation Vikings: Scandinavian Language Instruction and High School Mascots

As the years passed, Minnesota's immigrant population become increasingly aware that the survival of their cultural traditions depended upon the education of the next generation. This preoccupation began in the late 1860s as the Norwegian church promoted the faith and sought to "educate Norwegian Lutherans to minister to immigrants," and the church turned its attention to the common schools that provided education for all children.[27] While lay Norwegians welcomed the common schools and funded them through taxes, the Norwegian Evangelical Lutheran Synod's leaders feared them, calling them "religionless" and worrying that they taught in English.[28] This so-called "School Controversy" lasted for some twenty years, ending around 1880, with the synod accepting that parochial schools would be difficult to staff and that many prominent Norwegian Americans supported the learning of English in the common and high schools, seeing it as a commitment to their new country. However, as each successive generation became further removed from the mother tongue and old cultural traditions, Minnesotans became increasingly concerned with the loss of both. Beginning in 1900, there was a concerted effort to provide public school students with the opportunity to study Norwegian language, literature, and culture in school, most likely led by the Sons of Norway and similar organizations, which ramped up in the following decades.[29] In Minneapolis, a petition was submitted to the school board in 1910 signed by some seventy-five organizations, requesting that high schools add Scandinavian instruction to their offerings.[30] The school board approved this request, and by 1911 both South and East High Schools of Minneapolis offered Norwegian and Swedish. In 1915, twenty high schools in Minnesota offered Norwegian, eleven Swedish, and two Danish.[31]

With language instruction came instruction in history and culture. One of the first readers designed for Americans learning Norwegian was Carl Johan Peter Petersen's *Norwegian-Danish Grammar and Reader with a Vocabulary Designed for American Students of the Norwegian Language*.[32] To develop his readers' appreciation for medieval Scandinavia, Petersen included selections from various sagas, at least one from Snorri's *Heimskringla*, and poems written by later authors about medieval figures such as Canute. Petersen also presents readings about the discovery of Iceland and selections from *Erik the Red's Saga* and *Saga of the Greenlanders*, emphasizing the Norse discovery of America. In "Biographical Sketches," a later section of the book, students learn about Adam Oehlenschläger, the Danish Romantic poet mentioned above, who had read Snorri, won a prize for his use of Nordic mythology, and written poems and plays about the Norse gods, as well as prose texts such as *Orvarodds saga* and *Hroars saga* that are based loosely on Icelandic sagas.

Knud Throndsen's two-volume reader, *Norsk læsebog for børn og ungdom*, published in 1873 and 1876, contains stories from *Heimskringla*; a list of the Norwegian kings starting with Harald Fairhair and his descendants; poems written by Romantic authors on various medieval Scandinavian subjects; stories about St. Olaf and his conversion of Norway; and material taken from *Erik the Red's Saga* and *Saga of the Greenlanders*, called *Amerikas Opdagelse* (The discovery of America).[33] Another popular reader, Nordahl Rolfsen's *Læsebok for folkskolen*, first appeared in 1892, with a new edition in 1909.[34] The volumes of this title include much of Snorri's *Heimskringla*, selections from sagas such as *Gisli Sursson*, and material pertaining to the history of Norway. O.L. Kirkeberg's *Læsebog for Børn: Tredje trin* (1910) includes many readings from medieval Scandinavian texts that run a gamut: an account of missionaries to Scandinavia (St. Ansgar); an introduction to *Den ældre Edda*, followed by a selection from *Hávamál*; and then nearly all of *Fridtjovs saga*, including some of Tegnér's songs.[35] He introduces his readers to the Norse gods and to the medieval kings of Norway, including poems written in honour of such medieval figures as Olav Tryggvason in B. Björnson's "Olav Tryggvessøns død." J.A. Holvik's *Second Book in Norse: Literary Selections* (1912) complements Holvik's *Beginners Book in Norse*, providing reading texts and notes.[36] It contains *Gunnlaug Ormstunges saga* (*The Saga of Gunnlaug Serpent's Tongue*), *Norge samlet* (*The Unification of Norway*), B. Björnson's poem "Olav Tryggvessøn," and a twenty-page retelling of Norse mythology, *Den norske gudelære*. Holvik's reader is mentioned specifically in "Courses of Study in Scandinavian (Minneapolis High Schools)" that appeared in *Scandinavian Studies and Notes* in 1918. According to this article, which outlines three years of study in Norwegian and four in Swedish, texts that introduce Norse mythology, folklore, and history are studied in the second semester of the second year. In addition, students are expected to memorize five historical poems, among them *Island* (A. Munch), *Olav Trygvason* (Björnson), and *Kong Haakons gildehal* (Ibsen); *Snorres Kongesagaer* is the supplementary reading. In the Swedish sequence, in the second semester of the second year, students would intensively study Tegnér's *Frithiofs Saga*.[37] Regardless of which language was studied, high school students were introduced to many medieval Scandinavian works that included Vikings who travelled the seas on their dragon ships and dragons themselves, as well as visions of once-predatory Vikings reimagined as knightly icons of chivalric virtue.

Thus, it is not surprising that high school clubs like the Edda Literary Society, Viking Club, and Norwegian Club enjoyed active memberships, or that two of these published either fully Norwegian or half-Norwegian newspapers, each called *Vikingen*. Nor is it surprising that many Minnesota high schools further connected the descendants of the original Scandinavian settlers to their Scandinavian past through the names of their yearbooks and sports teams. In fact, sports teams provided a seemingly natural point of transmission between a medievalized Viking past and the present as high school athletics became more and more a part of an area's culture, regardless of whether the location was urban or rural, whether the high school was large or small. As Roy Yarbrough writes of school mascots, "A mascot is an identity, a source of entertainment, a rallying point"; he also notes, "Each [high school] desires to represent [its] school in a unique way forever hoping that [its] mascot will bring ... VICTORY on the field or court."[38] Small-town athletics together with school mascots produce a rallying point, an identity, and products for sale. Ross Bernstein, in a book about the development of football in Minnesota, observes that "by the 1920s, high school football was, in many cases, the biggest show in town for many small communities."[39]

Because of this, one of the ways to analyse the importance of the medieval in the Minnesota present is to examine the history of high schools and their team names and mascots. Ironically, none of the schools with Viking clubs had Viking mascots, either in the 1910s or more recently, and, of the earliest schools offering Scandinavian languages, it seems that only Milan and Pelican Rapids High Schools may have had both languages and Vikings mascots. This fact may also illustrate how deeply medieval Viking roots ran in Minnesota, as smaller or more rural schools denied the opportunity to study language and culture nevertheless expressed their Scandinavian identity in their choice of mascot. While not all of these modern medieval mascots – Vikings, knights, warriors, crusaders, dragons, and griffins – can directly be traced back to Scandinavian influence, all are medievalish and evoke one another, participating in a metonymic chain.[40] One mythical animal solicits images of another; one mounted mascot calls to another. Added to this imbrication is the fact that certain medieval mascots have been adopted explicitly to promote student codes of conduct based on the idea that medieval knights and others represented the epitome of good, virtuous behaviour, thus creating a temporal bridge from the ideal medieval Viking, knight, or warrior to the present well-behaved and well-rounded student athlete.

Just as the droves of Scandinavians who immigrated to Minnesota inscribed the landscape with Scandinavian place names, so they chose either the name Viking or Nordic for some of the earliest high schools in the state, connecting their students and community members to the once-feared raiders and explorers of medieval Europe. At one point, there were eighteen four-year high schools whose yearbooks, annuals, sports teams, or mascots were called the Vikings.[41] Place-name evidence for twelve of these Viking schools demonstrates their obvious connections to Scandinavia, eleven to Norway and one to Sweden, while the other six – Dassel, Kenyon, Golden Valley, Cook County, Hayfield, and Littlefork–Big Falls – do not have obvious Scandinavian immigrant connections. Eight of these twelve are in western counties in Minnesota, evidence of moves westward, paralleling medieval Viking travels first to Iceland, then to Greenland and Vinland.[42] In the northwest, there is Ada in Norman County, Climax in Vineland Township in Polk County, and Newfolden in New Folden Township – named after a seaport in northern Norway – in Marshall County. Vineland Township gets its name from Leif Erikson's name for North America. Norman County is named "for commemoration of the great number of Norwegian (Norseman or Norman) immigrants who had settled there. Norse delegates were a majority at the convention, and the name was selected on account of patriotic love and memories of their former homes across the sea."[43]

In the west and west central regions, while the name of the school does not always evoke a Scandinavian past, that past is there. In the west were Hitterdal, Kensington, and Pelican Rapids. Hitterdal was named for Bendt O. Hitterdal, the "original town proprietor," an emigrant from Norway.[44] Kensington, where Olof Ohman found the runestone, is a city in Solem Township, the latter named after a district in Norway.[45] Pelican Rapids had many Norwegian settlers, its first postmaster was born in Norway and served from 1872 to 1886, the high school yearbook frequently has Vikings on the cover, and the high school offered Norwegian (at least in 1917).[46] The west central region had Milan in Chippewa County and Sacred Heart in Renville County. Many settlers from Norway came to Sacred Heart as early as the 1860s.[47] Milan is a city in Kragero Township, the latter named after the seaport of Kragero in southern Norway. Milan High School, like Pelican Rapids, once offered Norwegian (in 1913).

Of the remaining four Viking high schools in counties with Norwegian connections, two of these are in the southwest (Minneota and Ruthton), one is in south central (Frost), and the last is in central Minnesota (North Branch).

Minneota, in Eidsvold Township, was settled in 1871, and "named by vote of its Norwegian settlers after a parish in Norway."[48] The high school, founded in 1900, is (still) the "Home of the Vikings." Ruthton is located in Aetna Township, with the latter named in honour of a Norwegian immigrant's stepdaughter.[49] The majority of Frost's settlers hailed from Norway.[50] Finally, North Branch Area is in Branch Township, where the first settler, a Swede, came in the late 1860s, and the high school's website promotes "Viking Pride."[51]

Of these eighteen Viking schools, two have closed their doors: Golden Valley and Frost. Six consolidated and changed their mascots: Ada, Dassel, Hitterdal, Newfolden, Milan, and Sacred Heart.[52] One, Big Falls, consolidated with Littlefork, which kept its Viking mascot. Three consolidated and took another medieval mascot, the Knights: Kenyon with Wanamingo; Kensington with Hoffman and then Hoffman-Kensington with West Central; and Ruthton with Russell and Tyler. One, Climax, changed its mascot from the Vikings to the Knights. Five never consolidated – Cook County, Hayfield, Minneota, North Branch, and Pelican Rapids – remaining active and with Viking mascots to this day.

Only five of these original Viking schools remain Vikings, but the spirit of the Viking and its connection to a romanticized medieval past is alive and well at Minnesota high schools. Indeed, across Minnesota, school mascots symbolize and uphold the ideal of a chivalric warrior in various other manifestations – knights and crusaders – with each of these manifestations crossing over and blending into each other. Let us begin with the knight. Sixteen schools feature a knight as their mascot. Of these sixteen, four – Climax, Kensington, Kenyon, and Ruthton – originally had a Viking and either changed their mascot (Climax) or merged with other schools. Seven schools had knight mascots from the beginning: Sleepy Eye St. Mary, Fisher, St. Paul Harding, Irondale, Martin Luther, Paladin, and Nova Classical.[53] One high school, Babbitt, originally opted for a knight as its mascot but after a series of mergers lost its knight mascot, the only such school. Finally, seven schools, all formed as a result of consolidation(s), chose a knight as their mascot. They are St. Michael-Albertville; Alden-Conger; Lake Crystal-Wellcome Memorial; Russell-Tyler-Ruthton; Kenyon-Wanamingo; Kingsland; and West Central Area (which includes Kensington).[54] Why is a knight the mascot of choice for many consolidated schools? When two schools merge, more often than not they choose a new mascot and new team colours so that the team can start afresh. For example, when St. Michael and Albertville merged in 1968, the students were given the choice of the Golden Eagles, the Marauders, and the Knights, choosing the Knights.[55] When Kenyon merged with Wanamingo, they also selected the Knights, as their website explains:

> Layers of positive relationships make K-W great! We are the Knights and we have blended Kenyon, Wanamingo, and parts of the surrounding area into a culture that

is symbolically represented by the traditional strengths displayed within a Knighthood. A Knight is not gender specific. Knights learn from their adult and upper classman role models about the core values of respect and service to others. Our Knights strive to be the best that they can be. They take pride in their school, their community, and are held to high standards.[56]

Kenyon-Wanamingo's explanation makes clear the significance of such a choice: Knights are chivalric, noble, respectful; they exhibit good sportsmanship on the field, show respect, and serve others. K-W Knights aspire to the values of those mythic Vikings who were "chivalrous, strong, pure, virtuous" and strongly connected to family and community.[57]

In fact, the image of the knight as *the* prototype of the medieval warrior is borne out in the visual and written depictions of other types of medieval-warrior mascots found in Minnesota high schools. Although the image of the warrior derives from both Native American tradition and the medieval past, the three Minnesota high schools with warrior mascots now hark back to the European and Scandinavian past. Henry Sibley's mascot resembles a warrior-Spartan, whereas West Lutheran's looks like a knight. Both of these schools were founded late enough (1971 and 1979 respectively) that a Native American warrior should not have even crossed the minds of school administrators and students.

The third school with a warrior mascot, Brainerd, was founded in 1884, and its original mascot was a Native American chief nicknamed, according to Brainerd's yearbook, Old Joe (see figure 7.2). Native Americans, specifically the Santee, a Sioux band known as the Sioux of the East, inhabited Crow Wing County and likely Brainerd from the seventeenth century onwards. In 1662, a fourteen-day feast was held in Minnesota, somewhere east of the Mississippi River, where warriors engaged in "plays, mirths, and battle for sport," in addition to games, physical contests, and dances.[58] From the early to the mid-nineteenth century, "the classic Western Sioux culture developed, shaping stereotypes that ultimately would define the Indian in American popular culture ... [as] one wearing a feathered headdress and fringed buckskin garments."[59] Brainerd's original warrior logo reifies this stereotype, which is not at all surprising; as Robert Berkhofer Jr. notes in *The White Man's Indian*, "For most Whites throughout the past five centuries, the Indian of the imagination and ideology has been as real, perhaps more real, than the Native American of actual experience and contact."[60] Both Brainerd's logo and code, the "Warrior Way," blend Euro-American stereotypes of and ideology about Native Americans; the ceremony and the stereotyped image mentioned above demonstrate the beginning of how sport, physical contests, and communalistic behaviour merge.

On 12 April 1993, in response to the Department of Education's request that schools critically examine their use of Native American names and mascots, the Brainerd school board decided that "the Warrior name be retained, that the

7.2. Old Joe, the Native American chief, and Brainerd's warrior mascot. Composite image courtesy of Elisabeth Carnell.

warrior logo be eliminated, and that a new logo … be instituted."[61] The mascot was changed to the Flying B, which remained the logo until 2014, when it was replaced by a bearded Viking warrior – the only Viking (or Viking-like) warrior mascot who does not wear a horned helmet.[62] No matter the mascot design, warriors ostensibly exemplify chivalric conduct and the willingness of student athletes to step onto a basketball court, a football field, or another sports arena and fight the opposing team for victory, for the glory and honour of the school, as exemplified by Brainerd High School's code: "The Warrior Way has become an inspiration to students. Instances have occurred when students have responded spontaneously to discourage behaviors that have put people down, and encouraged supportive, positive behavior."[63]

This code transcends the actual image chosen by Brainerd, linking their idea of the warrior to any mascot symbolizing such a code, such as the Nicollet Raiders and the Kenyon-Wanamingo Knights. Similarly, Nicollet High School, the one Minnesota high school whose raider mascot is not a pirate but a knight on horseback, encourages students to adhere to the tenets of "Raider Pride," a code of "behavior expectations" that emphasizes "be[ing] responsible, respectful, positive, and safe," not unlike a code of conduct for knights rewritten for the twenty-first century.[64]

One last example of the medieval-warrior mascot, the Crusader, is rapidly disappearing in some contexts but not in others. According to Joel Landskroener, executive director of Mayer Lutheran, one of the four high schools in Minnesota with this mascot, "Crusader is a common name for Christian schools of all shapes and sizes."[65] The image of the crusader, however, has shifted from a positive to a negative valence, as schools question the values associated with the Crusades and of those western Europeans who participated in them. Jody Veeker, examining problematic mascots, notes that "a crusading knight on a charging steed ... [might] be sending the wrong message about Christianity."[66] Jesse Carey explains further: "Considering the crusades aren't exactly a shining moment in church history, the medieval weapon-wielding knight is the mascot of way too many schools."[67] Two Christian colleges, Wheaton and Maranatha Baptist University, changed their mascots owing to this issue, although high schools have not yet followed their example.[68] What's in a name matters.

More recent schools, perhaps inspired by modern fantasy novel series such as *Harry Potter* and *The Lord of the Rings*, have turned from medieval-warrior figures to mythical creatures for their mascots and identity. Five dragon schools populate Minnesota: Adrian, Avalon School, Litchfield, Math and Science Academy, and Pine City; and one that burned down, Madison, was reborn via consolidation some years later as Lac qui Parle Valley High School. Dragons abound in medieval literature, from the Old English poem *Beowulf*, in which the dragon is Beowulf's third foe, through the *Eddas* and the *Saga of the Volsungs*, in which the dragon Fafnir is killed by Sigurd, to the *Nibelungenlied*, in which Siegfried is referred to as the dragon killer. It is possible that the more modern of these Minnesota schools chose the dragon because of familiarity with the dragons of their Scandinavian traditions, but it is also possible, especially given the late foundation dates of both the Avalon School and the Math and Science Academy (2000 and 1999, respectively), that their dragon mascot choices were influenced by students who had read the first three Harry Potter books; indeed, in personal communication with the Math and Science Academy, I learned that the students chose and developed their own mascot, Glaedr the Dragon, in 2014 (see figure 7.3).[69]

Similar to medieval Vikings, knights, and warriors in their function, dragons and other mythical beasts embody ideal traits and virtues, identities to be adopted by the students whom the mascots represent. The dragon in medieval heritage symbolizes "power, protection, and wisdom,"[70] and the griffin, employed as a mascot by Groves Academy, a charter school established in 1972 for students with learning disabilities, displays "death-defying bravery in battle."[71] Debbie Moran, Groves director of admissions, told me that the griffin was

7.3. Glaedr the Dragon.

chosen for the mascot because the mythical aspect appealed and because the griffin "is strong and mysterious." In 2005, a student won an essay contest about the significance of the griffin to Groves Academy students, writing, "Griffins are smart, they guard treasures, and test people with riddles. Our school has many smart students, our minds are treasures, and to some people how we do things is a mystery or riddle to them. Also, griffins are strong and at Groves Academy we have some very strong students."[72]

As this survey of high school mascots attests, while Minnesota medievalism evolved over the years, it is rooted in the languages and traditions of the state's Scandinavian settlers and early nineteenth-century portrayals of recuperated chivalric Vikings. Representing codes and expectations of behaviour (whether on a basketball court, on a football field, or in a classroom) that go back to the Middle Ages, Minnesota's medieval high school mascots imbricate the present with a Scandinavian past.

Marketing the Viking: The Runestone, Reality, and Tourism

This image of the chivalric Viking is not uncontested, and for many, the popular culture version of the Viking as "a brawny battle crazed berserker from comic books or the Monty Python movies" comes more readily to mind, which may explain why so many Minnesotans believe – or want to believe – that the dubious Kensington Runestone is real.[73] Olof Ohman, a Swede who immigrated to America in 1879 because, like so many immigrants, he wanted his own land, found this stone inscribed with runic writing in 1898.[74] Clearing his homestead outside the village of Kensington, he came upon the later-named Kensington Runestone among the roots of an aspen tree. This stone is 31 by 15 by 6 inches, looks a bit like a gravestone, and bears a twelve-line inscription in runes that states that eight Swedes and twenty-two Norwegians were on a discovery trip before some of their party were killed in 1362. If the runestone is not a fraud – and debate about this continues – it attests to the presence of Scandinavians in what would become Minnesota well before Christopher Columbus's arrival in North America in 1492. Regardless of the stone's authenticity, it connects all Scandinavians, particularly Minnesota's Norwegian immigrants, with their medieval past.

In "'Making' History: The Vikings in the American Heartland," authors Michael Hughey and Michael Michlovic "examine the specific social means and processes by which [believers] have endowed it with sufficient legitimacy that it has become not only a widely held popular belief but also an accepted version of reality in the region."[75] In early days, immigrants, subjected to discrimination and contempt, might have latched onto this idea because they felt defensive. With the English publication in the 1880s of *Erik the Red's Saga* and *Saga of the Greenlanders*, telling the story of Leif discovering North America (Vinland) around 1000 CE, and possibly contributing to the desire for and the replication of a Viking ship at the Chicago Columbian Exposition in 1893 – the idea that Vikings arrived in America before Columbus began to take hold. Ohman's 1898 discovery of the runestone seemed to confirm this idea and to lend Scandinavian immigrants reason to take pride in their history and their ancestors. This pride manifested itself, as we have seen, in the founding of the Sons of Norway, in Norwegian language classes in high schools and regional universities, Scandinavian folk festivals, and Syttende Mai celebrations.[76]

As time passed and small towns declined economically, this belief also led to business opportunities, with Minnesotans deploying their Scandinavian past to lure tourists to the region. The third chapter of David Krueger's book, *Myths of the Rune Stone: Viking Martyrs and the Birthplace of America*, is aptly titled "In Defense of Main Street: The Kensington Rune Stone as a Midwestern Plymouth Rock."[77] Another defence is ethnic commerce, and it is not surprising that "the Viking presence has become something of a regional industry and a mainstay in promoting institutional interests" as businessmen and various organizations "actively promoted the Viking visit as a historically factual episode."[78]

This same tendency can be seen in the result of a contest to name the professional football team awarded to Minnesota in 1960. According to reporter Dick Cullum, team owners planned to hold a contest "to choose the name which will reflect the character of the state, its history, and people." Suggestions included Miners, Chippewas, and Voyagers, but Vikings was chosen, writes Cullum, "to recognize the venturesome people who first populated the state."[79] Bernstein connects the concepts of "venturesome people" to stereotypes attributed to Vikings, most likely to demonstrate how the players on such a team would be expected to behave on the field as "barbaric and ruthless marauders."[80] To market the Kensington Runestone further – and to capitalize on the name Minnesota Vikings – in 1965, a 28-foot-tall statue of a Viking, called Big Ole, was built to draw attention to the artefact while on display at the 1964/65 World Fair. After the fair, Big Ole took up residence in downtown Alexandria, welcoming visitors with "Birthplace of America" written on his shield.[81]

Building on these developments, the Minnesota Department of Tourism in 1967, attempting to attract more visitors to Minnesota and to northwest Minnesota specifically, named a region of the state comprising seventeen counties "Vikingland"; this became one of the state's six tourism regions (see figure 7.4).[82] According to a spokesman for Vikingland USA,

> the name of Vikingland was selected because most people in the country equate Minnesota with three things: 10,000 lakes, Twins, and Vikings … We selected Vikingland because it can be easily tied in with this entire area. "It is expected that the Kensington Runestone and Alexandria area will become one of focal points [sic] for the region because of its close association with Viking promotion."[83]

Vikingland includes Douglas County (where Kensington and Alexandria are located) as well as Becker, Clay, Douglas, Grant, Otter Tail, and Polk Counties, worth mentioning because they each have rocks with holes, what Hjalmar Holand, the Kensington Runestone's earliest and most impassioned promoter, called Viking ship mooring holes.[84] A 1979 Minnesota Tourism brochure asks of Vikingland, "Did Columbus really discover America? No, according to the Kensington Runestone, found in Vikingland. The controversy continues, but the Kensington Runestone and other 14th century artifacts of Scandinavian design are on display in Vikingland's Alexandria … make up your own mind."[85] Krueger has eloquently rewritten the history of the Kensington Runestone not from the perspective of proving or disproving its veracity but to demonstrate the importance of the myth for those who lived first and foremost in Alexandria and nearby Kensington, and eventually for all Minnesotans. Promoters of Minnesota do not hesitate to capitalize on the runestone, whether they accept its veracity or not. Not only do Viking mascots continue to wear horned helmets without any historical evidence to buttress this image, but so too do Kensington Runestone believers continue to promote their "truth" that fourteenth-century Christian Vikings made their way to North America, all the way to Minnesota.

Is the Kensington Runestone responsible for high schools teaching Scandinavian languages or choosing medieval mascots for their athletic teams and yearbooks? No. The runestone, however, does keep the medieval – in the myth of Christian Vikings and an emphasis on a medieval, European past that

7.4. Minnesota's tourism districts, including Vikingland in the west.

includes Vikings, knights, warriors, crusaders, dragons, and griffins – alive in the present. The Scandinavian, particularly Norwegian, immigrants brought their cultural traditions to Minnesota, and their traditions merged with those from other European countries and those of Native Americans in Minnesota.

Norwegian Culture and Minnesota Medievalism

The medieval in Minnesota manifests itself in multiple ways and the present state of Minnesota's Scandinavian past figures prominently. For example, the city of Milan still prides itself on its Norwegian heritage. The Milan Village Arts School teaches Scandinavian crafts, and the town website proclaims, "Velkommen Til Milan, MN! Norwegian Capital USA," and mentions its founding by Norwegian immigrants in 1879. The city hosts a vibrant Syttende Mai celebration every year.[86] The Minnesota Vikings play on, hoping to one day win a Super Bowl. Norwegian, while no longer taught in most high schools, is taught in more colleges in Minnesota than in other states and can be studied at Concordia Village language camps and through Mindekirken's Norwegian Language and Culture Program. Ingebretson's Nordic Marketplace in Minneapolis, which opened in 1921, continues to sell "old country" items; promotes Norwegian history, culture, and tradition on its website; and offers classes in cooking, needlework, and knitting.

The Vikings, knights, warriors, crusaders, dragons, and griffins chosen by school districts or students bridge the past and present, demonstrate the ubiquitous ideas or ideals represented by certain figures, and capitalize on stereotypes. Whereas Native Americans fought against the use of mascots they found stereotypical and offensive, many Minnesotans embraced the Viking logos that still have horns. Because of the former's fight, high schools had to seek permission to keep their team names. Brainerd illustrates how a high school retained its name and code of behaviour but removed the offensive image, alighting finally on a Viking-like warrior who stands for both medieval and Euro-Americanized Native American values.[87] The stereotypical figure of the horned Viking, however, continues to appeal to many Minnesotans in spite of the error of that depiction, precisely because it has come to represent their culture, traditions, and myths. Medieval Minnesota, representing both European and Native American traditions, reveals itself in prominent symbolic figures, most noticeably in high school team mascots.

NOTES

1 Quoted in Odd Lovoll, *Norwegians on the Prairie: Ethnicity and the Development of the Country Town* (St. Paul: Minnesota Historical Society Press, 2006), 24.
2 Theodore Blegen, *Minnesota: A History of the State* (Minneapolis: University of Minnesota Press, 1963), 175; Lovoll, *Norwegians on the Prairie*, 33, 102.
3 Quoted in Blegen, *Minnesota*, 305. *Fritchof* is a variant spelling of *Friðþjófr*, the hero of *Friðþjófs saga hins frækna*, which was translated into English as early as 1839.
4 Lovoll, *Norwegians on the Prairie*, 37.
5 Blegen, *Minnesota*, 310.
6 The name *Swenoda* is formed from the first letters of Sweden, Norway, and Denmark. See Warren Upham, *Minnesota Place Names: A Geographical Encyclopedia*, 3rd ed. rev. (St. Paul: Minnesota Historical Society Press, 2001), 588.
7 I refer to the church here but later to a synod, the latter referring to the geographical and denominational area to which a church and its congregation belongs.
8 Esther Chilstrom Meixner, *The Teaching of the Scandinavian Languages and Literatures in the United States* (PhD diss., University of Pennsylvania, 1941), 36.
9 Leola Bergmann, *Americans from Norway* (Philadelphia: Lippincott, 1950), 71–3.
10 Carl Gustav Otto Hansen, *History of Sons of Norway: An American Fraternal Organization of Men and Women of Norwegian Birth or Extraction* (Minneapolis: Sons of Norway Supreme Lodge, 1944), 11, 58. See chapter 3, "The Masonic

Medievalism of Washington, D.C.," in this volume for a discussion of lodges, medieval guilds, and chivalric codes.
11 Quoted in Odd Lovoll, *Norwegian Newspapers in America: Connecting Norway and the New Land* (St. Paul: Minnesota Historical Society Press, 2010), 254.
12 See http://www.nsaaonline.org for a history of the group and http://www.nsaaonline.org/category/nsaa-member-organizations for individual member organizations (both accessed 11 Jan. 2019). The one still active in Minnesota is the Norwegian Glee Club.
13 Quoted in Einar Haugen, "The Struggle over Norwegian," *Norwegian-American Studies and Records* 17 (Jan. 1952): 1–35, at 21–2.
14 Hansen, *History of Sons of Norway*, 123 and 64.
15 Jan Ragnar Hagland, "The Reception of Old Norse Literature in Late Eighteenth-Century Norway," in *Northern Antiquity: The Post-Medieval Reception of Edda and Saga*, ed. Andrew Wawn (Middlesex: Hisarlik Press, 1994), 27–40, at 30 and 36.
16 Quoted in and translated by Hagland, "Reception of Old Norse Literature," 37.
17 The title character's name is spelled variously as Friðþjófr, Frithiof, and Fridthjof.
18 Andrew Wawn, "The Cult of 'Stalwart Frith-Thjof' in Victorian Britain," in Wawn, *Northern Antiquity*, 211–54, at 225.
19 Rasmus B. Anderson, *Viking Tales of the Norse: The Sagas of Thorstein, Viking's Son, and Fridthjof the Bold*, trans. Rasmus B. Anderson and Jón Bjarnason (Chicago: Griggs, 1877). See also Gerald H. Thorson, "First Sagas in a New World: A Study of the Beginnings of Norwegian-American Literature," *Norwegian-American Studies and Records* 17 (1952): 108–29.
20 Henry Wadsworth Longfellow, "Review of *Frithiofs Saga* (*The Legend of Frithiof*) by Esaias Tegnér: *Die Frithiofs-Sage* by Esaias Tegnér and Amalie von Helvig; *Frithiof's Saga, or the Legend of Frithiof*," *North American Review* 45, no. 96 (Jul. 1837): 149–85, at 151 and 152.
21 Longfellow writes: "The memory of Balder is still preserved in the flower that bears his name, and Freyja's spinning-wheel still glimmers in the stars of the constellation Orion. The sound of Strömkarl's flute is heard in tinkling brooks and his song in waterfalls" ("Review of *Frithiofs saga*," 152).
22 Wawn, "The Cult of 'Stalwart Frith-Thjof,'" 239.
23 Régis Boyer, "Vikings, Sagas, and Wasa Bread," in Wawn, *Northern Antiquity*, 69–81, at 71–2.
24 Boyer, "Vikings, Sagas, and Wasa Bread," 72.
25 Boyer, "Vikings, Sagas, and Wasa Bread," 73.
26 Boyer, "Vikings, Sagas, and Wasa Bread," 73.
27 "History," Augsburg University, https://www.augsburg.edu/about/history (accessed 8 Jan. 2019).
28 Frank C. Nelson, "The School Controversy among Norwegian Immigrants," *Norwegian-American Studies and Records* 26 (1974): 206–19.

29 Hansen, *History of Sons of Norway*, 11, 58.
30 Meixner, *Teaching of the Scandinavian Languages*, 73.
31 Hugh Graham, *The History of Secondary Education in Minnesota* (PhD diss., University of Minnesota, 1929), 258, table 61. "In August 2015, *Sønner af Norge* reported that Norwegian was being taught in more than 200 public schools in … Minnesota," a number that would presumably have included common schools (Hansen, *History of Sons of Norway*, 124).
32 Carl Johan Peter Petersen, *Norwegian-Danish Grammar and Reader with a Vocabulary Designed for American Students of the Norwegian Language* (Chicago: Griggs, 1872). See Einar Haugen, *The Norwegian Language in America: A Study in Bilingual America*, 2nd ed., vol. 1, *The Bilingual Community* (Bloomington: Indiana University Press, 1969), esp. chapter 7, part 3, "The Teaching of Norwegian"; and Anne Hvenekilde, "Readers for Norwegian-American Schools," *Norwegian-American Studies* 34 (1995): 135–69. It is noteworthy that of the four grammars and seven readers published between 1908 and 1919, all but two were published in Minneapolis (Haugen, *Norwegian Language in America*, 139). See also Meixner, *Teaching of the Scandinavian Languages*, 31.
33 Knud Throndsen, *Norsk læsebog for børn og ungdom*, 2 vols. (Decorah, IA, 1873, 1876).
34 Nordahl Rolfsen, *Læsebok for folkskolen*, 5 vols. (Kristiania, Norway: Jacob Dybwads Forlag, 1892–5).
35 O.L. Kirkeberg, *Læsebog for Børn: Tredje trin* (Minneapolis: Augsburg Publishing, 1910).
36 J.A. Holvik, *Second Book in Norse: Literary Selections* (Minneapolis: Augsburg Publishing, 1912).
37 Committee Report, "Courses of Study in Scandinavian (Minneapolis High Schools)," *Scandinavian Studies and Notes* 5 (1918): 33–40.
38 Roy Yarbrough, *Mascots: The History of Senior College and University Mascots/Nicknames* (Lynchburg, VA: Bluff University Communications, 1998), 13 and 12.
39 Ross Bernstein, *Pigskin Pride: Celebrating a Century of Minnesota Football* (Minneapolis: Nodin Press, 2000), 151.
40 To find Minnesota high school mascots, I relied on http://mascotdb.com (accessed 11 Jan. 2019) and a 2014 report on all the public and private high schools in Minnesota.
41 Because the logo for Marshall County Central is the same as the Minnesota Vikings team, I include the Nordics in the total of eighteen Viking schools. It is noteworthy that Viking images changed frequently and that not all of these images were horned Vikings: Viking ships and winged Viking helmets abounded, especially before 1961. In fact, Kensington's yearbook boasted both of these images at various times.
42 In the northwest are Marshall, Norman, and Polk; in the west are Clay, Douglas, and Otter Tail; and in the west central are Chippewa and Renville.
43 Upham, *Minnesota Place Names*, 408.

44 Upham, *Minnesota Place Names*, 121.
45 Upham, *Minnesota Place Names*, 182.
46 Pelican Rapids is in Otter Tail County, one with many Norwegian settlers.
47 Upham, *Minnesota Place Names*, 493.
48 Upham, *Minnesota Place Names*, 335.
49 Upham, *Minnesota Place Names*, 447.
50 Upham, *Minnesota Place Names*, 189.
51 Upham, *Minnesota Place Names*, 113.
52 Newfolden merged with schools in Holt and Viking to become Marshall County Central Schools.
53 In order of year founded: 1914, 1917, 1928, 1967, 1983, 2002, and 2009.
54 Schools listed in order of consolidation date: 1968; the next three all in 1987; 1990; 1992; and 1993.
55 Personal communication, Principal Robert Driver, April 2018.
56 "What Makes K-W Great!," Kenyon-Wanamingo School District, www.kw.k12.mn.us/district_office/what_makes_k_w_great (accessed 8 Jan. 2019).
57 Boyer, "Vikings, Sagas and Wasa Bread," 73.
58 Quoted in Raymond J. DeMallie, "Sioux until 1850," in *Handbook of North American Indians*, gen. ed. William C. Sturtevant, vol. 13, vol. ed. Raymond J. DeMallie (Washington, D.C.: Smithsonian Institution, 2001), 722–4.
59 DeMallie, "Sioux until 1850," 732.
60 Robert F. Berkhofer Jr., *The White Man's Indian* (New York: Knopf, 1978), 71.
61 Brainerd School Board Meeting Minutes, 12 Apr. 1993.
62 The receptionist who answered the phone at the high school described him as "a Viking-like warrior."
63 Brainerd School Board Meeting Minutes, 12 Apr. 1993.
64 Nicollet Public School, http://www.isd507.k12.mn.us/page/2656 (accessed 21 July 2018).
65 Personal communication with Joel Landskroener, 4 June 2018. The other three schools are First Baptist School, St. Croix Lutheran, and Mankato Loyola.
66 Jody Veenker, "Eagles, Crusaders, and Trolls – Oh My!," *Christianity Today*, 12 June 2000: 44, 7.
67 Jesse Carey, "Religious NCAA Mascots: The Definitive Ranking," *Relevant*, 20 Mar. 2015, www.relevantmagazine.com/current/religious-ncaa-mascots-definitive-ranking (accessed 13 July 2018).
68 Veenker, "Eagles, Crusaders, and Trolls," 18; Joshua R. Miller, "Christian College Drops 'Crusaders' Nickname in Bow to 'Global' Society," *Fox News US*, 2 Feb. 2014.
69 In conversation with Director John Gawarecki on 1 Aug. 2019, he confirmed that Glaedr was influenced by the Harry Potter books and told me that one of the school clubs is named the Order of the Phoenix.
70 Brenda Rosen, *The Mythical Creatures Bible* (New York: Sterling, 2009), 27.
71 Rosen, *Mythical Creatures Bible*, 118 and 26.

72 Personal conversation and emails with Debbie Moran, 31 July 2018.
73 William Fitzhugh, "Vikings: The North Atlantic Saga," *AnthroNotes* 22, no. 1 (2000): 1–9, at 7.
74 "Olof Ohman," Kensington Area Historical Society, http://kahsoc.org/ohman.htm (accessed 8 Jan. 2019).
75 Michael Hughey and Michael Michlovic, "'Making' History: The Vikings in the American Heartland," *Politics, Culture, and Society* 2, no. 3 (1989): 338–60, at 338–9.
76 Syttende Mai celebrations are held on 17 May in honor of the signing of a new constitution in 1814; Hughey and Michlovic, "'Making' History," 342.
77 David Krueger, *Myths of the Rune Stone: Viking Martyrs and the Birthplace of America* (Minneapolis: University of Minnesota Press, 2015).
78 Hughey and Michlovic, "'Making' History," 345, 344.
79 Dick Cullum, "Minnesota Is Designation of Pro Grid Team," *Minneapolis Tribune*, 6 Aug. 1960: 21.
80 Bernstein, *Pigskin Pride*, 24.
81 Hughey and Michlovic, "'Making' History," 346; Krueger, *Myths of the Rune Stone*, 137–9.
82 Ralph Thorton, "State Split in 6 Regions for Tourism Promotion," *Minneapolis Star*, 30 Oct. 1967: 9; see also *Minnesota's Lodging Industry: Statistics and Characteristics*, Extension Bulletin 386 – 1975, Hospitality Series No. 1, pp. 20–1.
83 "'Vikingland USA' Is Name of Tourism Group," *Daily Journal* (Fergus Falls, MN), 7 Sept. 1967: 10.
84 Krueger, *Myths of the Rune Stone*, 52.
85 "Minnesota. Lakes. And a Whole Lot More," Tourism Division, Minnesota Department of Economic Development, 1979.
86 City of Milan, Minnesota, http://www.milanmn.com (accessed 8 Jan. 2019); Ann Thompson, personal communication, 3 July 2018.
87 See the Brainerd School District's presentation, "Building a Compelling School Identity," http://www.mnmsba.org/Portals/0/PDFs/LC2014Handouts/Friday/2014QRClimateBrainerd.pdf, 62, for an explanation of what the Warrior symbolizes.

8 "I Yearned for a Strange Land and a People That Had the Charm of Originality": Searching for Salvation in Medieval Appalachia

ALISON GULLEY

"Medieval" Follies on a Highway

The Blue Ridge Parkway runs for 469 miles through the southern Appalachian Mountains, linking the Great Smoky Mountains National Park in North Carolina with the Shenandoah National Park in Virginia. As the most visited unit of the National Park Service since 1946, this scenic highway is driven by millions of people each year. Along this popular destination, a tourist to milepost 176 in Virginia can visit Mabry Mill, site of a restored gristmill and sawmill with a working miller who demonstrates the traditional Appalachian milling process. This stop draws several hundred thousand visitors a year, who are charmed not just by the mill but by the Matthews Cabin, described as an "outstanding example of mountain architecture and workmanship."[1] The Parkway was built beginning in 1935, and its designers, including landscape architect Stanley W. Abbott, aimed to provide "tourist recreation" as opposed to regional travel, envisioning the roadway as a venue through which travellers could view not only historical sites like Mabry Mill but also the pristine wilderness of the Appalachian region. "Like the movie cameraman who shoots his subject from many angles to heighten the drama of his film," wrote Abbott, "so the shifting position of the roadway unfolds a more interesting picture to the traveler." The artifice of the camera is an apt metaphor here because the result, and indeed the goal, was not the rich and varied reality of the region but a simulacrum of a pastoral idyll and an idealized past. The Park Service took care to eliminate, as Abbott put it, "parasitic and unsightly border development of the hot-dog stand, the gasoline shack, and the billboard."[2] The Park Service went beyond simply removing unsightly elements: all signs of development and industrialization were expunged or shielded from the view of passing tourists while the artefacts of real Appalachia were replaced with objects deemed more authentic. Clearly, it wasn't simply unspoiled nature that the designers pursued; they also sought to preserve – and to provide a glimpse of – a gentler, slower, Arcadian pre-modern existence. To this day, no billboards, stop signs, or traffic lights mar the landscape, and, aside from the occasional farm or craft centre and the visitors themselves, visitors see little evidence of human habitation. In 2010, on the occasion of the Parkway's seventy-fifth anniversary, *Smithsonian Magazine* could still report that "cruising along at the speed limit of 45 miles per hour is like taking a step back in time."[3]

In many ways, the Blue Ridge Parkway is not unique in its re-creation of the past. The desire to refashion and reframe history for public consumption recalls such medievalish spectacles as the follies of the seventeenth and eighteenth centuries, built to look like a past, in this case a specifically medieval one, that never exactly was. The great poet John Milton, for example, pulled down the ruins of Milton Abbey to construct a new house on the site and then used remaining stones to construct a Gothic sham on the grounds.[4] Horace Walpole's Strawberry Hill, probably the best-known example of a folly, did not seek to provide authenticity; instead, John Ganim says, it "embodied an imagined vision of the Gothic."[5] In this vision, Walpole saw not just "a little Gothic castle" but, as he writes in a 1753 letter to George Montague, a "castle (I am building) of my ancestors," indicating that he was also attempting to reconstruct his own history.[6] As Walpole makes clear, the impetus for such follies was a desire to reconstruct a past in keeping with one's present sense of self, not just at the individual level but also collectively.

Such identity formation came about partly through a medievalism that broadly served two purposes. First, the Middle Ages existed as an era to be rejected and as evidence of a more sophisticated present. For example, broadly speaking, to many Protestants during the Renaissance and Enlightenment, the Middle Ages represented pre-Reformation ignorance, superstition, and corruption.[7] In this line of thought, the architecture and art of the period were reminders of a "dark" age between the glories of the classical age and their own, and John Stewart argues that the follies served as a "warning to those who might attempt to rebuild a culture of abbeys and divine right kings in an age of reason that appropriated rather than worshipped the Gothic era."[8] Conversely, as illustrated in endeavours like Walpole's, the medieval stood for something quite different. Reginald Horsman notes that the "eighteenth-century English view of Anglo-Saxons was a mythical one produced by two centuries of religious and political conflict and reinforced by the image of the Germanic peoples that originated with Tacitus and was elaborated by a whole series of post-Reformation Continental writers."[9] Thus, Johann Gottfried Herder and other historians, drawing on Tacitus's *Germania*, developed "a myth of a free Germanic people" while Hegel perceived a Germanic "spirit" that emerged following the decline of Rome.[10] There came to be a growing political and popular sense of the medieval period as an era to be celebrated as the source of British liberty, a "democratic Saxonism" in a line of thought that assumed an "unbroken chain of government authority descending from the Gothic Saxons to the Gothic present."[11]

The Gothic revival of Britain was imported to America in the context of the French and American Revolutions, during which, as Roger Wood explains, political and intellectual figures re-envisioned the Middle Ages, "raising the startling possibility that it was not necessarily a completely 'dark' age but in fact offered a precursory glimpse of the political 'enlightenment' that dared to question the absolute authority of traditional monarchy."[12] Thomas Jefferson was merely one among the founding fathers and their nineteenth-century successors who idolized and mythologized the Anglo-Saxons, and he urged his compatriots at the Second Continental Congress to adopt a seal of the new United States that reflected his belief that the country was both blessed and ordained by God and also the genealogical bequest of freedom-loving Saxons. One side was to feature Moses parting the Red Sea, while the reverse would feature "Hengist and Horsa, the Saxon chiefs from whom we claim the honor of being descended, and whose political principles and form of government we have assumed."[13]

Within this broader context of American medievalism, the mythology of Appalachia similarly rewrote and repackaged history for political purposes. The kind of past represented by the Blue Ridge Parkway and the Mabry Mill site proved to be useful at a time when Americans, overwhelmed by industrialization, modernism, and their attendant ills, sought to establish a specific origin story through which they – like the English in the eighteenth century – could trace an unbroken line of political and cultural superiority. As frequently happens in times of social upheaval, America, specifically white America, looked for a scapegoat and found one in what were deemed immigrant hordes of dark races, against whom Appalachia proved to be a panacea. This remote Brigadoon, peopled with mountain whites who were supposedly vestiges of a pure Anglo-Saxon race and who epitomized the olden days and olden ways, held the key to salvation.[14]

This imagined and desired past appears in miniature at milepost 176, where park officials removed a kerosene engine that the Mabrys used to power the mill and later, in the early 1940s, restored the mill's waterwheel that had been nonfunctioning for years before the Park Service obtained the site. The Park Service also added a pond that reflected the mill to optimize its photogenic qualities.[15] Elsewhere along the Parkway, following the model set by Milton's reconstruction centuries earlier, common clapboard houses were destroyed in favour of log cabins, which were judged more representative of the "isolated and independent pioneers" of the region, and the Mabry Mill site was no exception.[16] In 1941 the two-story frame farmhouse built by Ed Mabry in 1914 was torn down, and in 1957 the Matthews Cabin that now stands on the site was relocated from Carroll County, Virginia. The cabin joined a whiskey still and a sorghum press, despite the fact that the Mabry family never used them on their property.

There was no public outcry over this destruction and re-creation of Appalachia, which later occurred at other spots along the scenic highway. As Phil Noblitt explains, "The lack of internal or public protest over the transformation of the mill and its history testifies to the power of the prevailing mythology about mountain culture. Hardly anyone questioned the integrity or relevance of the new and greatly altered mill because hardly anyone in the 1940s and 1950s could imagine an alternative past for the Appalachian South."[17] And yet, he argues, the designers did not deliberately set out to mislead the public. Instead, they meant to preserve a way of life that they feared was passing away. The *Blue Ridge Parkway News* in 1942 lamented that the "old dwellings and the barns hewed by hand from the forest itself are beginning to go ... The very picture which makes the Blue Ridge seem old and solid and early American and very different to the traveler is changing."[18] It is as if the designers and Park Service sought to freeze-frame, to return to the camera metaphor, the region and its inhabitants. A 1938 report from the Great Smoky Mountains National Park even recommended the establishment of what today sounds like a human zoo: so-called "pioneer culture" should be preserved with field exhibits of mills and farms, with real-live mountaineers living and working on the farms.[19] Never mind that this way of life may never have existed. For one thing, historically, as well as in the present, Appalachia was far more culturally diverse than popularly imagined. For example, about 300 miles south of Mabry Mill, at milepost 457.7, the Parkway enters the Cherokee Indian Reservation, with access to the town of Cherokee, home to many of the Eastern Band of Cherokee Nation. African American Appalachians have largely remained invisible to outside American eyes, yet today they make up approximately 10 per cent of the population, about the same as in the late nineteenth century, when the myth of a white Appalachia was developing.[20] Such a reality, however, didn't – and still doesn't – fit the accepted narrative socially or politically.

Gothic Medievalism: Appalachian Grotesque

Appalachia has long inhabited the geographical, political, and cultural edges of the United States, and the people themselves reside on the margins of American consciousness. In the American imaginary, Appalachia is a place not only of pioneer culture and log cabins but of dark primitivism; it is usually synonymous with rural and abject poverty, feuding clans, superstition, and moonshine, a word conjuring visions of illicit liquor as well as darkness, night, and even magical occurrences, reminiscent of some far-off and mystical time and place. Although the Appalachian mountain range stretches from northern Alabama to Canada, "Appalachia" as a cultural entity typically refers to the southern portion of the range and to its poor, rural white residents. Likewise, cultural Appalachia, for those not part of it, excludes such urban centres as Pittsburgh, Knoxville, and Birmingham in favour of mountains, "hollers," and small towns like Robbinsville, North Carolina, of Discovery Television's *Moonshiners* "reality" show fame. Although the wineries and craft breweries of Appalachia have gained a national following, moonshine and the farm stands selling "punkins" and "biled [boiled] p'nuts" represent real Appalachia to the many tourists who enjoy the region's offerings (and one suspects that at this point the signage is really a clever marketing ploy).

In the same way, for many, the "real" Middle Ages are indeed a Dark Ages, a time of superstition, ignorance, violence, and squalid poverty set against the tyranny and material excesses of church and state. In this view, as noted, Gothic follies and shams were not emblems of a desired, ideal past but rather a contemptuous and parodic nod to the medieval era, and they represented the triumph of the Renaissance and Enlightenment over a decidedly unscientific and undemocratic age. Thus, Andrew Elliott can point to a film like *The Advocate* (1993), set in fifteenth-century Burgundy, as a kind of shorthand for the way the medieval era is frequently portrayed and perceived:

> There is no doubt about it; we are back in the Middle Ages. It is the world of barbarity and squalor, in which dark forces sweep unchecked through defenseless villages, storm monasteries and ransack their way into the annals of history. It is the world of superstition and religious zeal, too, in which the earth is still flat and all phenomena – from comets to rainbows – are instantly ascribed to the ineffable Divine … It is of course a familiar world to us; we know the signs, we know how it operates, and we know – thanks to years of conditioning – vaguely what to expect from the dark primitivism of the Middle Ages.[21]

We know what to expect from Appalachia, too. In the tradition of the Appalachian grotesque, the region is evoked as a rejection of barbarity, ignorance, and squalor and a contrast to modern America as a land of prosperity and enlightenment. Nowhere is this more evident than in media representations of Appalachia, which, like those of the Middle Ages, continually play up and distort the sensationalistic perceptions of the land and its people. This hillbilly mythos has roots that began well before it showed up in popular-media caricature. Anthony Harkins traces three strands of literary and illustrative traditions that date from the colonial era – the "rural rube," the idea of the "poor whites" in the rural South, and images of Southern mountain folk – that "slowly coalesced through the nineteenth century into a new icon of complex and ambiguous geographic, racial, and cultural significance," primarily to be found in what by the end of the nineteenth century was called "Appalachia."[22]

Portraits of this hillbilly can be seen in the local colour writings of the late nineteenth and early twentieth centuries. One of the first essays in this genre establishing the mountains and the mountaineer as subaltern was Will Wallace Harney's aptly titled "A Strange Land and a Peculiar People." Although Harney praised the natural beauty of the region and the impoverished nobility of its inhabitants, he also noted the mountaineers' "peculiarities of ... anatomical frame" and the "disproportion of the extremities," along with their superstitious dependence on the influence of the moon in planting their crops.[23] A close cousin to the "peculiar" mountaineer is the mountaineer as an uneducated, backward, "poor white trash" hillbilly living in squalor. The Reverend Robert F. Campbell of the First Presbyterian Church in Asheville, a native of the region, pleaded for resources to help the poor mountain whites in his community. While professing a love for "his people," he nonetheless described a region in which "[old] women administer their herbs, and quacks practice their superstitious arts" and where the "most serious employment" of the mostly idle mountain men is "hunting, or fishing, or running illicit distilleries and imbibing the blood of John Barleycorn ... In some regions," he writes, "a young man has reached the summit of his ambition when he has learned to pick the banjo, owns a dog, and carries a pistol and a bottle of whiskey."[24] Years later, this image refuses to die: rumour has it that the statue of Yosef, the mountaineer mascot at my institution, Appalachian State University, was originally designed to feature a jug in one outstretched hand and a rifle in the other (see figure 8.1). Horace Kephart, a Pennsylvanian librarian, outdoorsman, and travel writer whose widely read 1916 book *Our Southern Highlanders* is generally considered an early departure from the stereotyping of local colour writing, nonetheless described hills peopled with men and women with grey eyes, "sometimes vacuous, but oftener hard, searching, crafty – the feral eye of primitive man."[25] These primitives lack sympathy for others, crowd around with morbid curiosity when someone is dying, and are a "perversely suspicious bunch."[26] This more sinister portrait of the region and "hillbillies" appeared previously, for example, in newspaper coverage of Breathitt County, Kentucky, home of the legendary Hatfields and McCoys, whose conflict began in the 1880s, and the site of more bloodshed in the first decade of the twentieth century. In this yellow journalism, families became "clans" and battles were "feuds," words that suggested their remove from modern society.[27] As Henry Shapiro puts it, "When the mountain people of Kentucky came to town with their rifles as they did in 1901, images of the mountaineer as pathetic ... gave way before a new set of images of mountaineers as feudists and desperadoes, criminals and social deviants."[28]

These early depictions are precursors to those found later in stereotypical representations of the region. This crowded field mostly includes fictional portraits of good-natured simpleton mountain folk such as Li'l Abner (featured in a comic strip of the same name running from 1934 to 1977) or Gomer Pyle of television's *The Andy Griffith Show* (1960–8) and its spinoff *Gomer Pyle, U.S.M.C.* (1964–9), but criminals and social deviants are common. *Deliverance* (1971, based on the novel by James Dickey) depicts Appalachian natives as not

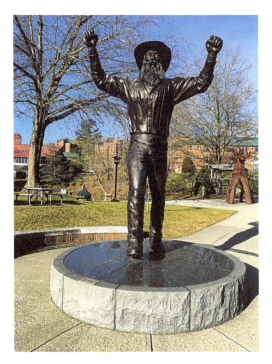

8.1. Yosef on the Appalachian State University campus. Author's photograph.

only illiterate and inbred but evil, but perhaps most egregious is the portrait of Appalachia in the king of the so-called hillbilly horror genre, *Wrong Turn* (2003), which features inbred cannibals in West Virginia bearing descriptive names like "Three Finger," "Saw Tooth," and "One Eye." Even nonfictional attempts at realism often follow a sensationalist tack. Notably, *Life Magazine*'s 1964 photo-essay "The Valley of Poverty" features an overly fertile and desperate people. As exhibit A in President Johnson's War on Poverty, the Appalachian people in John Dominis's photographs live in a "lonely valley," "in shacks without plumbing or sanitation"; they are "disease-ridden and unschooled … without jobs and even without hope."[29]

Saxon Medievalism and Appalachian Romance

Dominis's attempt at a realistic portrait, which in addition to grim-faced miners and despairing children also features large families gathered before a fireplace in a shack or laundry on the line backed by snow-covered mountains, bears the ghosts of another turn-of-the-century tradition running parallel to that of the Appalachian grotesque: romantic Appalachia. This paradox is similar to that found in perceptions of the medieval era. As illustrated by a Gothic revival that both embraces and rejects a medieval past, the medieval grotesque exists alongside what has been called the romantic Middle Ages: that is, the medievalism of knights and ladies, of a Middle Ages as a simpler, nobler time, described by David Matthews as a time "of romance, of chivalric deeds, but also of simple communitarian living and humanely organized labour, a pastoral time when the cash nexus was unknown," in short, "a Middle Ages revalued in largely positive ways."[30] Romantic Appalachia is likewise revalued in positive ways. Such images are part and parcel of another myth that holds Appalachia as "the land that time forgot." To Kephart, even the suspicious and primitive mountain man had a certain appeal: "When I went south into the mountains I was seeking a Back of Beyond ... I yearned for a strange land and a people that had the charm of originality."[31] These mountains were to him and his readers "a mysterious realm" and "terra incognita," covered with a "forest primeval" and even "an Eden still unpeopled and unspoiled." In short, he writes, "time has lingered in Appalachia."[32] Photographs from this earlier era show picturesque log cabins nestled at the foot of beautiful mountains, where women gather on the porch to churn butter or piece quilts (see figure 8.2). Other popular photographic subjects are bearded men and bonneted women standing beside their log cabins, homemade farm implements in hand. One 1935 book of essays and photographs, *Cabins in the Laurel* by Muriel Earley Shepherd, bears a photograph that in conjunction with its caption captures the perceived agelessness of mountain life: this picture shows an older bearded man leaning on a fence and bears the descriptor "To Uncle Rube Mosely the past is only the day before yesterday."[33]

This nostalgia for a past that never was took a distinctive twist, likening Appalachia and its people not simply to an older and simpler time, but – references to primeval forests and Eden aside – to one older, simpler, generally medieval, and, at times, specifically Anglo-Saxon. We find such images again and again in descriptions of the region from the turn of the century onwards. In 1899, William Goodell Frost, president of Kentucky's Berea College from 1892 to 1920, wrote an essay for *Atlantic Monthly* in which he described what he oxymoronically called "our contemporary ancestors." Frost compares a trip to the mountains to a trip to the past, a place where the residents have fallen into a Rip Van Winkle sleep, so that mountain men still use the "old English bow." The "Saxon arts" such as spinning and weaving continue to exist, as does the Chaucerian language with its strong verb forms ("holp" for helped, for example) and quaint vocabulary ("'pack' for carry and 'gorm' for muss").[34] According to the well-known writer and journalist Charles Morrow Wilson, Appalachia was "a land of high hopes and mystic allegiances, where one [could] stroll through the

188   Alison Gulley

8.2. "Maggie Lewis and Wilma Creech, Pine Mountain, KY," by Doris Ulmann, 1934, photograph on paper. Bequest of Doris Ulmann, Berea College Art Collection 150.140.2022.

forests of Arden and find heaths and habits like those of olden England."[35] The myth even crept into novelist James Lane Allen's paean to Kentucky bluegrass:

> One might well name it Saxon grass, so much is it at home in favorable localities of Saxon England, so like the loveliest landscapes of green Saxon England has it made other landscapes on which dwell a kindred race in America, and so near is itself to the type of nature that is peculiarly Saxon: being a hardy, kindly, beautiful, nourishing stock; loving rich lands, and apt to find out where they lie; uprooting inferior aborigines, but stoutly defending its new domain against all fresh invaders … and allying itself closely to any people whose content lies in simple plenty and habitual peace – the perfect squire-yeoman type of all grasses.[36]

In this context, photographs showing children plodding through the snow or men driving a cow through a cornfield are not simply artefacts of romantic Appalachia; they are also reminiscent of illuminated medieval books of hours

8.3. "Young Man Holding Reins to Two Plowing Horses; Man with Bucket," unknown photographer. *Appalachian State University Digital Collections*, omeka.library.appstate.edu/items/show/40484 (accessed 11 January 2018).

that record the passing of the seasons and show peasants, as described by Matthews, "contentedly performing honest manual labour according to ageless seasonal rhythms" (see figure 8.3).[37]

Similarly, a folklorist like William Chase could have his students demonstrate during the White Top Folk Music Festival – which took place in Virginia in the years 1931–9 and aimed to preserve a supposedly rapidly vanishing traditional music – how children of "'Merrie England' some 500 years ago danced and played on the village green."[38] Describing this festival, noted musicologist George Pullen Jackson claimed that such music continued a "tradition which goes back beyond 'Sumer Is Icumen In' and disappears in the cultural mists of the Angles, Saxons, and Celts."[39] The festival also provided the occasion for well-known musician and composer (and native Appalachian) John Powell to gush,

> Every visitor becomes instantly part of all that goes on, and his own traditional heritage pours into the general stream ... Thoughts fly back to Pioneer days, to sailing ships bearing immigrants from England to the New World, to Elizabethan merrymaking, to Chaucer and the Canterbury pilgrims, and at times to a remote

period which the mind of the race has long ago forgotten … There is a sense that we are a folk and that in that fact lies some of the secret of the Golden Age.⁴⁰

In these examples, Anglo-Saxon, medieval, Elizabethan, and Renaissance are all conflated, much as they are in a typical Renaissance faire. Historical accuracy is not the point; rather, general atmosphere and the notion of an idyllic old country are emphasized.

The synthetic nature of the music festival is representative of American medievalism in general, the trappings of which exhibited a peculiarly American bent compared to their overseas counterparts and which had been present from the very beginning. "'History' in the decorative arts had a kind of paste-on quality," writes Robin Fleming, "one in which any number of quasi-historical motifs would do."⁴¹ Apostles in Renaissance garb graced pressed-glass goblets, and cast-iron stoves featured Gothic window-paning and impressions of Jacques-Louis David's *Napoleon on Mont Saint-Bernard*. Decorative mantel sets included Rococo-styled objets d'art alongside Gothic cathedrals, as well as Ivanhoe and, curiously, Pocahontas and the quintessential American woodsman Daniel Boone. She notes that the mass production of such items led consumers "to have a highly eccentric and anachronistic relationship with the medieval past," which was "at once exotic and familiar" so that "the spirit of the age was more important than any empirical truth about it."⁴² This spirit of the age was also apparent in the American literary tradition. Alice Kenney and Leslie Workman point to the novels of Charles Brockden Brown, which represented the first such works in the new Gothic genre in America:

> Brown's six novels imitated the sensational best-sellers of Mrs. Radcliffe and "Monk" Lewis; but, rather than use their medieval artifices for creating terror, such as gloomy, labyrinthine castles and superstitions of diabolical influences, he chose to depict the terror of the American environment and of actual murders, Indian raids, and catastrophic epidemics. A particularly effective example of his use of American natural objects to arouse [emotions] occurs in *Edgar Huntley*, where a young man views the awesome scenery of the Delaware Water Gap while fleeing from marauding Indians, exhausted, in pain, lost in the forest at night, and apprehensive for the safety of his family.⁴³

Although the cultural concept of Appalachia had yet to be established, this early novel, set in the northern Appalachian range straddling the Pennsylvania and New York borders, not only ignited the American imagination but, along with the "Gothic"-inspired figure of the woodsman Daniel Boone described by Fleming, also implicated the Appalachian region in American medievalism from its earliest days. Kenney and Workman further suggest that to a young America, a medieval past had the added appearance of providing "stepping stones toward the accomplishments of a fabulous future."⁴⁴

The same patterns we find in the development of medievalism are present in creating the myth of Appalachia. On the one hand, as Frost notes enthusiastically, "Appalachian America may be useful as furnishing a fixed point which enables us to measure the progress of the moving world!"[45] On the other hand, just as they had earlier absorbed English and Continental traditions of Teutonic and medieval mythology, some Americans looked to Appalachia as representative of the golden age that Powell referenced and as a touchstone against which to create their own identity as the descendants of the Saxons. By the mid- to late nineteenth century the optimism illustrated by the juxtaposition of the medieval past with the prospects of a shiny future wore off as white Americans confronted the rapid influx of supposedly inferior immigrants. In the face of such anxiety, the Southern mountain white – like that hardy Saxon bluegrass that defended itself against "invading newcomers" – provided the possibility of salvation. Harkins argues that to outsiders, "[despite] their poverty, ignorance, primitiveness, and isolation, 'hillbillies' were 'one hundred percent' Protestant Americans of supposedly pure Anglo-Saxon or at least Scotch-Irish lineage."[46] An Appalachia peopled with pure Saxons (the Reverend Campbell claimed they were a "strain [of] white *par excellence* – fair in skin, hair, and eyes"),[47] even those perceived as uneducated and superstitious, gave hope to a nation that saw itself as overrun by immigrant hordes. As Emily Satterwhite notes, "The supposed existence in [the] Southeastern mountains of a pool of desirable 'Saxon' stock served to reassure elites that their vision of America could be replenished thanks to prolific white mountain people who … sustained a respectable 'pioneer' way of life in the face of modernity."[48] Frost highlights the importance of the mountaineer who is "part and parcel of the nation," and he recommends "breaking in upon this Arcadian simplicity" in the battle to retain control. "The question," he writes, "is whether the mountain people can be enlightened and guided so that they can have a part in the development of their own country, or whether they must give place to foreigners and melt away like so many Indians."[49] One quality of Appalachian people held particular promise in the battle for the soul of the nation: "While in more elegant circles American families have ceased to be prolific, the mountain American is still rearing vigorous children in numbers that would satisfy the patriarch. The possible value of such a population is sufficiently evident."[50]

Frost is not the only one to recommend intervention and exploitation of high birth rates for the betterment of America at large. *The Carolina Churchman*, newsletter for the Episcopal Diocese of North Carolina, recommended supporting the mission school at Valle Crucis, a small village in the northwestern mountains of the state, for that very reason:

> Those who long for the combination of the sturdy manhood and virtue and simplicity of the first half of the 19th century with the advantages attendant upon the wealth and enlightenment of today, might be satisfied with the result, and

combination, if the same amount of help proportionately were given these sturdy Highlanders that is given the well-to-do in the colleges and universities of the United States ... Another potent asset, that should appeal to the lover of America and American institutions, is that these Southern Appalachian mountains are giving to the nation every year 100,000 new citizens of the purest American type, which is no inconsiderable item when we know that fifty percent, [sic] increase in many of our large cities is made up of a low type of immigrants from the slums of Europe.[51]

There is no subtlety here: very clearly, the mythology of medieval Appalachia served to define a desired origin story for white America.

In demonizing immigrants and searching for salvation in a specific past, the author of the Episcopal newsletter engages in what Svetlana Boym, in her book *The Future of Nostalgia*, terms "restorative nostalgia." Unlike "reflective nostalgia," which dwells in "longing and loss, the imperfect process of remembrance" – and which we might understand by the example of the yearning for the idyllic, unchanged natural beauty of Appalachia or in the romanticized portraits of rural life – restorative nostalgia poses a danger. She writes, "This kind of nostalgia characterizes national and nationalist revivals all over the world, which engage in the anti-modern myth-making of history by means of a return to national symbols and myths ... Restorative nostalgia manifests itself in total reconstructions of monuments of the past."[52] One of the characteristics of such reconstruction, which can be seen in the Mabry Mill restoration or the performances at the White Top Folk Music Festival, is that the new traditions engendered by these movements "are characterized by a higher degree of symbolic formalization and ritualization than the actual ... customs and conventions after which they were patterned."[53] Restorative nostalgia can propagate benign cultural cohesiveness and a sense of security or, more insidiously, extreme examples of nationalism. Boym points to early twentieth-century Russian pogroms that were inspired by Judeo-Masonic conspiracy theories, but the result need not be so dramatic. What I propose that we see in Appalachian medievalism is instead a less flagrant but potentially no less destructive form of nostalgia. Boym distinguishes between cultural intimacy and political nationalism, both of which result from restorative nostalgia. The former is based on common social context rather than national or ethnic homogeneity. Relishing the natural beauty of the Smoky Mountains and appreciating the quietness of the rural life when compared to a hectic city life can draw Americans together; plotting to displace an undesirable foreign element by exploiting the high birth rate of uncultivated yet supposedly prototypical American mountain whites divides. As with medievalism, these kinds of nationalist reconstructions of the past are commonplace in times of rapid change or at times of political and cultural renegotiation, such as existed at in the late nineteenth and early twentieth centuries, so that it is no coincidence that some of the most enduring myths about a medieval Appalachia date from this period.

Boym additionally observes that "national awareness comes from outside the community rather than within. It is the romantic traveler who sees from a distance the wholeness of the vanishing world ... The vantage point of the stranger informs the native idyll."[54] It is worth noting that in contrast to other forms of medievalism that are usually purposefully engaged in by creators and practitioners, Appalachian medievalism is almost entirely manufactured by outsiders and imposed on the region and its inhabitants to cultivate a specific American identity. Louise D'Arcens suggests that medievalism can be broadly understood as falling into the categories of the "found" and the "made" Middle Ages, the former comprising the interaction with and interpretation of remnants of medieval culture, and the latter being the post-medieval creation of texts, objects, performances, and practices that rely on the perception or imagination of "the medieval" rather than actual historical category.[55] Appalachian medievalism straddles this divide, with early historians and writers fully believing that the mountains preserved not only the pure bloodline of the Anglo-Saxons but also a way of life originating in a hazy medieval and Elizabethan England. At the same time, the Mabry Mill site and especially the White Top Folk Music Festival show a conscious attempt to construct such a past, even as the planners claimed authenticity. For a society on the cusp of multicultural modernism yearning for the stability and simplicity of a conceptual ideal past, the mountain South existed as a vestige of a (mostly white) collective American past in which identity and even salvation could be forged.[56]

NOTES

1 "Mabry Mill, Milepost 176.1," Virtual Blue Ridge, http://www.virtualblueridge.com/parkway-place/mabry-mill (accessed 23 Aug. 2017).
2 Jim Morrison, "75 Years of the Blue Ridge Parkway," *Smithsonian*, 15 Sept. 2010, www.smithsonianmag.com/history/75-years-of-the-blue-ridge-parkway-61889786 (accessed 23 Aug. 2017).
3 Morrison, "75 Years of the Blue Ridge Parkway."
4 David Stewart, "Political Ruins: Gothic Sham Ruins and the '45," *Journal of the Society of Architectural Historians* 55, no. 4 (1996): 400–11, at 406.
5 John Ganim, "Medievalism and Architecture," in *The Cambridge Companion to Medievalism*, ed. Louise D'Arcens (Cambridge: Cambridge University Press, 2016), 29–44, at 30.
6 W.S. Lewis, ed., *Horace Walpole's Correspondence*, Yale ed., vol. 9, p. 149 (letter to George Montague, 11 June 1753). Walpole referred to Strawberry Hill as "a little Gothic castle" in a letter to Mann, 10 Jan. 1750, vol. 20, p. 111. The text is available

at http://images.library.yale.edu/hwcorrespondence/page.asp?vol=20&seq=127&br=ff (accessed 24 Aug. 2017).

7   Clare A. Simmons, "Romantic Medievalism," in D'Arcens, *Cambridge Companion to Medievalism*, 103–18, at 107.
8   Stewart, "Political Ruins," 400.
9   Reginald Horsman, *Race and Manifest Destiny: The Origins of American Racial Anglo-Saxonism* (Cambridge: Cambridge University Press, 1981), 15.
10 Simmons, "Romantic Medievalism," 104.
11 Sean R. Silver, "Visiting Strawberry Hill: Horace Walpole's Gothic Historiography," *Eighteenth-Century Fiction* 21, no. 4 (2009): 535–64, at 541.
12 Roger Wood, "The History Is Concisely This: Thomas Paine's Account of the Peasants' Revolt," in *Medievalism in North American*, ed. Kathleen Verduin (Suffolk, UK: D.S. Brewer, 1994), 5–20, at 6.
13 As documented in a letter from John Adams to Abigail Adams, 4 Aug. 1776, Adams Family Archive, Massachusetts Historical Society, http://www.masshist.org/digitaladams/archive/doc?id=L17760814ja (accessed 28 Jan. 2018). Hengist and Horsa were the reputed chieftains of the invading Angles, Saxons, and Jutes in the fifth century.
14 I am not the first to make this comparison to Brigadoon, the town in the 1949 Lerner and Loewe musical of the same name that appears once every hundred years in the Scottish Highlands and retains the traditions and appearance of two centuries earlier. A quick Google search yields bed and breakfasts in the region bearing the name Brigadoon, scholarly books and articles noting the comparison ironically, and earnest blogposts lacking irony.
15 Phil Noblitt, "The Blue Ridge Parkway and Myths of the Pioneer," *Appalachian Journal* 21, no. 4 (1994): 394–408, at 395.
16 Noblitt, "Blue Ridge Parkway," 394.
17 Noblitt, "Blue Ridge Parkway," 395.
18 Noblitt, "Blue Ridge Parkway," 398n8.
19 H.C. Wilburn, C.S. Creasman, and A. Stupka, "Report on the Proposed Mountain Culture Program for Great Smoky Mountains National Park," photocopy, National Park Service, Harpers Ferry Center Library, Harpers Ferry, West Virginia, p. 48; quoted in Noblitt, "Blue Ridge Parkway," 399.
20 Kelvin Pollard and Linda A. Jacobson, *The Appalachian Region: A Data Overview from the 2013–2017 American Community Survey*, 19 May 2019, https://www.arc.gov/wp-content/uploads/2020/06/DataOverviewfrom2013to2017ACS.pdf, p. 21 (accessed 18 Aug. 2019); and Althea Webb, "African Americans in Appalachia," Oxford African American Studies Center, https://oxfordaasc.com/page/featured-essay-african-americans-in-appalachia (accessed 18 Aug. 2019). William H. Turner notes that Black Africans made contact with the Native Americans in the region by 1526 and that African Americans thus predated the arrival of enslaved Africans in the Cotton South; see his *Blacks in Appalachia* (Lexington: University of Kentucky Press, 1985), xix.

21 Andrew Elliott, *Remaking the Middle Ages: The Methods of Cinema and History in Portraying the Medieval World* (Jefferson, NC: McFarland, 2010), 1.
22 Anthony Harkins, *Hillbilly: A Cultural History of an American Icon* (New York: Oxford University Press, 2004), 14.
23 Will Wallace Harney, "A Strange Land and a Peculiar People," *Lippincott's Magazine of Popular Literature and Science* 12, no. 13 (Apr. 1873): 429–37, at 431.
24 Robert F. Campbell, *Mission Work among the Mountain Whites* (Asheville, NC: Citizen, 1899), 5.
25 Horace Kephart, *Our Southern Highlands* (New York: Outing Publishing, 1916), 214.
26 Kephart, *Our Southern Highlands*, 12.
27 Harkins, *Hillbilly*, 30.
28 Henry Shapiro, *Appalachia on Our Mind: The Southern Mountains and Mountaineers in the American Consciousness, 1870–1920* (Chapel Hill: University of North Carolina Press, 1986), 102. Shapiro notes, however, that the mythology of moonshine and feuds was already present in outsiders' perceptions of Appalachia (104).
29 John Dominis, "The Valley of Poverty," *Life Magazine*, Jan. 1964: 54–5.
30 David Matthews, *Medievalism: A Critical History* (Rochester, NY: D.S. Brewer, 2015), 25.
31 Kephart, *Our Southern Highlands*, 30.
32 Kephart, *Our Southern Highlands*, 14, 31, 51, and 18.
33 Muriel Earley Shepherd, *Cabins in the Laurel*, with photographs by Bayard Wootten (1935; repr., Chapel Hill: University of North Carolina Press, 1991).
34 William Goodell Frost, "Our Contemporary Ancestors in the Southern Highlands," *Atlantic Monthly* 83 (1899): 311–19, at 312–13.
35 Charles Morrow Wilson, "Elizabethan America," *Atlantic Monthly* 144 (1929): 238–44, at 238–9.
36 James Lane Allen, "The Blue-Grass Region of Kentucky," *Harper's New Monthly Magazine* 72 (1885–6): 365–82, at 365.
37 Matthews, *Medievalism*, 40.
38 David Whisnant, *All That Is Native and Fine: The Politics of Culture in an American Region* (Chapel Hill: University of North Carolina Press, 1983), 202. Whisnant quotes an unidentified clipping from a Richmond newspaper that referred in fact to sword and morris dances, which, while of late medieval provenance, had never been a tradition of the Southern mountains.
39 George Pullen Jackson, "The White Top Music Festival Keeps Folk Music Alive," *Musical America* 53 (1933): 7–8, at 7. "Sumer Is Icumen In" dates from the mid-thirteenth century and is generally recognized as one of the earliest Middle English lyrics. As with the log cabins trucked in to establish "authenticity" on the Parkway, "hillbilly" music and country dancing were not necessarily in the tradition of the mountain folk themselves. Instead, organizers urged musicians to play music that was popularly supposed to harken from Appalachia and that had developed a following via radio barn dance shows. The most popular of these shows was Nashville's *WSM Barn Dance*, which later became the *Grand Ole Opry*. For a

discussion of the commercialization of traditional mountain music, see Whisnant, *All That Is Native and Fine*, chap. 3, especially 183–6.

40 John Powell, "Treasure Recovered (Folk Music)," in *Home and Garden Review*, Jul.–Aug. 1934 (Chicago: Home and Garden Review Publishing Company), 5, quoted in Whisnant, *All That Is Native and Fine*, 199.

41 Robin Fleming, "Picturesque History and the Medieval in Nineteenth-Century America," *American Historical Review* 100, no. 4 (1995): 1061–94, at 1067.

42 Fleming, "Picturesque History and the Medieval," 1068.

43 Alice Kenney and Leslie Workman, "Ruins, Romance, and Reality: Medievalism in Anglo-American Imagination and Taste, 1750–1840," *Winterthur Portfolio* 10 (1975): 131–63, at 148.

44 Kenney and Workman, "Ruins, Romance, and Reality," 163.

45 Frost, "Our Contemporary Ancestors," 313.

46 Harkins, *Hillbilly*, 7.

47 Campbell, *Mission Work*, 2.

48 Emily Satterwhite, "Romancing Whiteness: Popular Appalachian Fiction and the Imperialist Imagination at the Turn of Two Centuries," in *At Home and Abroad: Historicizing Twentieth-Century Whiteness in Literature and Performance*, ed. La Vinia Delois Jennings (Knoxville: University of Tennessee Press, 2009), 93–188, at 95. Note that this myth relies on another one, that of a white Middle Ages, highlighted in the United States by the appropriation of medieval symbolism and chivalry as popularly conceived by such white supremacist and white nationalist groups as the Ku Klux Klan, beginning in the immediate aftermath of the Civil War and continuing to the present day.

49 Frost, "Our Contemporary Ancestors," 319.

50 Frost, "Our Contemporary Ancestors," 318.

51 *The Carolina Churchman*, Mar. 1910, p. 6, https://archive.org/details/carolinachurchma12epis (accessed 27 Jan. 2018).

52 Svetlana Boym, *The Future of Nostalgia* (New York: Basic Books, 2008), 41.

53 Boym, *Future of Nostalgia*, 42.

54 Boym, *Future of Nostalgia*, 12.

55 Louise D'Arcens, "Introduction: Medievalism: Scope and Complexity," in D'Arcens, *Cambridge Companion to Medievalism*, 1–13, at 2.

56 I would like to thank my colleagues in the English and Appalachian Studies Departments at Appalachian State University, especially Jessie Blackburn and Zackary Vernon, for steering me towards appropriate scholarship on the region. Greta Browning in the ASU Library has been invaluable both in helping me find my way around Special Collections and, with the help of Graham Shelton, in searching through photographs.

9 Wounded Landscapes: Topographies of Franciscan Spirituality and Deep Ecology in California Medievalism

LOWELL GALLAGHER

I begin with a thought experiment, a critical variant of the road movie that sets its sights on California's coastal expanse for signs of an idiosyncratic medievalism – a California medievalism – that is hidden in plain view. The key to the coinage "California medievalism" turns on the suffix -*ism*, a morpheme so ingrained in parlance that it is easy to forget its provocative suggestiveness as both marker of membership in a group or entity and symptom of territorial conflict at the edges of felt belonging. In what follows, sites and trajectories that harbour traces of three legacies – pastoral and colonial extensions of Franciscan spirituality, ethical provocations of the deep ecology movement, and the seismic instability of California's tectonic geography – constellate into a topographical and figural apparatus for appreciating California medievalism's riven histories and envisioning its reparative futures. This assemblage invites attention as a late-stage permutation of a touchstone of medieval affective and visionary piety: the mystical wounding that transfigured the flesh of Francis of Assisi – the city of San Francisco's namesake – by marking the saint's body as a devotional species of fault zone between spiritual and material orders of being, a stigmatic flashpoint.

California's Seismic Frontier: Fault Line to Contact Zone

I am looking at a photograph of the San Andreas Fault and thinking about the geological scar's vexed association with the resilient myth of California as frontier of the future (see figure 9.1). The myth's resilience owes much to the portability of the frontier meme across a dizzying range of California-based cultural, political, entrepreneurial, and scientific innovations.[1] To this myth, the San Andreas Fault adds the silent provocation of an immemorial hazard – the region's susceptibility to geological disaster. Having gained recognition as one of several virtual shorthands of the California ethos – along with, for example, Hollywood, the Gold Rush, the Golden Gate Bridge, the Beat poets,

198 Lowell Gallagher

9.1. Aerial photograph of the San Andreas Fault in the Carrizo Plain. Copyright David K. Lynch, http://www.SanAndreasFault.org.

Cesar Chavez and the grape boycott, the Valley Girl Syndrome, and Silicon Valley – the San Andreas Fault uniquely harbours a species of medievalism. This claim is no doubt counterintuitive, and the burden of this chapter is to give it ballast by indicating the reach and cultural import of this geologically based medievalizing phenomenon.

To this end, instead of thinking about the fault line, let's think with it. Imperceptibly, it lays the groundwork, so to speak, for an undatable future calamity whose irruption has its origin in the convergence of two tectonic plates (the Pacific Plate and the North American Plate) in the middle Tertiary period, twenty-eight to thirty million years ago. Extending nearly 800 miles from Northern to Southern California, the fault system forms a synapse between an indeterminate peril to come (the "Big One") and a prehistoric event so remote in time as to defy precise calculation.[2] The synapse is meaningful, of course, only to humans, particularly California residents, for whom the rhythms of life in the Golden State consequently harbour an unstable temporality, a subliminal oscillation between practised forgetfulness and anxious anticipation of the predicted (but not fully predictable) magnum earthquake and the catastrophic events to follow.

This dynamic establishes the baseline for imagining the parameters of California medievalism. The aerial image of the tectonic rift's jagged interstices, carved across the length of the state, yields a simple yet suggestive figure: a topographical *medium aevum* born of the fissuring and interpretively opaque space-time of the in-between.[3] This space-time bears on the more conventional scholarly and popular mappings of medievalism (construed as either historical period or assemblage of creatively appropriated tropes and stylistic devices), but it does so in one respect only. The tangent appears through a kind of phenomenological reduction, touching on a characteristic mode of time awareness, both precarious and consoling, in pre-modern Christian cultures. I refer to the widely promulgated sense of ethically charged salvation history unfolding between alpha and omega points, from Creation and the Christ event to the divinely ordered eschaton. To recall Reinhart Koselleck's remark in *Futures Past*, the engines of secular modernity (reliance on contingent prognoses and the "political calculus of probability") have consigned this mode of time awareness, with its transcendent eschatology, to obsolescence or minoritarian status, leaving its contemporary adherents in the asynchronous condition of inhabiting a dominant globalized culture whose *lingua franca* hinges on the expectation of an immanentized eschaton – an earthly heaven or hell, depending on your vantage point.[4]

No argument with that, but let's not discount expressions of the baseline intuition of the *medium aevum* that subsist in displaced or altered avatars. The San Andreas Fault proves a suggestive instance precisely because its access to a schematic temporality of the in-between, inscribed in the fault system's seismic activity and unstable geomorphic signature, offers a tactical occasion to reboot the interpretive system for detecting and appraising other avatars that fall within geographic range of the fault system. My overarching premise, then, is that California medievalism harbours a frontier edginess with no essential ties to more familiar ways of looking for the medieval or the medievalizing gesture in California (as in art objects or manuscripts housed in California museums and archives, or the medieval simulations populating Disneyland and the Disney enterprise).[5] The ties that matter have to do with the critical volatility inherent to the concept and practice of medievalism, traits that carry over into two phenomena that constitute signature elements of California's cultural topography and recall, with different accents, the medieval genealogy of the state's mythos as a perpetually renewable, and perilous, frontier. The phenomena I have in mind, arguably close cousins, are the vexed material legacy of Franciscan spirituality in the California mission network and the controversial tenets of the deep ecology movement.

To bring these linkages into sharper focus, I wish to recast Mary Louise Pratt's concept of the "contact zone." For Pratt, contact zones are "social spaces where cultures meet, clash, and grapple with each other, often in contexts of highly asymmetrical relations of power, such as colonialism, slavery, or their aftermaths as they are lived out in many parts of the world today."[6] If contact zones come into view through a sociopolitical and ethnological lens attuned to conflict, Pratt complicates this perspective by attending to the generically diverse expressive and communicative gestures deployed along the contact zone's borders: "Autoethnography, transculturation, critique, collaboration, bilingualism, mediation, parody, denunciation, imaginary dialogue, vernacular expression – these are some of the literate arts of the contact zone. Miscomprehension, incomprehension, dead letters, unread masterpieces, absolute heterogeneity of meaning – these are some of the perils of writing in the contact zone."[7] According to this view, the multi-generic cast to the bustling activity at the contact zone catalyses an ethos of communicative and disciplinary pluralism, which entails forging illusions of settled expertise and embarking on the road to an engaged and self-critical cosmopolitanism that must, almost by default, face off and engage trials of literacy. Contact zones, as Pratt suggests, may lead to successful mediation and even transcultural innovation, but they cannot guarantee respite from the "perils" of distorted or defective literacies. In sum, contact zones are quintessential states of border anxiety, with no one-size-fits-all metric for knowing when the call to vigilance is warranted or moot.

The contact zone, in other words, is a nomadic concept, finding its first home in ethnographic literary studies but making itself equally at home as the umbrella figure for the nervous energies that course across the edges of the California earthquake fault network as well as the unsettled parameters of medievalism, deep ecology philosophy and activism, and the Franciscan institution. All these constitute a phenomenological cluster of stress points in the cultural topography of California.

Medievalism Meets Deep Ecology

Take medievalism, for starters, where the crux question is not *what* medievalism is but rather *where*. The academic profession has long coped with the inherent contestation built into the question. As Helen Young points out, medievalism is a "very slippery concept."[8] Slipperiness in this instance is the effect of the field's shuttling between polar regions: the direct study of materials dating from the medieval era, often with curatorial intent and sometimes with pretensions to scientific objectivity; and engagement with varied mediations of ideas and tropes associated with the medieval in intervening eras and host genres (e.g., contemporary channellings of Victorian medievalism, fantasy literature and films, historical reenactments by the Society for Creative Anachronism). Drawing on Stephanie Trigg's use of convergence theory in media and communications studies, Young argues further that medievalism is inherently "a practice of convergence as it brings together multiple ideas; modern ideas about and engagements with the medieval past do not bridge a gap in time from now to then but rather tunnel through the many intervening strata and are influenced by that journey."[9]

The metaphor of tunnelling through strata underscores how medievalism's methodological and conceptual convergences tend not to yield immaculate truths but rather to open onto contact zones that may be fractious and messy. Such features may indeed contribute to the contact zone's generative outcomes, even as they also precipitate what Kathleen Biddick calls "the shock of medievalism," the traumatic fault line running through medievalism's methodological contact zones and often inciting withering perceptions of the ersatz or undisciplined or improperly presentist or queer.[10] (There's a slippery slope for you.) *The Shock of Medievalism* came out over twenty years ago, but its core insight retains currency in quarters of the discipline. In part, the resilient shock element betrays the felt loss of cultivated access points to the heart of the medieval in its "hard-edged alterity." Too many "guideposts" to the past conduce to a maze of errors or distractions that pass for a garden of earthly delights.[11] Imagine the jolt such a view gets from the California Through My Lens website's endorsement of the Medieval Times Dinner & Tournament in Buena Park, California, ten minutes from Disneyland: "The campy goodness that is Medieval Times has not lost its charm."[12] In other words, border anxieties at medievalism's contact zones convert easily into a legitimation crisis (even if staged as no more than impatient bemusement).

On a different register, the same dynamic pulses through the deep ecology movement. The name's two words trace the circuit. "Ecology," a nineteenth-century coinage from the Greek *oikos* for home or environment, tacitly conjures its bracketed other – the not-home, the foreign. The "Age of Ecology," heralded by Rachel Carson's *Silent Spring* (1962), identified a quietly virulent contact zone by prompting broad awareness of techno-industrialized society's dangerous introduction of foreign chemical agents (pesticides, herbicides) into the biosphere and triggering a neoliberal, anti-environmentalist backlash with remarkable staying power.[13] The "deep" part comes from an influential lecture and essay-manifesto by one of the founders of the deep ecology movement, Norwegian philosopher Arne Naess.[14] Naess's argument identified a second-order contact zone, between "shallow" and "deep" positions, on the spectrum of advocacy and activism in modern environmentalism.

For Naess, the "shallow" position takes measures to fight "pollution and resource depletion" with the primary goal of sustaining the "health and affluence of people in the developed countries."[15] As David Keller argues, its "reasons for conserving wilderness and preserving biodiversity are invariably tied to human welfare, and it prizes nonhuman nature mainly for its use value." Essentially "an extension of European and North American anthropocentrism," this perspective also remains "typical of mainstream environmentalism."[16] By contrast, the "deep" position promotes a systemic and wholesale displacement of the "man-in-environment image" (and its static figure-ground gestalt) by "*the relational total-field image*" – a complex and dynamic global ecosystem.[17] Espousing "*biospherical egalitarianism* – in principle" and an ethos of "metaphysical holism," the "deep" dimension of ecological commitment recasts the "so-called struggle for life" mantra as a species of contact zone where "realistic practice," which "necessitates some killing, exploitation, and suppression," cedes its normative status to a wider "sense of the ability to coexist and cooperate in complex relationships, rather than the ability to kill, exploit, and suppress."[18] The radical character of deep ecological thinking turns therefore not on the advancement of a specific policy or programmatic action but rather on the aspiration to trigger ideological transformation on a global scale: "Not a slight reform of our present society, but a *substantial reorientation of our whole civilization*."[19]

True to Pratt's emphasis on the contact zone's stress points, the traction that deep ecology's tenets have gained has not come without contestation, denunciation, or misrecognition from both inside and outside the tent of environmental communities.[20] The relevant nuance in all this, given deep ecology's biospheric purview, is the temptation to read the frontier aspect of the movement's aspirations as an essentially spatial image (with local versus global, anthropocentric versus holistic foci). The lesson from medievalism's and the San Andreas Fault's temporo-historical axes, however, draws attention to the movement's longitudinal temporality, told in the punctuated genealogy of its developing insights.

Deep ecology's diverse foundational scenes point to multiple origins before the onset of the "Age of Ecology" in the mid-twentieth century. The genealogical tree includes formative figures such as Aldo Leopold (1887–1948), a shaping voice in environmental ethics and wildlife management; Robinson Jeffers (1887–1962), an important naturalized California voice, whose philosophy of inhumanism directly influenced deep ecology's holistic ethos; conservationist John Muir (1838–1914), another naturalized California voice, co-founder of the Sierra Club and early shaper of the US National Park Service; and several philosophical giants, including Martin Heidegger, Alfred North Whitehead, and Baruch Spinoza.[21]

The crucial contact zone in this genealogy takes us to 1967, with the publication of "The Historical Roots of Our Ecological Crisis" by Lynn White Jr., then professor of medieval history at UCLA (and hence another avatar of California medievalism). White famously – and controversially – argued that secular modernity's presumption to favour the human over and against nature derives in large part from the anthropocentric and hierarchically dogmatic character of orthodox Christianity. In White's account, the accelerating ecological depredations of the modern era are more than collateral damage from the nineteenth-century merger of science and technology. They are the long-range outworking of a precipitating factor, the "victory of Christianity over paganism" – pagan animism in particular – in late antiquity and the medieval era, which "made it possible to exploit nature in a mood of indifference to the feelings of natural objects."[22]

Rather than seek corrective direction from untapped legacies of modern science and technology or alternative Eastern religious traditions (Zen Buddhism, famously), White advocated a species of intramural ideological grafting by appropriating the intuitive legacy of a medieval saint, Francis of Assisi, "the greatest radical in Christian history since Christ."[23] As White explains,

> The key to an understanding of Francis is his belief in the virtue of humility – not merely for the individual but for man as a species. Francis tried to depose man from his monarchy over creation and set up a democracy of all God's creatures ... His view of nature and of man rested on a unique sort of pan-psychism of all things animate and inanimate, designed for the glorification of their transcendent Creator, who, in the ultimate gesture of cosmic humility, assumed flesh, lay helpless in a manger, and hung dying on a scaffold.[24]

White's argument prompted either denunciation or reexamination of previously held tenets in both scientific and theological communities, and the salient consequence was telling.[25] As George Sessions observes, "White claimed with some justification to have created 'the theology of ecology,'" crystallizing ambient perceptions of Francis's "ecological egalitarianism" as a medieval harbinger of the paradigm shift espoused by the deep ecology movement.[26]

Neither Francis's legend nor writings (namely, the ecologically suggestive *Canticle of the Creatures*) achieved the galvanizing force White anticipated for addressing the ecological crisis, although the saint's legacy has undoubtedly impacted the Franciscan order's modern-day pastoralism. A 2011 manifesto by the Order of Friars Minor reminds readers that Francis "was named patron saint of ecology by John Paul II in 1979 for a reason" – the reason being that while the itinerant mendicant "did not confront the same questions that we do ... his approach to the world and his relationship to nature ... remind us of the moral imperative to address the crisis that threatens our planet and all its inhabitants."[27] Secular historiography, however, has tended to view White's account of Franciscanism as compromised by an anachronistic hermeneutic, derived from romanticized nineteenth-century perceptions of Francis's affective piety and creaturely care.[28] Such critiques, while warranting consideration, miss the larger relevance of White's argument. For White, the appeal of Francis's egalitarian ethic lay in large part in its radical – that is, atypical – character and heretical potential (stemming from its implicit demotion of humans as the pre-eminent, if not sole, *imago dei*). Still more telling is White's inference of the abortive yet also incubating character of Francis's egalitarian intuitions – abortive in that they were barred from dogmatic endorsement, and incubating in that they provided fallow ground for emergent (or, as the Orders of Friars Minor manifesto puts it, "incipient") seeds of thought and practice that would later germinate new concepts (like deep ecology) after tunnelling through "many intervening strata," to recall Young's semaphore for the adventures of medievalism writ large. Reading the Franciscan archive, White sought in effect to inhabit a middle ground – a contact zone – between ethical generativity and epistemological accuracy.[29]

To this end, White's argument presented the idea of Franciscanism not as a coherent and unified field but rather as a networked relay of words and behaviours with fault lines running through it. The burden of ensuing scholarship on the Franciscan legacy has been to capture the varied faces of Franciscanism with analytical precision, without consigning the imaginative fecundity of the "eyes of the heart" to a hermeneutic hinterland.[30] The charge, then, is to cultivate critical and non-reductive attunement to the mutating constellation of Franciscanism's signature attributes.

Crucially, the Franciscans' profession of humility, advocacy of voluntary poverty and mendicant life, and emulation of the founder's exemplary affective piety sit oddly with the order's known complicity and participation in some of the most ruthless and predatory manoeuvres of the early modern ecclesial imperium. Julia McClure's recent study of the contradictory outworking of Franciscan pastoralism brilliantly isolates the core fault line:

> The romanticized legends of St. Francis, a man committed to poverty and humility … and who became the patron saint of animals, seem in conflict with the history of the Franciscan Order which became entangled with violence, the repressive processes of Inquisition, and the history of colonialism. Yet this is not a true paradox. The history of the Franciscan Order and the history of colonialism are interrelated in important ways that are hidden by the illusion of paradox. Peace and humility *and* discipline and violence all contributed to the Franciscan condition.[31]

McClure's meticulous unpacking of the Franciscans' "historically ambivalent relationship with power and authority" makes for persuasive reading, especially in chronicling how that ambivalence played out in the seemingly effortless extension of the friars' ascetic self-discipline. Franciscans espoused the "virtue of violence" as a vehicle of personal transcendence over earthly cares, which merged with the missionary cohort's "multidimensional programme" of subjugation and erasure of Indigenous "culture, language, and history" during the spiritual, ideological, social, and political colonization that extended across the Americas and into Alta California.[32]

I pause over the swift dispatching of the detected paradox as mere illusion. The paradox, I think, is not illusory because its terms do not reside in the historical circumstances per se. Where, then, is the paradox? It lies in the clarity of historical hindsight, which makes it nearly impossible for today's scholarship *not* to see more of the ruinous cultural effects and malignant ironies of the Franciscans' proselytizing program than the missionaries of the era could have recognized or owned up to (in terms conforming to modern critical tenets). Critical reflection's capacity to detect blind spots in the past is a truism, and a trivial one at that, but the point also carries the useful reminder that the work of critical reflection on the past carries its own blind spots. In the case of the vexed legacy of the Franciscans' evangelistic agenda, the tell lies in the ease with which the missionaries' devotional fervour and salvific aspiration solicit interest, at least in mainstream medievalism, either as ethnographic curiosity, historical artefact limned with the "hard-edged alterity" of the immeasurably other, or forensic clue pointing to something closer to home – the concerns shaping the *oikos* of secular modernity. As the history of the deep ecology movement and its contact zones amply shows, however, the *oikos* of the now is no simple thing. Its perspective on the past does not work like an intravenous line. Its angle of vision inherently includes lateral encroachments, dead ends, and anamorphic extensions, as well as impressions of congruence and unpredictable retrievals of seemingly dismantled or obsolete arcs of thought. On this score, the truth of the historical archive has an inherently divided character, as both bearer and reflection of unsettled energies, paradoxical convergences, unfinished outcomes, and unnavigated detours.[33]

Stigmatized Body as Contact Zone

The Franciscan archive contains a paradigmatic trope of the prospect and challenge I have just described: the paranormal contact zone that occurred during Francis's mystical experience at La Verna, reportedly two years before his death in 1226. Francis's vision of a mysterious and suggestively apocalyptic emissary, "a seraph with six wings," produced a kind of spiritual fibrillation ("joy and grief alternating within him") that manifested on his flesh in the form of stigmata resembling Jesus Christ's wounds of crucifixion.[34] I identify Francis's stigmatization as a unique species of contact zone to highlight the ferment of responses to the event during the Franciscan movement's formative decades, extending into the moment of the missionary-colonizing expedition to the Americas.

Initial accounts (notably Thomas of Celano's) include reports of consternation and wonder at the unprecedented character of the phenomenon ("miraculi novitas"), as well as the impulse to treat the event as the exemplar of a "new 'carnal' spirituality" disclosing the meritorious promise of devotional ardour, "a divine reward for a life of love and total commitment" and giving bodily testimony to the "rebirth of the apostolic spirit" in Francis's affective piety.[35] Later accounts emphasized the "cosmic and eschatological aspects" of the stigmata, even at the risk of theological provocation. By the beginning of the fourteenth century, two separate terms of the provocation — the view of Francis as *alter Christus* and alternatively as *alter angelus*, a second Christ and a second apocalyptic angel — fused to create the eventual template for translating the Franciscan "eremitic *habitus*" into the emergent landscapes of missionary colonial expansion.[36]

McClure traces the gathering momentum of this thought cluster, from Bonaventure's tempered apocalypticism in his influential biography of Francis, the *Legenda maior*, to the engaged millenarianism of important sixteenth-century Franciscan actors in the evangelization of New Spain, Gerónimo de Mendieta and Toribio de Benavente Motolinía.[37] For McClure, the connective tissue in the archive is the legible influence of Joachim of Fiore's eschatological theology of history and the rhetorical suggestiveness of its supersessionism: the "crucial element of Joachim's eschatological model of time was that the future age of the spirit was located within earthly time and so could be spatialised in the New World."[38] McClure's decisive gesture is to point out how "the stigmata are invested with this symbolic meaning": "This connection to the sixth seal invented St. Francis as the signifier of the transition to the new age of the spirit. Franciscans saw themselves as 'midwives to the millennium,' as important agents for the negotiation of the future."[39] The takeaway from McClure's observation, in my view, is to ask where and how to locate the figurative and material extensions of the stigmata in California, on condition that we respect the marks as unsettled contact zones between the legacies of eschatological aspiration and pragmatic futurism.

Stigmatic Viewing: A Museum Tour

Where are the stigmata to be found now in California? It depends on where and how you look. See what turns up when you begin with aesthetic objects, and then turn to figural extensions in California's cultural topography. Bear in mind the operative forensic hint that stigmata are to the body of Francis and cultural corpus of Franciscan devotional tradition what the San Andreas Fault is to the cultural topography of California: lesions that are less a symptom of a pre-existing irruptive condition than an opening onto an altered and complexly shaped phenomenological optics for reading the contact zones between medievalism and the California landscape.

Following our initial pause over the state's fissured geography, the next interpretive reboot required to grasp the provocations of California medievalism comes from scenes of devotional stigmatization housed in the expected setting for aesthetic appreciation: California's art collections. Consider two early modern paintings in the Los Angeles County Museum of Art's permanent collection: Giovanni Baglione's *The Ecstasy of Saint Francis* (1601) and Mariano

Salvador Maella's *Saint Francis of Assisi Receiving the Stigmata* (1787). Although Baglione's colour palette makes it hard to discern, the telling detail appears in the lower foreground (see figure 9.2). The visual narrative tells a straightforward story: the saint's devotional meditation has been interrupted by the mystical vision. The visual detail, however, harbours an iconographic surplus. The proximity of the stigmatized hand to the book suggestively identifies both book and wound as reading instruments.[40] Maella's painting gives a more explicit treatment of the stigmata's readerly endowment (see figure 9.3). Looking from left to right, we observe Brother Leo, Francis's secretary and confessor, poring over his devotional reading; Francis gazing upwards at the winged seraph, who appears in a sunburst; and Francis's stigmatized left hand, poised in the position of a prosthetic lens in front of an opened Bible.

Two manuscripts in the Getty Collection of medieval illuminations pick up the theme in the context of otherwise conventional late medieval visual homilies on the salvific merit of private devotional reading. The mid-fifteenth-century illumination in a book of hours by the Master of Sir John Fastolf makes striking use of saturated red pigment to compose the visual argument (see figure 9.4). Francis's reading matter, presumably sacred scripture, acquires a dual function, as textual source of the meditation on the axial event, the Crucifixion, and as member of the extended scene of somatized wounding-reading that marks the saint's access to the eschatologically charged event filling the star-studded night sky. The signature feature of the stigmatization scene in Taddeo Crivelli's *Gualenghi-d'Este Hours* is the rendering of the apocalyptic seraph, who appears ensconced in a multiform object, at once escutcheon, monstrance, solar oculus, and giant orb-wound (see figure 9.5). The riveting flying object doesn't shout reading device, but the vertical trajectory of the blood-red colour, targeting the opened book in Leo's hands, makes the argument.

The ensemble gathered thus far marks an important station in our itinerary by showing, within the confines of California's art museums, how the stigmata, considered as religiously evocative aesthetic icons, present not only as phenomena to be read about or looked at but also as optical and reading instruments whose symbolic fissuring action both incites and testifies to the onset of transformative perception. To connect this insight to more viscerally provocative aspects of California's topography, it bears recalling McClure's suggestion that the symbolic radiance of Francis's legendary stigmatization lent the mystical wounds privileged status in the Franciscan mental habitus as a sacred avatar of the Franciscans' missionary and colonizing efforts, casting the multifarious operation – including its violent effects – as salvifically and eschatologically tenable and necessary: a vehicle of Christian *novitas*. To discover the material signs of this legacy and the complex contact zones it carries today, the first step is to look again at the California landscape, this time through the mediation of two cartographic images (see figures 9.6 and 9.7).

9.2. Giovanni Baglione's *The Ecstasy of Saint Francis* (1601). Digital image courtesy of Los Angeles County Museum of Art, http://www.lacma.org.

Wounded Landscapes: Topographies of Spirituality in California Medievalism 209

9.3. Mariano Salvador Maella's *Saint Francis of Assisi Receiving the Stigmata* (1787). Digital image courtesy of Los Angeles County Museum of Art, http://www.lacma.org.

9.4. Master of Sir John Fastolf (Ms. 5, fol. 44v, 1430–1440). Color reproduction at http://www.getty.edu/art/collection/objects/2733/master-of-sir-john-fastolf-saint-francis-french-or-english-about-1430-1440. Digital image courtesy of the J. Paul Getty Museum.

9.5. Taddeo Crivelli, *Gualenghi-d'Este Hours* (Ms. Ludwig IX 13, fol. 201v, c. 1469). Color reproduction at: http://www.getty.edu/art/collection/objects/3827/taddeo-crivelli-the-stigmatization-of-saint-francis-italian-about-1469. Digital image courtesy of the J. Paul Getty Museum.

9.6. Map of San Andreas Fault. Copyright David K. Lynch, http://www.SanAndreasFault.org.

Wounded Landscapes: Topographies of Spirituality in California Medievalism 213

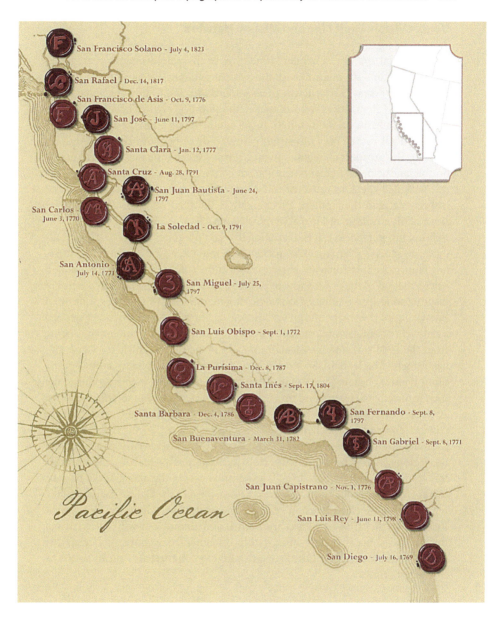

9.7. Map of California mission network. Digital image courtesy of California Missions Foundation, http://californiamissionsfoundation.org.

Double Vision: Fault Line and Mission Network

To the casual eye, the schematic rendering of the paired images presents an optical illusion – the alignment of the two seams along the coastal area is coincidental and betrays no structure of co-implication. The California Department of Parks and Recreation website makes the point nicely in declaring that the San Juan Bautista mission, ninety miles south of San Francisco along the El Camino Real route, "was unwittingly located directly above the San Andreas Fault."[41] The prospect changes, however, if you consider the two different marks on the landscape as a phenomenological contact zone. The paired geographical markings speak to adjacent inhabitings of an unruly spatio-temporalized in-between, and the ambient affect entails a shuttling between varied expressions of dissociation and projective aspiration.

From this perspective, it bears noting that contact zones are apt to trigger mutations. Francis's stigmatization turned him into *alter Christus* and *alter angelus*. Franciscan missionaries' participation in the colonial enterprise prompted a deformation of the order's vow of poverty, transforming the inherited ethos of dispossession into a subjugation tactic. Rotate the map 180 degrees. Common knowledge of the sociocultural turbulence caused by a seismic disaster opened a rich vein of entertainment material for the Hollywood film industry, ranging from the 1936 romantic musical drama *San Francisco* (a vehicle for Clark Gable, Jeanette MacDonald, Spencer Tracy, and the unintentionally campy eponymous theme song), to the 1974 disaster film *Earthquake* (which introduced the then innovative Sensurround process, with hyperrealistic sound effects), to the 2015 *San Andreas* (noted for its "idiotically hilarious dialogue" and "tons of computer-generated mayhem").[42]

Hence the pulse of life in the fault zone, veering between forgetfulness of the region's seismic precariousness (told in the generally uneven programming for "mitigation and preparedness") and immersion in the allure of the region's mythic frontier associations.[43] This is the heartbeat of the California dream, the region's secularized expression of eschatological hope. Along the El Camino Real, the pulse of forgetfulness and immersion sounds out with different but not unrelated accents. The most richly documented example concerns the still-resonant myth of California Spanish mission culture, ably summarized by Michelle Lorimer:

> Touring through the Spanish California missions today, many visitors learn about the early history of the state. Contemporary mission sites are graced with beautifully manicured gardens, tiled courtyards, fountains, large stone sculptures, and covered alcoves in which visitors can enjoy the relaxing environment created by mission stewards. The exhibitions in mission museums highlight the lives and accomplishments of Spanish Franciscan missionaries, especially Father

> President Junípero Serra, who pioneered these "civilizing" institutions … Many historical representations of California missions today neglect to acknowledge … vital components of Native life at the missions, including Native labor, resistance, sustenance, disease, punishment, and death. At the same time, they generalize or oversimplify the histories of Native peoples in the region and their connection to the land. Thus underneath the charming façade maintained at many contemporary mission sites is a more tumultuous history that, if told, would reflect poorly on the constructed "Spanish fantasy past" and mission myth in California.[44]

As Lorimer suggests, the "Spanish fantasy past" is a modern concoction. Its enabling condition was the secularization of the California missions in the mid-nineteenth century. The nominal break with the Spanish Catholic past was followed at the turn of the century by various stakeholders' Janus-faced "booster ideology."[45] Infused with a distinctively Protestant, not Catholic, pursuit of "order, acquisition, and the work ethic," booster ideology invented a composite practice of restoration and fabrication designed to install a "romanticized myth of the California missions" for consumers.[46] Brilliantly successful, the "resonance of the mission sites with a romanticized past continued through the twentieth century," as Elizabeth Kryder-Reid observes, "and the notion of traveling to see and experience the site in person, a pilgrimage to these historic shrines, became an iconic element of the California experience."[47]

The iconic element survives today in the state's mission tourism industry, whose aesthetic and historical airbrushing continues to purvey what is, in effect, a secular deformation of the supersessionist overlay that marked early modern Franciscan missionaries' redemptive and colonizing quest. In recent years, however, tectonic movements have been altering the shape and look of the contact zone, yielding yet another mutation of the first missionaries' eschatological dream of converting the Americas – of marking the land with the redemptive wounds of Christic suffering and sacrifice. Here, as Lorimer's overview suggests, the fissuring action opens prospects for a richer understanding of the complex admixtures of subjugation and complicity, among both colonizing and colonized populations.

In the main, the state's tourist industry has a long way to go in negotiating the switch between mythologizing the history of the missions and historicizing the myth, but momentum is growing in adjacent quarters, both secular and religious. In 2016, for example, the California State Board of Education adopted the California History–Social Science Framework's holistic guidelines for promoting historical and cultural literacy about the California missions at the grade four level. Consider the following excerpt:

> California's missions, presidios, haciendas, and pueblos should be taught as an investigation into the many groups of people who were affected by them. Sensitivity

and careful planning are needed to bring the history of this period to life. A mission lesson should emphasize the daily lives of the native population, the Spanish military, the Spanish–Mexican settler population, and the missionaries ... Once students have learned that they will investigate the multiple perspectives of people who lived during the mission period, the teacher presents carefully selected primary and secondary sources, as well as informational texts written for children that provide context about each of the groups of people ... The arrival of the Spanish, along with their imported flora and fauna, catalyzed a change in the region's ecosystem as well as its economy. What had once been a landscape shaped by hunter–gatherer societies became an area devoted to agriculture and the distribution of goods throughout the Spanish empire. Students can analyze data about crop production and livestock in order to better understand how people used the land and intensified the use of its natural resources.[48]

The template reads like an object lesson in attending to the wounding dynamics of the contact zones that played out on the edges of the California frontier on several fronts – social, cultural, political, religious, and ecological. If one accepts the mutational dynamics of the contact zone, the guidelines read very much like the unfurling of a twenty-first-century expression of a new age of the Franciscan stigmata in the public school system curriculum. The wounds' devotional and eschatological legacies have morphed into an attentive reading practice endowed with both critical and reparative instincts.[49]

All the more reason, then, to consider the adjacent dynamic among religious community stakeholders. In this domain, it is impossible to ignore the seismic event that occurred on 23 September 2015, the canonization of Junípero Serra, founding father of the California missions, by Pope Francis (who chose his papal name to honour Francis of Assisi, "the man of poverty, the man of peace, the man who loves and protects creation").[50] Serra's canonization was not a punctual decision – the momentum of his course to sainthood was evident after his beatification by John Paul II in 1988. Yet the ne plus ultra achievement of the eighteenth-century missionary to Alta California was received by many Native Californians and others as a double wound inflicted by institutional Catholicism, a humiliating and hypocritical disregard of Indigenous perspectives on the missionizing chapters of the region's history.

Even so, the very notoriety of the event catalysed renewed attention to the complex structure of dissension and misrecognition in the conflictual memories and histories of the mission system. In a 2016 article, Lee Panich notes that "the Diocese of Monterey, which subsumes a full third of California's 21 missions, has established a California Missions Coordinator position to engage various descendant communities in changes to public interpretation," while at the regional level, "the Catholic California Conference recently announced a formal review, led by Ohlone scholar Andy Galvan, of the interpretive programs at California mission sites under its jurisdiction as well as the relevant curriculum units in the state's Catholic elementary schools."[51] The CCC's 2015 curriculum for fourth-graders in the "CA Mission Project" already included evidence of careful negotiation of the conflicting perspectives in material covering the curricular program.[52] The "Biography of St. Junípero Serra" link eschews proselytizing bias, the "California Missions Native History" link uses instructional resources designed by the California Indian Museum and Cultural Center to showcase frank assessments of Indigenous perspectives on the missionary enterprise, and the "Words Can Hurt" link reminds students of the stigmatizing effects of using casually discriminatory language towards historically disenfranchised groups. In brief, what we see now, in both secular and religious California school systems, are the beginnings of a new reading practice, one focused on attending to wounds, with a mind to breaking the spiral of abreactions to a fissured memory of California's past.

California's Seismic Frontier Redux: Stigmatic Fault Lines

I am looking at Llagas Creek, a stream in Santa Clara County, California (see figure 9.8). The creek's headwaters are on the eastern side of Loma Prieta, the highest peak in the Santa Cruz Mountains, near the epicentre of the 1989 seismic disaster known as the Loma Prieta earthquake, the most devastating quake to hit the San Francisco Bay area since 1906. A strange adjacency: the benign and life-supporting cut of the stream traversing woodlands and chaparral on terrain moulded and creviced by the tectonic movements of the San Andreas Fault. What holds my thought, however, is the stream's name. *Llagas*, the Spanish word for "wounds," was chosen by Juan Crespí, the Franciscan missionary who accompanied the 1769 Portolá expedition to Monterey, to memorialize Francis's stigmatization in the rugged landscape of Nueva California. His diary records the inspiration: "Though the name of Saint Francis had been reserved for his famous town ... yet since this stream was not to be despised as the place for a fair little mission, I consecrated its name with that of his Stigmata."[53] Crespí's wish was to turn the Nueva California landscape into an optical mnemonic, to remind future travellers and sojourners of the eschatological dream that had materialized on the flesh of the order's founder and was now reappearing through the developing network of missionary enclaves along the California coast. His wish came true, in ways he could not have imagined. Considered under the aspect of their unfolding immanence, the stigmata are the most provocative expression of California medievalism, cutting through boundaries that define the disparate contact zones in California's topography – fault zone, mission network, deep ecology initiatives, and contemporary Franciscan pastoralism.

Reflecting on Llagas Creek, I hear converging echoes of two voices, a medieval historian's and an ecologist's, each marked with affective sympathy for the

9.8. Llagas Creek, California. View of Llagas Creek from bridge on Oak Glen Avenue in Morgan Hill, California. Photo taken 28 March 2017. By Wahn – Own work, CC BY-SA 4.0, https://commons.wikimedia.org/w/index.php?curid=57493013, https://creativecommons.org/licenses/by-sa/4.0/legalcode.

non-self. From Aldo Leopold's *A Sand County Almanac and Sketches Here and There*: "The cowman who cleans his range of wolves does not realize that he is taking over the wolf's job of trimming the herd to fit the range. He has not learned to think like a mountain. Hence we have dustbowls, and rivers washing the future into the sea."[54] From Aviad Kleinberg's *The Sensual God*:

> The Joachite idea of time has a spiral aspect built in it. The three ages, of Father, Son, and Holy Spirit, display recurring structures. But this recurrence is not a simple repetition; it is an evolution. The world is moving toward greater spirituality and each age surpasses the age that preceded it. Each age is restarted by an "epochal" event ... The stigmatization [of Francis] was not the humanization of God; it was the divinization of man. And paradoxically, the most radical expression of the divinization of man was, just as it was in the Age of the Son, carnal.[55]

Leopold's phrase "think like a mountain" remains a valuable mantra in the deep ecology movement, a resilient call to advance the claims of a holistic bioethics endowed with philosophical depth and pragmatic heft. The echo of Leopold's aphorism in Kleinberg's rendering of the Joachite "spiral" of time in the Franciscan cult of the stigmata issues another call. This is the call to think like the stigmata, with the understanding that this is no longer a call to devotion. It means keeping an ear to the ground, attuned to signs that the stories of the stigmata are not finished. So it is that the deep ecology movement may be seen as the outworking of an epochal transformation, an indeed carnal "divinization" of the human that materializes not as a paranormal event or radical co-option of the Anthropocene's excesses, but as a posthuman awakening to a broad-based ecological literacy, an everyday hermeneutic informed by an ethic of care for the biosphere and, in California, proactive recognition of the fault lines subsisting in the *political ecology* of the mission network.

To this end, it is important to recognize how the spiritual resonance and energy of the deep ecology movement sustain an ethos of creaturely care that remembers, even if through a refractive lens, the pastoral ideals of the early Franciscan movement. On a related front, recent statewide incentives in both secular and Catholic school systems to tell and honour more of the story of the California missions are ethically related to contemporary Franciscanism's reparative practices, as voiced in the 2011 Order of Friars Minor manifesto's declaration of the interconnectedness of the environmental crisis and social injustice. There is no mention of Francis's stigmata in this manifesto, but there does not need to be. The legacy of the wounding action survives in the manifesto's "invitation to all of us ... to take the time to study the reality of the world around us, to know the people involved and their problems, to feel the suffering of the earth and how it is related to the suffering of the people," including "problems relating to environmental justice."[56] That sounds to me like a medievalism for everyone.

NOTES

1 See, for example, Stacey L. Smith, *Freedom's Frontier: California and the Struggle over Unfree Labor, Emancipation, and Reconstruction* (Chapel Hill: University of North Carolina Press, 2013), and Lawrence Culver, *The Frontier of Leisure: Southern California and the Shaping of Modern America* (Oxford: Oxford University Press, 2012). Ross Douthat's *New York Times* opinion piece "Liberalism's Golden Dream" (25 Apr. 2018) opines that while "it is not an iron law that what happens in the Golden State *must* go national, you can tell a plausible story in which California is a harbinger of a delayed-but-still-coming Democratic wave."

2 Considered a datum of scientific inquiry, the age of the San Andreas Fault can be dated precisely. It was discovered in 1895 by UC Berkeley geologist Andrew Lawson, three years after the Sierra Club – another California touchstone – was founded by environmentalist John Muir.

3 Consideration of the rich philosophical investment in the notion of the in-between falls outside the scope of this essay. However, my use of the term is informed by Henk Oosterling's reflections on the term's significance for Jean-Luc Nancy and Gilles Deleuze. The San Andreas Fault materially resembles Oosterling's précis of the impact of the in-between on the dynamic of memory and anticipation. Memory "is no longer a matter of picking up the pieces of a scattered community, reconstructing a loss in order to produce a new identity or to fill in a gap ... Remembering is, in this sense, a creative process that nevertheless is embedded in past experiences ... Remembering, one could tentatively say, is eventually an effectuation of a new past in creating a 'world' right here and now" (Henk Oosterling, "From Interests to Inter-esse: Jean-Luc Nancy on Deglobalization and Sovereignty," *SubStance* 34, no. 1 [2005]: 81–103, at 99–100).

4 Reinhart Koselleck, *Futures Past: On the Semantics of Historical Time*, trans. Keith Tribe (New York: Columbia University Press, 2004), 21.

5 For a wide-ranging examination of the medievalizing aesthetic of Disneyland and the extended Disney operations, see Tison Pugh and Susan Aronstein, eds., *The Disney Middle Ages: A Fairy Tale and Fantasy Past* (New York: Palgrave Macmillan, 2012).

6 Mary Louise Pratt, "Arts of the Contact Zone," *Profession* (1991): 33–40, at 34.

7 Pratt, "Arts of the Contact Zone," 37.

8 Helen Young, "Approaches to Medievalism: A Consideration of Taxonomy and Methodology through Fantasy Fiction," *Parergon* 27, no. 1 (2010): 163–79, at 163.

9 Young, "Approaches to Medievalism," 166.

10 Kathleen Biddick, *The Shock of Medievalism* (Durham, NC: Duke University Press, 1998), 10.

11 Biddick, *Shock of Medievalism*, 10.

12 See "The Big List of Strange, Fun & Unique Attractions in Southern California," California through My Lens, last modified 14 Dec. 2020, https://californiathroughmylens.com/strange-fun-attractions-list.

13 See David K. Hecht, "How to Make a Villain: Rachel Carson and the Politics of Anti-Environmentalism," *Endeavor* 36, no. 4 (2012): 149–55. The expression "Age of Ecology" was coined by George Sessions, one of the leaders of the deep ecology movement; see his "The Deep Ecology Movement: A Review," *Environmental Review: ER* 11, no. 2 (1987): 105–25, at 105.

14 Arne Naess, "The Shallow and the Deep, Long-Range Ecology Movement: A Summary," *Inquiry: An Interdisciplinary Journal of Philosophy* 16 (1973): 95–100; repr. in *Deep Ecology for the Twenty-First Century: Readings on the Philosophy and Practice of the New Environmentalism*, ed. George Sessions (Boston: Shambhala, 1995), 151–5.

15 Naess, "Shallow and the Deep," 151.

16 David Keller, "Deep Ecology," in *Encyclopedia of Environmental Ethics and Philosophy*, ed. Baird Callicott and Robert Frodeman (Farmington Hills, MI: Macmillan Reference, 2008), 206–11, at 206.

17 Naess, "Shallow and the Deep," 151; italics in original.

18 Naess, "Shallow and the Deep," 151–2; italics in original.

19 Arne Naess, *Ecology, Community, and Lifestyle: Outline of an Ecosophy*, trans. David Rothenberg (New York: Cambridge University Press, 1989), 45; italics in original.

20 For overviews of the critiques of deep ecology's aims, see Bill Devall, "The Deep Ecology Movement," *Natural Resources Journal* 20, no. 2 (1980): 299–322, and Sessions, "Deep Ecology Movement."

21 See Bill Devall, "The Deep Ecology Movement," for a lucid account of the movement's complex genealogy. Without discounting the movement's international origins, Petr Kopecký argues for the robust inflection of California voices in the formative stages of the movement; see his *The California Crucible: Literary Harbingers of Deep Ecology* (Riga, Latvia: Lambert Academic Publishing, 2013).

22 Lynn White Jr., "The Historical Roots of Our Ecological Crisis," *Science* 155 (10 Mar. 1967): 1203–7, at 1205.

23 White, "Historical Roots," 1206.

24 White, "Historical Roots," 1207.

25 For a recent testament to the resilient suggestiveness of White's essay, see Todd LeVasseur and Anna Peterson, eds., *Religion and Ecological Crisis: The "Lynn White Thesis" at Fifty* (New York: Routledge, 2017).

26 Sessions, "Deep Ecology Movement," 106.

27 Order of Friars Minor, "Franciscans and Environmental Justice: Confronting Environmental Crisis and Social Injustice" (Rome: Office for Justice, Peace, and the Integrity of Creation, 2011), 2, at http://www.hnp.org/userfiles/EnvironmentalJustice.pdf (accessed 30 Sept. 2019).

28 See, for example, Andrew Cunningham, "Science and Religion in the Thirteenth Century Revisited: The Making of St. Francis the Proto-Ecologist, Part 2: Nature Not Creature," *Studies in History and Philosophy of Science* 32, no. 1 (2001): 69–98.

29 Francis's creaturely ethic "is an incipient invitation to care for the *habitat*, to protect the integrity of the ecosystem, thus guaranteeing the interrelationships that ensure survival" (Orders of Friar Minor, "Franciscans and Environmental Justice," 3).

30 I take the phrase from Jean-Bertrand Aristide's Franciscan- and liberation-theology-inflected *Eyes of the Heart: Seeking a Path for the Poor in the Age of Globalization* (Monroe, ME: Common Courage Press, 2002). The biblical source is Ephesians 1:18.

31 Julia McClure, *The Franciscan Invention of the New World* (Basingstoke, UK: Palgrave Macmillan, 2017), 119–20. See also Delno C. West, "Medieval Ideas of Apocalyptic Mission and the Early Franciscans in Mexico," *Americas* 45, no. 3 (1989): 293–313.

32 McClure, *Franciscan Invention*, 120, 129, 132.

33 On this point, see Steven Turley's reflections on the difficulty of gauging early modern Franciscans' ambivalence toward the punishing instruments of the missionary-colonial project, in *Franciscan Spirituality and Mission in New Spain, 1524–1599* (London: Routledge, 2016): "[The] physical, vocational, spiritual, and emotional struggles that the friars recounted ubiquitously in their correspondence ... were the predictable result of the interactions between their eremitic *habitus* and their radically new field of action ... in an entirely incompatible mission field" (188).

34 Thomas of Celano, *Vita Prima Francisci*, quoted in Aviad Kleinberg, *The Sensual God: How the Senses Make the Almighty Senseless* (New York: Columbia University Press, 2015), 106. As Kleinberg points out, "For many of his contemporaries and successors, Francis was to be identified as the Angel of the Sixth Seal of Revelation 7.2 ('And I saw another angel ascending from the east, having the seal of the living God'). He was the embodiment of Joachim of Fiore's hugely influential interpretation of this mysterious figure, as a messenger of the approaching third age of sacred history, the age of the Spirit" (107).

35 Kleinberg, *Sensual God*, 110, 119, 111.

36 Turley, *Franciscan Spirituality and Mission*, 188.

37 On the *Legenda maior*, see Jay Hammond, "Bonaventure's *Legenda Major*," in *A Companion to Bonaventure*, ed. Jay Hammond, J.A. Wayne Hellman, and Jared Goff (Leiden: Brill, 2013), 453–507.

38 McClure, *Franciscan Invention*, 161.

39 McClure, *Franciscan Invention*, 164–5. McClure cites Leonard Sweet's expression ("midwives to the millennium") in "Christopher Columbus and the Millennial Vision of the New World," *Catholic Historical Review* 72, no. 3 (1976): 369–82, at 378.

40 There is precedent for the optical stigmata trope. In the gigantic sonnet sequence with commentary on Christ's Passion by French poet Jean de la Ceppède, *Theorems on the Sacred Mystery of Our Redemption* (1613 and 1622), sonnet 60 (book 2, part 2) identifies Christ's wounds as components of a theological optics: "The three holes will serve as windows for our eyes / [so that] We may glimpse through them your secrets in Heaven" (*Les Théorèmes sur le sacré mystère de notre redemption: Réproduction de*

l'édition de Toulouse de 1613–1622, Travaux d'Humanisme et Renaissance, vol. 80 [Geneva: Librairie Droz, 1966], 293). With minor modifications I use the English translation supplied by John Porter Huston in *The Rhetoric of Poetry in the Renaissance and Seventeenth Century* (Baton Rouge: Louisiana State University Press, 1983), 182–3. La Ceppède's commentary establishes the trope's patristic genealogy by recalling its exemplary voicing in the twelfth-century meditation of Bernard of Clairvaux: "The nail has become for me a key to an opening so that I see the will of God … The nail cries out, the wound cries out, the secret of the heart [*arcanum cordis*] is visible through the holes in the body" (quoted in Huston, *Rhetoric of Poetry*, 295).

41 "The California Missions Trail," California Department of Parks and Recreation, http://www.parks.ca.gov/?page_id=22722 (accessed 6 Jan. 2019).

42 Peter Travers, "*San Andreas*: Not Even The Rock Can Save This Complete Disaster of an LA-Destroyed-by-Earthquake Movie," *Rolling Stone*, 27 May 2015, http://www.rollingstone.com/movies/movie-reviews/san-andreas-250600 (accessed 6 Jan. 2019).

43 On the difficulty of gauging the impact of a magnum earthquake in California, see James Fallows, "Living on the Fault Line," *Atlantic*, Oct. 1981, http://www.theatlantic.com/magazine/archive/1981/10/living-on-the-fault-line/303772 (accessed 6 Jan. 2019).

44 Michelle Lorimer, *Resurrecting the Past: The California Mission Myth* (Pechanga, CA: Great Oak Press, 2016). See also Phoebe Kropp's exemplary analysis of the Spanish mission ethos, in *California Vieja: Culture and Memory in a Modern American Place* (Berkeley: University of California Press, 2006), 47–102.

45 Kevin Starr, *Inventing the Dream: California through the Progressive Era* (New York: Oxford University Press, 1985), 76.

46 Thomas Bremer, "Tourists and Religion at Temple Square and Mission San Juan Capistrano," *Journal of American Folklore* 113, no. 450 (2000): 422–35, at 429.

47 Elizabeth Kryder-Reid, "Sites of Power and the Power of Sight: Vision in the California Mission Landscapes," in *Sites Unseen: Landscape and Vision*, ed. Dianne Harris and D. Fairchild Ruggles (Pittsburgh: University of Pittsburgh Press, 2007), 181–212, at 204.

48 "California: A Changing State," in *California History Social Science Framework* (Sacramento: California Department of Education, 2017), 76–7, www.cde.ca.gov/ci/hs/cf/documents/hssfwchapter7.pdf (accessed 6 Jan. 2019).

49 Perhaps the most newsworthy item in the guidelines is the recommendation to discontinue the established class assignment to build simulations of the missions, a practice that casually encouraged the perception of the past as a confectioner's dream: "Building missions from sugar cubes or popsicle sticks does not help students understand the period and is offensive to many. Instead, students should have access to multiple sources to help them understand the lives of different groups of people who lived in and around missions, so that students can place them in a comparative context … Students should consider cultural differences, such as gender roles and religious beliefs, in order to better understand the dynamics of Native and Spanish interaction" ("California: A Changing State," 76).

50 "Pope Francis Reveals Why He Chose His Name," *Catholic Herald*, 16 Mar. 2013, https://catholicherald.co.uk/pope-francis-reveals-why-he-chose-name (accessed 6 Jan. 2019).

51 Lee Panich, "After Saint Serra: Unearthing Indigenous Histories at the California Missions," *Journal of Social Anthropology* 16, no. 2 (2016): 238–58, at 252. Panich also observes that the California Missions Foundation "is adding a day of workshops for docents and other interpreters to its annual conference" (252).

52 See California Catholic Conference, "Resources for Students – CA Mission Project," 10 July 2015, https://cacatholic.org/article/resources-students-ca-mission-project (accessed 8 Mar. 2021).

53 Quoted in Bryan James Clinch, *California and Its Missions: Upper California*, vol. 2 (San Francisco: Whitaker and Ray, 1904), 37. See also Herbert Eugene Bolton, *Fray Juan Crespí: Missionary Explorer on the Pacific Coast, 1769–1774* (Berkeley: University of California Press, 1927).

54 Aldo Leopold, *A Sand County Almanac and Sketches Here and There* (New York: Oxford University Press, 1949), 132.

55 Kleinberg, *Sensual God*, 118–19.

56 Order of Friars Minor, "Franciscans and Environmental Justice," 19. An earlier version of this essay was delivered as a keynote address at the symposium "Between Humanity and Divinity: In Literature, Art, Religion and Culture" at National Chi Nan University, Taiwan, 19–20 October 2018, organized by the Taiwan Association of Classic, Medieval, and Renaissance Studies. I thank William Franke, Brian Reynolds, Carolyn Scott, and Francis K.H. So for their comments. For research assistance, I thank Kersti Francis.

Part Three

Playing in the American Middle Ages

10 Orlando's Medieval Heritage Project

TISON PUGH AND SUSAN ARONSTEIN

Orlando, Florida, and its outskirts may appear an odd space to find multiple fantasies of the European medieval past. Its landscape, featuring acres of scrub grass and miles of flat, straight roadways punctuated by strip malls and timeshare complexes, refutes popular conceptions of a romantic green and golden medieval world. Yet Orlando offers visitors plentiful opportunities to tour and play in a media-inspired Middle Ages: the Magic Kingdom's Cinderella Castle, Fantasyland's fairy-tale attractions, Epcot's Stave Church Gallery, the Wizarding World of Harry Potter's Hogsmeade and Diagon Alley, and Medieval Times's Castle and Village, as well as sundry roadside venues. These theme-park medievalisms, so central to Orlando's brand, all attest to the continued allure of medieval pasts, both real and imagined. Visitors flock to the city's crenellated and confected castles, eager to enter a fantasy realm where, thanks to a little technological wizardry, the Middle Ages of fairy tales and cinema – the Middle Ages as they imagine them to be – have been meticulously realized in resin and concrete.

While many critics and cultural pundits (including ourselves) have discussed Orlando's current popular medievalisms, the city's late nineteenth- and early twentieth-century turn to an imagined Middle Ages is less well known. Here, local historians recounted origin tales that invoked a romanticized Middle Ages to award this patch of Central Florida a medieval past. In this chapter, we explore the connections between these two Orlandian Middle Ages to consider the ways in which the city's fabricated medieval pasts transform Orlando from what social geographer Tim Cresswell calls *space*, a geographical locale with "fixed objective coordinates," into *place*, a site that "people have made meaningful" through narrative (the stories people tell about it), materiality (what is there and on display), and practices (embodied acts within that space). Places, Cresswell observes, "contribute to the production and reproduction of social memory" by "mak[ing] the past come to life in the present."[1] Thinking about Orlando's medievalisms as a place-making mechanism highlights a process that is often at play in America's medievalisms. This process first displaces the site's actual history – in Orlando's case, the relocation of the Seminole and Timucua peoples and the resulting Seminole Wars – in favour of a pseudo-European Middle Ages. It then grounds the space in persistent myths about the medieval past, producing and reproducing social memory, manufacturing heritage by drawing on our collective imagination to create collective memory. Displacing history in favour of fantasy, memory in favour of imagination, Orlando's heritage project illuminates processes at work at all heritage sites: the selection and creation of a past that suits the needs of the present, the ways in which expectations generated by popular media shape perceptions of authenticity, and the promise to bridge the gap between *then* and *now*.

We frame our discussion of Orlando's deployment of a fabricated medieval past as imagined heritage with a brief overview of more traditional heritage tourism, and then turn to the city's first "Middle Ages," a series of aetiological stories centred on how Orlando was named, examining the ways in which these narratives make the space of Orlando meaningful by connecting it to a romance of the Middle Ages. This romanticized past codes the land as "European," valorizes white colonial masculine identity, and presents the region's history and future as a tale of the advance of white civilization. This colonial progressive narrative coincides with Walt Disney's original plans for Orlando: an entertainment empire centred around a city of tomorrow, built by white men on land once occupied by the Seminole and Timucua. Disney's city of the future, however, was abandoned after his death in favour of Orlando's second Middle Ages. As we visit these Middle Ages, we examine the ways in which they create place not only through narrative but also through material (e.g., castles, attractions, and artefacts) and practice (the embodied experiences of the tourists who visit their sites). In Orlando's twenty-first-century Middle Ages, a "medieval" past offers not a path to the future but an escape, made possible through technology and consumption, into a fairy-tale past of romance, magic, and happy endings.

Space, Place, and Imaginary Cultural Heritage

"The past was never just the past, it was what made the present able to live with itself."[2] So muses Martha Cochrane in *England, England*, Julian Barnes's satirical send-up of the heritage industry. Barnes's novel centres around Sir Jack Pitman's quest to distil the English past – or what people imagine the English past to be – into "The Island," bringing "together within a single 155-square-mile zone everything that the Visitor might want to see in what we used to think of as England" (183). "After you've visited us," The Island's marketing materials promise, "you don't need to see Old England" (184). While Barnes's novel engages with the Disneyfication of Britain's heritage sites, it also serves as an appropriate starting point for our discussion of the medievalization of Orlando.

Pitman's commodification of England's history relies not, as he tartly observes, on history but on people's idea of history: "People won't be shelling out money to learn things. If they want to do that, they can go to a sodding library … They will come to us to enjoy what they already know" (74). As Pitman's wildly successful and wildly un-historical Island proves, heritage is not about the past; it is about "what people think they know." On The Island, Pitman constructs "the Fifty Quintessences of Englishness," including, among others, Big Ben, Stonehenge, Robin Hood, the White Cliffs of Dover, Harrods, Alice in Wonderland, the Tower of London, pubs, and thatched cottages (84), thereby distilling, in David Lowenthal's oft-quoted definition of heritage, "the past into icons of identity, bonding us with precursors and progenitors, with our earlier selves, and with promised successors."[3]

Barnes's entrepreneur understands that heritage tourism's "authenticity" resides, in the words of scholars Elizabeth Fine and Jean Speer, "not in the past but in the collective memory."[4] Heritage sites provide what Pierre Nora has famously termed *lieux de memoire*: "any significant entity, whether material or non-material in nature, which by dint of human will or the work of time has become a symbolic element of the memorial heritage of any community."[5] "Created by a play of memory and history," *lieux de memoire* fashion, validate, and perpetuate a nation's collective memory, shoring up national and civic identity.[6] As Nora recognizes, *lieux de memoire* "have no referent in reality, or rather they are their own referent: pure, exclusively self-referential signs. This is not to say they are without content, physical presence or history; it is to suggest that what makes *lieux de memoire* is precisely that by which they escape history."[7] In other words, in spite of the fact that heritage sites base their authenticity on the premise that history actually happened in this space – that here, as English Heritage promises, you can "stand where history happened" – what they actually offer are *signs* of history drawn from collective memory.[8]

In the case of the Middle Ages, that collective memory often relies more heavily on popular culture – on the collective imagination – than it does on history. This fact complicates the relationship between Nora's *lieux de memoire* and what Stijn Reijnders, in his discussion of media tourism, identifies as *lieux d'imagination*, sites "which are not so much concerned with collective memory, as collective imagination."[9] Medieval heritage sites imbue space with a past that is not just selected and commodified to meet the needs of the present, but one that has also taken a detour through media medievalism. History may have happened there, but that history has been staged.[10] Orlando's many Middle Ages take this staging to its logical end; they connect imagination "to specific locations and material objects [so that] something that is fundamentally immaterial can be pinned down, appropriated, and consumed," building a medieval past out of a collective imagination inspired by media medievalism.[11] Orlando has long relied on that collective imagination, materializing narrative (to extend Cresswell's discussion) to produce a place where visitors can engage in practices and embodied acts that both transport them to a medieval fantasy past and fabricate social memory. Thus, while Orlando's multiple Middle Ages, from its nineteenth-century origin stories to modern tourist attractions, are entirely "fake" – there is nothing historically real here, and the aetiological tales of yesterday and the castles of today point to no possible original – they nevertheless grant Orlando an "authentic" medieval heritage, one that conforms to our *image* of the Middle Ages.

Back to the Future: Orlando's Medieval Originary Myths

"Naming," Tim Cresswell observes, "is one of the ways space can be given meaning and become place."[12] And in 1857, the town of Jernigan, named after the area's first permanent settlers, cattlemen Aaron and Isaac Jernigan, was given a new meaning when it was renamed Orlando. While the name "Jernigan" had earlier transformed this geographical space into a meaningful place with its own narratives (the Jernigan family history and a very American tale of the taming of the frontier), materiality (a stockade and a post office), and practices (settlers and Aaron Jernigan's stint as Orange County's first state representative), "Orlando" inspired a different set of narratives. In telling the tale of how Jernigan was renamed Orlando, local historians turned to an imaginative medieval past to imbue this stretch of Florida with a new history and a new meaning. In this turn to the Middle Ages, these historians played into other American and specifically Southern nineteenth-century medievalisms, figuring the United States as the place in which Europe's lost Middle Ages, its golden and heroic past, was continually being reborn. Across the South, these medievalisms embraced Cresswell's qualities of place: material manifestations, such as neo-Gothic architecture (as evident on the University of Florida campus, established in 1853 in nearby Gainesville); narrative, resulting in, as Rollin Osterweis observes, a "Southern cult of chivalry [that] developed principally from a fusion of the tradition of 'The Virginia Gentleman' with those medieval notions best exemplified in the writings of [Sir Walter] Scott";[13] and practices, such as the Southern Ring Tournaments, in which Southern men demonstrated their chivalric masculinity in Walter-Scott-inspired medieval competition spectacles.[14]

Like all tales about the past, stories of Southern medievalism resonate in the present and argue for the future. Not only do they tell their (white) audiences who they are, but they transform the space of the South, coding it as a medieval *elsetime*, a chivalric utopia reborn on American soil, a transformation that either erases the land's native history or first displaces that history and then recodes it within a colonial narrative cloaked in chivalry. Orlando's conflicting founding stories provide an example of these techniques. One story is set in September 1857, when events culminated in the citizens of Jernigan renaming their town Orlando. This tale, promulgated by Donald A. Cheney, a former chairman of the Orange County historical commission, uses narrative to re-encode the materiality of Orlando's landscape, reading its wide and dusty streets and swampy margins as Shakespeare's idyllic Forest of Arden. Cheney records the story of Judge James G. Speer, a "gentleman of culture and an admirer of William Shakespeare," who saw "this area [as] a veritable Forest of Arden, the locale of *As You Like It*," where the protagonist Rosalind determinedly pursues and wins her beloved Orlando.[15] In Shakespeare's play, Arden represents a medieval world both green and golden. It is a fertile realm of regenerative comedy, in which old enmities fade away in favour of new beginnings and new romances, and a lost paradise of innocence and beauty, in which humanity lived harmoniously together. Charles the wrestler describes Arden as just such a paradise, detailing the pleasant life of the exiled duke and his courtiers: "They say he is already in the forest of Arden, and a many merry men with him; and there they live like the old Robin Hood of England. They say many young gentlemen flock to him every day, and fleet the time carelessly, as they did in the golden world."[16] Shakespeare's Renaissance comedy sees the Middle Ages as a lost playground ripe for rebirth, and in Florida's unlikely wilderness, a site of recurring battles with the Seminole, nineteenth-century townsfolk told a story about their place refracted through Shakespeare's vision of an idyllic past, casting it as a lost medieval paradise. The tale of Judge Speer's recognition of Orlando as the Forest of Arden erases both the chiefdoms of the Indigenous people who lived there before the Spaniards arrived and the dusty streets of Jernigan to code the city and its environs as a quasi-medieval paradise, a retreat that will engender the comic possibilities suggested in *As You Like It*'s concluding cavalcade of marriages: here Orlando's white citizenry can build a future.

Another of the city's founding narratives recounts the story of how a man named Orlando made this future possible. This tale attributes the city's name to Orlando Reeves, a US soldier fighting in the Seminole Wars who sounded the night alarm to alert his fellow soldiers of an ambush, despite sensing the fatal repercussions of this act. Writing in the 1930s, Orlando historian Kena Fries begins her account of these events with a rhetorical flourish that situates them in a fairy-tale medieval elsetime, despite the fact that Reeves died in 1835, merely a few decades before her birth in the late 1860s: "In the long, long, long ago Orlando Reeves, hero and martyr received the first Christian burial rites and had the first simple grave marker within the present limits of the city that bears his name."[17] In an elegiac valedictory to this lost soldier, who "fell pierced by more than a dozen poisoned arrows," Fries not only presents Reeves as the epitome of Southern chivalric masculinity but also uses images and language that recall those of medieval hagiographies to portray his death – the excessive suffering, his martyrdom for the (at least implicit) Christian missionary work congruent with territorial conquest, and his perpetual celebration, if not in a feast day, in his apotheosis into his town's eponymous and illustrious hero. A *lieu de memoire* – a plaque honouring Reeves that stands in Orlando's Lake Eola Park, erected by the graduates of a local high school in 1959 – declares and memorializes as historical fact what remains conjecture, demonstrating the ways in which this tale gave meaning to the space that is Orlando.

In a manner further congruent with medieval narrative, it is equally likely that neither of these accounts of Orlando's founding is true. At the very least, as Joy Wallace Dickinson notes, "when local researchers, including librarian Eileen Willis, dug into federal War Department records in the 1970s and 1980s, they found no Orlando Reeves in the thorough records of the territorial militia or regular army in that era."[18] A third hypothesis suggests that the town was named in honour of Orlando Savage Rees, a wealthy landowner with holdings in South Carolina, Florida, and Mississippi, yet no evidence conclusively resolves the vexing issue of why this particular Orlando should be lionized as the city's eponym, thereby relegating the other two Orlandos to the dustbin of Florida history.[19] This quandary, with its surprising multiplicity of Orlandos, productively links the city to a medieval past, for many medieval histories are, quite simply, full of lies, deceptions, and half-truths that bespeak a desire to create an appropriate heritage, and it demonstrates the narrative urge to record an account as it should have been rather than as it was. As Paul Strohm affirms of medieval narrative and historiography, "a text can be powerful without being true," documenting the ways in which "fictive elements teem within historical narratives, trial depositions and indictments, coroner's rolls, and other officially sanctioned accounts."[20] Whether it was named in honour of a character in one of Shakespeare's masterpieces or of one of several men named Orlando who may have lived there, the desire to rename Jernigan triggered various aetiological myths of an Orlando, all of which touch upon the medieval past.

Consuming Heritage: Orlando's Authentically Fake Middle Ages

As chivalric knight and martyred saint, Orlando Reeves – more than his competitor Orlando Savage Rees – is a character drawn from nineteenth-century "medieval" romance. His tale provides an origin narrative founded in conquest and colonialism, in a white heroism which made the city safe for its white citizens and set the stage for its progressive future. In the middle of the twentieth century, Walt Disney would come to Florida to build that future. Even before he unveiled his plans for an entertainment empire in Orlando, he told a story about this space. The occasion was the inaugural episode of *The Mickey Mouse Club* (3 October 1955), and the story was featured in the program's opening newsreel, "The News of Today for the Leaders of Tomorrow."[21] In "Boys Brave Buzz Boats," Mike Osceola, "great-grandson of the Seminole Indian chief," takes two tow-headed boys on a thrill ride into the Florida Everglades, guiding them through "hidden backwaters" where alligators lurk and snakes slither, following "secret paths" to Osceola's hidden village. Once there, the narrator tells us, Mike recounts the history of that village: how his great-grandfather was tricked into leaving, was captured, and died in prison. Rather than dwelling on this sad history of displacement and betrayal, the narrator abruptly shifts focus. "But it's time to leave!" he chirps, extolling the virtues of the "short trip back in the airboat." "Old Osceola," he exclaims, as the segment ends, "would really get a kick out of this. His great-grandson's airboat has conquered the Everglades!"

This segment tells a disturbingly cheerful story that echoes the main theme of the tale of Orlando Reeves: how white Floridians defeated the Seminole and made the land their own. It also embraces the progressive narrative implied in that tale: colonization and technology, the narrator implies, have benefited everyone. Thanks to the airboat, Osceola's great-grandson has conquered the Everglades and can now earn his living guiding those who took his great-grandfather's land on an adventurous trip into the past. Even great-granddad would approve. Civilization marches on, and Osceola's hiding place is transformed into a tourist attraction. As such, "Boys Brave Buzz Boats" dismisses the site's past in favour of its future, eerily predicting Walt Disney's later plans for Central Florida, which he unveiled to a national television audience in 1966. Here, Disney completes the process of overwriting the site's Native history, proposing a new start, a new origin story, one that abandons the past to look towards the future. In this story, the theme park and its tourist facilities are "but one small area of our Florida project." "The heart of it all" is the ever-evolving Experimental Prototype Community of Tomorrow – Epcot – the city of the future, to be inhabited by 20,000 Americans who would "actually live a life they can't find anywhere in else in the world." This city will owe nothing to the past but will instead "start from scratch on virgin land." "No city of today" (or yesterday), Disney asserted, "will serve as the blueprint of our city of tomorrow." Unlike Orlando's early historians, Disney expressed no desire to provide his new space with a past. Its attraction to him was that it ostensibly had no past, leaving him, his Imagineers, and American industry free to write "an exciting living blueprint of the future," featuring a "completely enclosed" and "climate-controlled" dynamic urban centre, state-of-the-art mass transit, and manicured single-family neighbourhoods. Disney wanted to write tomorrow on the empty spaces of Florida's swampland, a vision that would "influence the future of city living for generations to come."[22]

Disney died two months after his Epcot announcement, and his planned future was lost to history. Orlando was reborn not as a real community of tomorrow but as a playground of the fantasy past (and future). Instead of the "towering hotel" that Disney dreamed would provide the "visual center" for his new city, Cinderella Castle became the iconic centre of Disney's Florida project, the first of the many medieval-themed attractions that build a past on this flat Florida landscape. And, like Sir Jack Pitman, neither Disney nor the later builders of Orlando's medieval experiences express much interest in history per se; rather, they seek to provide visitors with what they think they know about the Middle Ages – the "50 Quintessences of Medievalness." Just as the fictional Pitman built an imaginative England on The Island, where Quality Leisure's guests could experience "everything you imagined England to be, but more convenient, cleaner, friendlier, more efficient" (186), so the creators of Orlando's Middle Ages provide tourists with a material space in which to interact – cleanly and efficiently – with everything they imagine the Middle Ages to be: a time of royalty and magic, love and bravery, and happily-ever-afters.

Fabricated from a pastiche of icons – castles, princesses, knights, wizards, dragons, horned helmets – that signify the "medieval" in our collective imagination, Orlando's themed attractions draw upon that imagination to offer what Umberto Eco identified in his 1975 essay, "Travels in Hyperreality," as "the Absolute Fake." Meticulously detailed, shiny, and solid, they seem real, but their "realness," like the Absolute Fakes that Eco encounters in his travels across the United States, relies on erasing the boundary between "Real World and Possible Worlds" through hybrid constructions pieced together from actual medieval artefacts and imitations of medieval originals, along with the make-believe or imaginative made "real." In a fairy-tale medieval past that never was, Orlando's medieval spaces provide visitors with a world in which "Good, Art, Fairy Tale and history, unable to become flesh, at least become plastic."[23] These Middle Ages derive their authenticity not from history but from various cultural media (e.g., Disney's animated films and J.K. Rowling's *Harry Potter* series) that have formed our vision of the Middle Ages.

If early accounts of the transformation of Jernigan into Orlando relied on medieval narrative to grant the city a usable past, modern themed attractions turn to narrative to transform the landscape itself, bringing fantasies of the past into the present. In this hyperreal reification, the intangible becomes tangible, the imagination is awarded a space, space is awarded a narrative, and thus space transforms into *place*: the Magic Kingdom, Medieval Times's Castle, the Wizarding World of Harry Potter. As Orlando's second Middle Ages make the intangible tangible, they bring along with them the social memory recounted in their originary narratives. In their new Ardens, visitors can enter into these stories, interact with them, and, as media and technologies advance, experience them through increasingly embodied acts of consumption.

In the rest of this chapter, we will visit Orlando's medieval *lieux d'imagination*, exploring them in the order in which they were built, from the Magic Kingdom and Epcot through Medieval Times to the Wizarding World of Harry Potter. Each of Orlando's medieval-themed attractions remediates and reifies a narrative about the Middle Ages, narratives that both create and confirm popular fantasies about the medieval past. In Disney's Magic Kingdom, visitors enter a time of romance and allure, of dreams come true and timeless gender-normative happily-ever-afters. Medieval Times gestures towards this narrative in its pageant and adds the fantasy of living "like royalty" in a distant "once-upon-a-time" of kings and princesses – one that, as so many popular medieval tales do, presents a Middle Ages where apparently everyone lives in a castle, without peasants or plague. While the Magic Kingdom and Medieval Times build their worlds on a fairy-tale Middle Ages of royalty and romance, Universal Studios' Wizarding World's medievalisms, like those of the *Harry Potter* series, are rooted in the more recent tradition of high fantasy, and here the medieval stands in explicit contrast to the modern: an era of magic and adventure that displaces the technological and the mundane. In Orlando, all of Cresswell's ways of transforming space into place – narrative, materiality, and practice – have been deployed to make that space meaningful for the multitude of guests who come to pay and play in Central Florida.

"When You Wish Upon a Star": Disney's Magic Kingdom and Epcot's World Showcase

To paraphrase Walt Disney's now-famous quote, it was all started by a castle.[24] On opening day, Cinderella Castle stood at the centre of the Magic Kingdom, the ultimate Disney weenie, drawing tourists down Main Street, through the castle, and into the medievalized space of Fantasyland. It still towers on the horizon, providing visitors with their first glimpse of the park. Perhaps even more important than the physical castle through which patrons of Disney World pass (the intangible made tangible), however, is the castle that stands emblazoned on all Disney films, perched atop its eponymous founder's name. Cinderella Castle materializes all that the logo stands for, awarding space a Disney past and touching the theme park's every endeavour with this fantasy of the past, no matter the chronological or thematic remove from the Middle Ages. As Martha Bayless suggests, Disney's castles project the illusion that "the content of the castle is all of Disneyland," giving pre-eminence to fairy tales as the park's defining and default narrative mode.[25] Cinderella Castle, in effect, metamorphoses all of Disney World into a "medieval" land of fairy tale and fantasy, suturing over the vast contradictions inherent in a theme park that combines a golden-age, fairy-tale past with Tomorrowland and that pays homage to the United States' history and declared exceptionalism in Liberty Square and Frontierland at the same time that it includes within its grounds the international goodwill represented in Epcot.

As we have observed elsewhere, Disney's fairy-tale past serves to create a Disneyfied collective memory, a Middle Ages that codes the corporation's stories about America's present and future as timeless and universal. Disney and his artists took this Middle Ages from the popular-media medievalism found in illustrated children's books and then repackaged and redeployed those medievalisms in the company's animated films. Fantasyland awards Disney's imagined world a space and, by so doing, awards the space on which it is built a narrative, creating a place where guests, in Reijnders's words, can "become themselves part of [Disney's] world of the imagination."[26] Its varied attractions, from rides to shopping, envelop tourists in Disney's Middle Ages through meticulously rendered hyperreal re-creations of the studio's animated fairy tales. Here, they re-experience Disney's fairy-tale films as they ride Prince Charming Regal Carrousel and Seven Dwarfs Mine Train, or enjoy a story (and a photo op) at Enchanted Tales with Belle; they dine at Cinderella's Royal Table or Gaston's Tavern; and they shop at Prince Eric's Village Market and Bonjour! Village Gifts. At Princess Fairytale Hall, they "join Cinderella when she welcomes Elena [of Avalor] to the land where 'a dream is a wish your heart makes.'"[27] Or they can indulge in the ultimate medieval fairy-tale fantasy at Bibbidi Bobbidi Boutique, where they can "transform into a Disney Princess or a Valiant Knight." In all of these experiences, visitors are, on the whole, passive consumers: the dominant mode of consumption is viewing and the dominant genre is cinema. Strapped into themed carts on a dark ride, they move through compressed versions of the rides' originary films; they walk through what is essentially a film set, posing with princesses and dining in medievalish spaces. Even when they embody the fantasy at Bibbidi Bobbidi Boutique or are invited to participate at Enchanted Tales with Belle, they either do so passively, sitting in the salon chair while the "fairy godmothers" work their Disney Magic, or merely reenact the film, like a kindergarten class performing a favourite book.

Fantasyland's passive mode of consumption in many ways suits the social memory that Disney's imagined Middle Ages works to produce, a fantasy of the medieval past as a time of romance that invokes a timeless, gender-normative happily-ever-after. As the classic tune from *Cinderella*, alluded to in the description of Princess Fairytale Hall, promises: "No matter how your heart is grieving / If you keep on believing / The dream that you wish will come true."[28] This song, played consistently throughout Fantasyland along with other Disney-dreaming songs – "When You Wish Upon a Star," "Some Day My Prince Will Come," "Once Upon a Dream" – tacitly reminds patrons of the uplifting narrative they now inhabit. As songwriters Al Hoffman, Jerry Livingston, Mack David, and a host of other Disney lyricists realized, the promise of fairy tales is the promise of fantasy dissolving the boundaries between dreams and reality, an apt assessment of the continued attraction of the medieval and fairy-tale past that one enters by walking through Cinderella Castle.

Visitors bring Fantasyland's Middle Ages with them to Epcot's World Showcase, an attraction that purports to give guests the world in miniature – a hyperreal, whirlwind global heritage tour undertaken in Disneyfied comfort. Here Disney's Imagineers have transformed the space on which Showcase

Plaza stands through meticulously replicated material manifestations of global medieval *lieux de memoire* – a Meso-American pyramid for Mexico, a stave church for Norway, St. Mark's Square for Italy – all located within easy strolling distance from one another. The World Showcase presents itself as a heritage site, bringing the past, or at least convenient replicas of the past, to Florida tourists. But those replicas look suspiciously like scenes re-created from Disney films: Pinocchio's village, Belle's town square, Elsa's Norwegian village. And the Disney animated characters who stroll side-by-side with the costumed international hosts – Elsa and Anna in Norway, Mulan in China, Pinocchio in Italy, Belle in France – further break down the barriers between the historical and geographical "real world" that Epcot purports to offer and the medievalized fantasy past of the Disney fairy tale. By blurring the boundaries between history and fantasy, the World Showcase authenticates the Disney Middle Ages, translating collective imagination into collective memory and setting the stage for other Middle Ages elsewhere in the city.

Celebrate (and Spend) Like Royalty: Medieval Times

Travelling seven miles down US 192 from the Magic Kingdom brings one to Medieval Times Dinner and Tournament and its sister attraction, the Medieval Life Village, located near a Walmart. Most guests visit for the feast and the jousting but tour the village before showtime. Like Epcot's World Showcase, the Medieval Life Village reproduces and deploys a purportedly real Middle Ages to offer patrons the media Middle Ages of our collective imagination, promising historical artefacts displayed in a reconstructed medieval space for the education and edification of consumers. According to *After Disney: The Other Orlando*, "Fortunately, the owner of … the popular Kissimmee dinner attraction … is a Spanish count. So it wasn't too much of a stretch for him to clear out the attics and the barns of his estates, buy up an old village on Majorca, and ship the whole lot to Central Florida." "The buildings are modern construction," the site admits, but assures us that "the doors, the wooden windows, the furniture, and many of the other objects to be found in the village are all originals, some of them 800 years old."[29]

The Medieval Life Village does indeed contain many old artefacts and consists of a series of residences and workspaces (for an architect, a weaver, and other such artisanal professions), a kitchen, and, improbably, the Dungeon. Each room is furnished with "originals" imported from Spain. However, this "medieval" village fails to distinguish between the actually medieval and the merely old, as signage in the village adumbrates, knowingly or not, the extension of the Middle Ages into the eighteenth century and the Age of Enlightenment. In the architect's bedroom, a book of hours stands anachronistically beside the architect's bed, dating, at "over 200 years old," from somewhere in the late eighteenth or early nineteenth century. Similarly, the weaver's room features a "medieval" loom, which a sign hanging over it describes matter-of-factly as "a 275-year-old factory loom," along with seventeenth-century silk stockings. Walking through these rooms, visitors are encouraged to code anything old, not-modern, as medieval. This blurring of the period between the thirteenth and the twentieth centuries into an unspecified medieval continues in the final "residence," the Dungeon, which features a parental advisory and a historical mash-up of torture devices. Here, patrons move from the simply not-modern to a display that confirms the association between the medieval and the abject in an exhibit that showcases "authentic" relics from the Dark Ages, thus confirming troubling suspicions about the medieval past, even if most of those relics are not, in fact, medieval.

The appearance of a dungeon, cheek-by-jowl with the village kitchen and the weaver's workroom, is as historically incongruous as the Disney characters wandering through the streets of the Epcot World Showcase, and yet guests seem to question neither. The authentic past cannot compete with the imagined past, and so a *lieu d'imagination* emerges, demonstrating the power to overwrite the meaning of any actual historical artefacts on display. The Medieval Times website fully deploys this confusion between history and imagination as it invites guests to enjoy an evening of "Chivalry, Rivalry, Revelry":

> Travel through the mists of time to a forgotten age and a tale of devotion, courage and love – at Medieval Times Dinner & Tournament. Imagine the pageantry and excitement that would have been yours as a guest of the royal court ten centuries ago. That's exactly what you will experience at North America's most popular dinner attraction. See our electrifying show featuring heroic knights on spirited horses displaying the astounding athletic feats and thrilling swordplay that have become hallmarks of this unique entertainment experience. Enjoy a "hands-on" feast as the dynamic performance unfolds before you. A sweeping musical score and brilliant lights provide a fabulous backdrop for this spellbinding experience that blurs the boundary between fairy tale and spectacle![30]

This invitation contrasts merely imagining the Middle Ages – with the "pageantry and excitement" of "ten centuries ago" – with experiencing the past, courtesy of Medieval Times and a show that promises to allow guests "to travel back in time" to become part of a narrative that dissolves any generic borders between history, fairy tale, and spectacle. The "past" guests experience at Medieval Times, however, is not so much a coherent construct as it is a grab bag of signifiers gathered from popular culture and the collective imagination, and largely inspired by Disney. Indeed, the attraction depends on its costumers' knowledge of the Disney Middle Ages, relying on medieval shorthand rather than engaging in fully realized medieval place-making. For instance, compared to the careful hyperreality of Cinderella Castle, constructed with painstaking attention to medievalish details such as whimsical gargoyles and elaborate mosaics, this castle is merely a "decorated shed,"[31] a big-box generic structure with a few details – an unconvincing stone façade, minimal crenellations, and neon faux-Gothic script – suggesting a Disneyfied Middle Ages. A tiny moat and drawbridge provide another out-of-scale nod to Disney's Castle, as does the medievalish arched-windowed ticket booth, where visitors can purchase various levels of show and merchandise packages.

Inside this decorated shed, "royal guests" pass through a tunnel decorated with a few torches and suits of armour to dine (without forks, of course) on a "feast" (chicken, bread, and corn on the cob) that also employs a truncated media medievalism to invoke a decidedly non-historical medieval past. While Disney's Magic Kingdom relies on the meticulous renderings of Disney narratives and characters that allow visitors to insert themselves into a Disneyfied Middle Ages, Medieval Times uses a special-effects spectacle to create a heightened experience that masks a flimsy narrative, involving a feast, a tournament, a Black Knight, a challenge, a contest, and a princess. Lights flash, mist swirls, music blares, but much of the dialogue is inaudible, even in the VIP seats. Unlike Disney's Middle Ages, the Middle Ages of Medieval Times is not primarily focused on the story – the happily-ever-after – and the social memory that story creates as a usable past for the present. Here, a return to the medieval past is about the purchased experience of being treated like royalty, being guests at the feast, being entertained with a show, and, for those who sprung for a "Celebrate like Royalty!" package, being "knighted" at its end.

At Medieval Times, the narrative (and practice) on offer is one that is particularly suited to late capitalism: experience through consumption. Visitors both shop and enter *and* shop and exit. Thus the glaring juxtaposition between the castle and the nearby Walmart, which deflates the attraction's medieval majesty, is not as glaring as it might seem. The castle stands defiantly, archaically, inviting tourists to escape modernity as incarnated in mass consumerism, but it merely displaces that mass consumption in favour of a medievalized consumerism. Whereas Disney's Magic Kingdom disguises the transactional nature of the guest experience in their parks through a seemingly democratic system of single-price admission (notwithstanding the purchase of add-ons such as VIP access to attractions) and its wristbands that eliminate the need for cash and credit cards, visitors' experience of the Middle Ages at Medieval Times Dinner Theater explicitly depends on their level of consumption. Ticket options range from general admission to the Royalty Package (an upgrade that includes priority access to the castle and seating, a cheering banner, and a VIP lanyard) and the Queen's Royalty Package (another upgrade that adds VIP front-row or centre seating and a group photo). After purchasing their tickets, guests enter into a medieval mall, one that, to paraphrase the website, blurs the boundary between spectacle and shopping. They can choose to "Celebrate Like [various levels of] Royalty! Get Knighted with the King, Don Carlos." The costs of these royal celebrations range from a basic package that includes a light sword and cheap goblet to an Engagement Knighting featuring two pewter goblets. If royal knighting is not to their taste, patrons can transport themselves back in time by imbibing a variety of medieval-themed drinks in souvenir glasses and goblets or purchasing "medieval" merchandise. The idea is not merely to imagine or witness the Middle Ages but to become embodied in them. These medieval props will allow you to "get medieval," and, as guests file out to return to the Florida suburbs and the world of modern commerce with the Walmart next door, they pass again through the gift shop, still open to allow them one more chance to buy the Middle Ages.

"Yer a Wizard!": The Wizarding World of Harry Potter

The relationship between narrative, material manifestations, and practice in the Middle Ages at Universal Studios' Wizarding World of Harry Potter is more complex than it is at either the Magic Kingdom or Medieval Times. The Magic Kingdom offers its visitors the chance to walk among the artefacts of the (medievalish) past through the stories that provide meaning to all of the other pasts – and visions of the future – found in the park. Medieval Times capitalizes on this Disney Middle Ages to create a medieval experience based in practice (shopping and cheering) more than place. Fantasyland functions as a media-medievalism heritage site, Medieval Times as a themed mall and cosplay opportunity. Taking advantage of new technologies and new media, the Wizarding World of Harry Potter offers consumers a re-created medieval past that merges both the Magic Kingdom's reliance on the narrative techniques of film and Medieval Times's consumption-driven embodiment in an experience that deploys the narrative and ludic structures of a video game. To this end, whereas Cinderella Castle provides a portal to the world of fantasy, metaphorically suggesting that all of the rest of the Magic Kingdom is contained inside, Hogwarts Castle – and the medieval fantasy world it suggests – represents but one "island of adventure," one stop among the multiple fantasies available in Universal's parks. Hogwarts, in its neo-Gothic splendour, looms over Hogsmeade alone, and to reach it, Universal's patrons must wend their way through a veritable maze, twisting and turning through Seuss Landing and the Lost Continent before passing through the gateway of the Wizarding World of Harry Potter into Hogsmeade. Similarly, when visiting Diagon Alley via Universal Studios' main entrance, patrons must first pass much of the park, and, even when arriving from Hogsmeade on the Hogwarts Express, they leave the station to find the Simpsons Ride, Duff Brewery, and Fast Food Boulevard in their direct line of sight before escaping into the Wizarding World.

As such, while Disney creates for Orlando and its environs a coherent if historically implausible narrative, Universal makes its spaces meaningful through multiple media narratives, providing visitors with a pastiche of *lieux d'imagination*, from *The Cat in the Hat* and *The Simpsons* to *Transformers* and *Jurassic Park*. As part of these media narratives, the Middle Ages on offer in the Wizarding World is based not on the general popular conceptions of the Middle Ages manifested in Orlando's origin stories, Fantasyland, and Medieval Times, but on Rowling's (and Warner Brothers') deployment of these and other medieval tropes in the *Harry Potter* series. Diagon Alley, Platform 9¾, Hogwarts, and Hogsmeade offer an escape from the mundane Muggle world of Privet Drive, and the magical world is coded as else*time*, but the historical referents, apart from the castle, are more Dickensian than Arthurian. The Wizarding World of Harry Potter, re-creating the film sets, offers guests a Hogsmeade and Diagon Alley inspired by an adaptation of *A Christmas Carol*: narrow streets, thatched cottages, half-timbered buildings, mullioned windows, even, at Hogsmeade, an improbable resin-coating of snow on roofs baking in the Florida sun. As evident in the Magic Kingdom and Epcot, it is not uncommon to conflate the tropes of the nineteenth century and of the medieval into a historical palimpsest signifying the fairy tale non-modern. The medieval in Harry Potter, however, is not merely part of this fantasy pastiche. It is the site of magic, the continuation of the past in the present both for wizards and for Muggles: dragons, gargoyles, ghosts, and incantations.

While the Magic Kingdom and Medieval Times build their worlds on a fairy-tale Middle Ages of royalty and romance, Universal's Wizarding World's medievalisms, like those of the *Harry Potter* series, are rooted in the more recent tradition of high fantasy. Rowling figures Harry as an epic fantasy hero (describing him as embodying a "sort of Galahad quality" because "the person who is leading the quest" tends "to have this weird purity about them"), whose destiny leads him away from the Muggle world and into the magical world of Hogwarts, an institution founded in the Middle Ages.[32] Rowling's Hogwarts eschews modernity: it is lit by torches, not electricity; students write their assignments with quill and parchment rather than on laptop computers. The Wizarding World of Harry Potter embodies Rowling's vision to some degree. Here, guests can visit a still-present past, a magical world just around the corner from Fast Food Boulevard, where they can become Harry Potter avatars, complete with robes, scarves, owls, and wands. Ollivander's Wand Shop welcomes "young wizards and witches [who] come in search of the most essential wizarding item: their wands." Once they purchase their unique wand – either one of the many non-technological accessories at a variety of price points or an interactive wand that allows them to "cast spells to create amazing magical experiences throughout Diagon Alley and Hogsmeade," they are ready to wander through a meticulously re-created Wizarding World that encourages them to continue to shop.³³ In Hogsmeade and Diagon Alley many of their favourite Potter-inspired places are disguised as commercial walk-through rides: Madam Malkin's Robes for All Occasions, Weasleys' Wizard Wheezes for magical gags, Magical Menagerie for (plush toy) owls and dragons, and, of course, Quality Quidditch Supplies for brooms and house fan gear. As they enter into the world of their imagination, guests will find it difficult to distinguish between the attraction and the goods, except by the price tag.

These shops/attractions are an integral part of the Wizarding World's embodied medieval experience. Like the villages and markets in medievally themed video games, they carry the narrative and provide guests/avatars with the goods and information needed to interact with the world of the game. A visit to a shop serves the same function as a cut-scene (e.g., Ollivander's Wand Shop begins with an interactive version of "the wand chooses the wizard" scene from *Harry Potter and the Sorcerer's Stone*); shops sell necessary supplies (such as robes and the interactive wands that enable consumers to reveal hidden artefacts and make objects move). These supplies allow guests to the Wizarding World of Harry Potter to truly experience this *lieux d'imagination* – to become avatars translated from pixels into flesh, outfitted in robes, armed with wands, perhaps carrying a white owl and munching on Chocolate Frogs. Costumed employees fill the role of NPCs (non-player characters) who expound on the narrative and direct guests along the way, giving would-be wizards the illusion of unrestricted movement as they explore the "map" of this limited free world.

Hogwarts Castle – which appears to emerge naturally from a rock at the end of Hogsmeade, with the use of forced perspective giving it a disproportional sense of height and majesty – and its extravagant ride, Harry Potter and the Forbidden Journey, allow its Harry Potter avatars to fight the final "boss," a fitting culmination for the Wizarding World's experiential video game. As tourists cross over the drawbridge from Hogsmeade, they enter the medievalized space of Hogwarts' torchlit castle, complete with a dungeon, unicorns, suits of armour, stained-glass windows, and tapestries; as it does in the *Harry Potter* novels, the medieval provides a background for mischievous adventure that leads to heroic action. Harry, Hermione, and Ron – in a filmed cut-scene – invite patrons to accompany them as they sneak out to view a Quidditch match. The ride then recaps a mishmash of plot points from the *Harry Potter* novels as guests fly unsteadily on their brooms through the Quidditch match, enter the Forbidden Forest where dwells the Acromantula Aragog (who "spits venom at" – sprays water on – the patrons), encounter Dementors and vanquish them with a Patronus spell, and then return to Hogwarts Great Hall as Dumbledore and their "classmates" cheer.

Hogwarts Castle offers guests an exaggerated hyperreality. Its culminating ride supplements the visual replica with a sensory one, which uses proprioceptive, vestibular, and visual cues to trick guests into believing that they really are flying through the wizarding world, replacing the relatively staid viewing of Disney's dark rides with an embodied experience that allows guests to insert themselves into Harry Potter's central narrative: the magic-fuelled battle between good and evil. This state-of-the-art technology in Hogwarts Castle transforms mundane space into a fantasy place where visitors, for the price of an admissions ticket (and perhaps a wand, a robe, and a handful of Bertie Bott's Every Flavour Beans), can reenact the stories that provide the Wizarding World's replicated and constructed Middle Ages with meaning. These stories allow them to escape from the everyday to the magical, from routine to adventure, from helplessness to power, from insignificant tourist to world saviour.

The Medieval Present

As a tourist mecca, Orlando could not prosper without tourists paying hotel and other taxes, and so the city's fiscal health depends upon people leaving the comforts of home for the thrills of theme parks and the pleasures of its quasi-medieval heritage project. Although one cannot presume to speak for all tourists, it is worth pondering their objectives in their journeys and the desires they seek to sate by leaving home. In a moment of comic irksomeness in *As You Like It* ridiculing the traveller's itch, the clown Touchstone complains, "Ay, now am I in Arden; the more fool I. When I was at home, I was in a better place, but travellers must be content."[34] While Touchstone may take the cynic's view of his journey to the medieval past as simulated in Arden, the simulation retains its appeal, and also perhaps proves the very uncertainty of the meaning of home. For certainly, when *As You Like It* ends with Duke Ferdinand's unexpected conversion and Arden's visitors returning to court, the unreality of the medieval simulation must by necessity infiltrate the reality of their prior lives: the simulation does not become the real but instead infects it. At some point in Orlando's history, from its foundation until today, it came to life as a site of unconstrained medieval simulation that somehow miraculously transformed into a real heritage for its citizens and the millions of tourists who visit annually. In other words, the city's twenty-first-century medieval heritage sites award this Floridian space a past that *produces* rather than *reproduces* the Middle Ages. Like Jack Pitman's Island, they give tourists, in Eco's words, "the reproduction so you will no longer feel the need for the original."[35] Orlando does not offer tourists the real Middle Ages, nor does it claim to. In Orlando, the Middle Ages is bigger, better, shinier; these past centuries both exceed and displace European history, providing one of many American medieval *lieux d'imagination* that stretch from Las Vegas to Orlando and beyond, allowing the United States to lay claim to a history and culture it never possessed.

NOTES

1. Tim Cresswell, *Place: A Short Introduction*, 2nd ed. (Chichester, UK: Wiley Blackwell, 2015), 121.
2. Julian Barnes, *England, England* (New York: Alfred Knopf, 1999), 6; cited parenthetically.
3. David Lowenthal, "Identity, Heritage, and History," in *Commemorations: The Politics of National Identity*, ed. John R. Gillis (Princeton, NJ: Princeton University Press, 1994), 41–57, at 42.
4. Elizabeth Fine and Jean Speer, "Tour Guide Performances as Sight Sacralization," *Annals of Tourism Research* 12 (1997): 73–95.
5. Pierre Nora, *Realms of Memory: The Construction of the French Past*, 2 vols. (New York: Columbia University Press, 1996), 1:xvii.
6. Pierre Nora, "Between History and Memory: Les Lieux de Memoire," *Representations* 26 (1989): 7–24, at 19.
7. Pierre Nora, "Between History and Memory," 23–4.
8. English Heritage, http://www.english-heritage.org.uk (accessed 4 Jan. 2019).
9. Stijn Reijnders, *Places of the Imagination: Media, Tourism, Culture* (Farnham, UK: Ashgate, 2011), ebook.
10. Dean MacCannell introduced the idea of staging history to conform to visitors' expectations of the past in "Staged Authenticity: Arrangements of Social Space in Visitor Settings," *American Journal of Sociology* 79, no. 3 (1979): 589–603.
11. Reijnders, *Places of the Imagination*.
12. Cresswell, *Place*, 17.
13. Rollin Osterweis, *Romanticism and Nationalism in the Old South* (1949; repr., Baton Rouge: Louisiana State University Press, 1967), 87.
14. On the Southern states' ring tournaments, see James B. Avirett, "Knights and Court Ladies: The Romantic Ultimate," in *The Romantic South*, ed. Harnett T. Kane (New York: Coward-McCann, 1961), 182–5. Visions of chivalry defined Southern masculinity in various cultural contexts, with this homage to the medieval past sparking inherent contradictions between ideal and enactment. On the inherent gender anxiety in Southern performances of chivalry, see Tison Pugh, *Queer Chivalry: Medievalism and the Myth of Southern Masculinity* (Baton Rouge: Louisiana State University Press, 2013), 26–52.
15. Joy Wallace Dickinson, *Orlando: City of Dreams* (Charleston, SC: Arcadia, 2003), 24.
16. William Shakespeare, *As You Like It*, in *The Riverside Shakespeare: The Complete Works*, ed. G. Blakemore Evans (Boston: Houghton Mifflin, 1997), 399–436, at 1.1.114–19.
17. Kena Fries, *Orlando in the Long, Long Ago ... and Now* (Orlando: Tyn Cobb's Florida Press, 1938), 4–5; punctuation correct to original.
18. Dickinson, *Orlando*, 24.
19. Dickinson, *Orlando*, 24.

20 Paul Strohm, *Hochon's Arrow: The Social Imagination of Fourteenth-Century Texts* (Princeton, NJ: Princeton University Press, 1992), 5–6.
21 "Boys Brave Buzz Boats!," 1955, on *Walt Disney Treasures: The Mickey Mouse Club*, DVD (Walt Disney Home Entertainment, 2004).
22 "EPCOT TV Special," 1966, on *Walt Disney Treasures, Tomorrow Land: Disney in Space and Beyond*, DVD (Walt Disney Home Entertainment, 2004).
23 Umberto Eco, *Travels in Hyperreality* (New York: Harcourt Brace, 1983), 57.
24 Walt Disney, "It Was All Started By a Mouse," 1954, *The Disneyland Story* on *Walt Disney Treasures: Disneyland USA*, DVD (Walt Disney Home Entertainment, 2001).
25 Martha Bayless, "Disney's Castles and the Work of the Medieval in the Magic Kingdom," in *The Disney Middle Ages: A Fairy-Tale and Fantasy Past*, ed. Tison Pugh and Susan Aronstein (New York: Palgrave Macmillan, 2012), 39–56, at 49. In this remark, Bayless refers specifically to Disneyland's Sleeping Beauty Castle, but her point holds for Disney World's Cinderella Castle as well.
26 Reijnders, *Places of the Imagination*.
27 "Meet Cinderella and Elena at Princess Fairytale Hall," Walt Disney World, https://disneyworld.disney.go.com/entertainment/magic-kingdom/character-meet-elena-fairytale-hall (accessed 30 Nov. 2017).
28 Walt Disney Company, *The Disney Collection: Best-Loved Songs from Disney Movies* (Milwaukee, WI: Hal Leonard, 1992), 32–3.
29 "Another Roadside Attraction: Medieval Life Village," After Disney: Exploring the Other Orlando, http://www.theotherorlando.com/contents/chapters/13/medieval.html (accessed 6 May 2016).
30 "Chivalry, Rivalry, Revelry: The #1 Dinner Attraction in North America," Medieval Times, http://medievaltimes.com (accessed 15 Dec. 2015).
31 This term is from Denise Scott Brown, Robert Venturi, and Steven Izenour, *Learning from Las Vegas*, rev. ed. (Cambridge, MA: MIT Press, 1977), 87.
32 Ian Parker, "Mugglemarch: J.K. Rowling Writes a Realist Novel for Adults," *The New Yorker*, 1 Oct. 2012 (accessed 4 Jan. 2019). See also Heather Arden and Kathryn Lorenz, "The *Harry Potter* Stories and French Arthurian Romance," *Arthuriana* 13, no. 2 (2003): 54–68, in which they connect Harry Potter to the Percival tradition.
33 "Ollivanders: Makers of Fine Wands since 382 BC," Universal Orlando Resort, https://www.universalorlando.com/web/en/us/things-to-do/shopping/ollivanders-diagon-alley (accessed 5 Jun. 2018).
34 Shakespeare, *As You Like It*, 2.4.16–18.
35 Eco, *Travels in Hyperreality*, 19.

11 Saints and Sinners: New Orleans's Medievalisms

USHA VISHNUVAJJALA AND CANDACE BARRINGTON

New Orleans is a city famous for its saints and sinners. On the saintly side of matters, its unofficial patron saint, St. Joan, the Maid of Orléans, receives eponymous honours. The St. Louis Cathedral dominates the French Quarter's Jackson Square, with nearby streets named in honour of St. Ann, St. Louis, and St. Peter. And, of course, the city's beloved football team is dubbed the Saints. On the sinful side, the city is recognized worldwide for its riotous, nearly notorious, Mardi Gras bacchanalias, so much so that it is nicknamed the Big Easy, which the *Times-Picayune* wrote in 1887 "refer[s] to the gentle pace of life and somewhat lax morals for which New Orleans is known."[1] A site of contrasts, New Orleans is home to sinners on Saturday and saints on Sunday, a duality encapsulated in the city's rousing anthem, "When the Saints Go Marching In," a song that had its roots as a spiritual but now is better known as a jazz classic, thus metonymically demonstrating the ways in which the sacred and the profane unite in New Orleans. New Orleans is also perhaps the most medieval of American cities, rooted in the Catholic Church, steeped in the Gothic, and famous for a Carnival tradition that stretches back to medieval Europe. Moreover, in New Orleans, medievalism represents a mélange of cultural traditions. Whereas most American cities adopted a particularly white, "Anglo-Saxon," Protestant, and aristocratic view of the Middle Ages, New Orleans enjoys a more complicated social history than many other US cities, particularly when it comes to its colonial history and the European aspects of its cultural heritage. The strong mix of Spanish, French, and English traditions in modern New Orleans's culture, along with Caribbean, African, Central American, and Native influences and those of today's robust immigrant communities, is evident in various aspects of the city's culture, including its food, music, and the language options printed on its parking metres (English, French, Spanish, and Vietnamese), as well as its architecture. These various cultural influences, past and present, are also evident in its competing medievalisms, ecclesiastical and carnivalesque. In the streets of the Big Easy, we find the Middle Ages invoked to shore up social hierarchy and (white) privilege, to glorify martial conquest, and to preserve race, gender, and class distinctions. But we also find another Middle Ages, an unruly Middle Ages that breaks down borders and celebrates the mingling of classes, races, and cultures. In the end, it is this Middle Ages, the carnivalesque past of the "sinners," that may well point the way for the new saints of the future.

This chapter examines New Orleans's competing Middle Ages and how each has been used to shore up political and social agendas. It begins with the saints, visiting two churches, the St. Louis Cathedral and the Immaculate Conception Jesuit Church, looking at the ways in which these edifices draw on the medieval past to offer a vision of New Orleans, the first rooted in crusader glory and linked to a retrograde nostalgia for the city's antebellum past, and the second in the ideal of medieval Spain and the *convivencia*, the free mingling of cultures and ideas. It then moves out from the church and into the streets to look at the multiple medievalisms of Mardi Gras. This exploration begins with one of the city's founding moments, when Pierre Le Moyne laid claim to the area in 1699, naming it Pointe du Mardi Gras. It then traces the history of Mardi Gras in New Orleans from its first days when, as a religious festival grounded in medieval Catholicism, it connected the New World to the Old through its early incarnation as a time of carnivalesque misrule that provided the Creole social elite the opportunity to turn to the chivalric past in spectacles that shored up their power and privilege. In post–Civil War New Orleans, white residents appropriated this chivalric vision of Mardi Gras, in which its romanticized medievalisms worked to construct and affirm the city's "Southern" identity: a white identity in which both Black people and women were relegated to their "proper" antebellum roles. Our study of Mardi Gras medievalisms concludes with the return of comic and carnival medievalisms, which began after the First World War and continues today, as new krewes, which better represent New Orleans's multicultural past and present, take to the streets and the parade routes to challenge old hierarchies.

Crusade or *Convivencia*: Medievalism at Church

Among the saints, two Catholic houses of worship demonstrate the mix of cultural influences that characterizes both New Orleans's medievalisms and the city's multicultural present, but their respective relationships to medieval Europe and to contemporary politics could not be more dissimilar. Their medievalisms and their divergent modern politics are related: as John Ganim observes, "even in their most playful moments, medieval architectural revivals made political gestures or claims, however inconsistent these claims might be."[2] The divergent medievalisms of the St. Louis Cathedral in the French Quarter and the Immaculate Conception Jesuit Church in the Central Business District exemplify Ganim's claims. Although they are located less than a mile apart and jointly draw on medieval history and culture, these two houses of worship

11.1. Looking north at the St. Louis Cathedral from the Mississippi riverbank, with Jackson Square in front.

represent very different pictures of medievalist New Orleans: the former celebrates the martial history of its medieval namesake and overlooks racial divisions in US history, while the latter celebrates medieval exchange between cultures and the modern blending of cultures through immigration.

The St. Louis Cathedral, which was first built in 1717 and is the oldest Catholic cathedral in continuous use in the United States, is a prominent, centrally located, and notably visible landmark in New Orleans (see figure 11.1). This cathedral evokes a transtemporal and transcultural presaging of a Disney castle, with its spires towering over Jackson Square evoking a lost past. Street performers entertain the crowds and local artisans set up their booths in the pedestrian-only street that runs between the front of the cathedral and Jackson Square, with tourists gathering on the sidewalk in front of the cathedral to watch them. Stepping inside the cathedral seems at first to offer a markedly different environment from the carnivalesque atmosphere outside, with the quietness, cool air, and smell of incense providing a reprieve from the sensory overload that permeates the French Quarter. The visuals inside the cathedral, however, can be overwhelming too, and serve to highlight divisions in both medieval Europe and the Southern United States.

The inside of the cathedral celebrates the life of its medieval namesake, King Louis IX of France (1214–1270), also known as the "Sainted King" or the "Crusader King." Louis is a complicated figure, and the cathedral does not shy away from representing the more violent aspects of his reign. His moniker "Crusader King" comes from the fact that, although the Crusades had been ongoing for 130 years when he took the throne in 1226 at the age of twelve, and despite the fact that they had been disastrous for the French Crown, he swore in 1244 that he would begin a new one if he recovered from an illness.[3] After returning from the failed Seventh Crusade, he centralized judicial power under the Crown, strengthened existing restrictions on Jews in France, and instituted new punishments against blasphemy.[4] He eventually led an Eighth Crusade and died in what is now Tunisia in 1270. As James Naus notes, he was the first French king to take the crusading vow twice, rather than expressing his piety in the ways earlier French kings had, such as founding new monastic orders.[5]

Churches are named in honour of Louis IX all over the world, and while some of them obscure his crusader identity, celebrating his patronage of the arts or his charity for the hungry, the St. Louis Cathedral commemorates his more violent acts. The cathedral contains stained-glass scenes and frescoes depicting events from Louis's life, and the painting over the altar, the most prominent of them, depicts his announcement of the Seventh Crusade (captioned in French in case anyone doubts what they are seeing), stressing that for this cathedral, Louis's role as an instigator of crusade is his most important one. This emphasis is echoed in the aspects of US political allegiance and history the cathedral celebrates: the central passage of the ceiling, which contains paintings of Louis's childhood, is lined on both sides with flags (see figure 11.2). On one side, flags display the insignias of bishops of the cathedral, many of whom are buried there. On the other side, the flags are more overtly political and include various historical versions of the US flag, the Confederate flag, the French flag, and the Louisiana flag, linking the life of Louis IX with both Louisiana and the Confederacy (see figure 11.3).

The cathedral's website continues this theme of celebrating the martial history of both King Louis and the United States, and more explicitly links the two when it gives the following introduction to the building's history and significance:

> The St. Louis Cathedral is one of New Orleans' most notable landmarks. This venerable building, its triple steeples towering above its historic neighbors, the Cabildo and the Presbytere[,] looks down benignly on the green of the Square and General Andrew Jackson on his bronze horse and on the block-long Pontalba Buildings with their lacy ironwork galleries. Truly, this is the heart of old New Orleans.[6]

11.2 and 11.3. The flags along the ceiling of the St. Louis Cathedral, including multiple iterations of the US, Louisiana, and Confederate flags.

The strange juxtaposition of "venerable" and "benignly" suggests both an expression of power and a need to rhetorically mitigate that power. The reference to the statue of Andrew Jackson, which has become the subject of great dispute since then-mayor Mitch Landrieu had other controversial statues, including the prominent one of Robert E. Lee in Lee Circle, removed in 2017, suggests either an ignorance of the statue's current controversy or a deliberate link to this controversial figure. Like Louis, Andrew Jackson's legacy is a complicated one. He is frequently credited with saving New Orleans from British troops during the War of 1812 and for bringing that war to an end. But this locally celebrated military victory is, for many in and outside New Orleans, outweighed by his support for and role in forcibly removing Native Americans from their land and killing countless of them in the process. By linking Louis to Jackson's prominent statue in this statement, the cathedral connects – or even conflates – Louis's crusading with Jackson's destruction of Native communities, and veers close to celebrating them both.

In the back of the cathedral opposite the altar stand two medievalist figures: a statue of Louis, with a high-quality copy of his personal Bible, made in 2000; and a statue of Joan of Arc noting the year of her canonization (1920). Although they are likely there to link the cathedral to its namesake and New Orleans (with Joan representing Orléans, France, which she helped to reclaim from English troops in 1429), these statues contribute to the cathedral's appeal to the Middle Ages as part of its contemporary political identity. The statue of Joan may also indicate a pro-French, anti-British sentiment that has long served to distinguish Louisiana from the rest of the United States, and which reinforces the celebration of Jackson as someone who defended this city from the British.[7]

Such a distinction from British-only colonialism is present in a very different way in the other medievalist Catholic church in downtown New Orleans. Less than a mile away from the St. Louis Cathedral, the Immaculate Conception Jesuit Church is situated on Baronne Street on the eastern (or downriver) edge of the Central Business District, less than two blocks from Bourbon Street, but it represents a very different New Orleans than both the cathedral and Bourbon Street. A brick building nestled between a hotel and an apartment building and set flush with the fronts of the other buildings on the block, it is easy to miss and seems unassuming until one looks closely enough to see the intricate tile, glass, and stone work on its front and the plaque commemorating it as a historic building (see figures 11.4 and 11.5).

The Immaculate Conception Church, known colloquially as the Jesuit Church, is not as old as the St. Louis Cathedral; it was built in the 1850s and almost entirely rebuilt in the early twentieth century following structural damage. Although it does not attract nearly as many tourists as the St. Louis Cathedral, it is more representative of the multicultural city it serves, and it reflects

11.4 and 11.5. Two views of the Immaculate Conception Jesuit Church from across Baronne Street.

the multiculturalism of the medieval church as well. Rather than paying homage to the church's history of war with other religions, or war between Christian nations or proto-nations in the Middle Ages, it celebrates a vision of the medieval church as one that existed in and benefited from a mix of cultures, religions, and varying expressions of belief. That mixture is represented both in the church's architecture and in the public welcome on its website, which contains the following paragraph:

> The church's architectural style is Moorish (Islamic). Both the interior and exterior of the church are adorned with symbols that reflect Christian, Jewish, and Islamic sensibilities. This decision of the original architect, Jesuit Father John Cambiaso, was inspired by a period in Spain's history when Muslims, Christians, and Jews lived together peacefully and exchanged freely their cultural and intellectual treasures. This mélange of Islamic architecture with Jewish and Christian symbols invites people of various religious backgrounds to explore the church. The building itself stands as a reminder and challenge to all people of faith to respect each other and work together for the greater glory of the one true God.[8]

While the idea of a medieval Spain in which religions existed without friction is somewhat of an oversimplification, the choice to represent a state frequently understood through the concept of *convivencia* is a notable one, especially in a city where three colonial powers mixed with the cultures of Native and enslaved peoples. The church was originally constructed in the 1850s, when Catholicism in New Orleans was very much aligned with the French and Spanish rule of Louisiana, which included different slave codes and a significant free Black population compared with much of the rest of the United States. In that context, this statement suggests that its architect's appeal to what he understood as a time of coexistence and harmony between religions and ethnicities was one intended to resist what many saw as a British (and therefore Protestant) imposition of stricter codes concerning the rights of non-Europeans.[9]

The choice of neo-Venetian or Venetian Gothic architectural features, too, reflects a different sort of engagement with medievalism. A style of architecture that reflected a mix of Gothic, Moorish, and Byzantine styles, it was also, as Ganim notes, a "tool of social critique and ethical investigation" in John Ruskin's work in the 1850s.[10] Although, Ganim writes, Venetian architecture in this period was shifting away from its "socially symbiotic origins," the Jesuit Church's statement about its own origins suggests that Father Cambiaso was invested not only in those multicultural origins but in defending or propagating that particular aspect of Venetian Gothic architecture.[11] Perhaps, then, the Jesuit Church was not only drawing on this aspect of this style of architecture but also intervening in the way its social significance was evolving in the mid-nineteenth century.

The Jesuit Church's multicultural vision is evident in the flags that decorate the inside of the church. Like the cathedral, it contains the US and French flags, but it also contains flags of many other countries, which represent the immigrant histories of the local Catholic community. Images of these flags feature prominently on the church's website gallery, under the category "Church Interior." Moreover, the Jesuit Church looks very much like a neighbourhood church, and its function seems to be that of a local centre for the Catholic community, rather than a seat of power like the cathedral. For example, its website contains a host of useful logistical information, including links with instructions for recent or prospective converts to Catholicism and those new to New Orleans; explanations of the sacraments and instructions for how to arrange a wedding, baptism, and first communion; and contact information for staff and the parish council. Although similar information is available on the website of the St. Louis Cathedral, it is mixed with tourist information, an online gift shop (which includes the category "Holy Land Gifts," echoing the Crusades imagery inside), and a history of the cathedral up to 1849, including references to the military victories of Andrew Jackson and Zachary Taylor.

These two houses of worship offer different forms of outreach, different rhetoric on their websites, and different physical surroundings. Beyond those differences, though, they also offer different forms of engagement with the Middle Ages. Both celebrate the medieval aspects of their heritage, with the St. Louis Cathedral depicting a medieval past of war, crusades, and the exercise of power, whereas the Jesuit Church depicts one of cultural exchange, coexistence, and hospitality. These two different visions of the medieval past also reflect two different ways of seeing contemporary New Orleans. As with many medievalisms, the past we look to determines the present and future we make, both inside and outside a church's doors.

Lords of Misrule and Keepers of Order: Mardi Gras Medievalisms

The history of Mardi Gras, like the competing medievalisms on display at the St. Louis Cathedral and the Jesuit Church, demonstrates the multivalence of the Big Easy's medieval past, presenting an unruly array of Mardi Gras medievalisms, all of which were linked to the political desires of their historical moments. Unlike many American medievalisms, Mardi Gras can trace an unbroken, diachronic lineage back to the European Middle Ages. Derived from pagan rituals absorbed by the Roman church, Mardi Gras acquired during its passage through the Middle Ages certain features distinctive enough to be labelled "medieval" when they are revitalized or appropriated.[12] These evolving yet continuous features, which arrived with the founding of New Orleans and persisted for a century before being modified by Protestant reforms, include incorporation into the Christian calendar (the day before Lent), gluttonous and libidinous excesses, and carnivalesque levelling of social hierarchies. Woven within this diachronic medievalism are multiple medievalisms that borrow elements not associated with Mardi Gras during the Middle Ages but are nevertheless now associated with the Middle Ages (rightly or wrongly) and deemed essential to Mardi Gras in New Orleans. These borrowed elements include chivalric medievalism (and its attendant justifications for enforcing class and gender hierarchies), courtly love medievalism (closely related to the chivalric and borrowed from medieval literature and art), and comic medievalism (with its embrace of transgression and the absurd). For over three centuries, New Orleans's citizens have manipulated these modes of diachronic and borrowed medievalisms, adjusting their relationship to one another depending on contemporaneous sociocultural and political demands.

Diachronic Medievalism

New Orleans and the medieval holiday Mardi Gras have been intertwined from the beginning. Auspiciously enough, when Pierre Le Moyne claimed an area near the mouth of the Mississippi River in 1699 on the day before Ash Wednesday, he named it Pointe du Mardi Gras. This first affiliation between New Orleans (destined to become the South's greatest port city) and Mardi Gras (the final day of Carnival – observed from Epiphany, January 6, until the beginning of Lent on Ash Wednesday) conjoined an "Old World" religious holiday and a "New World" city, a link that did not lie dormant for long.

By the mid-eighteenth century, the New Orleans Creole community (Spanish and French colonialists' descendants comprising elite families of bankers, planters, and brokers) reinforced its ties with the metropole by promoting the city's earliest observations of Carnival. Drawing on medieval Catholic traditions of personal and social misrule during the days preceding Lent, the city's celebrations allowed everyone to abandon decorum with outrageous behaviour and sexual escapades. The city's leadership even condoned widespread festivities by allowing separate Carnival celebrations of music and dance (restricted to Congo Square) for the city's large population of people of colour, some enslaved, some freed.[13] For themselves, however, the Creole elite created an exclusive space to celebrate excess via theatrical amusements, operas, ballets, concerts, maskings, and (beginning in 1743) fancy dress balls. Early on, Carnival (culminating with its exclusive Mardi Gras ball) was simultaneously the height of elite society's social season and an extended period of civic abandon with street music, dancing, drinking, and public balls.

When New Orleans's elite and public Mardi Gras celebrations came together in 1837 with the first recorded "cavalcade," modelled on parades that the young male Creoles had observed in Paris, they triggered another carry-over from the Middle Ages: aristocratic display.[14] In contrast to the spontaneity defining previous masses of revellers, the cavalcade of costumed Creole elites was planned and announced beforehand, so that "thousands of maskers and spectators lined the streets and crowded cast-iron balconies" to view the costumed marchers on their way to the private Mardi Gras ball at the St. Louis Hotel.[15] With these public parades (where the social elites flaunted their status) and their final *bals masques* (where elaborate and expensive costumes "gave an air of grandeur which is difficult to imagine"), the Creoles accidentally anticipated how chivalric and courtly love customs (which persisted in Creole culture) were later marshalled by Mardi Gras parades and balls to reinforce social and gender hierarchies.[16]

Chivalric Medievalism

These latent medievalisms were more intentionally mobilized when American businessmen and tradesmen sought to establish their dominance over New Orleans's established Creoles. From the time Louisiana was annexed in 1803, the Creoles and Americans viewed each other with suspicion. The Creoles saw themselves as aristocratic, refined, and educated, while dismissing the Americans as plebeian, brutish, and money-grubbing. The Americans, on the other hand, judged the Creoles as stuck in the past – slothful, inexperienced in self-government, and reliant on inherited wealth and slave labour – while seeing themselves as purveyors of a new world order requiring ambition, civic participation, and skill in such professions as law, medicine, education, and commerce.[17] The newcomers, however, appreciated the powerful message sent by Creole myths of aristocratic prerogative and natural chivalry, and in 1857, a group of Americans styling themselves as the Mistick Krewe of Comus organized a parade and ball using the models established by the Creoles' traditional events but elevated to unforgettable spectacles created by the infusion of money and the visible overlay of chivalric and (eventually) courtly love elements.[18] In New Orleans's first procession to limit participation (but not observation) to members, masked krewe members paraded at night with a torchlight procession featuring Satan (from Milton's *Paradise Lost*) and his court of demons, who represented the enticements (and dangers) of the Seven Deadly Sins.[19] Not only did this spectacle raise the ante for what Mardi Gras in New Orleans would look like, but it also illustrated the Protestant businessmen's ability to appropriate a Catholic festival for their own purposes. The Creoles had established their exclusivity via Mardi Gras cavalcades and balls that nostalgically reached back to a continental past; the Americans, in turn, amplified the Creole traditions to announce their economic and political dominance. By appropriating the chivalric medievalism inherent in Creole culture, the Americans challenged the old regime and made themselves "the refined products of a vanished civilization."[20]

After the Civil War, Carnival became less about Creole versus American and more about establishing a New Orleans identity separate from that of the military government imposed during Reconstruction. In this era, "conservative white New Orleanians revived the Carnival tradition, innovated within it, and used it as a theater of protest" against the imposed government and the newly emancipated Black people.[21] An important weapon in this battle was the myth of chivalric honour, a central element of Southern identity and the emblem of the Cult of the "Lost Cause." The chivalric myth used medievalist war tropes to "support supposed age-old and elemental antimonies of light and dark, good and evil, pure and polluted," helping to rework the war to the losers' advantage.[22] The Yankee aggressors may have won, but the defeated Rebels retained their honour, a rhetorical strategy that allowed medievalizing discourse to imbue the South with secular and spiritual heroism while projecting brutality and depravity onto their enemies.[23] Mardi Gras parades and tableaux focused on topics that distinctly excluded ties to American culture, drawing instead on Southern traditions purportedly upholding chivalric honour. By importing medieval themes and chivalric tropes, Mardi Gras ritualized the recognition of the white gentleman's entitlement to status, wealth, and respect. In their chivalric guise, New Orleans's modern-day knights formed secret societies, such as the Mistick Krewe of Comus, the Krewe of Proteus, the Knights of Momus, the Twelfth Night Revelers, and Rex. They rode on papier-mâché floats pulled by mules caparisoned in emulation of horses ridden by medieval knights. They formed tableaux on those floats depicting contemporary visions of orientalist and medievalist exoticism.[24] They relegated Black people to the most subservient roles, such as the night-time procession of Black men carrying heavy torches to light the parade route.[25] And under the cover of Carnival and Mardi Gras spectacle (and thus under the protection of the law), they continued promiscuous masking, an otherwise illegal activity associated with illegal vigilante activities such as lynching and Ku Klux Klan rallies.

This "public ceremony of pomp and bombast, with mystery, artistry, and ritual splendor," required lavish spending and secretive, year-long preparations.[26] The mobile tableaux of the parade floats were magnificent – and purposely intimidating – expressions of New Orleans nobility's exquisite taste, extensive wealth, and arcane erudition. Rather than provide opportunities for role reversals, these highly regulated activities maintained social order by feeding on fantasies of an "imaginary Southern, Creole-French way of life which placed high value on chivalrous conviviality."[27] In a more limited way, the Comus revelries also sought to control the large influx of revellers and tourists – approximately 100,000 annually as early as 1910 – lured to New Orleans during Carnival and Mardi Gras by the promise of sexual promiscuity, social licence, and racial mixing. Although tourists were encouraged to trespass the boundaries of social and moral norms, the theatrics of Comus and his Krewe made certain that the tourists understood how far to push their transgressions. Through "total civic participation" involving locals and visitors alike "in a collective cultural performance," the krewes reasserted and enforced for another year their undemocratic yet "historic claims of entitlement, priority, and exclusivity."[28]

Courtly Love Medievalism

Arguably a subset of chivalric medievalism, courtly love medievalism deserves its own consideration because the krewes relegated it to its own sphere: the extremely private arena of the Carnival balls. These affairs limited attendees to prominent New Orleans families who received the exquisite die-cut or, later, engraved summons to the ball.[29] Although Carnival was the most exclusive social season for New Orleans, and the balls held by the old-line krewe were "paramount" in fashion and exclusivity, women had very little input regarding their themes or organization.[30] Instead, the krewes' male membership determined the year's theme and tapped young women (selected for their beauty and their luck for being the daughter of a prominent man) to fill the honorific membership of that particular krewe's royal court, becoming important props whereby the parade turned into a "king's procession through the city" on his way to a royal ball, representing, in turn, the king's "retreat from public space to semiprivate space."[31] In this secluded space, young women and debutantes chosen from among the daughters of New Orleans's finest families served as queens and maids of the royal court.[32] These few women and the masked krewe participating in the parade were the only dancers at the ball; the other guests merely served as spectators attending the ball by exclusive invitation.

Whereas the parades regulated class divisions in public spaces with chivalric medievalism, the Carnival balls monitored gender roles with a form of courtly love medievalism, insisting that the young women were so pure, so innocent, that their courtship role must be limited to being chosen by a worthy "knight." At the Carnival balls, a young unmarried woman could flirt or demur, but how she did so came from a carefully prescribed repertoire of movements and protocols. Moreover, the repurposed theatres serving as ballrooms were "a new kind of social space, something neither private nor public, something between the parlour and the streets" that allowed "the display of the social elite to the social elite," thereby enforcing "social discipline on the families of the elite."[33] Women were invited to be observed and chosen. A young woman's marriage prospects could be determined by her ability to adhere to the restricted conventions. With each woman's movements susceptible to the condemnation or approbation of those who could determine her future, the ballrooms were an ideal site for maintaining and enforcing gender roles – and, similar to ways their medieval predecessors realized, for the young woman "to manipulate the royal image and carve out some sense of personal power."[34]

Comic Medievalism

Although the carnivalesque was never absent from New Orleans Mardi Gras, the old-line krewes worked diligently to keep the topsy-turvy in its place. From the earliest years, impropriety was kept away from the main corridors and ballrooms the krewes controlled. If there were to be social satire in the form of parading figures reminiscent of grotesques atop cathedrals and in manuscript marginalia, the parody's targets were determined by the city's elite.[35] The control wielded by elite krewes of white New Orleans diminished (and nearly disappeared) after the First World War; they would no longer predominantly determine the tone and tenor of official Mardi Gras. Perhaps the money spent and the mysterious masking could not hide the fact, as Mark Twain caustically observed, that New Orleans's Mardi Gras magnificence was based on "sham grandeurs, sham gauds, and sham chivalries."[36] Most likely, though, the medieval roots of Mardi Gras in bacchanalian exuberance prevailed, and the carnival was again dominated by the wild abandon that lured tourists and locals alike. Elements long kept on the back streets gained prominence in the parade routes. Black social clubs, working-class organizations, and women's groups used comic absurdity to counterbalance the formalism of the elite old-line krewes.[37] Tourists and locals embraced the new Zulu parade floats, dancing Mardi Gras Indians, women's krewes, and truck parades. In their evolution, parades, balls, and street festivals have not diminished their dazzling spectacle. After nearly a century of chivalric and courtly love medievalisms dominating Carnival and Mardi Gras, these new krewes, social clubs, and carnival organizations released the carnivalesque aspects the old-line krewes had sought to control. For the past century, Mardi Gras celebrations have been a mode for expressing "anxieties about such issues as social change and historical progress, political and religious structures and culture tolerance."[38]

In the wake of Hurricane Katrina's devastations in 2005, the Great Recession of 2008, and emboldened white supremacists, it will be comic – not chivalric or courtly love – medievalism that will generate the cultural energy of New Orleans's Mardi Gras celebrations, even if such a comic sensibility is achieved simply through the vibrant refusal to allow tragedy to triumph. Today in New Orleans, "When the Saints Go Marching In" is played raucously through the streets, and many times, it heralds the New Orleans Saints, celebrating their own kind of modern crusade – one on the football field rather than the battlefield. Following Katrina, after a season played away from their home city, the Saints returned to New Orleans in 2006, and in the newly renovated Superdome, Drew Brees took the Saints to victory against the Atlanta Falcons. That night, Monday Night Football opened to the strains of "Amazing Grace" and the image of a cross; the camera then moved inside New Orleans's First Emmanuel Baptist Church, to cross-cut between the Reverend Charles Southall III with his congregation and shots of the devastation Katrina wrought on New Orleans's African American citizens. "In spite of the flood waters of Katrina, in spite of pumps that don't work, and walls that were built inferior, in spite of neighborhoods that were shattered, we are still right here," Southall proclaims. "We must never, ever forget. Now we must move forward … because our resolve will never, ever diminish." "Tonight," he continues, as the segment cuts to the Superdome, "our future burns brighter than ever. Regardless of your affiliation or domination, regardless of your social or economic status, regardless of whether you are wearing red and black or black and gold, tonight we are one." The congregation breaks into "When the Saints Go Marching In," singing and dancing as Southall exclaims, "We are here, we are here, we are still here."[39] St. Louis, the crusader, is replaced by new saints: a multicultural New Orleans and a powerhouse team, one that had long been derided as a laughingstock of the league. And when the Saints won that night, the city spilled into the streets, in a carnival of cheers and hurricanes (the ones that come in a tall glass), celebrating as the Saints had indeed come marching in. The parties were even more raucous four years later when the Saints won the 2010 Super Bowl. More subdued, though still evidence of the irrepressible New Orleans spirit, the 2021 parades during the COVID-19 pandemic were transformed from floats travelling along prescribed routes to stationary displays adorning the city's stoops, porches, balconies, and yards, displays which celebrants could safely enjoy from their automobiles as they followed the ad hoc route.[40]

In considering New Orleans and its saints and sinners, we would be remiss not to conclude with Joan of Arc, the Maid of Orléans from whom the city takes its name and with whom we began this chapter. New Orleans's Joan of Arc statue stands on Decatur Street in the French Quarter, a gift from the French unveiled in 1972. A martyr for her faith, Joan of Arc models a fervent piety that, ironically, the Big Easy is more known for eschewing than embracing. Of course, medievalisms themselves are neither holy nor unholy, neither sacred nor profane; it is the uses to which they are put that involve human values. Could the Maid of Orléans have foreseen amongst her fifteenth-century visions that a likeness of her would stand centuries later in a then unknown land and that she would be painted in gold and recruited to represent the city's fandom for its football team? (see figure 11.6). In the city of New Orleans, medievalisms, even those of Joan of Arc herself, are more often conscripted as an excuse for a party rather than as a reminder of piety, no matter how many saints might be tut-tutting in the heavens.

11.6. The Maid of Orleans, rooting for the New Orleans Saints. Photo courtesy of Dr. Robert Sanford, physicist and New Orleanian.

NOTES

1. Melinda Daffin, "What Do You Call New Orleans? 11 of the Good, Bad and Silly Nicknames for an Iconic City," *Times-Picayune*, 3 Oct. 2017, http://www.nola.com/living/index.ssf/2017/10/new_orleans_nicknames_the_good.html (accessed 11 Jan. 2018).
2. John M. Ganim, "Medievalism and Architecture," in *The Cambridge Companion to Medievalism*, ed. Louise D'Arcens (Cambridge: Cambridge University Press, 2016), 29–44, at 30. See also Elizabeth Emery, "Postcolonial Gothic: The Medievalism of America's 'National' Cathedrals," in *Medievalisms in the Postcolonial World: The Idea of "the Middle Ages" Outside Europe*, ed. Kathleen Davis and Nadia Altschul (Baltimore: Johns Hopkins University Press, 2009), 237–64.
3. Sean L. Field and M. Cecilia Gaposchkin, eds., *The Sanctity of Louis IX: Early Lives of Saint Louis by Geoffrey of Beaulieu and William of Chartres* (Ithaca, NY: Cornell University Press, 2014), 6.
4. Field and Gaposchkin, *The Sanctity of Louis IX*, 9. See also William Chester Jordan, *Men at the Center: Redemptive Governance under Louis IX* (Budapest: Central European University Press, 2012), 101–2.
5. James Naus, *Constructing Kingship: The Capetian Monarchs of France and the Early Crusades* (Manchester: Manchester University Press, 2016), 2.
6. "Our History," Cathedral-Basilica of Saint Louis, King of France, http://www.stlouiscathedral.org/our-history (accessed 12 Sept. 2018).
7. Joan has also been the subject of right-wing medievalisms, as detailed by Nadia Margolis, "The 'Joan Phenomenon' and the French Right," in *Fresh Verdicts on Joan of Arc*, ed. Bonnie Wheeler and Charles T. Wood (New York: Garland, 1996), 265–88.
8. "I'm New to the Parish," Immaculate Conception Jesuit Church, https://www.jesuitchurch.net/to-the-parish (accessed 12 Sept. 2018).
9. For more on the differences between English colonial rule and French/Spanish colonial rule in the Americas, and their different types of engagement with Protestant and Catholic theology, see James Muldoon, "Discovery, Grant, Conquest, Discovery, or Purchase: John Adams on the Legal Basis for English Possession of North America," in *The Many Legalities of Early America*, ed. Christopher L. Tomkins and Bruce H. Mann (Chapel Hill: University of North Carolina Press, 2001), 25–46.
10. Ganim, "Medievalism and Architecture," 33.
11. Ganim, "Medievalism and Architecture," 33.
12. Claire Sponsler, "A Response to Candace Barrington," *American Literary History* 22, no. 4 (2010): 831–7, at 835–6.
13. Henri Schindler, *Mardi Gras: New Orleans* (Paris: Flammarion, 1997), 130–1.
14. Henri Schindler, *Mardi Gras Treasures: Float Designs of the Golden Age* (Gretna, LA: Pelican, 2001), 8.
15. Schindler, *Mardi Gras: New Orleans*, 27.
16. Schindler, *Mardi Gras: New Orleans*, 27, quoting Louis Fitzgerald Tasistro.
17. Joseph Tregle, "Creoles and Americans," in *Creole New Orleans: Race and Americanization*, ed. Arnold Hirsch and Joseph Logsdon (Baton Rouge: Louisiana

State University Press, 1992), 131–85, at 134–46; and Charles Henry White, "New Orleans," *Harper's Magazine*, Dec. 1906: 121–30, at 126.
18 Candace Barrington, "'Forget What You Have Learned': The Mistick Krewe's 1914 Mardi Gras Chaucer," *American Literary History* 22, no. 4 (2010): 806–30.
19 Schindler, *Mardi Gras: New Orleans*, 35.
20 James Gill, *Lords of Misrule: Mardi Gras and the Politics of Race in New Orleans* (Jackson: University Press of Mississippi, 1997), 143.
21 Reid Mitchell, *All on a Mardi Gras Day: Episodes in the History of New Orleans Carnival* (Cambridge, MA: Harvard University Press, 1995), 79.
22 Andrew Lynch, "Medievalism and the Ideology of War," in D'Arcens, *Cambridge Companion to Medievalism*, 135–50, at 139.
23 Catherine Clinton, *Tara Revisited: Women, War, and the Plantation Legend* (New York: Abbeville Press, 1995), 19; Lynch, "Medievalism and the Ideology of War," 139.
24 Schindler, *Mardi Gras Treasures*.
25 Joseph Roach, *Cities of the Dead: Circum-Atlantic Performance* (New York: Columbia University Press, 1996), 269–70.
26 Schindler, *Mardi Gras: New Orleans*, 35. Comus ceased parading when city regulations forbade sexual/racial segregation in 1991.
27 Samuel Kinser, *Carnival, American Style: Mardi Gras at New Orleans and Mobile* (Chicago: University of Chicago Press, 1990), 250.
28 Roach, *Cities of the Dead*, 245.
29 Schindler, *Mardi Gras Treasures*.
30 Robert Tallant, *Mardi Gras: As It Was* (Gretna, LA: Pelican, 1989), 9; Mitchell, *All on a Mardi Gras Day*, 100.
31 Mitchell, *All on a Mardi Gras Day*, 98–9.
32 Mitchell, *All on a Mardi Gras Day*, 98–9, 102–5.
33 Mitchell, *All on a Mardi Gras Day*, 99; Roach, *Cities of the Dead*, 245.
34 Jennifer Atkins, "'Using the Bow and the Smile': Old-Line Krewe Court Femininity in New Orleans Mardi Gras Balls, 1870–1920," *Louisiana History* 54, no. 1 (2013): 5–46, at 6.
35 Schindler, *Mardi Gras Treasures*, 18–24 passim.
36 Mark Twain, *Life on the Mississippi*, Oxford Mark Twain, ed. Shelley Fishkin (1883; repr., New York: Oxford University Press, 1996), 467–8.
37 Kinser, *Carnival, American Style*, 83.
38 Louise D'Arcens, *Comic Medievalism: Laughing at the Middle Ages* (Cambridge: D.S. Brewer, 2014), 6.
39 "MNF [Monday Night Football] Opening, Sept. 2006 before Falcons at Saints," ESPN Front Row, 25 Sept. 2006, https://vimeo.com/183338842 (accessed 13 Jan. 2019).
40 Doug MacCash, "'Float Houses' Are Now Popping Up All Over New Orleans for Mardi Gras 2021," *Times-Picayune*, 2 Jan. 2021, https://www.nola.com/multimedia/photos/collection_57b3b908-54fb-11eb-af5d-8b79d450f1c0.html (accessed 1 Mar. 2021).

12 Sherwood Forest Faire: Evoking Medieval May Games, Robin Hood Revels, and Twentieth-Century "Pleasure Faires" in Contemporary Texas

LORRAINE KOCHANSKE STOCK

The Sherwood Forest Faire (hereafter SFF) located in McDade, Texas, belongs to the popular culture category of historically grounded, immersive entertainments termed "Renaissance faires."[1] Putatively, such nomenclature renders my subject irrelevant to a scholarly appraisal of American expressions of *medievalism*.[2] Although many such faires throughout the United States adopt (or have applied to them) the sobriquet "Renaissance," most of these venues promote and encourage their patrons' celebration of European culture covering a broad temporal spectrum well beyond the narrowly defined "Renaissance" era. Joking about the multi-periodicity and multiculturalism of the 1970s Marin "Renaissance Pleasure Faires" in California, Sam Blazer observes, "'Renaissance' ... means medieval and Elizabethan England with a convenient recognition of falafel."[3] In the four decades since Blazer described early faires in America, this mixture of "historical" periods and concessions to current popular taste has continued. Activities featured and costumes worn by faire employees and patrons/playtrons (elaborately costumed repeat fair-goers) at these entertainments span a period of over a millennium, ranging from the earliest so-called Dark Ages of European history (c. sixth century) through the Renaissance (with a c. seventeenth-century *terminus ad quem*) to twenty-first-century fictional worlds. For example, the 2018 Cloisters "Medieval Festival," held on the grounds of the Cloisters Museum of medieval art in New York City's Fort Tryon Park, attracted more than 60,000 visitors who dressed in garb that could qualify them as *Game of Thrones* extras and travelled to the festival on the subway to "watch professional stunt actors joust and clang swords" and "eat highly inauthentic turkey legs (the turkey, native to the Americas, did not exist in medieval Europe)."[4]

In other words, these seasonal faires offer their guests a chance to visit neither the Renaissance nor the Middle Ages but an eclectic once-upon-a-time that borrows from both while mixing historical clichés with notions about the period(s) originating in popular film and television. These faires are more medieval than they might first appear, medieval in function if not in form, as America's Renaissance faires are rooted in the timeless vernal festivities that cohered as the local parochial May games and Whitsun ales of late medieval England. In their incorporation of these festivals' carnivalesque aspects and spirit of social resistance, today's Renaissance faires represent an intersection of cultural forces extending from fifteenth-century England to present-day America. More so, the medieval qualities of these events are often bolstered by their inclusion of Robin Hood, the English outlaw whose legendary career motivated a name change for the May games and Whitsun ales into "Robin Hood" revels. While most faires merely nod to the outlaw of Sherwood, SFF adds an additional and uniquely historical layer to its American medievalism by celebrating his legend, bringing Sherwood Forest to central Texas.

In this chapter, I situate SFF in the context of both medieval and American faires, beginning with a discussion of the late medieval springtime festivities and the history of their association with Robin Hood, who, as a figure aligned with eternal springtime in the greenwood, was a natural fit for these medieval "going-a-Maying festivities." From here, I turn to the rise of American "Renaissance" faires in the 1960s and the coterminous development of the Society for Creative Anachronism (SCA), discussing the ways in which the anti-establishment status of the outlawed yeoman Robin Hood made him a suitable mascot both for the carnivalesque aspects of the original May games and Whitsun ales and for the spirit of social resistance that inspired these anti-establishment and counterculture American medievalisms in 1960s California. I conclude by describing several trips to SFF, examining the faire within the history of the Robin Hood legend and the theoretical context of "serious leisure" to illuminate the ways in which it keeps the spirit of the greenwood alive and well in Texas.

From May Games and Whitsun Ales to "Robin Hood" Revels

Faires such as SFF that are characterized by medievalism originated from similar recreational activities practised during the actual medieval period. Late medieval and early modern people celebrated seasonal May festivities reflecting pre-Christian fertility rituals practised at Beltane (1 May). These revelries inspired activities performed during the rite of "going a-Maying": gathering verdure and flowers from woodlands; erecting a large felled tree that served as a maypole; and making love.[5] Equally important in late medieval England's festive calendar was the Christian holy day of Pentecost, falling variously between mid-May and mid-June. Dubbed "Whit-Sunday" (shortened to "Whitsun"), the feast initiated seven days of Whitsuntide, during which agricultural workers enjoyed time off from their labours. All rural parish members thus enjoyed the leisure to participate in parochial-sponsored religious processions, secular games, lay and religious drama, morris dancing, moneymaking gambits (the sale of floral garlands, Robin Hood's livery badges, food, and ale), and general revelry.[6]

At Whitsun ales, timed during May through June to reflect the moveable feast of Pentecost, patrons paid to attend lavish community feasts offering various edible delicacies and fresh-brewed ale. Money collected from the sale of these meals supported coverage of the parish's financial emergencies.[7] A Mock-King, Lord of Misrule, or Summer Lord originally presided over the Whitsun ales and the May games; Robin Hood fulfilled this role alongside his consort Maid Marian and their down-market "court" of Little John and the Merry Men.[8] Once this happened, the May games and Whitsun ales inevitably became the "Robin Hood revels." In addition to folk plays that adapted the ballads about the outlaw and the Merry Men, guild members of the parishes played the roles of Robin and Marian at rural and urban May games, Whitsun ales, and staged professional dramas. Eventually, "Robin Hood, Little John, Friar Tuck, and Maid Marian, although not constituent parts of the original English morris [dance], became ... so blended with it, especially on the festival of May-day, that ... they continued to be the most essential part of the pageantry."[9]

The identification between Whitsun ales and Robin Hood revels occurred gradually over the course of the fourteenth through seventeenth centuries. Illustrating this identification, *The Practice of the Divell* (c. 1577) praised the "merry" past, when "Robin Hood's plays [were] in every town, the Morrice and the Fool, the Maypole and the Drum," all listed of a piece.[10] Similarly, describing the theatrics at the Robin Hood/May games and Whitsun ales in *Albion's England* (1612), William Warner claimed, "At Paske [Easter] begun our Morris, ere Pentecost [Whitsun] our May, / When Robin Hood, Litell John, Friar Tuck, and Marian deftly *play*."[11] Here "play" references Robin Hood dramas, such as *Robin Hood and the Curtal Friar*, performed by members of the parish, who inhabit the roles of the usual greenwood principals plus Friar Tuck and Maid Marian, the morris figures who became associated with Robin Hood through the dance's identification with the outlaw.[12] Furthermore, a Marprelate tract alludes to a boy in church responding interchangeably to "either a Summer Lord with his Maygames, or Robin Hood with his Morris dance."[13]

Whether the Robin Hood ballads were the catalyst for or the result of simultaneous urban and rural interest in May games and other country games, they enjoyed a symbiotic relationship.[14] When early printers William Copland and Edward White published their separate 1560 and 1594 editions of the ballad *A Mery Geste of Robyn Hode*, each appended to the ballad text "a new playe for to be played in Maye games, very plesaunte and full of pastyme."[15] These *Geste*-plus-play texts illustrate how professional writers or text compilers provided dramatic scripts to be performed at May games. Although J.M. Steadman posits the ballads as unique sources for the plots of early plays performed at May games,[16] John Forrest suggests that to construct his play about Robin meeting his match in Friar Tuck, Copland "cobble[d] together a text from [various] folk plays ... in his possession."[17] Considering W.E. Simeone's assertion that Robin Hood's three-centuries-long association with the May games was "the most important episode in the history of the legend," these scanty extant textual remnants may represent a previously numerous corpus of now-lost dramatizations of Robin Hood narratives enacted at the fifteenth- through seventeenth-century May games or Whitsun ales.[18]

These narratives' celebration of the mythic outlaw's stealing of money from his victims reflected the fundraising function of the late medieval revels; the connection between these festivities and Robin Hood was intrinsically symbiotic, and thus Robin Hood naturally became their iconic patron. Scholars account for this reciprocal interrelationship between the greenwood outlaw and the May games in three ways: the seasonal approach, the carnival theory, and the economic explanation. The seasonal approach constructs Robin as "May Lord of the May-games," associated with vernal renewal and personifying what is now called the "Green Man." As Ronald Hutton notes, the May games and attendant Robin Hood–related activities were an important aspect of the spring/summer season of "Merry" England's "ritual year."[19] In his 1603 *Survey of London*, John Stow reported that on May Day morning everyone "would walk into the sweet meadows and green woods, there to rejoice their spirits with the beauty and savour of sweet flowers," and would bring back floral and foliate tokens to adorn their homes.[20] David Wiles associates the greenwood outlaw with the maypole, "an emblem of summer and the natural world," which lent itself to deeming Robin as "Summer Lord," "May King," or "Lord of the greenwood."[21] John Matthews details associations between May games, maypoles, the morris dance, and Robin Hood, the "Green Lord of the Wildwood," while Lorraine Stock connects Robin Hood with the period's other mythic figures, the Green Man and the Wild Man, who were also "Lords of the Wildwood."[22] Finally, the evocation of the "somer" forest in the month of May as the temporal backdrop and physical setting for nearly all early Robin Hood ballads underscores the seasonal identification between the outlaws' activities and the natural world "under the grene wode tre."[23]

Rather than figuring Robin Hood as the greenwood's May king, advocates of the Bakhtinian carnival theory construct the outlaw as the embodiment of disorder and misrule. Medieval games or revels associated with Robin Hood registered their participants' embrace of his outlawry through conscious subversion of authority. The mayhem perpetrated by Robin Hood, the violent outlaw, qualified him for the position of both May king and the Lord of Misrule at May games and other seasonal celebrations. Assessing his role as Lord of Misrule, Bakhtinian-inspired critics emphasize Robin Hood's signification of anti-establishment transgression, violence, and especially the carnivalesque inversion of official social structures. According to Wiles, the large trees used to fabricate maypoles for the Robin Hood revels were stolen from the forests of the wealthy. Such illicit acts reinforced associations between Robin Hood's reputation for robbing from the rich and the practices of the May games. Wiles concludes, "in the figure of Robin Hood two elements are combined, the outlaw who ignores the requirements of society [by inspiring the theft of timber for maypoles], and the green man, the incarnation of spring."[24] Peter Stallybrass highlights how "gender-inversion and transvestism," transgressive aspects of the outlaw's legend, also illustrate the May games' carnivalesque aspects.[25] Just as the morris dance's Maid Marion figure crossdressed, Robin's May queen, Maid Marian, wore male armour for disguise and violated the period's gender norms by matching the outlaw's fighting skills.[26] Moreover, May-time's "freedom of the forest," which inspired the sexual licence that Stubbs excoriated, provided the greenwood habitus that attracted to Robin Hood "masterless men seeking a meagre subsistence, ... cottagers and squatters, ... outlaws and religious dissenters," which prompts Stallybrass to equate Robin Hood and the May games with heterodoxy.[27] For Christine Richardson, the May games' symbiosis between the transgressive outlaw and the games' otherwise law-abiding civilian participants exemplified the "characteristically carnival aspect ... [that] eliminates boundaries between performers and spectators, making the 'performance' a universalizing, participatory event, removing also the barriers between art and life, ... seen as a game."[28]

According to the third explanation of the May games' significance, the economic/parochial theory, social gatherings honouring Robin Hood (known for taking his victims' money) pragmatically employed the outlaw for purposes of fundraising – to underwrite repairs to the local church's fabric in rural parishes, to support parochial religious guild activities, and to offer financial relief to the poor. This reliance on the Robin Hood legend to support the parish's poor reifies the final lines of *A Gest of Robyn Hode* about the ballad's protagonist: "For he was a good outlawe / And dyde pore men moch god."[29] As Peter Greenfield notes, Robin Hood–themed May games were "charitable fund-raisers, authorized and organized by local officials," that typically "culminated in a communal feast."[30] Paul Whitfield White agrees that the staging of "numerous parish revels featuring Robin Hood" raised money to fund individual guilds' "devotional observances," the "general parish fund," or "a new rood loft or image."[31] During Robin Hood–themed "gaderyngs" in Cornwall's parishes of Bodmin and Stratton, the citizen playing "Robin hoode" – along with men posing as Little John, Friar Tuck, and other "hoodsmen," all costumed in the Kendal (or Lincoln) green livery of the outlaw's band – collected money either door-to-door or at a church ale.[32]

Collectively, the seasonal, carnivalesque, and economic interpretations of the ubiquitous late medieval and Renaissance Robin Hood revels demonstrate the pre-eminence of the English outlaw's central role in what I maintain were the early period forerunners of contemporary American medieval/Renaissance faires. Although Robin Hood "gatherings" (communal get-togethers and collecting of contributions) were fundraisers, John Marshall notes that they were also *"fun*-raisers"; the Robin Hood revels' thus balanced a "contribution to parochial finances and social cohesion" with "the sheer fun to be had from dressing up in Lincoln green and brandishing a bow and arrows with a few friends."[33] Given the English outlaw's prominent function in the historic antecedents of what have developed into American early period faires, it is little wonder that SFF's organizers chose a Robin Hood theme as the focus of their faire in twenty-first-century Texas.

The Medieval Roots of Twentieth-Century American Renaissance Faires

If medieval festivities such as springtime games, ales, and fairs were the implicit temporal forerunners of American Renaissance early period faires, they also provided explicit models for content. The first Renaissance faire, organized in California in 1963, was conceived as a celebration of medieval European culture. Phyllis Patterson, a teacher whose pedagogical success at rendering history and literature engaging was matched by her savvy organizational skills, spearheaded this faire, modelling her event upon the medieval period's market fairs – moveable and temporary commercial events comprising an annual circuit of opportunities for travelling merchants to buy, sell, and trade domestic and imported wares. In this spirit, later incarnations of American faires also looked back to the Middle Ages. The Marin Renaissance Pleasure Faire incorporated a medieval market cross in their faire-ground's layout, a feature dating from the seventh through the fifteenth centuries that was erected to designate the market square, a place granted by a king or a high-ranking ecclesiast for a town to hold local markets or to host travelling fairs. In Marin, "Ye Market Cross" greeted patrons upon entering the faire-ground, while a procession of larger-than-life figures representing various guilds participating in the faire entertained them, just as these figures had been employed during the medieval period as greeters in royal entries, over bridges into London, and in parades like the Lord Mayor's procession.[34] The second iteration of the Southern California Renaissance Pleasure Faire, held in 1965, reflected not only medieval market fairs in general but also a specific medieval "historical precedent," the Old Woodbury Hill Fair in Dorset, England, which developed before 1200 and continued throughout the Renaissance and intermittently thereafter until 1951. To better educate patrons, promotional material and programs distributed to faire-goers at the 1965 event emphasized this connection to a historical medieval market fair by "offering brief histories of English fairs such as the Old

Woodbury Hill Fair." The 1965 faire attempted to re-create the Woodbury Fair's "combination of vendors and entertainment" and featured costumed actors portraying such historical figures as Queen Elizabeth I, Sir Francis Drake, and Sir Walter Raleigh.[35]

From market crosses and historical referents to a sense of seasonal carnival, the early California faires incorporated a heavy dose of the medieval within their version of the Renaissance. Because medieval travelling fairs "arrived in town during the springtime when the roads were dry and the local market established," Patterson timed her first faire in Los Angeles to reflect the medieval model. Concerning these spring market fairs, Patterson presumed "an interactive environment where everyone, from the theatre players to the vendors and visitors, were engaged in a lively exchange of words and wares." This set-up, which reproduces the blurred boundaries between performers, vendors, and patrons at the medieval May games, provided a paradigm for her first and subsequent faires. Reflecting the "temporary nature of these mercantile gatherings," Patterson's early faires, which were planned to "lend a seasonal and therefore historically correct impermanent quality to the gathering," comprised temporary structures that could be changed each year. They were timed to "coincide with the May festivals" and the Robin Hood–themed gatherings of medieval and early modern England, thus duplicating the timing of similar immersive entertainments enjoyed by audiences participating in the aforementioned May games and Whitsun ales.[36]

In addition to being medieval in form, these early period faires and a similar organization that arose coterminous with them, the Society for Creative Anachronism, proved to be also medieval in function. Similar to the financial parochial function of late medieval Robin Hood revels, in May 1963, the inaugural Renaissance Pleasure Faire presented in the Los Angeles area was organized as a fundraiser for KPFK Pacifica radio station. Furthermore, as Rachel Rubin documents, the faires were mirrors and catalysts of social developments of the 1960s, both inspired by and contributing to America's socially revolutionary climate. Indeed, Rubin identifies the faires as a "point of origin" in helping to "invent the Sixties."[37] The faires encouraged, almost demanded, that their patrons engage in "play," a word faire-goers employ "more often than is common in American English." Moreover, the 1960s youth culture, then branded "hippies," used "play" both as "a rather direct repudiation of the status quo" and to "upend *all* cultural identities." Kevin Patterson, husband of Phyllis and co-founder of the California faires, asserted that "getting people to 'play' was the Renaissance faire's strategy for effecting social change" by contributing to an "artistic manifestation of a protest gathering."[38]

Reflecting the same countercultural climate in 1960s California, a group of fans of medieval fantasy literature hosted a May-day Tournament of Chivalry near San Francisco on 1 May 1966. This was the foundational moment of the SCA.[39] Although the "chivalry" in the event's title belies the association, the SCA was rooted in the same local intent to challenge the norms of then-contemporary society that inspired other expressions of social resistance arising in the San Francisco Bay area in the 1960s: hippies, the Grateful Dead, the Black Panthers, and the Renaissance Pleasure Faires. As Michael Cramer recounts, several medieval theme parties hosted in the Bay Area by the founders of the SCA – Ken de Maiffe, David Thewlis, Diana Paxson, and writers Marion Zimmer Bradley and Poul Anderson – catapulted (pun intended) the gatherings into a massive organization of medieval and Renaissance enthusiasts that expanded throughout the United States. Besides participating in the general countercultural movement in 1960s California, Cramer asserts, the SCA is the very definition of a counterculture in that its membership adopts a lifestyle that, even if for temporary periods, rejects the dominant values and behavioural norms of contemporary twentieth- and now twenty-first-century culture. While putatively striving to re-create and practise life as it *was lived* in the medieval period, some SCA members prefer to "recreat[e] the Middle Ages as they *should have been*" (emphasis added). In addition to studying the material culture, activities, and attitudes of medieval European people to adopt medieval personae, dress the part, and act out their lives, SCA members "refer to their game as 'The Current Middle Ages,' placing themselves not in history but as a part of a contemporary utopian counterculture ... so that what they end up with is a fantasy about the Middle Ages rather than an accurate representation."[40]

Just as he was for the carnivalesque medieval festivals that bore his name, Robin Hood was the perfect fit for these 1960s counterculture revels – as viewers of the 1950s television series, *The Adventures of Robin Hood* would have known. Although the series was filmed in England with a cast of mostly British actors, it was produced by an American red-leaning expatriate, Hannah Weinstein, who hired a group of highly esteemed, Oscar-winning Hollywood scriptwriters working under pseudonyms. These American writers, some of whom belonged to the notorious "Hollywood Ten," included Waldo Salt, Ring Lardner Jr., and others blacklisted from Hollywood by the House Un-American Activities Committee (HUAC) after being persecuted in Joseph McCarthy's infamous 1950s communist "witch hunts." Reminiscing about his experience of writing for *The Adventures of Robin Hood*, Lardner admitted that he and his American compatriots took comfort in their exile by coding the British hero as a subtext about their own persecution, in which the thinly disguised Sheriff, inspired by McCarthy, plagued them, Robin's Merry Men. So arguably, although produced in Britain, this series written by exiled American writers and created by a similarly red-sympathetic American producer, was culturally just as American as British and was received equally enthusiastically on both sides of the pond.

Given the vogue for celebrating the adventures of the social bandit Robin Hood on the increasingly influential medium of television immediately preceding the rise of the SCA and early period Pleasure Faires in 1960s counterculture California, it is surely no coincidence that both incorporated allusions to or appropriations of this infamous figure of social and political resistance. Rubin illustrates the second (1964) iteration of the Pattersons' California faires with a photo of Art Kunkin distributing the inaugural issue of the *Los Angeles Free Press* (dubbed the *Faire Press*). This paper was an early example of the new counterculture underground press of the 1960s and 1970s. The paper's hawker is costumed in garb reminiscent of Robin Hood, especially the pointed feathered forester's cap worn by the epitome of medieval resistance to the status quo in many Hollywood versions of the outlaw. Another patron of the 1964 event described his enthusiasm about the faire as "my robin hood [*sic*] hat took over." Moreover, a photo epitomizing the typical faire experience, published by the *Los Angeles Times* in 1966, illustrates a crowd watching a Robin Hood show. Many of the audience are dressed in garb, with one man in the foreground sporting a peaked, feathered Robin Hood hat while watching a dramatic representation of the outlaw's adventures.[41] Within this uniquely American form of entertainment, born from the rebellious spirit of the 1960s, the past collided with the present and then spread throughout the United States.

Bringing Sherwood Forest to Texas

While the early Renaissance Pleasure Faires embraced Robin Hood as a key part of their eclectic medievalish past, SFF places Robin Hood at the historical, narrative, and ideological centre of their expansive revels, which include over 40 stage acts, 130 merchant "shoppes," various categories of food for sale, and assorted entertainments for the whole family.[42] Located in McDade, a thirty-minute drive east of Austin, SFF specifies the iconic locale associated with a particular medieval British folk hero, the outlaw Robin Hood, who made Sherwood Forest in Nottinghamshire a lair for himself and his fellow outlaws, the Merry Men.

Why should a Robin Hood–themed faire be especially appropriate for Texas? From the late 1930s through the 1950s, a vogue for Hollywood movies and television series portraying the British folk hero popularized him for an American audience. Perhaps still the definitive Robin Hood film, *The Adventures of Robin Hood* (1938) starred the swashbuckling Errol Flynn as the outlaw and Olivia de Havilland as Maid Marian at the height of their respective film careers. Through the intervening decades, Flynn's engaging portrayal of the violent British figure as an attractive Americanized anti-hero inspired a series of pale imitation, B-movie feature films, including such titles as *The Bandit of Sherwood Forest* (1946), *The Prince of Thieves* (1948), and *Rogues of Sherwood Forest* (1950). Mid-twentieth-century American television audiences became reacquainted with the exploits of Robin, his Merry Men, the plucky, tomboyish, crossdressing Maid Marian, the evil Sheriff of Nottingham, the heroic King Richard the

Lionheart, and the nefarious Prince John through Walt Disney's 1952 feature film, *The Story of Robin Hood and His Merrie Men*, which garnered an even wider audience when it was re-edited in two parts and broadcast on *The Magical World of Disney* television series on 2 and 9 November 1955.[43] Presented in black and white on the same new medium, *The Adventures of Robin Hood*, a five-season series comprising 143 half-hour episodes, was broadcast from 1955 to 1960. Starring British actor Richard Greene, the series achieved enormous popularity in both Britain and America and was the version of Robin Hood that introduced most baby boomers, including myself, to the legend.

Coinciding with the rise of movies and TV series about Robin Hood in the 1940s and 1950s occurred the popularity of movies about cowboys in America's Old West. These were exemplified by western-themed series like *The Lone Ranger* (1949–57), *The Roy Rogers Show* (1951–7), and the long-running *Bonanza* (1957–73). Countless feature films followed, including a franchise of B-movie westerns starring Texas-born cowboy crooner Gene Autry and the "King of the Cowboys," western singer Roy Rogers. The simultaneous popularity and intersection of Robin Hood films and westerns resulted in a peculiar hybrid genre, the Robin Hood western, typified by Roy Rogers's *Robin Hood of the Pecos* (1941) and *Trail of Robin Hood* (1950). Matching these Roy Rogers vehicles were films starring the equally popular Gene Autry, typified by *Robin Hood of Texas* (1947). Arguably, the 1960 film *The Magnificent Seven*, one of the last successful westerns before the genre went into a decline, was another remaking of the Robin Hood legend, with a cast of gunslinger Merry Men who use their outlaw skills to champion an oppressed Mexican village. Whether involving a band of American cowboy gunslingers or skilled Sherwood Forest archers, the theme of benevolent outlaws prosecuting more despicable criminals unites the western genre and the medieval Robin Hood legend. Thus, a nexus of interconnections of Texas, western films about American outlaws and their cowboy antagonists, and the British outlaw figure Robin Hood renders a Robin Hood–themed faire featuring medievalism in Texas almost inevitable.

This connection between Hollywood, Robin Hood, Texas, and American faires finds a fortuitous illustration in the early history of Southern California's 1963 Renaissance Pleasure Faire, which was moved in 1965 to the Paramount Ranch, an exterior lot that had been used for location shooting for Robin Hood movies as well as westerns. If this locale for the faire was not Nottinghamshire's authentic Sherwood Forest boasting its famous "Major Oak," Paramount Ranch was "dotted with 500-year-old oak trees," the next best thing.[44] Similarly, although "Major"-sized oak trees do not shade the site of the still fairly new SFF, its grounds are landscaped with many pines and other trees that are gradually maturing in size.

Having visited the putative home of the British outlaw, the real Sherwood Forest in Nottinghamshire, England, and SFF three times apiece, I attest that the Texas version holds up very well in comparison to its British exemplar. Once a royal hunting forest controlled by such Plantagenet figures in Robin Hood's orbit as King Richard I and Prince John, England's Sherwood Forest is now a 1,000-acre national nature preserve, open to the public and overseen by English Nature. Fabled oak trees, especially the eight- to ten-centuries-old "Major Oak" (the purported hideout of Robin Hood), an educational Visitor Centre, a comprehensive gift shop, and an Art and Craft Centre annually attract up to a million British and foreign tourists. If not precisely a for-profit theme park resembling Disneyland, Sherwood Forest nevertheless is equal parts nature preserve and commercial operation. It also, like its Texas namesake, participates in a faire-based medievalism, holding an annual week-long Robin Hood Festival in August that both reflects facets of the original Robin Hood revels of the late medieval period and offers many of the same features as American faires: jousts, demonstrations of medieval martial combat, period-costumed minstrels, storytellers, reenactors demonstrating medieval crafts and occupations, and, of course, the opportunity for visitors to try their hand at Robin's famous skill, archery.

Thus, the ways in which SFF stages its authenticity differs little from those on display in the "real" Sherwood Forest. Like the original Sherwood Forest in England, SFF, through its explicit evocation of Sherwood Forest, balances its goal of being a profitable commercial entertainment enterprise with an attempt to achieve historical and literary authenticity via a medievalism ironically filtered through popular culture by placing its faire in the era of Richard I and the Plantagenets. In embracing this "historical" version of Robin Hood, the operators and enthusiastic patrons of SFF draw on traditions stretching from early modern ballads through Robin Hood–themed plays to twentieth- and twenty-first-century movies and TV series that locate the British bandit temporally in the late twelfth century. Even if the intersection of Richard I's reign and the literary character Robin Hood is spurious, the association between Robin, the Plantagenets, and Richard has been a fixture of literary and cinematic medievalism about the greenwood outlaw since Anthony Munday's plays *The Downfall of Robert, Earl of Huntington* and *The Death of Robert, Earl of Huntington* (1598) gentrified the formerly yeoman-class Robin Hood as the Earl of Huntington. SFF's co-owner George Appling explained to me the faire's working philosophy and its temporal vision of history:

> We advance our year each year. So, we started in 1189 and are now in 1195. We will reset to 1189 after King Richard dies in 1199. We always have some solid nods to history in each year's [plays]. In this one, patrons see a ceasefire negotiated between Richard and King Philippe [of France]. Of course, it all goes awry and Robin Hood saves the day! ... We also have a full contact jousting tournament Saturday, which is going to be epic. King Richard lifted the ban on tournaments in England in 1195 so this is quite a nod to history as well.[45]

In programming the events, plays, and performances for each succeeding season and reflecting the temporal span from 1189 to 1199, SFF adroitly blends medieval literary tropes about Robin Hood, gestures towards historical accuracy, and encourages their patrons' participation in their literary/historical re-creation of Robin Hood's Sherwood Forest. As I told Appling, SFF's desire for a degree of historical authenticity sets it apart from other medieval or Renaissance faires like the Texas Renaissance Festival, and I look forward to seeing how the faire portrays the 1199 death of King Richard I, which occurred (surprisingly) not in a blaze of glory battling the Muslim occupiers of the Holy Land at the Third Crusade but at the Battle of Château de Châlus-Chabrol, where Richard oversaw a siege perpetrated by his mercenary Mercadier against a minor castle in France that was part of his feudal fiefdom. During the siege, Richard was inadvertently wounded by a crossbow-bolt in the shoulder, which developed gangrene; two weeks later, he died ignominiously of the infected wound in Châlus, not on the battlefield in Jerusalem. Medieval chroniclers disagree about the historic event, and Richard's humiliating death has been folded into narratives about Robin Hood, who is portrayed as a loyal supporter of Richard.[46]

Besides the chronological arc of Richard I's career that it mirrors in its yearly program of dramatizations, SFF presents facets of the purported history between the Earl of Huntington/Loxley/Robin Hood and the literary construction of his invented interactions with Plantagenet royalty – King Richard, Prince John Lackland, and Queen Eleanor of Aquitaine – blending literary fantasy with the arc of "history." Just as the adventures of the outlaw Robin Hood were re-created in various categories of ludic entertainment performed at May games, some of the most successful entertainments at SFF are dramatic adaptations of episodes from the medieval Robin Hood ballads, enacted on designated named stages or in the general space of the faire-grounds, where the actors interact with patrons and playtrons in impromptu improvisation. On my first visit, I particularly appreciated the staged adaptation of the ballad *Robin Hood and Guy of Gisborne* and *The Wedding of Robin Hood and Maid Marian*, which culminated the day in the structure called Maid Marian's Chapel. At my request, SFF owners Zane Baker and George Appling shared with me the scripts of plays they had performed before my first visit in 2011, including adaptations of ballads such as *Robin Hood and the Potter*; *Robin Hood and Little John* (their quarterstaff fight); *Robin Hood and Alan a Dale*; Baker's original ballad titled "Little John Meets a Coward in the Woods"; and some invented plots (not based on medieval ballads) involving Arthurian characters like Nimue and Merlin, and even a conversation between Maid Marian and William Shakespeare.[47]

What separates SFF from its Texas faire peers is its success at achieving a balance between more than a modicum of historical and literary authenticity and broad appeal to adults and to children, who want not only to have their faces painted by a glitter-speckled fairy but also to watch live plays that often spill offstage into the audience, thrilling the youngsters. To give both audiences what they want, the team adapts their medieval source material to make it family friendly. For instance, the original ballad *Robin Hood and Guy of Gisborne* is noteworthy for over-the-top violence: Robin kills Guy, decapitates him, mutilates the corpse by cutting off his face, and impales his head on his bow. Robin then exchanges his usual Lincoln green clothing for Guy's strange "Capul-hyde" disguise, which may be the flayed hide of a live horse worn by the bounty hunter Guy and then donned by his escaping quarry Robin. In their dramatic adaptation, SFF's writers tame the ballad's savage equine grotesquerie by having Robin not kill the horse-man Sir Guy but rather make an "ass" of him by covering him with a donkey hide instead of the bizarre horsehide. Adults familiar with the ballad understand what is being encoded; children laugh as Robin renders Guy a fool. If the Middle Ages and frontier-era Texas share a pop-culture stereotype, both being a time and a place of lawless violence, the SFF exploits but tames these traditions that their patrons and playtrons expect.

"Serious Leisure": Sherwood Forest Faire's "Medieval" Community

SFF's Robin Hood performances provide a contemporary version of the carnivalesque interactions of actors portraying Robin and his Merry Men, costumed playtrons, and casual patrons that marked the medieval May games and Robin Hood revels. And, indeed, over the years the faire itself has come, for its playtrons, to function in much the same way as these medieval springtime revels, echoing their communal traditions. This function illuminates playtrons' attachment to full participation in the faire experience, one that requires a substantial degree of financial and temporal commitment to the enterprise of being "at faire." For the playtrons, SFF (and any Renaissance festival) is what sociologist Robert Stebbins terms "serious leisure" (as opposed to "casual leisure," which includes passive diversions like talking with friends, walking in the park, or watching television). "Serious leisure," Stebbins claims, is the "steady pursuit of an amateur, hobbyist, or career volunteer activity that captivates its participants with its complexity and many challenges. It is profound, long-lasting, and invariably based on skill, knowledge, or experience," or a combination of all three, "with no significant remuneration." In lieu of monetary payback, serious leisure enthusiasts attain personal rewards, such as "fulfilling one's human potential, expressing one's skills and knowledge, having cherished experiences, and developing a valued identity." While achieving these rewards, serious leisure practitioners "typically become members of a vast social world, a complex mosaic of groups, events, networks, organizations, and social relationships." By so immersing themselves in their serious leisure pursuits, these participants can temporarily forget "worrisome cares and woes plaguing them in other parts of their lives," such as being overworked in their Monday-through-Friday unfulfilling day jobs.[48]

Stebbins's concept of serious leisure describes the passion motivating the most ardent playtrons of medieval festivals and Renaissance faires as well as SCA members, all of whom can be said to "recognize each other and to some extent are recognized by the larger community for the distinctive mode of leisure life they lead." Playtrons and SCA enthusiasts attempt to re-create the medieval and Renaissance past as personal recreation. Re-creating early history provides pleasurable recreational activities for these playtrons.[49] Significantly, the emphasis on the avoidance of the "mundane" aspects of workaday life undertaken by serious leisure practitioners reflects the dichotomy between the costumed playtrons and the civilian-clothed mundanes who inhabit the space of these early period faires.

SFF provides its playtrons with the promised escape and community of the faire, offering a serious leisure that forms, for a season, a new community, one based on putatively medieval and counterculture values. It does so by first constructing the "medieval" space of the faire itself and filling it with the appropriate people, activities, and food so that its visitors can participate in a material past. In keeping with its twelfth-century setting, SFF gives visitors a chance to view – if not rub elbows with – Plantagenet royalty. King Richard I and Queen Eleanor of Aquitaine attend the joust, ensconced in the royal viewing stand across from the audience of playtrons, patrons, and mundanes, and participate in various plays and skits on stages or in the faire-grounds. King Arthur's Round Table, surrounded by all manner and periods of garbed knights, is also on offer. For the amusement of playtrons and mundanes, SFF features jousting; mud-wrestling; wench-like laundresses who embarrass adult male patrons by getting them to contribute their underwear for washing; a first-rate falcon and predatory bird show; and various demonstrations of medieval fighting skills like archery and swordsmanship. The grounds also contain a maypole, one of the requisite fixtures of the medieval May games and Whitsun ales, and, as ale-brewing, imbibing, and community feasting were important culminations of the parish-based medieval Whitsun ales and May games, SFF continues this tradition. Of course, as at other early period faires throughout the United States, obligatory concession booths sell turkey legs, sausages-on-a-stick, cotton candy, and other such anachronistic "medieval" edibles.

Many of SFF's extended family of repeat-visit playtrons flock to this medieval space both days of every weekend for two months to play in the past. Like their equivalents at other faires, in addition to dressing in medieval garb, SFF's playtrons represent themselves as Vikings, pirates, various fantasy warriors, and even mythological creatures like minotaurs or centaurs. Walking around dressed as a centaur in Texas's spring heat (already on 3 April, it was 93°F in the shade), or garbed in a velvet-and-brocade Elizabethan ensemble complete with farthingale, or in handmade chain mail, is physically challenging. The playtrons I interviewed at SFF offered a variety of motives for attending in elaborate garb. A male playtron, costumed as a Viking warrior, explained that, having toiled Monday through Friday at a stultifying, mechanical job, he spent Saturday and Sunday at SFF dressed to express his secret self among like-minded fellow playtrons and weekend friends. A young woman I chatted with over a beer at SFF's re-creation of Nottingham's "Trip" tavern was garbed in the complete ensemble of a twelfth-century Norman lady, which she had laboriously hand-sewn and hand-embroidered using period-correct natural linen and silk fabrics. I was startled out of my cynical presumption that she was living out a secret fantasy of being Robin's fiancée Matilda Fitzwater/Maid Marian when she confessed that throughout her childhood and adolescence, her late mother, who had recently succumbed to cancer, had been an avid "Rennie," attending faires in other states in complete costume, accompanied by her young daughter. Since moving to Texas, her now-adult daughter attended SFF every weekend in "Norman lady" garb to honour the memory of her mother's enthusiasm for being at faire.

For both of these playtrons, SFF was a place not just of play but of community; this community was also in evidence at SFF's unique replica of Nottingham's extant Ye Olde Trip to Jerusalem, arguably the oldest tavern in England, set beneath the hill topped by Nottingham Castle, home of the sheriff.[50] In SFF's airy outdoor pub, nicknamed the "Trip," mundanes and playtrons gather, particularly in the evening as the faire's day draws to a close. There I witnessed a ceremony commemorating one of the actors from SFF's regular troupe, who had died between faire seasons. The group, both regular staff and playtrons who knew the actor, sang select songs honouring him and danced to his honour onstage, concluding with this toast to their fallen comrade: "May we always be merry and our enemies know it." I was profoundly moved as the crowd in the "Trip" fondly remembered this individual, with some tears and a lot of quaffed ale.

Paralleling the community-grounded paradigm of the late medieval Robin Hood revels, these playtrons comprise a secular "parish" of sorts, a group of like-minded and like-spirited members, many of whom become "Friends of the [SFF] Faire," entitling them to admission for the entire two-month season, a camping place, markdowns on purchases from faire vendors, discounted subscriptions to *Renaissance* magazine, and other perquisites. Obviously, these friends *of* the faire also become friends *with* one another, reflecting the motivations of loyal patrons and playtrons at all Renaissance faires, per Stebbins's theory of serious leisure. Off-season, SFF also sponsors a medieval summer camp for youths, adults, and families and organizes weekend gatherings at which SFF community members volunteer their service, preparing the faire-ground for the next season. This too contributes a sense of community and social cohesion among these friends, similar to the camaraderie experienced by late medieval parish members who contributed communally to the local Whitsun ale, as Marshall described earlier. During the faire, for an additional cost beyond admission, patrons can attend a special end-of-day dinner, Robin's Feast, held at the "castle," another opportunity that closely parallels the community feasts that culminated the late medieval Whitsun ales celebrating Robin Hood.

Another facet of SFF aligning with the May games and Robin Hood revels that were a fixture of parish life of the late medieval and early modern periods is its fundraising. Recall that critics subscribing to the economic/parochial theory about the origins of the May games posit that the games or gatherings (overseen by a local resident playing Robin Hood) pragmatically employed the outlaw figure, noted for taking money from his victims, as an effective fundraiser. Collected money allowed rural communities to repair their parish church, support local guilds, and give succour to the poor. If SFF's proprietors George Appling and Zane Baker do not use their Robin Hood–themed faire to refurbish the local parish church, they do allocate some of their profits to ongoing construction of new structures on the faire-grounds for their playtrons' enjoyment. Such new venues, like the castle providing the architectural structure for the battle between King Richard and the three kings, also will attract the mundanes to revisit the faire in subsequent years.

Moreover, very much in the spirit of the medieval May games' fundraising function, SFF donates a portion of its revenues to charitable organizations, such as the Make-a-Wish Foundation, which pays to grant wishes, like a visit to Disneyland, to children suffering from life-threatening medical conditions. To collect money for Make-a-Wish, SFF positions a wishing well just inside the front gate, where it attracts the attention (and generosity) of those entering and leaving the faire. Typically, patrons deposit about $500 in change per season, which the SFF owners match, donating a total of $1,000 to Make-a-Wish. Even closer to the original medieval parish paradigm, SFF donates to the RESCU Foundation, an acronym for Renaissance Entertainers Services Crafters United, a non-profit organization established "to promote and maintain the health and medical well-being of the participants of Renaissance Faires, historical performances, and other artistic events through financial assistance, advocacy, education and preventive programs." Many employed in these faires are itinerant and seasonal workers who have no medical insurance.[51] In 2016 SFF raised $35,000 for RESCU through an auction. Compared to larger faires like the Texas Renaissance Festival, SFF is midsized; yet, according to SFF's owners, it is the largest contributor to RESCU nationwide.

For two months a year, SFF brings the Middle Ages to Texas, in a manner both similar to and unique among the various medieval and Renaissance faires held throughout the United States. With patrons and playtrons reenacting the legends of Robin Hood and other medievalish narratives, the outlaw legend is reconceived anew and imbued with particularly American sensibilities reflective of medieval festival practices and Hollywood films of the frontier West. Everything is bigger in Texas, the old saying goes, and the SFF succeeds in its grand ambitions to bring the Middle Ages into the state's present.[52]

NOTES

1 Rather than the modern word "fair," "faire" is the preferred antiquated spelling, which I employ unless directly quoting a source using the modern spelling. Being "at faire" (as opposed to "at *the* faire") signifies participating, in any capacity, in the faire's community as staff member, vendor, performer, or patron.
2 Over the more than half-century during which these historically grounded entertainments have developed, the collective organizers, performers, craftspeople, food providers, and volunteers hosting these faires, as well as the patrons attending them, both in and out of period costumes, have generated a lexicon indigenous to the faire experience and the Society for Creative Anachronism. Throughout this essay, definitions of the terms used by and about participants at such faires and SCA members are informed by Kimberly Tony Korol-Evans, *Renaissance Festivals: Merrying the Past and Present* (Jefferson, NC: McFarland, 2009); Michael Cramer, *Medieval Fantasy as Performance: The Society for Creative Anachronism and the Current Middle Ages* (Lanham, MD: Scarecrow Press, 2010); and Rachel Lee Rubin, *Well Met: Renaissance Fairs and the American Counterculture* (New York: New York University Press, 2012).
3 Sam Blazer, "The Renaissance Pleasure Faire," *Drama Review* 20, no. 2 (1976): 31–7, at 31.
4 John Leland, "Taking the A Train to the Middle Ages – Medieval Festival in Fort Tryon Park Is Quite a Scene: Jugglers, Jousting Knights and New Yorkers Thirsting for Mead," *New York Times*, 5 Oct. 2018.
5 Prudence Jones and Nigel Pennick, *A History of Pagan Europe* (New York: Routledge, 2013), 124; Ronald Hutton, *The Pagan Religions of the Ancient British Isles* (Oxford: Blackwell, 1991), 182–3; and Ronald Hutton, *The Stations of the Sun: A History of the Ritual Year in Britain* (Oxford: Oxford University Press, 1996), 226–43.
6 Ronald Hutton, *The Rise and Fall of Merry England: The Ritual Year 1400–1700* (Oxford: Oxford University Press, 1994), 52; Hutton, *Stations of the Sun*, 237.
7 Hutton, *Rise and Fall of Merry England*, 113.
8 Hutton, *Stations of the Sun*, 270–4.
9 N.A., "Shakespeare and His Times: May-day," *Atheneum* 3 (1818): 10–11, at 11.
10 Barbara Lowe, "Early Records of the Morris in England," *Journal of the English Folk Dance and Song Society* 8, no. 2 (1957): 61–82, at 68.
11 William Warner, *Albion's England [1612]* (Hildesheim, Germany: Georg Olms, 1971), 121.
12 On the association between the morris dance and "Robin Hood," see Lorraine Kochanske Stock, "Canonicity and 'Robin Hood': The Morris Dance and the Meaning

of 'Lighter than Robin Hood' in the Prologue to Fletcher and Shakespeare's *The Two Noble Kinsmen*," in *Robin Hood and the Outlaw/ed Literary Canon*, ed. Alexander L. Kaufman and Lesley Coote (London: Routledge, 2019), 109–31.

13 Lowe, "Early Records," 69.
14 John Forrest, *The History of Morris Dancing, 1458–1750* (Toronto: University of Toronto Press, 1999), 217–18.
15 See Thomas Ohlgren and Lister Matheson, eds., *Early Rhymes of Robyn Hood: An Edition of the Texts ca. 1425 to ca. 1600* (Tempe, AZ: ACMRS, 2013), 228–37. Compare Copland's version to the play appended to Edward White's 1594 edition, 303–7.
16 J.M. Steadman, "The Dramatization of the Robin Hood Ballads," *Modern Philology* 17 (1919): 9–23. On texts of the plays, see George Parfitt, "Early Robin Hood Plays: Two Fragments and a Bibliography," *Renaissance and Modern Studies* 22 (1978): 5–12.
17 Forrest, *History of Morris Dancing*, 218.
18 W.E. Simeone, "The May Games and the Robin Hood Legend," *Journal of American Folklore* 64 (1951): 265–74, at 274.
19 Hutton, *Rise and Fall of Merry England*, 27–35.
20 John Stow, *A Survey of London*, ed. Charles Lethbridge Kingsford (Oxford: Oxford University Press, 1908), 90.
21 David Wiles, *The Early Plays of Robin Hood* (Cambridge: D.S. Brewer, 1981), 18, 56.
22 John Matthews, "The Games of Robin Hood," in *Robin Hood: Green Lord of the Wildwood* (Glastonbury: Gothic Image, 1993), 81–102; Lorraine Kochanske Stock, "Lords of the Wildwood: The Wild Man, the Green Man, and Robin Hood," in *Robin Hood in Popular Culture: Violence, Transgression, and Justice*, ed. Thomas Hahn (Cambridge: D.S. Brewer, 2000), 239–49.
23 See the opening stanzas of *Robin Hood and the Monk* in Stephen Knight and Thomas Ohlgren, eds., *Robin Hood and Other Outlaw Tales* (Kalamazoo, MI: TEAMS Middle English Texts, 1997), 37. The ballads consistently open in a springtime setting.
24 Wiles, *Early Plays*, 19.
25 Peter Stallybrass, "'Drunk with the Cup of Liberty': Robin Hood, the Carnivalesque, and the Rhetoric of Violence in Early Modern England," *Semiotica* 54 (1985): 113–45, at 122.
26 Knight and Ohlgren, *Robin Hood and Other Outlaw Tales*, 494–6.
27 Stallybrass, "'Drunk with the Cup,'" 126.
28 Christine Richardson, "The Figure of Robin Hood within the Carnival Tradition," *Records of Early English Drama Newsletter* 22, no. 2 (1997): 18–25, at 18.
29 Knight and Ohlgren, *Robin Hood and Other Outlaw Tales*, 128.
30 Peter Greenfield, "The Carnivalesque in the Robin Hood Games and King Ales of Southern England," in *Carnival and the Carnivalesque: The Fool, the Reformer, the Wildman, and Others in Early Modern Theatre*, ed. Konrad Eisenbichler and Wim Hüsken (Amsterdam: Rodopi, 1999), 19–28, at 19–20.

31 Paul Whitfield White, "Holy Robin Hood! Carnival, Parish Guilds, and the Outlaw Tradition," in *Tudor Drama before Shakespeare, 1485–1590*, ed. Lloyd Edward Kermode, Jason Scott-Warren, and Martine van Elk (New York: Palgrave Macmillan, 2004), 67–89, at 69–71.
32 White, "Holy Robin Hood!," 74, quoting from Rosalind Conklin Hays et al., eds., *Dorset Cornwall: Records of Early English Drama* (Toronto: University of Toronto Press, 1999), 521.
33 John Marshall, "'Comyth in Robyn Hode': Paying and Playing the Outlaw at Croscombe," *Leeds Studies in English* 32 (2001): 345–68, at 360.
34 Blazer, "Renaissance Pleasure," 32, 36; for a map of the Marin faire-grounds showing the market cross, see 33.
35 Rubin, *Well Met*, 33.
36 Duke Shadow, "A Brief History of the Renaissance Faire," *Renaissance* 6, no. 3 (2001): 33–40, at 35–6.
37 Rubin, *Well Met*, 6. Space limitations prohibit more than summarizing what Rubin demonstrates at length.
38 Rubin, *Well Met*, 10–11.
39 For the early history of the SCA and its counterculture tendencies, see Cramer, *Medieval Fantasy as Performance*, 1–4.
40 Cramer, *Medieval Fantasy as Performance*, xi.
41 Rubin, *Well Met*, 39, fig. 1.6; 45; 48, fig. 1.7.
42 For a full account of the attractions at SFF, see the official website: http://www.sherwoodforestfaire.com. SFF is but one of many Texas faires. The fall faire circuit includes: the Canterbury Renaissance Festival, presented in Mount Pleasant in September; the Texarkana Renaissance Festival, mounted for one weekend in September; and the Magical Medieval Fantasy Festival, staged for one weekend in early October. Concluding the fall season is the largest and most famous of such faires in the entire United States, the Texas Renaissance Festival, held every weekend throughout October and November. Texas's spring faire season includes the Avalon Faire in Kilgore in April and the Scarborough Renaissance Faire in Waxahachie from April through the end of May.
43 For *The Story of Robin Hood and His Merrie Men* (1952) see the IMDb entry at https://www.imdb.com/title/tt0045197. For the 1955 edited TV version, *The Story of Robin Hood: Parts 1 and 2*, see https://www.imdb.com/title/tt0561359. This live-action film should not be confused with the 1973 animated, animal-cast Disney film *Robin Hood*, starring a wily fox as the benevolent outlaw.
44 Shadow, "Brief History," 36.
45 Email to the author from George Appling, 5 Oct. 2016.
46 See John Gillingham, "The Unromantic Death of Richard I," *Speculum* 54, no. 1 (1979): 18–41; John Gillingham, *Richard I* (New Haven, CT: Yale University Press, 2002), 323–31.

47 Email to the author with attachments of scripts from Zane Baker, 5 Apr. 2011. If sceptics object to the otherwise temporally impossible intermixing of Arthurian characters with the greenwood outlaws, recall that T.H. White created the same anachronism in *The Once and Future King*. As to the evocation of the Bard, Shakespeare and John Fletcher referenced Robin Hood in the prologue of their Chaucerian adaptation, *The Two Noble Kinsmen*.
48 Robert Stebbins, "Serious Leisure," *Society* 38, no. 4 (2001): 53–7, at 53–4, 56. See also his "Serious Leisure: A Conceptual Statement," *Pacific Sociological Review* 25, no. 2 (1982): 251–72.
49 Robert Stebbins, "Cultural Tourism as Serious Leisure," *Annals of Tourism Research* 23, no. 4 (1996): 948–50.
50 See "Welcome to the Oldest Inn in England: Ye Olde Trip to Jerusalem," http://www.greeneking-pubs.co.uk/pubs/nottinghamshire/ye-olde-trip-to-jerusalem (accessed 10 Jan. 2019).
51 For information about RESCU's support of faire employees, see RESCU Foundation, Inc.: Renaissance Entertainers Services and Crafters United, http://www.rescufoundation.org (accessed 10 Jan. 2019).
52 While this chapter was in press, the COVID-19 pandemic that disrupted all aspects of American life throughout most of 2020 caused the cancellation of SFF's entire 2020 season. For their disappointed patrons and playtrons, SFF staged and filmed some of the planned performances and plays, providing them on YouTube. Notwithstanding the pandemic-caused demise of many entertainment organizations, SFF mounted its 2021 season, scheduled a few months later than usual. The programmed schedule of weekends from 3 April through 23 May serendipitously and appropriately positions 2021's faire in the traditional Maytime of the late medieval May games presided over by Robin Hood.

13 Las Vegas: Getting Medieval in Sin City

LAURIE A. FINKE AND MARTIN B. SHICHTMAN

"Radix malorum est cupiditas"

Despite the city's glorification of the new, the modern, the latest, despite its garish neon signs and towering gleaming casinos, Las Vegas teems with re-creations of the medieval: most obviously the Excalibur Hotel, with its Lego-like castle façade, suits of armour, stained-glass windows, medieval-themed slot machines (Robin Hood, Stonehenge, Dungeons and Dragons), and Sword in the Stone Bar. More medievalisms can be found in the Tournament of Kings, with its celebration of medieval aristocratic blood sports; off-Strip accommodations like the castle-shaped Manor Suites, with its ersatz tapestries, swords, and suits of armour, and its reproduction of Edmund Leighton's "The Accolade";[1] Gothic-quoting wedding chapels; and in details as small as madrigal performers in the Venetian or Italian coats of arms on tables in a café in the Bellagio. But Vegas is full of re-creations of all times and places: New York City, Venice, Paris, ancient Egypt, classical Rome. Vegas caters to all fantasies and, in doing so, reduces all of our fantasies of the past to a single fantasy. It offers what Umberto Eco calls the hyperreal, where imitations do not just reproduce originals but improve on them, and what Fredric Jameson calls pastiche, "the cannibalization of all styles of the past, the play of random stylistic allusion ... amputated of the satiric impulse."[2] "Where else," write Barbara and Myrick Land in *A Short History of Las Vegas*, "could [visitors] take a long walk past King Arthur's Camelot, the Statue of Liberty, several ornate palaces, and an erupting volcano – all without leaving the sidewalk?"[3] Vegas's monuments (i.e., casinos) are both bigger than life to awe us and more compact to save us time and travel.

In exploring Las Vegas's medievalism, however, we are not going to dwell on its representations of the Middle Ages nor on its deployment of medieval iconography.[4] We believe Las Vegas's medievalism may be more structural than these monuments to the hyperreal might suggest. Instead, taking our lead from Robert Venturi and Denise Scott Brown's classic *Learning from Las Vegas*, we investigate Vegas as the City of Scenography, where pedestrians "circulate ... within a stage-set." Vegas is a city "whose *Space* between buildings is the stage where [visitors] circulate, whose *Scale* accommodates pedestrian perception from up close."[5] Vegas's built medievalisms are another layer of unironic pastiche through which visitors are invited to circulate.

The idea for this chapter came from listening to the pitch of a timeshare salesman in Las Vegas.[6] In exchange for free tickets to the Tournament of Kings (a $73 value) at the Excalibur – and perhaps the worst breakfast we ever consumed – we were required to attend an "information session" where "Jimbo," as he called himself, regaled a room of about thirty "marks" for two hours, attempting to convince us to buy vacation time in his company. What struck us is how much Jimbo's twice-daily performances resembled that of Geoffrey Chaucer's Pardoner, the salesman of salvation whose Canterbury tale begins by condemning the sins of the tavern: "riot, hasard, stywes," and drinking (6.465).[7] Las Vegas's medievalism, we suggest, resides less in its hyperreal reproductions of medieval sites, pastimes, or objects than in its structural function in creating and maintaining a pilgrimage site for sin, where desperate people flock to be healed of their sickness, to strike it rich the easy way, and to indulge in pleasures condemned in other less liminal spaces – in fact, to indulge in the aforementioned pleasures of the tavern: "riot, hasard, stywes," and drinking. Like the Canterbury pilgrimage, the Vegas pilgrimage promises to heal – or, at least, temporarily remove – its adherents from the "sickness" of the everyday by putting them in some fantastical in-between place. It is never about arriving – "life is a pilgrimage."[8] It is about relishing liminality, being neither here (the horrors of home) nor there (the terrors of consummation). How might an analysis of Jimbo's performance return us to the *Canterbury Tales* to think about the desperation of the Canterbury pilgrims, on the road but never finally arriving in Canterbury? Pilgrimage offers a space where anything and everything becomes possible – sex, love, marriage, wealth, fame, miracles – and it is where anybody can be a winner of the game, even the hapless Geoffrey Chaucer, who never realizes what a mope he is.[9]

Welcome to the Desert of the Hyperreal

Although this chapter does not focus on the hyperreality of Las Vegas's re-creations of the Middle Ages, a few words describing how the city became a pilgrimage destination are in order. We might begin by asking, why all of the city's opulence simply in the service of gambling? After all, a casino is a casino. And gambling is pretty much gambling, wherever you do it. Even in Vegas the casinos themselves are depressingly similar. Why such extravagant surroundings? Prior to the mid-1940s, Las Vegas was a motel town, a transit point on the westward route to Los Angeles. Garish neon signs pointed to Fremont Street, where travellers might partake in some uninspired but legal, or, in some cases, illegal but unenforced, western saloon fantasies – mostly attached to drinking, gambling, and prostitution.[10] All that changed in 1946, when Benjamin "Bugsy" Siegel, along with partner Billy Wilkerson, transformed Vegas into America's premier adult pilgrimage space and playground, opening the palatial Flamingo Hotel, an all-purpose resort that would attract lowbrow consumers – people willing to part with about $100 of their hard-earned capital – about $1,350 in 2021 dollars. Siegel, a visionary thug, spent wildly on his project ($6.5 million), determined to envelop ordinary Americans in extravagance, a luxury they could barely imagine – beautiful surroundings and top-flight entertainment. Plumbers, gas station attendants, teachers, and accountants would mix it up with famous gangsters and Hollywood stars in the finest mansion this side of Heaven. Siegel's dream likely cost him his life; it would take quite a while for his gangster patrons to understand the potential of such an outlandish investment, to recognize that the promise of the Las Vegas experience could be much more profitable if it extended beyond the casino floor.[11]

By the 1990s, Las Vegas's mega-hotels had moved well beyond the fantasy of the Old West; Vegas began playing to every possible fantasy, including that of time travel. New luxury casino/hotels, financed by tycoons like Jay Sarno, Kirk Kerkorian, and Steve Wynn, featured "classic images from all of Western civilization."[12] Journalist Michael Ventura commented in a television interview, "It's as though Western history had come here for one last party."[13] Las Vegas is in a constant, relentless, and fevered state of creating new ways to repackage nostalgia, to provide tourists with a sense of elegance, well-being, ease, and certainty, even as their pockets are being picked. Even the discarded remnants of the old Vegas do not disappear entirely; they are co-opted into the pastiche. They become relics, consigned to museums to take their proper place in the tourist economy. The Fremont Street Experience repackages old Vegas for contemporary tourist consumption; the Neon Boneyard preserves the city's storied neon signs as so many relics of a bygone Vegas; the Mob Museum re-creates a time when organized crime, rather than corporate interests, ruled the city.

Las Vegas, in the words of one casino spokesman, "is not just about gambling. It's about fantasy. People come here to play-act."[14] Middle-class consumers can, for a few days each year, think themselves Roman emperors, Italian lords, medieval ladies. In so many ways, the hyperreality of Caesars Palace, Bellagio, and Excalibur are of a piece. The luxury and opulence of Vegas's hyperreal set up a relay between hope and desperation that is the lifeblood of gambling. It encourages the belief that one can "strike it rich," a belief that runs counter to the Protestant ethic of hard work and disciplined saving that, as T.J. Jackson Lears argues, offers "the faith that we can master chance through force of will, and that rewards will match merits in this world as well as the next."[15] As Bugsy Siegel presciently grasped, Vegas's hyperrealism offers ordinary people the kind of luxury they cannot afford, the kind represented so compellingly in *The Queen of Versailles*, Lauren Greenfield's 2012 documentary about Jackie and David Siegel (no relation to Bugsy), founder of Westgate Resorts, a timeshare company that once owned Planet Hollywood Towers in Las Vegas. In the film, the couple's display of wealth – like Vegas's – is ostentatious, the wealth of the parvenu, conspicuous display for its own sake. If the Siegels can imagine themselves a latter-day Sun King and Marie Antoinette, for a price, and a relatively small one, Vegas casinos can offer more than an escape from the everyday. They can hint at some realm of infinite pleasure, some paradise of inexhaustible entertainment, alcohol, gambling, and sex in fantastically beautiful surroundings. Vegas offers the lure of glamour, which as Laura Cook Kenna, following John Berger, suggests, "accrues to objects or places or people not because they look good but because of what they bring out in us: a bit of envy."[16] In Vegas, a college English teacher can imagine himself, just for a short while, James Bond at the roulette wheel. David Seigel, the "timeshare king," quips, "Everyone wants to vacation like a Rockefeller. If they can't be rich, the next best thing is to feel rich."

Pilgrim's Progress

Las Vegas, then, is the modern-day equivalent of the pilgrimage, a destination where tourists imbibe high-culture reproductions while indulging in various pleasures, hoping for some kind of redemption. Furthermore, once there, to indulge in the particular kinds of pleasure on offer, the tourist, as both the Lands and Venturi and Brown suggest, must be peripatetic, must be constantly on the move in pursuit of the pleasures that Vegas promises but cannot really provide. In this sense, perhaps in every sense, Sin City is the flip side of the Heavenly City. Vegas is a pilgrimage site – different from Jerusalem, Mecca, Rome, or, of course, Canterbury in one sense only: it is a pilgrimage site for sin. However, to think of it as some version of Hell's capital, Dis, is somewhat misleading, given the egregious sinning performed by medieval pilgrims searching for Jerusalem, Mecca, Rome, and Canterbury, as well as the sheer volume of churches in Vegas. As NBC News reports, "Some surveys over the years have even included Las Vegas among lists of cities with the most churches per capita. A recent Internet search revealed listings for more than 500 churches in the city."[17] Like Chaucer's Canterbury pilgrims, Vegas visitors want the pleasures of the flesh, of the tavern, and yet also like the Canterbury pilgrims, they seek some kind of expiation for their sins. More to the point, even if Sin City represents the flip side of the Heavenly City, the fantasies are frequently identical. Both Sin City and the Celestial Jerusalem promise excess; they offer to more than fill us, to overload our capacity for enjoyment.

Las Vegas is a pilgrimage site for the hopeless and hopeful – and every Vegas pilgrim is, at one time or another, both of these simultaneously; everywhere there is desperation and the promise of a deliverance that must, by necessity, always be insufficient. (Just as medieval pilgrimage sites – including Jerusalem – no matter their promise, could never be the heavenly city on the hill.) The kinds of emptiness that promote the need for pilgrimage can never be filled. The insufficiency of the pilgrim experience is to be always wanting and always to long for the next, better return to the site – or to some alternative pilgrimage site – where satiation might be delivered. During the Middle Ages, pilgrims like Margery Kempe and Chaucer's Wife of Bath would collect pilgrimage experiences along with their badges, souvenirs of their travel. Certainly, both women revelled in the exhilaration of tourism and in the pleasure of boasting (in all Christian humility) of the wondrous religious sites they visited. But both also possessed a longing that could never be entirely gratified, an emptiness resulting, in Margery's case, from raising at least fourteen children, her many frustrations negotiating medieval England's mercantile economy, and her difficulties with the Catholic Church.[18] Chaucer's Wife displays the gregariousness of the well-seasoned traveller off on another journey:

> And thries hadde she been at Jerusalem;
> She hadde passed many a straunge strem;
> At Rome she hadde been, and at Boloigne,
> In Galice at Seint-Jame, and at Coloigne.
> She koude muchel of wandrynge by the weye. (1.463–7)

Five-times married (and looking for number six), an international woman of mystery,[19] Chaucer's Wife has engaged in "wanderings" that seem to encompass everything from international tourism to sexual experimentation. Her appetites both for faith and for pleasure remain unsatisfied – and she is growing no younger. But we would like to suggest that she is not atypical of the Canterbury pilgrims, except insofar as she is a trifle wealthier than some and more "experienced" (the word she uses to describe herself) than most. For the Wife and for the other pilgrims, there is a wound that cannot be healed, an ache that cannot be relieved, an absence that cannot be remedied. She has vacillated between religiosity – but, sorry D.W. Robertson, this did not help (any more than it brings complete solace to Margery Kempe) – and risky behaviours.[20] She is left on the road, glib and endlessly amusing, but also fearful and desperate. She and her Canterbury-bound colleagues are prime targets for someone promoting a new product that promises to ease their desperation, someone of the Pardoner's skill.

The medieval pilgrimage always represented a kind of wager: the pilgrim places herself – and perhaps her faith – on the line hoping to reap the enormous return of salvation. Pilgrimage sites come replete with stories of big winners, from the first miracles that gave the particular site its reputation for holiness and grace to contemporary reports of the blind who now can see, the deaf who now can hear, the lame who now can walk, lepers literally made whole again. According to Benedict of Peterborough and William of Canterbury, who chronicled Thomas Becket's canonization, 703 miracles were recorded during the ten years immediately following his death.[21] That sounds like an impressive number. However, a site like Canterbury was a hugely popular destination; in 1420 alone, more than 100,000 visitors made their way to Becket's church.[22] With these odds, the miracles sought were a gamble long enough (0.7 per cent) to rival modern state lotteries. Margery and the Wife of Bath have become pilgrimage addicts, drawn no doubt both to the thrill of the adventure and to play against the overwhelming odds set against them. Their touristic excitement is enhanced by the nearly impossible prospect of a personal miracle.

What Vegas offers is only a slightly different hope and disappointment, the opportunity to "beat the house" or, at very least, to make oneself, as the gamblers say, "whole again," literally to "break even."[23] But, as Dostoyevsky – and so many other gamblers – would testify, "whole again" is impossible. No gambler is ever satisfied; no gambler can ever be whole enough. The next hand of cards, the next roll of the dice, the next pull of the slot machine arm always holds out a promise of something more, of striking it rich, of sex, booze, glamour, excitement. It holds out the promise of transformation, the do-over. Las Vegas, filled with fortune tellers, faith healers, tanning lounges, health clubs, hair and nail salons, and walk-in clinics, is a town dedicated to the promise of transformation (or conversion). Visitors come seeking a degraded – but no less efficacious – version of Chaucer's "hooly blisful martir ... / That hem hath holpen whan that they were seeke" (1.17–18). But the sickness remains, in the streets filled with the homeless and the hungry, the two-bit peddlers like the man dressed in a *Sesame Street* costume holding a sign imploring "Ernie needs a drink," the oxygen-tank-sucking grandmas and grandpas zipping in battery-powered wheelchairs towards the next slot machine, the children on street corners handing out escort-service advertisements. The pilgrimage city holds plenty of opportunity for that American avatar, the confidence man, whether he is dressed in a cheap suit, like Jimbo, or in clerical robes.

The Art of the Steal

Like Chaucer's Pardoner who offers an institutionally sanctioned scam – his pardons (or indulgences) "comen from Rome al hoot" (1.687) – Jimbo sells a corporate product guaranteed to provide eternal joy for the largely underclass victims in attendance. To be sure, timeshares are aggressively marketed in vacation spots throughout the world; the company Jimbo represents, as he constantly reminded us, owns properties all over the globe. We do not claim that timeshare sales are any more unique to Vegas than gambling is. Instead we are interested in the peculiar mélange Vegas serves up that weds the "sins of the tavern," paradisiacal luxury, and pilgrimage to gambling as a means of selling "grace," the chance of a life-altering transformation. How does Vegas's marketing of the "timeshare" (consider the very word) compare to the medieval church's practice of selling its own brand of grace as a cure-all for sin? While critics like Alastair Minnis, who writes about the Pardoner, separate the doctrine of indulgences from the abuses and fraud of the Pardoner, in fact, as with the timeshare, the scam is already inherent in the nearly incomprehensible complexity of the entirely legal instrument.

Our precedent for thinking about indulgences as an economic instrument comes from Robert Ekelund and his colleagues' *Sacred Trust: The Medieval Church as an Economic Firm*, in which they argue that the church's indulgences provided "the choice of paying for sins with money rather than with deeds."[24] In fact, more interesting than the abuses revealed by the Pardoner's prologue is the theological justification for the practice.[25] This justification employed a nearly Byzantine economic metaphor of capitalist accumulation that would not sound all that strange to a timeshare salesman like Jimbo. The theology rests on a "treasury of merit," a bank filled with an "inexhaustible fund" that is "sufficient to cover the indebtedness contracted by sin."[26] The pardon is based not on the merits of the sinner but rather on the "merit" that accrues from Christ's sacrifice, from the "works" of the Virgin Mary, and from the works, virtues, and suffering of the saints, to which sinners can apply as if seeking a loan from a bank (release from indebtedness).[27] Despite the fact that this fund is inexhaustible, it is perpetually renewed by the very souls that have been saved by pardons as a kind of interest: "The more numerous are the people reclaimed through the use of its contents, the more it is augmented by the addition of their merits."[28] If the Pardoner is selling salvation as an "entrepreneurial opportunity," Jimbo is selling a "consumption alternative" as salvation.[29] As Jimbo is quick to point out, the purchase of timeshares backed by a major hotel provider assures not only the purchaser but his (and it is always his) family of a sure thing: if Jimbo can't quite promise Paradise, he can guarantee a penthouse on Paradise Island – a guarantee every bit as ephemeral as a mansion in God's kingdom.

The Pardoner's prologue is also a veritable "art of the deal," and it is worth looking at the striking similarities in the ways in which the Pardoner and Jimbo deploy rhetoric to close their deals. We can discern in their pitches five elements; they must 1) identify an audience, 2) identify the lack in that audience, 3) never reveal the fine print, 4) instead sell the dream, and 5) tell a good story.

Both scams begin with the right audience, an audience whose specific forms of greed makes them susceptible to the pitch. The Pardoner is selling pardons to sinners who want to think themselves worthy of salvation. Early on he warns "Goode men and wommen,"

> If any wight be in this chirche now
> That hath doon synne horrible, that he
> Dar nat, for shame, of it yshryven be,
> Or any womman, be she yong or old,
> That hath ymaked hir housbonde cokewold,
> Swich folk shal have no power ne no grace
> To offren to my relikes in this place. (6.378–84)

To remain silent in the face of such a challenge would be to admit that one had committed a sin so shameful it could not be pardoned or so scandalous it would threaten the sinner's reputation. More to the point, the Pardoner needs sinners who prefer to buy their stairways to Heaven rather than to do penance on earth or in Purgatory. He does not require that his audience be able to afford his wares:

> I wol have moneie … ,
> Al were it yeven of the povereste page,
> Or of the povereste wydwe in a village,
> Al sholde hir children sterve for famyne. (6.448–51)

The Canterbury pilgrims constitute a ready-made audience for the Pardoner because they are already in the market to buy what he is selling. They are travelling on the road to Canterbury, at least in part, because they believe salvation possible. They are on pilgrimage to seek an indulgence and will likely also purchase relics as well. If you obtain one indulgence, why not more? If you buy one relic, why not a whole passel? Why not buy the Pardoner's?

Jimbo, the timeshare salesman, is also pitching to those whose greed makes them susceptible to the pitch, to those for whom a free breakfast and complimentary show tickets make them feel as if they are getting luxury for nothing. "If you'll spend ninety minutes and see what we have to offer, you'll get free Disney tickets," says a saleswoman in Greenfield's *The Queen of Versailles*. The ideal mark, we learn from the film, is a married couple with at least $60,000 in income; like the Pardoner's audience, not wealthy by any measure. Jimbo is also pitching to family, but more specifically to the putative father of a very traditional nuclear family (heterosexual or not). As both Siegel and Jimbo suggest, they are the group most likely to need (or desire) the space he describes, not a cramped hotel room where kids and parents sleep in the same space and fight over the television and bathroom, but a nice condominium with a full kitchen, living and dining rooms, and separate bedrooms and bathrooms for parents and kids. Jimbo interpellates the father repeatedly in his performance with only occasional nods to the wives and children in the room as bit players. The unmarried, the childless are nowhere addressed by the pitch, even though, when we attended, there were plenty in the audience (including members of our group).

Once he finds his captive audience, the salesman (whether of salvation or vacation) must create the lack that his product will meet. He must preach sin, and that sin must generate insufficiency. Ironically the one sin he cannot address is greed, although his pitch depends on it. The *Pardoner's Tale* begins with a harangue on the sins of the tavern, describing

> … yonge folk that haunteden folye,
> As riot, hasard, stywes, and tavernes,
> Where as with harpes, lutes, and gyternes,
> They daunce and pleyen at dees bothe day and nyght,
> And eten also and drynken over hir myght,
> Thurgh which they doon the devel sacrifise
> Withinne that develes temple in cursed wise
> By superfluytee abhomynable. (6.464–71)

Like the Canterbury and Vegas pilgrims, the Pardoner's revellers temporarily inhabit a liminal space that allows for physical gratification but not much more. They are desperate; they visit the tavern because they are miserable, mourning the death of a friend, almost certainly to plague. Theirs is a desperation that cannot be remedied, and the Pardoner understands this. His game is to make an example of their unquenchable desire – a desire shared by his pilgrim audience – and their failure to find anything other than betrayal and death in their quest for solace. He can then offer his travelling congregation a new alternative: redemption in the form of fake religious relics and indulgences. He is the gift shop, the timeshare sales point, where weary pilgrims pause, take inventory of how little happiness they have encountered on their journeys, and purchase something perhaps more substantial.

Jimbo is also quick to point out the sins of his captive audience: the harried fathers, how they have failed to prepare for their families' vacation well-beings, how they have been so very penny-wise with their few pennies that they have neglected to make an investment in paradise. In *The Queen of Versailles*, Richard Siegel encourages his salespeople to sell "the breakdown of the family." Families no longer spend time together. The wife is surfing Facebook, the husband watching sports, and the kids off playing – you guessed it – video games. Only on vacation can the family heal this rift, can parents and children come to know one another in any meaningful way. In no sense are these Vegas hucksters selling property. They are selling time, the right to occupy luxury accommodations for a certain number of days a year. But they don't say that; instead, Jimbo and the Siegels sell pardon for failed lives, to people who are in Vegas for the very purpose of trying to exorcise the hauntings of failure.

What the pitchman cannot say is every bit as important as what he says. He cannot under any circumstances reveal the fine print. He must avoid quoting costs or unpacking the legal intricacies of the purchase. The doctrine of indulgences that supports the Pardoner's scam bears a remarkable resemblance to the legal details that underlie Jimbo's timeshare pitch. In both cases, backed by a powerful corporate institution, the salesman is selling nothing more substantial than time. If Jimbo's or the Pardoner's audiences do not read the fine print, it is because it is intentionally long and nearly incomprehensible. Timeshare ownership is "a generic term that describes an interest in property whereby a number of persons own, or have the exclusive right to use, a piece of property for a specified time period."[30] Or as Richard Siegel phrases it in *The Queen of Versailles*, selling a timeshare is selling the same property fifty-two times.[31] But the situation is even more complicated than that, since there are many different kinds of timeshares, each carrying its own distinct set of legal requirements and complications.[32] Timeshares break down into two general categories: fee interest, in which the buyer owns a particular unit for a specific number of days or weeks each year; and non-fee interest – vacation leases or club memberships – in which the buyer owns no part of the property but only the right to occupy certain spaces for a specified amount of time. A new wrinkle in the latter type is the points program that sells not units, not even time, but points that buyers can spend each year anywhere the company has properties (provided, of course, that the buyers have enough points). The number of points required for any particular stay depends on the season, the demand for the property, the size of the accommodation, and the number of nights desired.[33]

Indulgences also granted time – or time off from suffering in Purgatory. The ecclesiastical small print of the indulgence offers up the rhetoric of the scam; because time is not measurable in either Purgatory or Heaven, the speed of escape from one to the other is impossible to determine. An easier way to understand what the Pardoner is selling is to explain it as spiritual points. The *Catholic Encyclopedia* defines an indulgence as "the extra-sacramental remission of the temporal punishment due, in God's justice, to sin that has been forgiven, which remission is granted by the Church in the exercise of the power of the keys, through the application of the superabundant merits of Christ and of the saints, and for some just and reasonable motive."[34] That is, according to the doctrine of confession, sin brings with it guilt (*culpa*) and punishment (*pena*). The sacrament of penance, and that alone, can forgive guilt and transmute damnation to temporal punishment (absolve sin). However, the papal bull *Unigenitus*, pronounced in 1343 by Clement VI, offered sinners remission of some of that temporal punishment if they performed certain devotions, worshipped in particular churches, donated money to particular causes, or went on pilgrimage. Such indulgences could be granted only by the pope, who, in turn, licenced that power to representatives known as *quaestores* or pardoners. The pardons carried by these officials (salesmen really) could not absolve sins, although Chaucer's Pardoner claims on several occasions that he can; they could only remit the punishment (in Purgatory) due for sins that had been repented and confessed. And since there is no time in Purgatory, such remission had to be calculated in terms of earthly time; that is, the sinner would receive as much relief from the punishments of Purgatory as she would have received if she had done penance on earth for 600 days or 50 years or whatever time was specified in the indulgence. "The issue of time became malleable in the hands of ecclesiastical policy makers," so much so that we might as well think of pardons as selling points towards salvation, towards a room in God's house.[35] It is little wonder that the Pardoner could so easily convince his marks that he was selling salvation, when even learned theologians had difficulty understanding the finer details of doctrine on this subject.[36] The Pardoner's pitch to the pilgrims contains none of these theological subtleties, just as the timeshare salesman must on no account reveal the true cost of the purchase – including financing and maintenance fees, potential legal liabilities, or complications arising from partition, resale, or inheritance of a timeshare.

Instead the pitchman must focus repetitively on the dream and its fulfilment. The Pardoner's relics, he tells his audience, can heal the sick, increase wealth, cure jealousy. The "clouts" or rags that he sells may have particular resonance for Canterbury pilgrims. The first miracle recorded after Thomas Becket's murder involved rags that had been used to wipe his blood and brains from the altar healing the sick.[37] Arthur Stanley writes in his 1889 book on Canterbury memorials that Becket's blood was "endlessly diluted, was kept in innumerable vials, to be distributed to the pilgrims; and thus, as the palm was a sign of a pilgrimage to Jerusalem, and a scallop-shell of the pilgrimage to Compostela, so a leaden vial or bottle suspended from the neck became the mark of a pilgrimage to Canterbury."[38] The full impact of the blood itself is diluted so that it can be distributed to the masses. In effect, like timeshares, the same object – or relic – can be sold over and over again, increasing the profits but with perhaps diminishing returns for the buyer.

The Pardoner also claims for himself the ultimate power to absolve sinners of their sins, a promise he iterates frequently:

Myn hooly pardoun may yow alle warice,
So that ye offre nobles or sterlynges,
Or elles silver broches, spoones, rynges.
Boweth youre heed under this hooly bulle!
Cometh up, ye wyves, offreth of youre wolle!
Youre names I entre heer in my rolle anon;
Into the blisse of hevene shul ye gon.
I yow assoille, by myn heigh power,
Yow that wol offre, as clene and eek as cleer
As ye were born. (6.906–15)

The Pardoner makes wild claims at the close of his tale, that his pardons can "cure," that those who subscribe will be absolved (assoiled[39]) of sin, and that they will enter into the "blisse of hevene." These promises of salvation are skilfully interwoven with reminders of sin and insufficiency. The Pardoner preaches on the theme *radix malorum est cupiditas* (1 Timothy 6:10)[40] and, by repeatedly circling around the sins of the pilgrims, he is able "to make hem free / To yeven hir pens, and namely unto me" (6.401–2).

Jimbo too has a dream to sell. Those in attendance at the timeshare seminar are looking for escape from the soulless degradations of late capitalism. Like the peasants deceived by Chaucer's Pardoner, this is an audience of victims, likely to blame their suffering on themselves, innocents convinced to focus constantly on their own sins rather than on the sins of their masters. They are miserable in their work, humiliated in their homes, looking for some respite in their brief time in motion, on vacation. *The Queen of Versailles* captures Richard Seigel in a training session with his timeshare sales force. He opens, "Why are we here?" The room shouts back, "To save lives!" The timeshare salesman sells vacations, and vacations are healthy; the research "proves" it. People (read men) who go on vacation are less likely to suffer from heart attacks. The timeshare salesman is selling salvation as vacation – and vacation as salvation – as David Lodge's return to Eden, where families are made whole again. "Make a sale, save lives," Seigel concludes.

Finally, if the pitchman can wrap up all of these rhetorical tactics (know your audience, hype the sin, avoid details especially cost, and sell the dream) into a story or stories, so much the better. Because "lewed peple loven tales old," the Pardoner explains, "Thanne tell I hem ensamples many oon / Of olde stories longe tyme agoon" (6.435–7). The Pardoner does not tell just one story about three revellers who seek to kill Death, he gives us stories within stories, exempla of sin. His tale begins with a long digression that relates famous stories about gluttony – the drunkenness of Lot and Herod, Attila and Lemuel, and the gambling of King Demetrius of Parthia – before he returns again to the three revellers.

Jimbo connects with his audience by telling stories about the drudgery of his work experience before becoming a salesman and about buying points for his own family. Jimbo narrativizes himself as a hapless, 1950s-sitcom father, so caught up in his labour that he ignores his family's various frustrations. When he attended his first sales pitch, he tells us, he informed his wife that he could not afford a timeshare. But she convinced him otherwise: "We'll cut something else out of our budget." He describes the amazing vacations he has experienced in Hawaii and in Disney World, paid for with his points. He makes up hypothetical stories of families squashed into too-small hotel rooms with little room to move, of fights over the television or the bathroom. At the climax of this performance, to drive home his point, Jimbo squatted down on his haunches and held an imaginary paper up to the crowd. We turned to one another marvelling, "Is he miming taking a dump?" According to Jimbo, most families participate in a kind of vacation Purgatory. Having escaped the hell of the workweek, they find themselves still punished by claustrophobic quarters and lack of privacy. A timeshare purchases a Heaven of space and comfort. It provides the suffering family, but mostly the suffering, emasculated father (who cannot even find alone time in a cramped bathroom), with the paradise he has earned and the happiness his wife and children so richly deserve.

What marks both the Pardoner and Jimbo as master salesmen is the utter cynicism they evince, telling their marks that they are fleecing them at the moment they do it. Their metacommentary on their own tactics attests to the cynicism in both cultures about the corporate entities these salesmen represent. The Pardoner explicitly admits on several occasions that he is swindling:

> That it is joye to se my bisynesse.
> Of avarice and of swich cursednesse
> Is al my prechyng, for to make hem free
> To yeven hir pens, and namely unto me.
> For myn entente is nat but for to wynne,
> And nothyng for correccioun of synne.
> I rekke nevere, whan that they been beryed,
> Though that hir soules goon a-blakeberyed! (6.399–406)

Jimbo works into his performance his expectation that the audience will think he is swindling them. So does David Seigel: "The wife is saying 'Don't you dare buy anything.' The husband is saying 'Don't you worry, they won't sell me anything.'" The salesman's job is to expect and neutralize resistance, to grant scepticism and undermine it at the same time. After they see the model penthouse, a penthouse that almost no one who sits through these pitches will ever stay in, says Seigel, "that motel room, if it looks bad before, looks twice as bad after."

Desperate Pilgrims

In his famous rebuke to the Pardoner, Harry Baily doesn't bite at the Pardoner's pitch, even though he has been identified as "mooste envoluped in synne" (6.942), and instead curses:

> … By the croys which that Seint Eleyne fond,
> I wolde I hadde thy coillons in myn hond
> In stide of relikes or of seintuarie.
> Let kutte hem of, I wol thee helpe hem carie;
> They shul be shryned in an hogges toord! (6.951–5)

How do we account for Baily's response, his disturbance of the peace? After all, it financially benefits the tavern owner to maintain good fellowship and order among the pilgrims, to keep them eating and drinking in his establishment. Is his outbreak just our hypermasculine host's way of exposing a fraud, or is something more than gender panic going on here? Perhaps Harry Baily understands better than most of the pilgrims the double misery of seeking a relief that is never on offer, neither from the tavern nor from a corrupt church. We would like to suggest that Baily suffers not from anger but rather from the frustration he shares with the other desperate pilgrims.

Perhaps we take Harry Baily a bit too literally when he insists, "For by my trouthe, if that I shal nat lye, / I saugh nat this yeer so myrie a compaignye / Atones in this herberwe as is now" (1.763-5). Baily sets the pilgrimage scam in motion, understanding the desperation of the Canterbury travellers and offering, as some small distraction, the sins of his tavern, the Tabard: "He served us with vitaille at the beste; / Strong was the wyn, and wel to drynke us leste" (1.749-50). Chaucer's companions are all failures: broken-down soldiers, a lovelorn widow, soulless clergy, hapless businessmen, cuckolded husbands, hucksters, fraudsters, and buffoons; they are suckers ready for fleecing. But Baily is not the master confidence man here. Like the timeshare clerks (and they are almost inevitably men) who tantalize Vegas pilgrims with their free event tickets and breakfast, Baily is the set-up guy (even if he doesn't know it). The closer, the real pro on the Canterbury pilgrimage, is the Pardoner, a confidence man's confidence man: a medieval timeshare salesman who with all the self-irony he can muster tells his world-weary marks they are about to be taken even as he runs his game.

Chaucer is writing during a time of extreme desperation – even if his constantly ironic tone seems to suggest otherwise. In "knitting up the feast" of the *Canterbury Tales*, the Parson's sermon, recounting those "thynges [that] destourben penaunce," namely "drede, schame, hope, and wanhope, that is, desperacioun" (10.1057), identifies the relay between desperation and hope that we have been tracking in this chapter. It is difficult to imagine the Canterbury pilgrims as having remained untouched by the ravages of bubonic plague, the little ice age, the Peasants' Rebellion, or the Hundred Years' War.[41] Such disruptions – and the suffering that ensued – substantially undermined England's economy, governance, even faith itself. Travel to Canterbury represented a time away from the misery of the everyday and provided solace in compact fashion – why take the time and trouble to journey to Rome or Jerusalem when the same rewards reside just a short trip down the road? (Why, indeed, travel to Paris, Venice, or Egypt when all their delights can be found in an easily accessed Nevada desert town?) The very wretchedness that provides the conditions for the Canterbury pilgrimage (a journey that vacillates between decadent vacation, spiritual passage, and swindle) creates a lush environment for the confidence game. As Chaucer notes of his Pardoner, the most unfortunate – those made most unfortunate by failures of the economy, the government, and the church – are the most vulnerable:

> But with thise relikes, whan that he fond
> A povre person dwellynge upon lond,
> Upon a day he gat hym moore moneye
> Than that the person gat in monthes tweye. (1.701–4)

Chaucer's Pardoner promises his unwitting public an opportunity to acquire authorized relics: the bones of saints, objects made holy by their proximity to blessed persons. He promises his listeners indulgences sanctioned and sanctified by the pope, guaranteed, beyond any doubt, by the Holy Church. The sucker's desire for an easy path is part of what makes her a sucker, and the Pardoner baits his trap accordingly. The Pardoner's switch convinces his listeners that junk has value, that all one needs is enough money to buy a seat at God's table. As the fourteenth century winds down, as England is buffeted by one catastrophe after another, Chaucer suggests that a little bit of suspicion might be in order, that salvation might not be purchasable, like so many souvenirs. As our time with Jimbo came to an end, we were offered a glimpse at one of the timeshares up for sale. It was lovely, perhaps not quite heavenly, but awfully luxurious. Still, we were staying in one of the timeshares in the same building, and ours looked nothing like the one on display. Did our salesman think we would be so readily duped? We insisted that we were not going to be taken by a bait-and-switch ploy – we had, after all, read the *Canterbury Tales*! Our salesman smiled knowingly. Pilgrims coming to Las Vegas never get what they want.

NOTES

1. A citation of a citation of the medieval.
2. See Umberto Eco, *Travels in Hyperreality*, trans. William Weaver (New York: Harcourt, Brace, Jovanovich, 1983); and Fredric Jameson, *Postmodernism, or, the Cultural Logic of Late Capitalism* (Durham, NC: Duke University Press, 1991), 18.
3. Barbara Land and Myrick Land, *A Short History of Las Vegas* (Reno: University of Nevada Press, 2004), 1.
4. Nor are we going to explore, though we might, Vegas's indigenous Middle Ages and its occupation by the Anasazi, who mysteriously disappear around 1150, about the time Geoffrey of Monmouth was writing his *History of the Kings of Britain* (Land and Land, *Short History of Las Vegas*, 10).
5. Robert Venturi and Denise Scott Brown, *Learning from Las Vegas* (London: Routledge, 2007), 75; their emphasis.

6 Our on-site research for this essay was conducted in Las Vegas between 12 and 16 Oct. 2016.
7 Jimbo's performance is certainly not unique. How many similar performances are enacted all over Vegas every day? Indeed, Jimbo's rhetoric duplicates with uncanny similarity the instructions given to salespeople by Richard Siegel, son of David Siegel, billionaire owner of the timeshare enterprise Westgate Resorts Ltd., in the documentary film *The Queen of Versailles* (dir. Lauren Greenfield, 2012). Subsequent quotations of David Siegel are taken from this source. Quotations from Chaucer's *Canterbury Tales* are taken from *The Riverside Chaucer*, ed. Larry D. Benson, 3rd ed. (Boston: Houghton Mifflin, 1987), and are cited parenthetically.
8 Vegas's famous strip is not even in Las Vegas, as David Schwartz documents: "Even today, the resorts of the Strip are not part of the City of Las Vegas, much to the consternation of city officials. From the start, they identified themselves as essentially antiurban and leagues apart from the downtown gambling halls of Fremont Street" (*Suburban Xanadu: The Casino Resort on the Las Vegas Strip and Beyond* [New York: Routledge, 2003], 6). The Strip resides in the unincorporated town of Paradise. For a detailed description of the failure of the city to annex the resorts on the Strip, see Eugene P. Moehring, *Resort City in the Sun Belt: Las Vegas, 1930–2000* (Reno: University of Nevada Press, 2000), 69–71.
9 We are not the first to suggest this comparison between pilgrimage and tourism. In David Lodge's novel, *Paradise News* (New York: Penguin, 1993), one of his characters, Roger Sheldrake, an anthropologist of tourism who teaches at the fictional South-West London Poly, notes that "sightseeing is a substitute for religious ritual. The sightseeing tour as secular pilgrimage. Accumulation of grace by visiting the shrines of high culture. Souvenirs as relics. Guidebooks as devotional aids" (61).
10 They did so in casinos with evocative names like El Rancho, the Last Frontier, the Horseshoe, and the Golden Nugget. Fremont Street in Old Vegas was known as Glitter Gulch.
11 Land and Land, *Short History of Las Vegas*, 93–9.
12 Land and Land, *Short History of Las Vegas*, 186; see also 160–77.
13 Land and Land, *Short History of Las Vegas*, 186.
14 Land and Land, *Short History of Las Vegas*, 193.
15 T.J. Jackson Lears, *Something for Nothing: Luck in America* (New York: Penguin, 2003), 2.
16 Laura Cook Kenna, "The Promise of Gangster Glamour: Sinatra, Vegas, and Alluring, Ethnicized, Excess," Center for Gaming Research Occasional Paper Series 6, https://digitalscholarship.unlv.edu/cgi/viewcontent.cgi?article=1015&context=occ_papers (Aug. 2010): 3 (accessed 1 Mar. 2021). John Berger writes, "The happiness of being envied is glamour" (*Ways of Seeing* [New York: Penguin, 1973], 132).
17 Chris Rodel, "Sin City's Dirty Little Secret: It's Full of Churches," NBC News, 29 Mar. 2011, https://www.nbcnews.com/id/wbna42074829 (accessed 2 Mar. 2021).

18 For Margery's story, see Margery Kempe, *The Book of Margery Kempe*, TEAMS Middle English Texts, ed. Lynn Staley (Kalamazoo, MI: Medieval Institute Publications, 1996).
19 Is she a murderess? See Mary Hamel, "The Wife of Bath and a Contemporary Murder," *Chaucer Review* 14 (1979): 132–9.
20 D.W. Robertson's *Preface to Chaucer* (Princeton, NJ: Princeton University Press, 1963), drawing upon the system of interpretive readings of scriptures developed by the church fathers, promoted exegetical (allegorical) readings of *The Canterbury Tales* that focused on Christian love or *caritas*. In the 1970s this approach was both popular and highly controversial.
21 Robert E. Scully asserts that this number is probably inflated because there were two registers recording miracles at the site ("The Unmaking of a Saint: Thomas Becket and the English Reformation," *Catholic Historical Review* 86 [2000]: 579–602, at 582).
22 Scully, "Unmaking of a Saint," 582–4.
23 Lears, in a chapter entitled "Gambling for Grace," plumbs the connections we are probing in this essay between religious belief and gambling that have haunted the American ideologies of hard work and moral rectitude: "What is sorely missing from American public debate is a sense, historical and spiritual, of this connection between gambling and grace" (*Something for Nothing*, 9).
24 Robert Ekelund, Robert Tollison, Gary Anderson, Robert Hébert, and Audrey Davidson, *Sacred Trust: The Medieval Church as an Economic Firm* (New York: Oxford University Press, 1996), 155. For a discussion of indulgences, see 154–8.
25 Minnis cites scholars who argue that the practice of indulgences allowed the church to build cathedrals, to repair churches and roads, and to support schools and hospitals; see his "Reclaiming the Pardoner," *Journal of Medieval and Early Modern Studies* 32 (2003): 311–34, at 313.
26 William Kent, "Indulgences," in *The Catholic Encyclopedia*, vol. 7 (New York: Robert Appleton Company, 1910), www.newadvent.org/cathen/07783a.htm (accessed 30 May 2017).
27 On the theology of the "treasury of merit," see Kent, "Indulgences," and J.J. Jusserand, *English Wayfaring Life in the Middle Ages*, 8th ed. (London: T. Fisher Unwin, 1891), 311–37; Robert Shaffern, "Images, Jurisdiction, and the Treasury of Merit," *Journal of Medieval History* 22 (1996): 237–47; and Minnis, "Reclaiming the Pardoner."
28 Shaffern, "Images, Jurisdiction, and the Treasury of Merit," 238.
29 These terms come from Robert Ekelund et al., *Sacred Trust*, who describe the medieval church as an "economic firm" (155).
30 Tom Eastman, "Time Share Ownership: A Primer," *North Dakota Law Review* 57 (1981): 151–62, at 152.
31 As James Scavo observes, "Timeshare developers have high profit expectations. For example, rather than a single sale of a condominium unit, the sale of a vacation

ownership or timeshare interest means potentially fifty-two interests sold in each unit" ("Marketing Resort Timeshares: The Rules of the Game," *St. John's Law Review* 73 [1999]: 217–45, at 217).

32 Ellen Peirce and Richard Mann's essay defining the various types of timeshare arrangements and their legal consequences runs to fifty-three dense, footnote-packed pages; see "Time-Share Interests in Real Estate: A Critical Evaluation of the Regulatory Environment," *Notre Dame Law Review* 59 (1983): 9–60.

33 By 1995, according to one source, almost 50 per cent of resorts were offering some kind of "flexible use plan" (Scavo, "Marketing Resort Timeshares," 220).

34 Kent, "Indulgences."

35 Ekelund et al., *Sacred Trust*, 155.

36 For an excellent analysis of learned theological debates over the efficacy of indulgences, see Minnis, "Reclaiming the Pardoner."

37 Scully, "Unmaking of a Saint," 582.

38 Arthur Stanley, *Historical Memorials of Canterbury* (London: J.M. Dent, 1889), 114.

39 "Assoile": "to absolve of sin by divine or sacerdotal authority; grant remission of sins or penance." In its definition, the *Middle English Dictionary* cites the traditional Latin phrase *a pena et a culpa*.

40 English translations of the Bible from the King James Version onwards translate this phrase as "the love of money is the root of all evil."

41 For a popular account of the "calamitous" fourteenth century, see Barbara Tuchman, *A Distant Mirror: The Calamitous Fourteenth Century* (New York: Random House, 1978).

Selected Bibliography

This selected bibliography compiles major works on medievalism, geography, and cultural studies as cited in this volume and as relevant to these overlapping fields. See each chapter for articles, reviews, and additional sources specific to the iteration of American medievalism that it addresses.

Aberth, John. *A Knight at the Movies: Medieval History on Film.* New York: Routledge, 2003.

Alexander, Michael. *Medievalism: The Middle Ages in Modern England.* New Haven, CT: Yale University Press, 2007.

Archibald, Elizabeth, and Ad Putter, eds. *The Cambridge Companion to the Arthurian Legend.* Cambridge: Cambridge University Press, 2009.

Aronstein, Susan. *Hollywood Knights: Arthurian Cinema and the Politics of Nostalgia.* New York: Palgrave Macmillan, 2005.

Ashton, Gail, ed. *Medieval Afterlives in Contemporary Culture.* London: Bloomsbury, 2015.

Aubrey, Elizabeth. "Medievalism in American Musical Life." In *Reflections on American Music: The Twentieth Century and the New Millennium,* edited by James R. Heintze and Michael Saffle, 55–63. Hillsdale, NY: Pendragon Press, 2000.

Bachelard, Gaston. *The Poetics of Space.* Translated by Maria Jolas. 1969. Boston: Beacon Press, 1994.

Barrington, Candace. *American Chaucers.* New York: Palgrave Macmillan, 2007.

Biddick, Kathleen. *The Shock of Medievalism.* Durham, NC: Duke University Press, 1998.

Bloch, Howard, and Stephen Nichols, eds. *Medievalism and the Modernist Temper.* Baltimore, MD: Johns Hopkins University Press, 1996.

Boym, Svetlana. *The Future of Nostalgia.* New York: Basic Books, 2008.

Brooks, Chris. *The Gothic Revival.* London: Phaidon, 1999.

Brown, Catherine. "In the Middle." *Journal of Medieval and Early Modern Studies* 30, no. 3 (2000): 547–74.

Brownlee, Marina, Kevin Brownlee, and Stephen Nichols, eds. *The New Medievalism*. Baltimore, MD: Johns Hopkins University Press, 1991.

Casey, E.S. *Remembering: A Phenomenological Study*. Bloomington: Indiana University Press, 1987.

Chandler, Alice. *A Dream of Order: The Medieval Ideal in Nineteenth-Century English Literature*. Lincoln: University of Nebraska Press, 1970.

Chazan, Robert. *Medieval Stereotypes and Modern Antisemitism*. Berkeley: University of California Press, 1997.

Cohen, Jeffrey Jerome, ed. *The Postcolonial Middle Ages*. New York: St. Martin's, 2000.

Cosgrove, Denis. *Geography and Vision: Seeing, Imagining, and Representing the World*. London: Taurus, 2008.

Cram, Ralph Adams. *Church Building: A Study of the Principles of Architecture in Their Relation to the Church*. Boston: Small, Maynard & Company, 1901.

– *The Gothic Quest*. New York: Baker and Taylor, 1907.

– *The Ministry of Art*. Freeport, NY: Books for Libraries Press, 1914.

Cramer, Michael. *Medieval Fantasy as Performance: The Society for Creative Anachronism and the Current Middle Ages*. Lanham, MD: Scarecrow, 2010.

Creighton, Oliver. *Designs upon the Land: Elite Landscapes of the Middle Ages*. Martlesham, UK: Boydell and Brewer, 2013.

Cresswell, Timothy. *Place: A Short Introduction*. 2nd ed. Chichester, UK: Wiley Blackwell, 2015.

D'Arcens, Louise, ed. *The Cambridge Companion to Medievalism*. Cambridge: Cambridge University Press, 2016.

Davis, Kathleen, and Nadia Altschul, eds. *Medievalisms in the Postcolonial World: The Idea of "the Middle Ages" Outside Europe*. Baltimore, MD: Johns Hopkins University Press, 2009.

Dinshaw, Carolyn. *How Soon Is Now? Medieval Texts, Amateur Readers, and the Queerness of Time*. Durham, NC: Duke University Press, 2012.

Eco, Umberto. *Travels in Hyperreality: Essays*. Translated by William Weaver. San Diego: Harcourt, 1983.

Elliott, Andrew. *Medievalism, Politics, and Mass Media*. Cambridge: D.S. Brewer, 2017.

– *Remaking the Middle Ages: The Methods of Cinema and History in Portraying the Medieval World*. Jefferson, NC: McFarland, 2010.

Emery, Elizabeth, and Richard Utz, eds. *Medievalism: Key Critical Terms*. Cambridge: D.S. Brewer, 2014.

Finke, Laurie A., and Martin B. Shichtman. *Cinematic Illuminations: The Middle Ages on Film*. Baltimore, MD: Johns Hopkins University Press, 2010.

– "Remediating Chivalry: Political Aesthetics and the Round Table." In *Mediality/Intermediality*, edited by Martin Heusser, Andreas Fischer, and Andreas H. Jucker, 139–60. Tübingen, Germany: Gunter Narr, 2008.

Forni, Kathleen. *Chaucer's Afterlife: Adaptations in Recent Popular Culture*. Jefferson, NC: McFarland, 2013.

Fraser, John. *America and the Patterns of Chivalry*. New York: Cambridge University Press, 1982.
Fugelso, Karl, ed. *Defining Neomedievealism(s)*. Studies in Medievalism 19. Cambridge: D.S. Brewer, 2010.
Ganim, John. *Medievalism and Orientalism: Three Essays on Literature, Architecture, and Cultural Identity*. New York: Palgrave Macmillan, 2005.
Giamatti, Bartlett, ed. *Dante in America: The First Two Centuries*. Binghamton, NY: Center for Medieval and Early Renaissance Studies, 1983.
Gillis, J.R., ed. *Commemorations: The Politics of National Identity*. Princeton, NJ: Princeton University Press, 1994.
Girouard, Mark. *The Return to Camelot: Chivalry and the English Gentleman*. New Haven, CT: Yale University Press, 1981.
Graham, Brian J., and Peter Howard, eds. *The Ashgate Research Companion to Heritage Identity*. Hampshire, UK: Ashgate, 2008.
Harty, Kevin J., ed. *Cinema Arthuriana: Twenty Essays*. Jefferson, NC: McFarland, 2010.
–, ed. *The Holy Grail on Film: Essays on the Cinematic Quest*. Jefferson, NC: McFarland, 2015.
– *The Reel Middle Ages: American, Western and Eastern European, Middle Eastern and Asian Films about Medieval Europe*. 2nd ed. Jefferson, NC: McFarland, 2006.
–, ed. *The Vikings on Film: Essays on Depictions of the Nordic Middle Ages*. Jefferson, NC: McFarland, 2011.
Harvey, John. *Mediaeval Gardens*. Portland, OR: Timber Press, 1982.
Holsinger, Bruce. *Neomedievalism, Neoconservatism, and the War on Terror*. Chicago: Prickly Paradigm Press, 2007.
James-Chakraborty, Kathleen. *Architecture since 1400*. Minneapolis: University of Minnesota Press, 2014.
Jameson, Fredric. *Postmodernism, or, the Cultural Logic of Late Capitalism*. Durham, NC: Duke University Press, 1991.
Joy, Eileen, Myra Seaman, Kimberley Bell, and Mary Ramsay, eds. *Cultural Studies of the Modern Middle Ages*. New York: Palgrave Macmillan, 2007.
Kelly, Kathleen Coyne, and Tison Pugh, eds. *Chaucer on Screen: Absence, Presence, and Adapting the "Canterbury Tales."* Columbus: Ohio State University Press, 2016.
Koselleck, Reinhart. *Futures Past: On the Semantics of Historical Time*. Translated by Keith Tribe. New York: Columbia University Press, 2004.
Kruger, Steven F. "Gay Internet Medievalism: Erotic Story Archives, the Middle Ages, and Contemporary Gay Identity." *American Literary History* 22, no. 4 (2010): 913–44.
Kudrycz, Walter. *The Historical Present: Medievalism and Modernity*. London: Continuum, 2011.
Lears, T.J. Jackson. *No Place of Grace: Antimodernism and the Transformation of American Culture, 1880–1920*. Chicago: University of Chicago Press, 1981.

Looney, Dennis. *Freedom Readers: The African American Reception of Dante Alighieri and the Divine Comedy*. Notre Dame, IN: Notre Dame University Press, 2011.

Lowenthal, David. "Identity, Heritage, and History." In *Commemorations: The Politics of National Identity*, edited by John Gillis, 41–57. Princeton, NJ: Princeton University Press, 1994.

Lupack, Alan. "American Arthurian Authors: A Declaration of Independence." In *The Arthurian Revival: Essays on Form, Tradition, and Transformation*, edited by Debra Mancoff, 155–73. New York: Garland, 1992.

– "Arthurian Youth Groups in America: The Americanization of Knighthood." In *Adapting the Arthurian Legends for Children: Essays on Arthurian Juvenilia*, edited by Barbara Tepa Lupack, 197–216. New York: Palgrave Macmillan, 2004.

Lupack, Alan, and Barbara Tepa Lupack. *King Arthur in America*. Cambridge: D.S. Brewer, 1999.

Mancoff, Debra. *The Return of King Arthur: The Legend through Victorian Eyes*. New York: Abrams, 1995.

Mathis, Andrew. *The King Arthur Myth in Modern American Literature*. Jefferson, NC: McFarland, 2002.

Matthews, David. *Medievalism: A Critical History*. Cambridge: D.S. Brewer, 2015.

McClure, Julia. *The Franciscan Invention of the New World*. Basingstoke, UK: Palgrave Macmillan, 2017.

Moreland, Kim. *The Medievalist Impulse in American Literature: Twain, Adams, Fitzgerald, and Hemingway*. Charlottesville: University of Virginia Press, 1996.

Murphy, Kevin D., and Lisa Reilly, eds. *Skyscraper Gothic: Medieval Style and Modernist Buildings*. Charlottesville: University of Virginia Press, 2017.

Nora, Pierre. "Between Memory and History: *Lieux de memoire*." *Representations* 26 (1989): 7–24.

Palmgren, Jennifer, and Loretta Holloway, eds. *Beyond Arthurian Romances: The Reach of Victorian Medievalism*. New York: Palgrave Macmillan, 2005.

Pugh, Tison. *Queer Chivalry: Medievalism and the Myth of White Masculinity in Southern Literature*. Baton Rouge: Louisiana State University Press, 2013.

Pugh, Tison, and Susan Aronstein, eds. *The Disney Middle Ages: A Fairy-Tale and Fantasy Past*. New York: Palgrave Macmillan, 2012.

Pugh, Tison, and Angela Jane Weisl. *Medievalisms: Making the Past in the Present*. New York: Routledge, 2013.

Reijnders, Stijn. *Places of the Imagination: Media, Tourism, Culture*. Farnham, UK: Ashgate, 2011.

Rosenthal, Bernard, and Paul Szarmach, eds. *Medievalism in American Culture*. Binghamton, NY: Medieval and Renaissance Texts and Studies, 1989.

Rubin, Rachel Lee. *Well Met: Renaissance Faires and the American Counterculture*. New York: New York University Press, 2012.

Shippey, Tom. "Medievalisms and Why They Matter." *Studies in Medievalism* 17 (2009): 45–54.
Simmons, Clare, ed. *Medievalism and the Quest for the "Real" Middle Ages*. London: Cass, 2001.
Sponsler, Claire. *Ritual Imports: Performing Medieval Drama in America*. Ithaca, NY: Cornell University Press, 2004.
Staines, David. *Tennyson's Camelot:* The Idylls of the King *and Its Medieval Sources*. Waterloo, ON: Wilfrid Laurier University Press, 1982.
Stanton, Phoebe B. *The Gothic Revival and American Church Architecture: An Episode in Taste, 1840–1856*. Baltimore, MD: Johns Hopkins University Press, 1968.
Stewart, Susan. *On Longing: Narratives of the Miniature, the Gigantic, the Souvenir, the Collection*. Baltimore, MD: Johns Hopkins University Press, 1984.
Taylor, Laurie, and Zach Whalen, eds. *Playing the Past: History and Nostalgia in Video Games*. Nashville: Vanderbilt University Press, 2008.
Utz, Richard. *Medievalism: A Manifesto*. Kalamazoo, MI: Arc Humanities Press, 2017.
Venturi, Robert, and Denise Scott Brown. *Learning from Las Vegas*. London: Routledge, 2007.
Voigtländer, Nico, and Hans-Joachim Voth. "Persecution Perpetuated: The Medieval Origins of Anti-Semitic Violence in Nazi Germany." *Quarterly Journal of Economics* 127, no. 3 (2012): 1339–92.
Weisl, Angela Jane. *The Persistence of Medievalism: Narrative Adventures in Contemporary Culture*. New York: Palgrave Macmillan, 2003.
Whitaker, Cord J., and Matthew Gabriele. "Mountain Haints: Towards a Medieval Studies Exorcized." *Postmedieval: A Journal of Medieval Cultural Studies* 10, no. 2 (2019): 129–36.
Whitaker, Muriel. *The Legends of King Arthur in Art*. Cambridge: D.S. Brewer, 1990.
Wickham, Chris. *Medieval Europe*. New Haven, CT: Yale University Press, 2016.
Williams, Peter W. *Houses of God: Region, Religion, and Architecture in the United States*. Urbana: University of Illinois, 2000.
Young, Bonnie. *A Walk through the Cloisters*. New York: Metropolitan Museum, 1988.
Young, Helen. "Approaches to Medievalism: A Consideration of Taxonomy and Methodology through Fantasy Fiction." *Parergon* 27, no. 1 (2010): 163–79.
Ziolkowski, Jan M. *The Juggler of Notre Dame and the Medievalizing of Modernity*. 6 vols. Cambridge: Open Book, 2018.

Contributors

Susan Aronstein, Professor of English at the University of Wyoming, is the author of *Hollywood Knights: Arthurian Cinema and the Politics of Nostalgia* and the co-editor of *The Disney Middle Ages: A Fairy-Tale and Fantasy Past*. She has also published several articles on artefacts of medievalism and popular culture, including Disneyland, Excalibur Hotel, *Monty Python and the Holy Grail*, and *The Da Vinci Code*.

Candace Barrington, Professor of English at Central Connecticut State University, pursues two research interests: the legal and literary discourses of medieval England, which resulted in multiple articles and the recently co-edited *Cambridge Companion to Medieval English Law and Literature*, and Chaucer's popular reception, which resulted in her monograph *American Chaucers* and numerous articles. With Jonathan Hsy, she directs Global Chaucers, a project collecting and studying non-Anglophone appropriations and translations of Chaucer's works. She is a founding member of the editorial collective publishing the *Open Access Companion to The Canterbury Tales*, a free, online introduction reaching Chaucer's global audience of English readers.

Laurie A. Finke, Professor of Women's and Gender Studies at Kenyon College, has published seven books, including her most recent, *Cinematic Illuminations: The Middle Ages on Film*, with her frequent collaborator Martin Shichtman. Her articles have appeared in *Theatre Survey, Signs, Theatre Journal, Exemplaria, Arthuriana*, and other venues, and she is currently the medieval editor of the *Norton Anthology of Criticism of Theory*.

Lowell Gallagher is Professor of English at the University of California, Los Angeles, where he teaches courses in Renaissance literature, critical theory, and queer and feminist approaches to biblical studies. He is the author of *Medusa's Gaze: Casuistry and Conscience in the Renaissance* and *Sodomscapes: Hospitality in the Flesh* and editor of several essay collections, including *Redrawing the*

Map of Early Modern English Catholicism and, with Shankar Raman, *Knowing Shakespeare: Senses, Embodiment, and Cognition*.

Alison Gulley is Professor of English at Appalachian State University in Boone, North Carolina, where she teaches courses in medieval literature and the history of the English language. She is the author of *The Displacement of the Body in Ælfric's Lives of the Virgin Martyrs* and the editor of *Teaching Rape in the Medieval Literature Classroom: Approaches to Difficult Texts*. Her research focuses on Old English hagiography as well as medievalism.

Kevin J. Harty, Professor and former longtime chair of English at La Salle University in Philadelphia, has published widely in the areas of Medieval Studies and Medievalism, especially on cinematic representations of the Middle Ages. His previous publications include *Medieval Women on Film*, *The Holy Grail on Film*, *The Vikings on Film*, *The Reel Middle Ages*, *King Arthur on Film*, *The Chester Mystery Cycle: A Casebook*, and *Cinema Arthuriana*. His current project is *Cinema Medievalia: New Essays on the Reel Middle Ages*.

Kathleen Coyne Kelly is Professor of English at Northeastern University. She is co-editor (with Marina Leslie) of *Menacing Virgins: Representing Virginity in the Middle Ages and Renaissance*; co-editor of *Queer Movie Medievalisms* and *Chaucer on Screen: Absence, Presence, and Adapting* the Canterbury Tales (both with Tison Pugh); and author of *A.S. Byatt* and *Performing Virginity and Testing Chastity in the Middle Ages*.

Tison Pugh, Pegasus Professor in the Department of English at the University of Central Florida, is the author of *Queering Medieval Genres* and *Chaucer's (Anti-)Eroticisms and the Queer Middle Ages*, among others. In the field of medievalism, he has published *Queer Chivalry: Medievalism and the Myth of White Masculinity in Southern Literature* and, with Angela Jane Weisl, *Medievalisms: Making the Past in the Present*. He has also edited such volumes as *Chaucer on Screen: Absence, Presence, and Adapting* the Canterbury Tales (with Kathleen Coyne Kelly) and *Race, Class, and Gender in "Medieval" Cinema* (with Lynn Tarte Ramey).

Jana K. Schulman is Professor of English and director of the Medieval Institute at Western Michigan University. Recent essays include "*Beowulf* in the Context of Old Norse" in *Teaching "Beowulf" in the Twenty-First Century*; "Old Norse-Icelandic Sagas" in *Oxford Bibliographies Online: Medieval Studies*; and "Retelling Old Tales: Germanic Myth and Language in Christopher Paolini's *Eragon*" in *Year's Work in Medievalism 25*.

Martin B. Shichtman is Director of the Center for Jewish Studies and Professor of English at Eastern Michigan University. His books include *Cinematic Illuminations: The Middle Ages on Film* and *King Arthur and the Myth of History*, both co-authored with Laurie A. Finke, and *Culture and the King: The Social Implications of the Arthurian Legend*, with James P. Carley.

Lorraine Kochanske Stock, Professor of English at the University of Houston, teaches courses on Chaucer, Arthurian literature, the Real/Reel Middle Ages, and Robin Hood. Commenting upon cinematic medievalism in *King Arthur* and *Kingdom of Heaven*, she appeared on the A&E documentary series *History vs. Hollywood*. She is completing her book *The Medieval Wild Man: Primitivism and Civilization in Twelfth- and Thirteenth-Century French Literature* and is researching a follow-up volume, *Wild Men or Noble Savages? Primitivism and Civilization in Fourteenth- through Sixteenth-Century English Culture*. For creating her undergraduate Hybrid Chaucer course, she was awarded the University of Houston's prize for Innovative Use of Technology in Teaching.

Alfred Thomas is Professor of English at the University of Illinois, Chicago. His books include *Anne's Bohemia: Czech Literature and Society, 1310–1420*; *A Blessed Shore: England and Bohemia from Chaucer to Shakespeare*; *The Bohemian Body: Gender and Sexuality in Modern Czech Culture*; *Prague Palimpsest: Writing, Memory, and the City*; and *Shakespeare, Dissent, and the Cold War*.

Richard Utz is Chair and Professor in the School of Literature, Media, and Communication at the Georgia Institute of Technology. He succeeded Leslie J. Workman and Tom Shippey as the third president of the International Society for the Study of Medievalism and currently serves as editor of *Medievally Speaking*. In 2017 he published *Medievalism: A Manifesto*, in which he challenges his colleagues to reconnect with the general public that has allowed medievalists to become, since the late nineteenth century, a rather exclusive clan of specialists who communicate mostly with each other.

Usha Vishnuvajjala received her PhD in English from Indiana University. Her research focuses on late medieval literature and culture, women's writing, and medievalism. She is currently a lecturer at Cardiff University, where she is teaching medieval literature, completing her monograph *Feminist Medievalisms*, and completing work on the volume *Women's Friendship in Medieval Literature*, co-edited with Karma Lochrie.

Index

Adams, Henry, 59n14, 86
Adams, John, 194n13, 262n9
Adventures of Robin Hood, The (1938 film), 272
Adventures of Robin Hood, The (1950s TV series), 271, 273
African Burial Ground (NYC), 149–51
Alighieri, Dante, 8, 31, 74–5, 141–2
American Poets' Corner, 139, 141
Amiens Cathedral, 54, 58
Andy Griffith Show, The, 185
anti-Semitism, 95, 147. *See also* racism
Appalachia, 14, 181–4, 186–7, 190–3
Aquinas, Thomas, 75
Arch Street Methodist Church (Philadelphia), 55
architecture: Chicago, 63, 65–7, 72–4; Classical Revival, 46, 66, 72, 74, 86, 91, 121, 212; Gothic, 21–2, 30, 33–4, 37, 46–57, 72, 84, 86, 89, 91–2, 94, 95, 103–4, 105, 112, 120, 130, 132, 134, 136–9, 142–3, 145, 147–51; Romanesque Revival, 21, 33, 62n54, 72, 89, 96, 120, 130, 134, 143, 145–6
Arts and Crafts movement, 12, 23, 34, 38, 89, 90, 92, 95, 101
Atlanta History Center, 122–3

Atlanta Race Riots, 112, 117–19, 122
Augustine, 75
Autry, Gene, 273

Bachelard, Gaston, 25
Bandit of Sherwood Forest, The, 272
Barnes, Julian, 228–9
Becket, Thomas, 289, 294
Belles Heures of Jean de France, duc de Berry, The (Limbourg Brothers), 136
Bernard of Clairvaux, St., 223n40
Biddick, Kathleen, 201
Birth of a Nation, 113. *See also* racism
Black Lives Matter, 124
Black Madonna, 139
Black people, 15, 66, 80n29, 117–19, 194n20, 247, 253, 257, 259
Bloomfield, Morton, 5
Blue Ridge Parkway, 180–3
Boccaccio, Giovanni, 26
Bonanza, 273
Boone, Daniel, 190
Bourdieu, Pierre, 132
Boym, Svetlana, 192–3
Braveheart, 7
Brown, Catherine, 16
Brown, Charles Brockden, 190
Brown, Dan, 64, 75, 77

Brown, Denise Scott, 284, 287
Brown, Michael, 138–9
Bryn Athyn Cathedral, 13, 45, 47, 49–55, 56, 60–1
Burp Castle (NYC), 152

Cabell, James Branch, 117
California Spanish missions, 213–16, 219, 223–4
Camelot, 8
Canterbury Cathedral, 46
Canterbury Tale, A, 114
Canterbury Tales (Chaucer), 7, 12, 15, 26–7, 115, 285, 287, 297–8
Cardiff Castle, 55
carnivals and the carnivalesque: Bakhtinian carnivalesque, 6, 265, 267, 268, 270, 271, 276, 281, 282; Mardi Gras, 15, 246–7, 254–60
Carson, Rachel, 201
castles, 3, 8, 10, 11, 15, 17n19, 68, 119–22, 181, 234, 239, 248, 278–9
– Burp Castle (NYC), 152
– Cardiff Castle, 55
– Cinderella Castle, 227–8, 233–5, 240 (*see also* Disney; Disney, Walt)
– Hogwarts Castle, 240, 242–3 (*see also* Harry Potter; Wizarding World of Harry Potter)
– Karlstein Castle, 89
– Nottingham Castle, 278
Cathedral Basilica of Saints Peter and Paul (Philadelphia), 45–6, 48, 50
Cathedral of Saints Peter and Paul (Providence), 62
Cathedral of St. John the Divine (NYC), 49, 50, 139–43
Cathedral of St. John the Evangelist (Cleveland), 62n54
Cathedral of the Blessed Sacrament (Detroit), 62n54

Cathedral of the Holy Cross (Boston), 62n54
cathedrals and churches
– Amiens Cathedral, 54, 58
– Arch Street Methodist Church (Philadelphia), 55
– Bryn Athyn Cathedral, 13, 45, 47, 49–55, 56, 60–1
– Canterbury Cathedral, 46
– Cathedral Basilica of Saints Peter and Paul (Philadelphia), 45–6, 48, 50
– Cathedral of Saints Peter and Paul (Providence), 62
– Cathedral of St. John the Divine (NYC), 49, 50, 139–43
– Cathedral of St. John the Evangelist (Cleveland), 62n54
– Cathedral of the Blessed Sacrament (Detroit), 62n54
– Cathedral of the Holy Cross (Boston), 62n54
– Chartres Cathedral, 32, 54, 84, 139, 142
– Christ the King Cathedral (Atlanta), 111
– Church of Heavenly Rest (NYC), 143–5
– Church of St. Paul the Apostle (NYC), 145–6
– Church of the Most Precious Blood (NYC), 149, 151
– Church of the New Jerusalem (*see* New Church)
– Cologne Cathedral, 58n4
– Episcopal Church of St. James the Less (Philadelphia), 47–8, 60n24, 62n64
– Erol Beker Chapel of the Good Shepherd (NYC), 146
– First Chinese Presbyterian Church (NYC), 149
– First Emmanuel Baptist Church (New Orleans), 260

– General Church of the New Jerusalem (*see* New Church)
– Gloucester Cathedral, 49
– Holy Cross Church (NYC), 143
– Holy Name Cathedral (Chicago), 62n54
– Holy Trinity Episcopal Church (Philadelphia), 48–9
– Immaculate Conception Jesuit Church, 247, 251–4
– National Cathedral (Washington, DC), 50, 64–5, 125
– National Shrine of the Assumption of the Blessed Virgin Mary (Baltimore), 62n54
– Rheims Cathedral, 54, 58n4
– Sainte-Chapelle (Paris), 86, 88 (illus.), 89
– San Carlo al Corso (Rome), 45
– St. Clement's Episcopal Church (Philadelphia), 48–9
– St. James's Chapel (Chicago), 86, 89
– St. Louis Cathedral (New Orleans), 246–54
– St. Mark's Episcopal Church (Philadelphia), 47, 48, 50, 59n24, 62n64
– St. Michael's Church (Cambridgeshire), 47
– St. Michael's Episcopal Church (NYC), 142
– St. Patrick's Cathedral (Detroit), 62n54
– St. Patrick's Cathedral (NYC), 58n4, 62n54, 146
– St. Peter in Chains Cathedral (Cincinnati), 62n54
– St. Thomas Episcopal Church (NYC), 49
cavaliers, 114–16, 121
Center City and Centre Square (Philadelphia), 46, 48
Chandler, Alice, 5

Chartres Cathedral, 32, 54, 84, 139, 142
Chaucer, Geoffrey, 8, 26, 27, 189, 285, 287–91, 297–8. See also *Canterbury Tales*
Chazan, Robert, 7
chivalry, 10, 70–1, 113–14, 162–3, 196n48, 230, 244n14, 270–1. See *also* knights
Chrétien de Troyes, 5–6
Christ the King Cathedral (Atlanta), 111
Church of Heavenly Rest (NYC), 143–5
Church of St. Paul the Apostle (NYC), 145–6
Church of the Most Precious Blood (NYC), 149, 151
Church of the New Jerusalem. *See* New Church
Cinderella Castle, 227–8, 233–5, 240. See *also* Disney; Disney, Walt
cinematic medievalism, 138, 183
City Hall (Philadelphia), 45, 46, 55, 58n3
civic organizations and societies: Freemasons and Freemasonry, 13, 46, 64–78; guilds, 27, 68–9, 266, 279; Knights of Columbus, 111; Norwegian Singers Association, 160–1; Sons of Norway, 160–1, 163, 172
civic spaces
– African Burial Ground (NYC), 149–51
– American Poets' Corner, 139, 141
– Blue Ridge Parkway, 180–3
– Center City and Centre Square (Philadelphia), 46, 48
– City Hall (Philadelphia), 45, 46, 55, 58n3
– Fort Tryon Park (NYC), 133, 152, 264
– George Washington Masonic Memorial, 64, 72–5, 77
– Great Smoky Mountains National Park, 180–1, 183, 192

- Hunting Park (Philadelphia), 47–8
- Independence Hall (Philadelphia), 45, 58n3
- Jackson Square (New Orleans), 246, 248
- Liberty Bell (Philadelphia), 45
- Library of Congress (Washington, DC), 63
- Masonic Temple (Philadelphia), 46, 55, 59n10
- National September 11 Memorial (NYC), 152
- Palazzo Barbaro, 30
- Palazzo Vecchio, 97, 100
- Printers Row (Chicago), 91, 96–7, 104
- Queen Eleanor's Garden, Winchester Cathedral, 26
- Rhodes Hall (Le Rêve), 119–23, 125
- Rittenhouse Square (Philadelphia), 48–9
- Shenandoah National Park, 180
- Steele Garden and Cloister Garden, Society of St. John the Evangelist, 23, 24, 25, 33–8, 41
- Stone Mountain (Georgia), 112–14, 115, 119, 122–4
- Supreme Court Building (Washington, DC), 56, 63, 65
- Thomas Jefferson Memorial, 65, 73
- Tribune Building (Chicago), 84, 86 (illus.), 91
- Washington Monument, 65
- Ye Olde Trip to Jerusalem (Nottingham tavern), 278

Civil War (US), 71, 112–15, 122–5, 247, 257; Confederacy, 7, 114–15, 120–1, 123–5, 249; "Lost Cause," 13, 112, 114, 120, 122–3, 125, 257; Reconstruction, 116, 121–2, 257
Classical Revival architecture, 46, 66, 72, 74, 86, 91, 121, 212
Clement VI, 293

Clifford, Derek, 26
Cloisters, The (NYC), 26, 103, 132–6, 139, 141–2, 264
Cole, Teju, 130–1, 153
Cologne Cathedral, 58n4
Columbia University, 132, 139
Columbus, Christopher, 172, 173
comic medievalism, 255
convivencia, 247, 253
Coolidge, Calvin, 73
Cosgrove, Denis, 24
courtly love (medievalism), 255–6, 258. *See also* chivalry
COVID-19 pandemic (2021), 260–1, 283n52
Cram, Ralph Adams, 22, 33–4, 49–51, 60n37, 61n48. *See also* Gothic Revival
Creoles (New Orleans), 255–9
Crespí, Juan, 217
Cresswell, Tim, 3, 227, 230, 235
Crivelli, Taddeo, 207, 211 (illus.)
Crusades, 7, 70, 86, 167, 170, 247, 249, 251, 254, 260, 275

D'Arcens, Louise, 4–5, 193
Dante Alighieri, 8, 31, 74–5, 141–2
Dark Ages, 14, 184, 238, 264
Davis, Jefferson, 114, 120–1
Davis, Kathleen, 132
decadence and the Decadent movement, 10, 90, 94–6, 105
Deliverance, 185–6
diachronic medievalism, 254–5
Disney (Disneyland, Walt Disney World, and the Disney corporation), 3, 199, 201, 228, 232–9, 248
Disney, Walt, 3, 228, 232–9, 248, 273
Dixon, Thomas Jr., 113
Douglass, Frederick, 63–4, 66, 78n3
dragons, 3, 163, 165, 170, 171, 174–5, 234, 241

Dukes, Mark, 138–9
Dutch West India Company, 133, 149

Earthquake, 214
East Harlem Giglio Dance and Feast, 152
Eco, Umberto, 3, 6, 12, 32, 57, 234, 284
ecology and the deep ecology movement, 40–1, 123, 197, 199–205, 217, 219
Eleanor of Aquitaine, 275, 277
Elliott, Andrew, 184
Enlightenment, 63–5, 67–8, 181–2, 184, 237
Epcot, 227, 233, 235–8, 241. *See also* Disney; Disney, Walt
Episcopal Church of St. James the Less (Philadelphia), 47–8, 60n24, 62n64
Erik the Red's Saga, 164, 172
Eriksson, Leif, 21, 158, 161, 166, 172
Erol Beker Chapel of the Good Shepherd (NYC), 146
Excalibur, 8
Excalibur Hotel, 284–6

fairs, faires, and festivals
 – East Harlem Giglio Dance and Feast, 152
 – market fairs (medieval), 269, 270
 – Medieval Festival (Fort Tryon Park, NYC), 133, 152, 264
 – Old Woodbury Hill Fair (Dorset), 269–70
 – Renaissance faires, 6, 190, 264–5, 269, 270–3, 277–9, 280n1
 – Sherwood Forest Faire, 264, 269, 272, 274, 275, 276
 – Stone Mountain Highland Games, 123–4
 – Tournament of Kings (Las Vegas), 284–5
 – White Top Folk Music Festival, 189–90, 192–3
fairy tales, 227–8, 231, 234–8, 241
Federalist Papers, The, 9–10

feudalism, 65–6, 96–7, 116, 275
films and television
 – *Adventures of Robin Hood, The* (1938 film), 272
 – *Adventures of Robin Hood, The* (1950s TV series), 271, 273
 – *Andy Griffith Show, The*, 185
 – *Bandit of Sherwood Forest, The*, 272
 – *Birth of a Nation*, 113
 – *Bonanza*, 273
 – *Braveheart*, 7
 – *Camelot*, 8
 – *Canterbury Tale, A*, 114
 – *Deliverance*, 185–6
 – *Earthquake*, 214
 – *Excalibur*, 8
 – *First Knight*, 7
 – *Gomer Pyle, U.S.M.C.*, 185
 – *Gone with the Wind*, 13, 112–16, 122
 – *Joan the Woman*, 8
 – *King Arthur*, 7, 8
 – *King Arthur: Legend of the Sword*, 8
 – *Knights of the Round Table*, 8
 – *Lone Ranger, The*, 273
 – *Magnificent Seven, The*, 273
 – *Prince of Thieves, The*, 272
 – *Queen of Versailles, The*, 287, 291–3, 295
 – *Robin Hood*, 8
 – *Robin Hood of Texas*, 273
 – *Robin Hood of the Pecos*, 273
 – *Rogues of Sherwood Forest*, 272
 – *Roy Rogers Show, The*, 273
 – *Story of Robin Hood and His Merrie Men, The*, 273, 282n43
 – *Trail of Robin Hood*, 273
First Chinese Presbyterian Church (NYC), 149
First Emmanuel Baptist Church (New Orleans), 260
First Knight, 7
First World War, 71, 84, 86, 247, 259
Flamingo Hotel, 286

Florence (Italy), 84, 90–1, 96–7, 100 (illus.), 101, 103, 136
Fordham University, 132
Fort Tryon Park (NYC), 133, 152, 264
Foucault, Michel, 65, 67
Francis (pope), 216, 224
Francis of Assisi, St., 197, 203–11, 214, 216, 217, 219
Franciscan Order, 14, 197, 199–200, 203–7, 214–17, 219
Franklin, Benjamin, 45, 64, 69, 101
fraternity, 64, 66–9, 71–3, 77
Freemasons and Freemasonry, 13, 46, 64–78
Frithiofs Saga (Tegnér), 162–3, 165
Frost, William Goodell, 187, 191

Gabriele, Matthew, 7
gallantry, 116, 121, 126n9
gambling, 285–6, 289, 290, 300n23
Ganim, John, 181, 247, 253
Gardner, Isabella Stewart, 13, 23, 27–8, 30–3, 39, 92. *See also* Monks Garden of the Isabella Stewart Gardner Museum
gender and gender roles, 66, 114–15, 168, 223n49, 235, 258–9, 268, 297. *See also* masculinity
General Church of the New Jerusalem. *See* New Church
General Theological Seminary (NYC), 147–8
George Washington Masonic Memorial, 64, 72–5, 77
Glencairn (Pennsylvania), 13, 45, 47, 49, 55–7. *See also* Pitcairn, Raymond
global medievalism, 132, 141, 145, 147, 148–53
Gloucester Cathedral, 49
Gomer Pyle, U.S.M.C., 185
Gone with the Wind (Mitchell), 13, 112–16, 122

Goodyear, William, 51–2, 56
Gothic Revival, 8, 21–2, 30, 46, 112, 120, 130, 132, 143–8, 149, 153, 181, 184, 246, 253
grace, 37, 290, 299n23
Graham, Wade, 22, 23
Great Smoky Mountains National Park, 180–1, 183, 192
Green, Nicola, 146
Greenblatt, Stephen, 6, 17n9
Greenfield, Lauren, 287, 299n7
griffins, 165, 170–1, 174
Griffith, D.W., 113
guilds, 27, 68–9, 266, 279

Habermas, Jürgen, 68
Hamilton, Alexander, 9–10
Hancock, John, 64
Haring, Keith, 141
Harkins, Anthony, 184, 185, 191
Harry Potter, 3, 15, 170, 178n69, 227, 234–5, 240–3. *See also* Hogwarts Castle; Wizarding World of Harry Potter
Hartsfield, William, 115
Hatfields and McCoys, 185
Hegel, Georg Wilhelm Friedrich, 181
Heimskringla (Snorri), 161, 164
heritage sites. *See* museums and heritage sites
High Museum of Art (Atlanta), 111
hillbillies, 184–6, 191
Hiram Abiff, 69, 75
Hogwarts Castle, 240, 242–3. *See also* Harry Potter; Wizarding World of Harry Potter
Holsinger, Bruce, 7
Holy Cross Church (NYC), 143
Holy Name Cathedral (Chicago), 62n54
Holy Trinity Episcopal Church (Philadelphia), 48–9

homosexuality and queerness, 94, 95, 149, 201
Hoover, Herbert, 73
hotels and casinos: Excalibur Hotel, 284–6; Flamingo Hotel, 286; Knights Inn, 111; Venetian Hotel, 284
Hugh of St. Victor, 75
Hunting Park (Philadelphia), 47–8
Hurricane Katrina (2005), 259–60
hyperreal, 15, 234–5, 239, 242, 284–6

identity, 70, 105, 113, 165, 170, 228–9, 247, 257, 276
Immaculate Conception Jesuit Church, 247, 251–4
immigration, 91, 131, 157–8, 160–1, 163, 165–7, 171–2, 174, 248
Independence Hall (Philadelphia), 45, 58n3
indulgences, 289–95, 298, 300n25

Jackson, Andrew, 249, 251, 254
Jackson, Thomas "Stonewall," 114, 120, 125
Jackson Square (New Orleans), 246, 248
Jacob, Margaret, 67, 69
Jameson, Fredric, 284
Jay, John, 9–10
Jefferson, Thomas, 182
Jerusalem, 32, 63, 74, 131, 287–8, 294, 297
Jewish Museum (NYC), 145
Joachim of Fiore, 206, 222n34
Joan of Arc, 251, 260
Joan the Woman, 8
John Paul II (pope), 203, 216
John the Evangelist, St., 53

Karlstein Castle, 89
Kempe, Margery, 288–9
Kenney, Alice, 190

Kensington Runestone, 157, 166, 171–3
Kha, Tommy, 149
King, Martin Luther Jr., 123
King Arthur, 7, 8
King Arthur: Legend of the Sword, 8
Kleinberg, Aviad, 219, 222n34
knights, 70–1, 116–19, 163, 165–8, 170, 232, 236, 239–40, 257. *See also* chivalry
Knights Inn, 111
Knights of Columbus, 111
Knights of the Round Table, 8
Knights Templar, 46
Kraitz, Gustav, 147
Ku Klux Klan, 113–15, 120–4, 196n48, 257. *See also* racism; white nativism and nationalism; white supremacy

La Ceppède, Jean de, 222n40
Land, Barbara and Myrick, 284, 287
Le Moyne, Pierre, 255
Lears, T.J. Jackson, 11, 90, 92, 286, 300n23
Lee, Robert E., 114, 120, 123, 125, 251
Leighton, Edmund, 284
L'Enfant, Pierre Charles, 63–4
Leon, Rodney, 150–1
Leopold, Aldo, 202, 219
Leslie-Lohman Museum of Gay and Lesbian Art (NYC), 149
Liberty Bell (Philadelphia), 45
Library of Congress (Washington, DC), 63
lieux de memoire, 3, 229, 237
lieux d'imagination, 3, 4, 229, 234, 241–3
Limbourg Brothers, 136
Lincoln, Abraham, 56
Locke, John, 66
Lodge, David, 295, 299n9
Lomuto, Sierra, 8
Lone Ranger, The, 273

Longfellow, Henry Wadsworth, 162–3, 176n21
Lorimer, Michelle, 214–15
Los Angeles County Museum of Art, 206
Louis IX (king of France), 86, 89, 249, 251, 260

Mabry Mill (Appalachia), 180–3, 192, 193
Madison, James, 9–10
Maella, Mariano Salvador, 206–7, 209 (illus.)
Magnificent Seven, The, 273
Magruder, Michael Takeo, 143–4
Margaret Mitchell House (Atlanta), 122. See also *Gone with the Wind*; Mitchell, Margaret
market fairs (medieval), 269, 270
Marshall, John, 64
masculinity, 7, 64, 67–70, 72, 74, 77, 95, 105, 113–14, 157, 162–3, 228, 230–1. *See also* gender and gender roles
Masonic Temple (Philadelphia), 46, 55, 59n10
Master of Sir John Fastolf, 207, 210 (illus.)
Matthews, David, 113, 187, 189
McClure, Julia, 204, 206–7
Mecca, 63, 287
Medici family, 86, 90–1, 96, 103
Medieval Festival (Fort Tryon Park, NYC), 133, 152, 264
Medieval Times, 15, 17n19, 111–12, 152, 201, 227, 234–5, 237–41
medievalisms
– cinematic, 138, 183
– comic, 255
– courtly love, 255–6, 258
– diachronic, 254–5
– global, 132, 141, 145, 147, 148–53
– history and theories of, 4–8, 24, 90, 95, 105, 132–3, 152–3, 193, 200–4, 229–30, 254–5

– nineteenth-century medieval revival, 10–12, 49–50, 52, 182, 186–7, 190
– political, 7–8, 17n16, 64–5, 67, 112, 113, 116, 117–19, 153
– residual, 132–3, 137–53
– Southern, 13, 116
– transplanted, 132–6, 145
– tycoon, 132
– vanished, 152–3
Mergenthaler, Ottmar, 91, 97
Metropolitan Museum of Art (NYC), 132–3, 145
Michael Van Valkenburgh Associates, 28, 31–2
Milton, John, 181, 182, 256
Minnis, Alastair, 290
Mitchell, Margaret, 112–13, 115–17, 122, 125n6. See also *Gone with the Wind*; Margaret Mitchell House
Mob Museum (Las Vegas), 286
Monks Garden of the Isabella Stewart Gardner Museum (Boston), 22–5, 27–33, 39–41
Mont-Saint-Michel, 47, 86
Morgan Library and Museum (NYC), 132
Morris, William, 23–4, 37–41, 89, 90
Munday, Anthony, 274
museums and heritage sites
– Atlanta History Center, 122–3
– Cloisters, The (NYC), 26, 103, 132–6, 139, 141–2, 264
– Glencairn (Pennsylvania), 13, 45, 47, 49, 55–7
– High Museum of Art (Atlanta), 111
– Jewish Museum (NYC), 145
– Leslie-Lohman Museum of Gay and Lesbian Art (NYC), 149
– Los Angeles County Museum of Art, 206
– Mabry Mill (Appalachia), 180–3, 192, 193

– Margaret Mitchell House (Atlanta), 122
– Metropolitan Museum of Art (NYC), 132–3, 145
– Mob Museum (Las Vegas), 286
– Monks Garden of the Isabella Stewart Gardner Museum (Boston), 22–5, 27–33, 39–41
– Mont-Saint-Michel, 47, 86
– Morgan Library and Museum (NYC), 132
– National Gallery of Art (Washington, DC), 73
– National Portrait Gallery (Washington, DC), 63
– Philadelphia Museum of Art, 45
– Sherwood Forest, 15, 265, 272–4
– Smithsonian Institute, 58n2, 64–5, 145

Naess, Arne, 201
National Cathedral (Washington, DC), 50, 64–5, 125
National Gallery of Art (Washington, DC), 73
National Portrait Gallery (Washington, DC), 63
National September 11 Memorial (NYC), 152
National Shrine of the Assumption of the Blessed Virgin Mary (Baltimore), 62n54
Native Americans, 148, 168–9, 174, 175, 183
Nevelson, Louise, 146–7
New Church, 13, 52–7, 60n31
NFL (National Football League): Minnesota Vikings, 14, 157, 172–4, 177n41; New Orleans Saints, 259–60
nineteenth-century medieval revival, 10–12, 49–50, 52, 182, 186–7, 190
Nora, Pierre, 3, 229

Norwegian Singers Association, 160–1
nostalgia, 11, 89–90, 112, 187, 192–3, 247, 286
Notman, John, 45, 48–9
Nottingham Castle, 278

Obama, Barack, 146
Oehlenschläger, Adam, 161–2, 164
Ohman, Olof, 157, 166, 171–2
Old Woodbury Hill Fair (Dorset), 269–70

Paine, Thomas, 64–5
Palazzo Barbaro, 30
Palazzo Vecchio, 97, 100
Penn, William, 45, 46, 56, 58n7
Philadelphia Museum of Art, 45
Pike, Albert, 71, 76, 81n45
pilgrims and pilgrimages, 32, 63–4, 130–3, 215, 285–95, 297, 299n9
Pitcairn, Raymond, 13, 47, 49–57, 60n37. *See also* Bryn Athyn Cathedral; Glencairn
plantation culture, 114–16, 121, 123. *See also* Civil War (US)
Poetic Edda, 161–3, 170
political medievalism, 7–8, 17n16, 64–5, 67, 112, 113, 116, 117–19, 153
Porter, Kingsley, 51–2, 56, 57
Powell, Michael, 114
Pratt, Mary Louise, 199–200
Pre-Raphaelite school, 11, 89, 90
Pressburger, Emeric, 114
Princeton University, 22, 49
Printers Row (Chicago), 91, 96–7, 104
Prose Edda (Snorri), 161–3, 170
Protestant Reformation, 47–9, 52–3
Purgatory, 144, 149, 291, 293–4, 296

Queen Eleanor's Garden, Winchester Cathedral, 26
Queen of Versailles, The, 287, 291–3, 295

racism, 7, 113, 117–19, 122, 125, 136; Atlanta Race Riots, 112, 117–19, 122; plantation culture, 114–16, 121, 123; segregation, 112, 119; slavery, 112, 114, 116, 121–2; white nativism and nationalism, 7, 17n15, 113, 196n48; white supremacy, 118, 122, 124, 136, 196n48, 259

Reijnders, Stijn, 3, 229, 236

relics, 75, 86, 89, 134, 238, 286, 291–2, 294, 298

Renaissance, 5–6, 22, 30, 33, 86, 89, 95, 184, 264

Renaissance faires, 6, 190, 264–5, 269, 270–3, 277–9, 280n1

residual medievalism, 132–3, 137–53

Revelation, Book of, 54, 56, 222n34

Rheims Cathedral, 54, 58n4

Rhodes Hall (Le Rêve), 119–23, 125

Rice University, 49

Richard I (the Lionheart), 272, 274, 275, 277

Rittenhouse Square (Philadelphia), 48–9

Robertson, D.W., 74, 288, 300n20

Robin Hood, 8

Robin Hood ballads and legends, 8, 15, 229, 231, 264–83. *See also* Sherwood Forest Faire

Robin Hood of Texas, 273

Robin Hood of the Pecos, 273

Rogers, Roy, 273

Rogues of Sherwood Forest, 272

Roman de la Rose, 12, 26

Romanesque Revival architecture, 21, 33, 62n54, 72, 89, 96, 120, 130, 134, 143, 145–6

Romanticism, 113, 115, 121–2, 161, 162, 164

Rome, 45, 63, 66, 96, 181, 284, 287, 297

Ruskin, John, 21, 89–90, 95, 99, 104, 253

sagas, 158, 161–4, 170; *Erik the Red's Saga*, 164, 172; *Frithiofs Saga* (Tegnér), 162–3, 165; *Heimskringla* (Snorri), 161, 164; *Saga of the Greenlanders*, 164, 172; *Saga of the Volsungs*, 163, 170

Sainte-Chapelle (Paris), 86, 88 (illus.), 89

San Carlo al Corso (Rome), 45

San Gimignano (Italy), 84, 86, 87 (illus.), 101

Second World War, 147

segregation, 112, 119

Selznick, David O., 115

serious leisure, 265, 276–8

Serra, Junípero, St., 215–17

Sessions, George, 203, 221n13

Shakespeare, William, 231–2, 275, 283n47

Shenandoah National Park, 180

Sherwood Forest, 15, 265, 272–4

Sherwood Forest Faire, 264, 269, 272, 274, 275, 276

Shippey, Tom, 7

Siegel, Benjamin "Bugsy," 286

Silvestris, Bernardus, 75

Sixties counterculture, 270–2, 277

slavery, 112, 114, 116, 121–2. *See also* Civil War (US)

Smithsonian Institute, 58n2, 64–5, 145

Society for Creative Anachronism, 9, 200, 265, 270–2, 277

Song of Solomon, 26

Southern medievalism, 13, 116

St. Clement's Episcopal Church (Philadelphia), 48–9

St. James's Chapel (Chicago), 86, 89

St. Louis Cathedral (New Orleans), 246–54

St. Mark's Episcopal Church (Philadelphia), 47, 48, 50, 59n24, 62n64

St. Michael's Church (Cambridgeshire), 47

St. Michael's Episcopal Church (NYC), 142

St. Patrick's Cathedral (Detroit), 62n54
St. Patrick's Cathedral (NYC), 58n4, 62n54, 146
St. Peter in Chains Cathedral (Cincinnati), 62n54
St. Thomas Episcopal Church (NYC), 49
Stebbins, Robert, 276–8
Steele, Fletcher, 23, 33–7, 39
Steele Garden and Cloister Garden, Society of St. John the Evangelist, 23, 24, 25, 33–8, 41
Stone Mountain (Georgia), 112–14, 115, 119, 122–4
Stone Mountain Highland Games, 123–4
Story of Robin Hood and His Merrie Men, The, 273, 282n43
Sturluson, Snorri (Snorre), 161, 163–5
Suger, 50, 60n34
Supreme Court Building (Washington, DC), 56, 63, 65
Swedenborg, Emanuel, 13, 52–4

Tacitus, 181
Taft, William Howard, 73
Tegnér, Esaias, 162–5
Tennyson, Alfred, Lord, 3, 11
Thomas Jefferson Memorial, 65, 73
Tournament of Kings (Las Vegas), 284–5
Trachtenberg, Alan, 86, 101, 105
Trail of Robin Hood, 273
translatio horti, 22, 23
transplanted medievalism, 132–6, 145
Très Riches Heures du Duc de Berry, 26
Tribune Building (Chicago), 84, 86 (illus.), 91
Trigg, Stephanie, 154n10, 200
Twain, Mark, 3, 8, 11–12, 90, 259
tycoon medievalism, 132

universities: Columbia University, 132, 139; Fordham University, 132; General Theological Seminary (NYC), 147–8; Princeton University, 22, 49; Rice University, 49; University of Chicago, 103–4; University of Pennsylvania, 46–7
University of Chicago, 103–4
University of Pennsylvania, 46–7
Utz, Richard, 4

vanished medievalism, 152–3
Venetian Hotel, 284
Venturi, Robert, 284, 287
Vikings, 14, 21, 157–8, 162–3, 165, 168, 170, 171–5, 277–8. *See also* sagas

Walpole, Horace, 21, 181
Washington, George, 34, 63–4, 75
Washington Monument, 65
Whitaker, Cord J., 7
White, Lynn Jr., 202–4, 221
white nativism and nationalism, 7, 17n15, 113, 196n48
white supremacy, 118, 122, 124, 136, 196n48, 259
White Top Folk Music Festival, 189–90, 192–3
Wickham, Chris, 90–1
Wilde, Oscar, 92, 94–6, 105
William of Canterbury, 289
Wilson, Woodrow, 22
Windrim, James H., 46, 59n10
Wizarding World of Harry Potter, 15, 227, 234–5, 240–3. *See also* Harry Potter; Hogwarts Castle
Workman, Leslie, 190
World War I. *See* First World War
World War II. *See* Second World War

Ye Olde Trip to Jerusalem (Nottingham tavern), 278
Young, Helen, 200, 204